God, Foreknowledge, and Freedom

GOD,

FOREKNOWLEDGE, AND FREEDOM

Edited, with an Introduction, by

JOHN MARTIN FISCHER

Stanford University Press, Stanford, California

Stanford University Press, Stanford, California
© 1989 by the Board of Trustees of the Leland Stanford Junior University
Printed in the United States of America

Original printing 1989
Last figure below indicates year of this printing:
01   00   99   98   97   96   95   94   93   92

CIP data appear at the end of the book

Contents

Contributors

Marilyn McCord Adams, Professor, Department of Philosophy, University of California, Los Angeles.

William P. Alston, Professor, Department of Philosophy, Syracuse University.

Martin Davies, Reader in Philosophy, Birkbeck College, University of London.

John Martin Fischer, Associate Professor, Department of Philosophy, University of California, Riverside.

Alfred J. Freddoso, Associate Professor, Department of Philosophy, University of Notre Dame.

William Hasker, Professor, Department of Philosophy, Huntington College.

Joshua Hoffman, Associate Professor, Department of Philosophy, University of North Carolina, Greensboro.

Nelson Pike, Professor, Department of Philosophy, University of California, Irvine.

Alvin Plantinga, O'Brien Professor of Philosophy, Department of Philosophy, University of Notre Dame.

Gary Rosenkrantz, Associate Professor, Department of Philosophy, University of North Carolina, Greensboro.

David Widerker, Assistant Professor, Department of Philosophy, Bar-Ilan University.

Eddy Zemach, Professor, Department of Philosophy, The Hebrew University of Jerusalem.

God, Foreknowledge, and Freedom

CHAPTER ONE

Introduction: God and Freedom

John Martin Fischer

Imagine that in some remote part of Connecticut there is a computer that has stored in its memory all truths about your life—past, present, and future. The computer contains all the information about what has happened to you, what is happening to you, and what will happen throughout your life, including the most minute details. Of course, in all likelihood there is no such computer, and some would argue that there could not be such a computer. But I simply ask you to suppose that there were this sort of computer. If so, would you be free to do other than what the computer says you will do? For instance, if the computer says that you will retire at the age of sixty, will you be free to refrain from retiring at sixty? Or would it follow from the fact that the computer now contains the true proposition that you will retire at sixty that you will not be able to refrain from retiring at sixty?

Suppose, now, that a very wise monk in Tibet knows exactly the same information contained in that imaginary computer. The monk knows everything about your life. Again, if this were so, would you be free to do other than what the monk now says that you will do? (Surely there is no difference, as regards your freedom, between the case of the computer and the monk.)

I wish to thank Norman Kretzmann and William Alston for their suggestions and for their support of this project from its inception. Also, I am very grateful to Philip Quinn, Mark Ravizza, and David Widerker for their insightful and helpful comments on previous versions of the Introduction.

And now imagine that God knew in some year before you were born all the facts about your life. Again, if this were the case, would you ever be free to do other than what you actually do? Would there be any difference, as regards your freedom, between the cases of the computer and the monk, on the one hand, and God, on the other?

These cases raise a cluster of traditionally vexatious philosophical questions. One such question is: If a presently true proposition states that you will do something in the future, can you nevertheless be free to do otherwise? Another question is: If some human being now knows that you will do something in the future, can you nevertheless be free to do otherwise? A third question is: If God now knows that you will do something in the future, can you nevertheless be free to do otherwise?

In this volume the focus is on the final question. The authors in this collection attempt to articulate an argument that, if sound, would show that God's foreknowledge is incompatible with human freedom to do otherwise. They do not all agree that the argument is sound, but they attempt to state precisely *why* one might worry that God's foreknowledge is incompatible with human freedom. Some of the authors also distinguish the argument for the incompatibility of God's foreknowledge and human freedom from similar arguments for the incompatibility of the present truth of propositions about the future and human freedom, and also for the incompatibility of human foreknowledge and human freedom.

In this introduction I shall begin by giving three related but different versions of what I call the "Basic Argument" for the incompatibility of God's foreknowledge and human freedom. I shall explain how this argument is related to those concerning the present truth of propositions about the future and human freedom, and about human foreknowledge and human freedom. Here I shall argue that God's knowledge of the future poses a *distinctive* problem for human freedom. I shall then summarize various different responses to the Basic Argument.

In explaining the strategies of response to the Basic Argument, I shall attempt to give the reader an understanding of different ways of arguing that God's foreknowledge is compatible with human freedom. The various compatibilistic responses help to chart an analytical and historical map of the issues involved in the debates about foreknowledge and freedom.

I hope that this conceptual map helps the reader to locate the articles in this anthology within the larger context of the historical and contemporary debates about these issues. I have not selected readings that represent all of the strategies of response to the Basic Argument. Rather, the readings largely (though not exclusively) discuss a particular strategy of response associated with William of Ockham. Many of the readings represent a kind of conversation about Ockham's approach, and a major goal of this collection is to give the reader a deep understanding of this approach. And although the main focus of the discussion is on Ockham's strategy, the readings touch on many aspects of the cluster of issues pertaining to God's foreknowledge and human freedom.

The Basic Argument

In this section I wish to present three different versions of what might be called the Basic Argument for the incompatibility of God's foreknowledge and human freedom. The authors of the articles in this collection present arguments that are in some respects similar to the arguments I shall put forth, but they are also in some respects different from these arguments. Whether one should say that there are three different versions of the same argument or three different arguments is unclear, but nothing important depends on this "counting" issue. Before I give the various formulations of the argument, I shall set out certain assumptions that all three have in common.

"God" is to be construed as a proper name, rather than a "title-term." Further, "God" names a person who has the divine attributes (such as eternality, omniscience, moral perfection, and so forth) *essentially*. That is, an essential feature of the person who is God (if He exists) is that He is, for example, omniscient; any actual or possible person who is not omniscient is not God.

For the purposes of the Basic Argument, I shall assume that among the divine attributes are (at least) eternality and omniscience. Of course, these do not exhaust the divine attributes, but they are the only properties needed in order to generate the

Basic Argument.[1] The properties of eternality and omniscience will be assumed to be "nested" within the total set of divine attributes.[2]

There are two different ways of understanding God's eternality. On the first approach, God is understood to be within the same temporal framework as humans are, and God's eternality consists in His existence at all times. On this view, God is "sempiternal": He has always existed, exists now, and will always exist. Further, God is essentially eternal insofar as He is sempiternal in all possible worlds in which He exists. The assumption that God is essentially eternal is weaker than—and entirely compatible with—the assumption that God exists necessarily. This temporal interpretation of eternality is the one that I will employ in order to generate the Basic Argument.[3]

In contrast, some philosophers understand God's eternality as atemporal eternality. On this interpretation God does not exist within the same temporal framework as the one in which humans exist.[4] God is here conceived of as outside of time altogether, or perhaps simply outside of human time. It should be clear that such a God could not have "foreknowledge," although He could arguably be omniscient. Some philosophers have adopted this atemporal conception of eternality in part as a response to the Basic Argument, and I shall consider this position below.

God is taken to be omniscient. A person is omniscient just in case he believes all and only true propositions. It will be useful here to assume that propositions can be true (or false) *at times*. Now the definition of omniscience (as regards a *temporal* being) can be given more sharply: a person is omniscient just in case for any time t and proposition p, he believes that p at t if and only if p is true at t. Further, a person is essentially omniscient insofar as it is necessarily true that, if he exists, then he is omniscient— that is, he is omniscient in every possible world in which he exists.

At least two aspects of this account of omniscience are worth mentioning here. First, it assumes that propositions can be true (or false) at particular times, and it will become clear below that certain philosophers would deny this possibility. Second, omniscience is understood in terms of true *belief*, and it might have been thought that the definition of omniscience would require

that an omniscient being *know* all true propositions. It is, however, a reasonable assumption that when a person knows some
proposition *p*, then he believes that *p*. Normally, knowledge is
analyzed in terms of belief. Thus the account of omniscience
given above would at least seem to specify a necessary condition
for omniscience, even if it does not give a sufficient condition,
and this necessary condition is all that is required by the Basic
Argument. But it should be noted that some philosophers might
claim that God's knowledge, unlike that of other knowers, does
not involve belief at all. This approach would deny one of the
assumptions of the Basic Argument.[5]

Now it is appropriate to present an important assumption
shared by all three versions of the argument for incompatibilism.
This assumption attempts to capture the intuitive idea that the
past is currently "fixed" and "out of our control." The idea is
that we do not now have any "control over" or "choice about"
certain facts about the past. For example, I do not now have any
choice about the fact that George Washington was the first president of the United States, or that the State of Israel was founded
in 1948. One way of putting the idea is this: no person can now
act in such a way that some fact about the past would not have
been a fact. So, for instance, I cannot now (in 1988) so act that
the stock market would not have crashed in October 1987, even
if I (dearly) wanted to!

A refinement needs to be introduced into the assumption
of the fixity of the past. There is an intuitive distinction between facts that are genuinely and solely (or strictly) about the
past, and facts that are not both genuinely and solely about
the past. Facts of the first sort are now "fully accomplished and
over-and-done-with," whereas facts of the second sort are not. I
shall call those facts that are genuinely and solely about a certain
time "hard facts" about the time. In contrast, those facts that are
not genuinely and solely about the time in question will be
called "soft facts." Much more will be said about the distinction
(and a related one between those facts that are now "fixed" and
those that are not) below, but it is sufficient here to note that we
can identify fairly clear cases of hard facts and soft facts, and
that we tend to think that the hard facts about the past are now
fixed, whereas the soft facts about the past may not now be
fixed. So, for example, the fact that George Washington was

the first U.S. president is a hard fact about the past, and it is now fixed: I cannot now so act that it would not have been a fact. However, the fact that George Washington was president prior to my going to a restaurant tomorrow is a soft fact about the past, and, insofar as it seems to be within my power not to go the restaurant tomorrow, it is not now fixed: I can so act tomorrow (i.e., refrain from going to the restaurant) that it would not have been a fact that George Washington was president prior to my going to the restaurant tomorrow.

This distinction having been made, we need to refine the interpretation of the fixity of the past. We can say: no person can now act in such a way that some hard fact about the past would not have been a fact. The assumption can be made more explicit (and general) as follows:

(FP) For any action Y, agent S, and time t, if it is true that if S were to do Y at t, then some hard fact about the past (relative to t) would not have been a fact, then S cannot do Y at t.

First Version

The first version of the Basic Argument is the "modal version." It makes use of an important and fundamental modal principle, which might be called the "Principle of the Transfer of Powerlessness." When a proposition p obtains and a person S does not have it in his power so to act that p would not obtain, p is "power necessary" relative to S. Power necessity is that kind of necessity which implies that a person does not have control over whether a proposition obtains. When a proposition is power necessary relative to a person, he has "no choice" about whether the proposition obtains. The abbreviation "$N_t^S (p)$" will be used to stand for: it is power necessary for S at t that p—that is, p obtains and S is not free at t to perform any action such that if S were to perform it, p would not obtain.[6]

Consider the following rule of inference involving the power necessity operator:

If: (a) $N_t^S(p)$

and (b) N_t^S(If p, then q),

then: (c) $N_t^S(q)$.

This rule of inference is the Principle of the Transfer of Powerlessness. Roughly, it says that if a person is powerless over one thing, and powerless over that thing's leading to another, then the person is powerless over the second thing. More carefully, the principle says that if a person S cannot so act that p would be false, and S cannot so act that it would be false that if p then q, then S cannot so act that q would be false. It is difficult to know how to prove such a principle, but it at least appears to be reasonable.[7]

For example, imagine that it is true that it will rain this afternoon and there is nothing you can do about it; that is, there is no action that you can perform this afternoon which is such that if you were to perform it, it would not rain this afternoon. Further, imagine that if it rains this afternoon, the streets will get wet, and that there is similarly nothing you can do about the fact that if it rains this afternoon, the streets will get wet. It seems to follow from these facts that the streets will get wet this afternoon and that you cannot prevent this from happening—you cannot do anything such that if you were to do it, the streets would not get wet this afternoon. Thus, the Principle of the Transfer of Powerlessness, interpreted as above, appears to be valid.

Now we are ready for the argument. Suppose that a person S fails to perform some "ordinary" act X at time t_2. (The act in question could be mowing the lawn, eating a cheese omelette, helping someone fix a flat tire, and so forth.) Assume, further, that God exists and has the properties sketched above. Because S does not perform X at t_2, it seems to follow that it was true at some prior time t_1 that S would not do X at t_2. (Of course, this assumes both that propositions can be true at times and, more specifically, that "future contingent propositions," such as that S will not do X at t_2, can be true at prior times.) It follows from God's eternality and omniscience that He believed at t_1 that S would fail to do X at t_2. Now, since God's belief at t_1 appears to be a hard fact about t_1, it follows from (FP) that S cannot at t_2 act in such a way that God would not have believed at t_1 that S would refrain from doing X at t_2. That is,

(1) $N_{t_2}^{S}$ (God believed at t_1 that S would not do X at t_2).

Further, in virtue of God's essential omniscience, we have:

(2) $N_{t_2}^{S}$ (If God believed at t_1 that S would not do X at t_2, then S would not do X at t_2).

Now it follows from the Principle of the Transfer of Powerlessness that

(3) $N_{t_2}^s$ (S does not do X at t_2).

That is, the conclusion of the argument says that S refrains from doing X at t_2 and that S *cannot* do X at t_2. But this result is obviously generalizable to any human action. Thus we have an argument (employing the idea of the fixity of the past and also the Principle of the Transfer of Powerlessness) that God's foreknowledge is incompatible with human freedom to do otherwise.

One might, however, challenge the Transfer Principle.[8] For this reason, and because it is illuminating to consider whether the intuitive ideas behind the Basic Argument can lead to the same conclusion via different routes, it will be useful to develop some alternative formulations of the Basic Argument.

Second Version

The second version of the Basic Argument makes exactly the same assumptions about God as does the first version. Also, I shall again assume that S does not perform some "ordinary" act X at time t_2. As above, it follows that God believed at a prior time t_1 that S would not do X at t_2. Now imagine that S can at t_2 do X at t_2. If this is so, it would appear that there are the following three possibilities:

(1) S can at t_2 bring it about that God held a false belief at t_1;
(2) S can at t_2 bring it about that God did not exist at t_1;
(3) S can at t_2 bring it about that God held a different belief from the one He actually held at t_1, i.e., S can at t_2 bring it about that God would have believed at t_1 that S would do X at t_2.

Although it seems correct that one of these three possibilities follows from S's having the power at t_2 to do X at t_2, it is unclear what general principle underwrites this inference. To become clear about the underlying principle, notice that when S can at t_2 do X at t_2, then S can at t_2 bring it about that S does X at t_2. So the general principle that underwrites the inference may govern the notion of "bringing it about that p." One such principle would be:

(PP) If S can bring it about that p, and if it is true that if p were the case, then q would be the case, then S can bring it about that q.

Call this principle the "Power Principle." If the Power Principle is valid, then it would seem that we could justify the inference from S's having it in his power at t_2 to X at t_2 to the truth of one of the three possibilities above. This is because the three possibilities pertain to different states of affairs that might be thought to obtain, were S to do X at t_2. Yet it is controversial whether the Power Principle is valid, and I shall briefly discuss this issue below. For now I shall put aside the question of the validity of the Power Principle and simply assume that it is valid.

So on the assumption that S is free at t_2 to X, there are three apparent possibilities: (1), (2), and (3). But (1) is not a real possibility in virtue of God's essential omniscience. And (2) can be ruled out as well. First, it might be thought that (2) can be ruled out in virtue of (FP). This may be so, but it will depend on whether the fact that God exists at t_1 is properly construed as a hard fact about t_1. But even if it is not obvious that God's existence at t_1 is a hard fact about t_1, I believe that (2) can be ruled out by the intuitive idea that God's existence should not depend on human action. God is, after all, the Supreme Being, a being "than which nothing greater can be conceived," in St. Anselm's words. It seems plausible, then, to think that such a being's existence should be "counterfactually independent of possible human action" in the following sense:

(CI) If God exists, then no human agent can act in such a way that God would not exist.

It clearly follows from this "counterfactual independence" assumption that if God exists at a time and it is true that if S were to perform some act then God would not exist at the time, then S cannot perform the act in question. Thus, (CI) would rule out (2) even if (FP) did not.

Finally, (3) would appear to be ruled out in virtue of (FP) together with the assumption that God's belief at t_1 is a hard fact about t_1. Because all three possibilities have been dismissed, we can conclude that, contrary to our hypothesis, S cannot do X at t_2. (Again, this result is straightforwardly generalizable to any human action.)

Note that the second version of the Basic Argument does not employ the Principle of the Transfer of Powerlessness (unlike the first version). But it does employ the Power Principle. Because of the controversial status of such principles as the Power Principle, it will be useful to develop a third version of the Basic Argument.

Third Version

The third version of the Basic Argument makes exactly the same assumptions as are made by the first two versions. And again let us suppose that S does not do X at t_2. Now it is plausible to say that one of the following three "conditionals" must be true:

(1) If S were to do X at t_2, then God would have held a false belief at t_1.
(2) If S were to do X at t_2, then God would not have existed at t_1.
(3) If S were to do X at t_2, then God would have held a different belief from the one He actually held at t_1, i.e., God would have believed at t_1 that S would do X at t_2.

But (1) must be false, in virtue of God's essential omniscience. This claim can be made more explicit by employing an attractive and widely held semantics for conditionals.[9] On this sort of semantics, a conditional—"If p were the case, then q would be the case"—is true (roughly) just in case in the possible world(s) most similar to the actual world in which p is true, q is also true. Now it is obvious that (1) must be false, since in the closest (indeed in all) possible worlds in which S does X at t_2, God does not have a false belief at t_1.

Further, if (2) were true, then it would follow that S cannot do X at t_2. This is certainly so in light of (CI), and it may also be true in virtue of (FP), depending on whether God's existence at t_1 is a hard fact about t_1. Finally, if (3) were true, then it would seem to follow in virtue of (FP) that S cannot at t_2 do X at t_2, if (as it is at least reasonable to suppose) God's belief at t_1 is a hard fact about t_1.

The structure of the third version of the Basic Argument is as follows. There are three apparent possibilities: (1), (2), and (3). But (1) is not a genuine possibility: it cannot be true. And if (2) or (3) were true, it would follow that S cannot do X at t_2. Thus S cannot do X at t_2, and this result is easily generalizable to any human action.

The third version of the Basic Argument does not rely (at least in any obvious way) on such principles as the Principle of the Transfer of Powerlessness or the Power Principle. This suggests that the intuitive ideas that drive the Basic Argument could be employed to generate the worrisome conclusion that there is no human freedom to do otherwise, even if the two principles—the Transfer Principle and the Power Principle—were invalid. Of course, some assumptions shared by all versions of the argument will have to be examined more closely below: that God is within time, that "future contingents" can be true prior to the times they are about, that God's beliefs are hard facts about the times at which they are held, that hard facts about prior times are fixed now, and so forth. But even if some of these assumptions are controversial, it is useful to see how the three versions of the argument can seem to "triangulate" on the conclusion that if God exists, there is no human freedom to do otherwise.

Comments on the Basic Argument

In order better to understand the Basic Argument, I wish to contrast it with certain similar arguments: for fatalism, for the incompatibility of human foreknowledge and freedom to do otherwise, and for the incompatibility of causal determinism and human freedom to do otherwise. But first I wish to emphasize a point about the conclusion of the Basic Argument.

The Basic Argument concludes that if God exists, then no human is ever free to do other than what he actually does. Notice that the kind of freedom pertinent to the Basic Argument is "freedom to do otherwise." Some philosophers have held that one can "act freely" even if one does not have the power to do otherwise.[10] If indeed it is possible to act freely without having the freedom to do otherwise, then the Basic Argument cannot be used to generate the conclusion that if God exists, then no human ever acts freely. Further, it is controversial what the relationship is between moral responsibility and freedom to do otherwise. If moral responsibility requires freedom to do otherwise, then the Basic Argument provides a threat to human moral responsibility. If, however, moral responsibility does not require freedom to do otherwise (but perhaps only acting freely), then the Basic Argument does not in itself generate a threat to moral responsibility. Of course, even if the Basic Argument does not threaten moral responsibility, it is, nevertheless, important and unsettling. We human beings are practical reasoners and planners, and in these contexts we seem genuinely to presuppose that we are free to do otherwise—that we have more than one genuinely open path into the future. It is important to distinguish different sorts of freedom, but we seem to care not just about acting freely (and moral responsibility), but also about freedom to do otherwise.

Fatalism

I now wish to sketch an argument for fatalism and compare it with the first version of the Basic Argument. Fatalism is the doctrine that it is a logical or conceptual truth that no person is ever free to do otherwise. The conclusion of the fatalistic argument is the same as that of the Basic Argument, but the fatalist claims that the conclusion can be derived from "logical" and "conceptual" facts alone, apart from any special assumptions (such as that God exists or that causal determinism obtains).

Imagine, again, that S refrains from doing something ordinary X at t_2. It follows (according to the fatalist) that it was true at t_1 that S would not do X at t_2. But (the fatalist claims) it must be the case that if it was true at t_1 that S would not do X at t_2, then S does not do X at t_2. And thus S cannot do otherwise at t_2. The argument can be set forth more carefully as follows.

(1) It was true at t_1 that S would not do X at t_2.
(2) $N_{t_2}^S$ (If it was true at t_1 that S would not do X at t_2, then S does not do X at t_2).
Thus: (3) $N_{t_2}^S$ (S does not do X at t_2).

But once the argument is regimented in this fashion, it can easily be seen to be invalid. Specifically, the argument is of this form:

(1) p
(2) N_t^S (If p, then q)
Thus: (3) N_t^S (q),

rather than the (apparently) valid form:

(1') $N_t^S (p)$
(2) N_t^S (If p, then q)
Thus: (3) $N_t^S (q)$.

That is, the fatalist's argument, as presented above, is *not* underwritten by the Principle of the Transfer of Powerlessness, and there is simply no reason to think that it is valid. (Note that the parallel form for logical necessity is invalid. If it were valid, we could straightforwardly prove that all true propositions are logically necessary.) Thus it can be seen that the fatalistic argument presented above commits a modal fallacy.

There are two obvious ways of attempting to improve the argument: strengthening (1) or strengthening (2). Let us first consider strengthening (2) to:

(2') If it was true at t_1 that S would not do X at t_2, then $N_{t_2}^S$ (S does not do X at t_2).

(2') in conjunction with (1) does indeed generate the relevant conclusion, (3). But whereas the argument now is valid, its soundness is dubious. It is important to distinguish the uncontroversial (2) from the highly questionable (2'). (2) expresses the "necessity of the consequence," whereas (2') expresses the "necessity of the consequent." Aquinas was careful to distinguish the analogous claims with regard to God's omniscience:

(2G) $N_{t_2}^S$ (If God believed at t_1 that S would not do X at t_2, then S does not do X at t_2).
(2G') If God believed at t_1 that S would not do X at t_2, then $N_{t_2}^S$ (S does not do X at t_2).[11]

The situation here is precisely the same as the situation with the fatalistic argument. (2G) is uncontroversial, but it does not render the relevant argument valid, and whereas (2G') does render the argument valid, it is not uncontroversial.

Consider now the attempt to patch up the fatalistic argument by strengthening the first premise to:

(1') $N_{t_2}^S$ (It was true at t_1 that S would not do X at t_2).

Whereas the argument would now become valid, its soundness would (again) be dubious, since (1') would seem to be false. If the fatalist tried to justify (1') by adducing (FP), it would be a questionable move because it is doubtful that "It was true at t_1 that S would not do X at t_2" is a hard fact about t_1. Here we have an interesting difference between the Basic Argument and the (improved) fatalistic argument: whereas it is relatively clear that "It was true at t_1 that S would not do X at t_2" is a soft fact about t_1, it is not so evident that "God believed at t_1 that S would not do X at t_2" is such a fact. Although it is an open question whether (FP) can appropriately be used by the Basic Argument, it is relatively clear that it cannot be so employed in the fatalistic argument.

It should be evident, then, that the distinction between hard and soft facts can help us to respond to the fatalist's argument, and perhaps also to distinguish it from that of the incompatibilist about God's foreknowledge and human freedom. Various authors in this book note this point. In Chapter 5, for example, David Widerker employs a related but distinct strategy for distinguishing the argument for fatalism from the incompatibilist's argument. Widerker distinguishes between having the power to bring about the non-occurrence of a past event and the power to bring it about that a past event would have had a different temporally relational property from what it actually had. Widerker claims that the fatalist is implausibly supposing that we do not have the power to bring it about that a past event would not have had a temporally relational property that it actually has. In contrast, Widerker claims, it is reasonable to think that the incompatibilist's argument need only employ the plausible principle that one cannot now bring it about that some event that actually occurred would not have occurred. Here, then, is another approach to distinguishing the argument for fatalism from the argument for incompatibilism, one that presupposes a distinction parallel to the distinction between hard and soft facts; this distinction is between temporally non-relational and temporally relational *properties*. (I shall have more to say about this distinction among properties below.)

Human Foreknowledge

Consider also a parallel argument for the incompatibility of *human* foreknowledge and freedom to do otherwise. The situation, I believe, is similar to that of the argument for fatalism.

Someone might argue in the following way. If a human being, say Smith, really *knew* at t_1 that S would not do X at t_2, then S *must* not do X at t_2, and S is not free at t_2 to do X at t_2. More carefully, the argument is:

(1) Smith knew at t_1 that S would not do X at t_2.
(2) $N_{t_2}^S$ (If Smith knew at t_1 that S would not do X at t_2, then S does not do X at t_2).
Thus: (3) $N_{t_2}^S$ (S does not do X at t_2).

As with the original fatalistic argument, it is clear that this argument is invalid: it is not of a form appropriate to the Principle of the Transfer of Powerlessness. And if one attempts to secure the validity of the argument by claiming that the first premise is "power necessary" in virtue of the fixity of the past, one has the same problem as with the fatalistic argument: it is highly dubious whether "Smith knew at t_1 that S would not do X at t_2" is a hard fact about t_1.

This point highlights an important difference between God's foreknowledge and human foreknowledge. If Smith knows at t_1 that p, then Smith believes at t_1 that p. Now if S can at t_2 bring about the falsity of p, then it seems that S can bring it about that Smith had a false belief at t_1 (and thus that Smith did not have knowledge at t_1). Thus positing that S can do otherwise at t_2 does *not* require saying that S can so act that some person would not have held a *belief* that he actually held in the past. But this may well be what is required if one says that S can at t_2 do otherwise, even though God believed at t_1 that S would not do X at t_2. So there is an obvious difference between the argument for the incompatibility of God's foreknowledge and human freedom to do otherwise and the argument for the incompatibility of human foreknowledge and freedom to do otherwise. This difference derives from the fact that God is *essentially* omniscient, whereas no human is.

The above point is consistent with claiming that there is another argument (not, apparently, proceeding from the fixity of hard facts about the past) to the conclusion that human foreknowledge is incompatible with freedom to do otherwise. For example, it might be claimed that knowledge that p requires evidence that p, and thus that if Smith knows at t_1 that S will not do X at t_2, then Smith possesses evidence at t_1 that implies that S

will not do X at t_2. Further, the claim would be that this evidence, if it really implies that S will not do X at t_2, is inconsistent with the genuine possibility of S's doing X at t_2. To justify this claim, one might say that Smith's evidence must consist of conditions obtaining at t_1 (or before), and if conditions obtaining at t_1 (or before) imply that Smith will not do X at t_2, then Smith cannot do X at t_2.

I do not have a knock-down objection to the incompatibilistic position just sketched. I do, however, believe that humans can have genuine knowledge that p without possessing evidence that entails p. If this is so, then it should also apply to human knowledge of the future (and, in particular, to human knowledge of "future contingents"). This sort of conception of human knowledge seems to leave room for human freedom to do otherwise. But if one believes that the only way in which one could have genuine knowledge about a future event would be to have good evidence that current conditions will *causally necessitate* the future event, then human freedom may well be jeopardized. In this case, however, the threat to human freedom would not come from human foreknowledge *per se*, but from causal determination. It will be useful now briefly to sketch an argument parallel to the sorts of arguments discussed above for the incompatibility of causal determinism and human freedom to do otherwise.

Causal Determinism

Let us imagine that casual determinism obtains. That is, let us say that it is true that, for any given time, a complete statement of the hard facts about the world at that time, together with a complete statement of the laws of nature, entails every truth as to what happens after that time. Imagine, as is our habit, that S does not do X at t_2. It follows (from causal determinism) that some condition C obtained at t_1, which, together with the natural laws L, entails that S does not do X at t_2. So we have:

(1) $N_{t_2}^S$ (C obtained at t_1)

in virtue of the fixity of the past. And we have:

(2) $N_{t_2}^S$ (If C obtained at t_1, then S would not do X at t_2),

in virtue of the intuitively reasonable idea that the laws of nature are fixed. Thus, we can conclude, by the Principle of the Transfer of Powerlessness:

(3) $N^S_{t_2}$ (S does not do X at t_2).[12]

This argument does seem to be valid and clearly parallel to the argument for the incompatibility of God's foreknowledge and human freedom to do otherwise—the Basic Argument. The argument is interestingly different from the parallel arguments for fatalism and the incompatibility of human foreknowledge and freedom to do otherwise insofar as the pertinent fixity-of-the-past premise is clearly more plausible. Whether there is a close similarity between the Basic Argument and the argument for the incompatibility of causal determinism and freedom to do otherwise depends on whether God's belief at t_1 about the future is, like the obtaining of condition C at t_1, a hard fact.

I wish to note a few points about the argument from causal determinism. First, the argument claims that causal determinism would rule out freedom to do otherwise *in virtue of* requiring (for such freedom) that the past not be fixed or that the laws not be fixed. Thus the "problem" that causal necessitation poses for freedom to do otherwise is that if it occurs, then freedom to do otherwise requires violation of the fixity of the past or the fixity of the natural laws. So, this argument suggests that the reason why causal determinism would threaten freedom to do otherwise is not *simply* that it would imply that each act is causally necessitated, but that the existence of such necessitation would imply that if there were freedom to do otherwise, the past or the laws would not be fixed. It is not claimed that causal necessitation *in itself* rules out freedom to do otherwise, and I shall return to this point below.

Also, it should be noted that even if the incompatibilistic arguments (with regard to causal determinism and with regard to God's foreknowledge) are on a par with respect to the fixity of the past, the second premises of the arguments are different. Thus someone could deny the second premise of the argument from causal determinism without denying the second premise of the (first version of the) Basic Argument. That is, one could deny the fixity of the natural laws, but it seems unassailable that, since God is essentially omniscient, one cannot so act that God would have held a false belief.[13]

Bringing About the Past

In this section I hope to sharpen our understanding of the Basic Argument by focusing on the notion of "bringing about the past." It will emerge that there are importantly different conceptions of bringing about the past, and it might be the case that one's evaluation of the soundness of the Basic Argument will depend on the particular interpretation of this notion that is employed.

We can begin by looking again at the second version of the Basic Argument. One form of compatibilistic response to this argument proceeds by distinguishing between a "causal" (or "strong") interpretation of "bringing it about that p" and a "non-causal" or "weak" interpretation. (At this point I simply operate with a vague distinction between causal and non-causal interpretations of "bringing it about that p"; below, I shall be more precise about the distinction between the two interpretations.) The theorist who insists on this differentiation (let us call him a "Difference Theorist") might claim that on the causal interpretation, the Basic Argument is invalid, and on the non-causal interpretation, the argument is unsound. (The precise content of this move will become clear below.) I shall refer to *anyone* who believes that there is a difference between the causal and non-causal interpretations as a Difference Theorist, and I should emphasize that some (although not all) Difference Theorists are *also* compatibilists. Perhaps the two most prominent Difference Theorists are John Turk Saunders and Alvin Plantinga.[14]

A compatibilistic Difference Theorist will say that, on the causal interpretation of "bringing it about that p," the second version of the Basic Argument is obviously invalid. This is because it is claimed that, on the causal interpretation, the Power Principle is clearly invalid. (Remember that the Power Principle says that if I can bring it about that p, and if it is true that if p were the case then q would be the case, then I can bring it about that q.) This point can allegedly be seen in the following types of examples. Imagine that I can go to the store tonight. It is true that if I were to go to the store tonight, then two plus two would equal four. But it seems that I cannot bring it about that two plus two equals four. Similarly, imagine that I can do any "ordinary" thing tomorrow, such as play softball. And of course it is true that if I were to play softball tomorrow, then the sun would not flicker out tomorrow. But I cannot bring it about that the sun continue to shine tomorrow.[15]

So it is claimed that, on the causal interpretation, the argument is invalid. And it is also alleged that, on the non-causal interpretation of the crucial idea, whereas the argument would be valid, it would not be sound, because possibility (3) could not be ruled out. The compatibilistic Difference Theorist will admit that no person can at t_2 initiate a causal sequence issuing in the occurrence of some event (which did not actually occur) at t_1, but he will claim that it is *not* incoherent (or problematic) to claim that a person can at t_2 perform some act such that if he were to perform it, the past (at t_1) would have been different from what it actually was. Of course, it is possible to agree with the Difference Theorist that there is a difference between the causal and non-causal senses of "bringing it about that p" but to deny that this difference *makes* a difference to the argument. That is, an incompatibilistic Difference Theorist would claim that, just as one cannot at t_2 initiate a backward-flowing causal chain, so one cannot at t_2 perform some act such that if one were to perform it, the past would have been different from what it actually was.

An incompatibilistic Difference Theorist thus claims that, on the non-causal reading, version three of the Basic Argument is the proper analysis of version two, and that the argument is sound. A compatibilistic Difference Theorist, on the other hand, can agree that version three is the proper analysis of version two (on the non-causal reading), but he claims that the argument is unsound. The Difference Theorist's claim that version three is the proper analysis of version two is based on two alleged facts: (i) the key locution, "bringing it about that p," can be analyzed as a conjunction of a certain sort, and (ii) once (i) is granted, the Basic Argument can be developed *without* the Power Principle. In contrast, the No-Difference Theorist claims that the causal reading is the only relevant reading of "bringing it about that p" and thus that version three cannot be construed as the appropriate analysis of version two. Further, an incompatibilistic

No-Difference Theorist will insist that there is *some* valid Power Principle that underwrites the validity of version two, and that version two is sound.

It seems to me that the Difference Theorist is correct (whether or not the difference *makes* a difference to the soundness of the argument). What I wish to do now is briefly consider one possible route to a No-Difference Theory. This route is suggested by part of William Hasker's paper, "Foreknowledge and Necessity" (Chapter 11), but Hasker is explicitly addressing an apparently different issue. In any case, it will be useful to consider whether Hasker-type considerations could yield a No-Difference Theory. This will help to bring out exactly what the two interpretations of the crucial locution—"bringing it about that *p*"—are.

Hasker is addressing himself not to the issue, as I put it, of whether there is a difference between a causal and a non-causal sense of "bringing it about that *p*," but whether there is a difference between "bringing about the past" and "counterfactual power over the past." Hasker denies that there is any such difference, and this denial is justified by what Hasker claims is a valid "Power Entailment Principle."

Hasker is concerned to show that

(A) God believed at t_1 that S would not do X at t_2 and S has it in his power at t_2 to do X at t_2

entails

(B) S has it in his power at t_2 to bring it about that God believed at t_1 that S would do X at t_2.

The claim that (A) entails (B) is supposed to follow (in part) from this power entailment principle:

(PEP3) If (a) it is within S's power to bring it about that p is true, and (b) it is within S's power to bring it about that p is false, and (c) p entails q and not-p entails not-q, then it is within S's power to bring it about that q is true.[16]

Further, Hasker attributes to Plantinga the claim that (A) does not entail (B), but only:

(B') S has it in his power at t_2 to perform some act such that if he were to perform it, God would have believed at t_1 that S would do X at t_2.

Hasker points out that if (PEP3) is valid, then the claim that he attributes to Plantinga—that (A) does not entail (B), but only (B')—is false. It would follow, then, according to Hasker, that there is no difference between "bringing about the past" (captured by (B)) and "counterfactual power over the past" (captured by (B')). There would be no difference between the two notions at least in this sense: it is necessarily the case that whenever (A) is true, then (B) is also true (as well as (B')).

Now someone might say that, if there is no difference between Hasker's two notions, "bringing about the past" and "counterfactual power over the past," then it would follow that there is no difference between what I have called the causal and non-causal senses of "bringing it about that *p*." But this is precisely what I wish to deny. I wish to maintain that even if everything that Hasker says is correct, and thus that (A) entails (B) as well as (B') (and that there is no difference between bringing about the past and counterfactual power over the past), there is still an interesting and clear difference between the causal and non-causal senses of bringing it about that *p*. It is important to see this because the point preserves the original distinction that Difference Theorists such as Saunders and Plantinga were making.

My response to the No-Difference Theory that is based on Hasker-type considerations is really very simple. The response is that even if Hasker's Power Entailment Principle (PEP3) is valid and thus (A) entails (B), there are still two interestingly different interpretations of (B), since there are two distinct interpretations of the phrase, "bringing it about that *p*," which occurs in (B). More specifically, I claim that these two interpretations can be seen to generate two ways in which (B) could be made true; thus the existence of the two interpretations is perfectly compatible with Hasker's claim that (A) entails (B).

Let us suppose that *p* is the proposition that some event *E* occurs at time t_1. Now we can distinguish two interpretations of "(at t_2) bringing it about that *p*":

Causal: At t_2 *S* brings it about that *p* if and only if *S* performs some act at t_2 which initiates a causal sequence issuing in *E*'s occurrence at t_1.

Non-causal: At t_2 *S* brings it about that *p* if and only if *S* performs some act at t_2 which is such that, if he were to perform it at t_2, then *E* would have occurred at t_1.

Now, applying this general point to (B), we can generate a causal and a non-causal interpretation:

(Bc) S has it in his power at t_2 to perform some action that would initiate a causal chain issuing in God's believing at t_1 that S would do X at t_2.

(Bn-c) S has it in his power at t_2 to perform some action such that, if he were to perform it, God would have believed at t_1 that S would do X at t_2.

Note first that (Bn-c) is the same as (B'). Now my point is that both (Bc) and (Bn-c) = (B') are possible readings of (B). That is, both (Bc) and (Bn-c) = (B') are ways in which (B) could be true. I think then that the dialectical situation is as follows. It is plausible to say that (A) implies (Bn-c) = (B'). But since (Bn-c) = (B') is one way in which (B) could be true, (Bn-c) = (B') is sufficient for (B). This explains Hasker's claim that (A) implies (B). But of course it would not follow that (A) implies (Bc), and this is the crucial issue. Both (Bc) and (Bn-c) are sufficient for (B), but it has not been established that they are both necessary for (B). Thus one can have (Bn-c) without having (Bc), and one can have (A) without having (Bc). On this way of understanding the situation, Plantinga's point is *not* properly construed as the claim that (A) does not entail (B), but only (B'); rather, his claim is that (A) does not entail (Bc), but only (Bn-c) = (B').

The above considerations imply that even if (PEP3) is valid and there is no difference between Hasker's "bringing about the past" and "counterfactual power over the past," there are still two interestingly different interpretations of "bringing about the past": a causal interpretation and a non-causal interpretation. Thus I do not believe that one could employ "Hasker-type" considerations to generate a No-Difference Theory about "bringing it about that p." I believe, then, that I have defended the basic point that Saunders and Plantinga were attempting to make.

I wish finally to suggest a reason why one might mistakenly think that the No-Difference Theory is true. Such locutions as "bringing it about that p" and "causing it to be the case that p" are "causal" locutions. Both imply, in my view, that the agent causes *something*. Seeing this, one might fail to notice that there are (at least) two interestingly different interpretations of the locutions, depending on exactly *what* is supposed to be caused. If p is the proposition that some event E occurs, then on the causal interpretation, one is required to cause E. In contrast, on the non-causal interpretation, one is required to cause *something else*, which is such that were it to occur, E would have occurred. Hiding behind a causal locution, then, are two different ideas.

I have been concerned to establish that we cannot reach the No-Difference Theory via a Power Entailment Principle (of a certain sort). Also, I have attempted to specify exactly what the difference is between the two interpretations of "bringing it about that p." But I wish to emphasize that even if we are Difference Theorists, this does not imply that we are compatibilists. Remember that there are both compatibilistic and incompatibilistic Difference Theorists; one's approach here will depend on whether one thinks that the difference in question *makes* a difference to the soundness of the Basic Argument. In what follows, I shall assume that the Difference Theory is correct, and I shall simply assume that the appropriate interpretation of "bringing it about that p" is the non-causal interpretation. On this interpretation, it is not evident to me that the Power Principle is invalid, and thus it is not evident to me that version two of the Basic Argument is invalid. Further, as I said above, on the non-causal interpretation it is plausible to take version three as an *analysis* of version two. The question, then, in what follows will be whether the Basic Argument, understood as version (3), is sound.

The Future Is Not Real

The first way of responding to the Basic Argument (in all its versions) that I shall investigate denies that the future is "real." Of course, this is an extremely vague formulation of the position, and various different strategies fall under this rubric.

Geach's Strategy

The first approach to denying the reality of the future is associated with Peter Geach.[17] Geach claims that some statements that are apparently about the future are really only about the present. His claim is about the *content* of statements putatively about future contingent events. So, for example, Geach would claim that a statement such as "S will not do X at t_2," when made at t_1, really means that conditions present at t_1 tend toward S's not doing X at t_2. In general, Geach's strategy is to re-interpret claims that are apparently about the future as claims that are "really" about the present. Along these lines, the propo-sitions, "God believes at t_1 that S will not do X at t_2" and "God believes at t_1 that S does not (tenselessly) X at t_2" are inter-preted as: God believes at t_1 that the world at t_1 is "tending to-ward" S's not doing X at t_2. Such an interpretation makes "God believes at t_1 that S will not do X at t_2" compatible with "S does X at t_2," because the world's tending at t_1 toward S's not doing X at t_2 is compatible with S's doing X at t_2. This fact opens the possibility of a response to the Basic Argument. The response simply points out that S's doing X at t_2 does *not* require that God have a different belief from the one He actually had (and it does not require that God have a false belief at t_1, and so forth). Let us suppose that S, although he does not do X at t_2, *can* do X at t_2. On one way of understanding this sort of claim, there exists some non-actual possible world (suitably related to the actual world) in which S does X at t_2. Applying Geach's strategy, in this non-actual world God holds the true belief at t_1 that the world at t_1 is "tending toward" S's not doing X at t_2.

There are, I believe, various problems with Geach's approach. (Some of the problems are shared by the other approaches that deny the reality of the future.) One very basic problem is that it denies to God any knowledge of what "really" will happen in the future. This picture of God, although certainly not incoher-ent, portrays God's omniscience as very restricted. Insofar as one wishes to preserve a more robust conception of God's om-niscience, one will want to reject Geach's approach. The point here is not that Geach does not construe God as omniscient; rather, the point is that, on Geach's view, God's omniscience does not involve His knowing anything about the future. Thus God's omniscience would not constitute a sufficiently robust awareness of the world, according to one picture of God.

Further, it is implausible to think that statements apparently about the future are "really" only about the present. In our de-liberation about the future, we certainly *think* that we are con-cerned with the *future* (and not simply with present tendencies), so a strong case would have to be made in order to justify "re-interpreting" and "re-constructing" our ordinary views. I think that we can point to the implausibility of Geach's approach by considering the following proposition:

(P) Although the world is now tending toward event E's occurring tomorrow, event E will not in fact occur tomorrow.

Proposition (P) seems to be consistent, but, on Geach's approach, it is evidently logically inconsistent. This is because, on Geach's approach, (P) is to be understood as:

(P*) The world is tending now toward event E's occurring tomorrow, and the world is not in fact now tending toward E's occurring tomorrow.

And (P*) is obviously inconsistent. Insofar as we think (P) is logically consistent, then, we will want to resist Geach's approach.[18]

Future Contingents Are Not True

Geach's strategy is to deny the reality of the future by denying that statements apparently about the future are really about the future. Other philosophers are willing to say that statements apparently about the future are really about the future, but they nevertheless wish to deny the reality of the future. Such philosophers deny that there are any *true* propositions (or statements) about "future contingent events" (or future free actions). Some of these theorists wish to maintain that all future contingent propositions are false prior to the times they are about.[19] Other such theorists hold that all future contingent propositions are neither true nor false; they are "indeterminate" in truth value (prior to the times they are about).[20] If this approach is plausible at all, it is precisely because it denies Geach's claim and insists that future contingents are genuinely about the future. On this approach, however, the future is not "already there" to ground the truth of the propositions in question. (It should be evident how this strategy provides an escape from the conclusion of the Basic Argument.)

Philosophers who deny that any future contingents are true now are likely to argue as follows. In order for a proposition to be true now, some conditions must obtain now in virtue of which the proposition is "metaphysically grounded."[21] If no such condition obtains, then it makes no sense to say that the future contingent proposition is true now. And if some such condition obtains, then the contingency of the statement is destroyed. There is a trade-off, then, between the putative truth and contingency of the relevant propositions. Some philosophers thus insist that there are no true statements that are both genuinely about the future and genuinely contingent. In particular, there are no statements that are currently true and are of the form, "*S* freely performs some action in the future."

The sorts of propositions we have been discussing might be called "absolute future contingents." Some philosophers have made arguments parallel to the one sketched above to the conclusion that there are no true "conditional future contingents," propositions of the form, "If in circumstance *C*, *S* would freely do *X*." (Such propositions are sometimes called "counterfactuals of freedom.") A classic formulation of this position is that of Robert Adams, and it will be useful to cite Adams at some length:

This passage [concerning David and Saul] was a favorite proof text for the Jesuit theologians. They took it to prove that God knew the following two propositions to be true:

(1) If David stayed in Keilah, Saul would besiege the city.
(2) If David stayed in Keilah and Saul besieged the city, the men of Keilah would surrender David to Saul. . . .

I do not understand what it would be for (these) propositions to be true, given that the actions in question would have been free, and that David did not stay in Keilah. I will explain my incomprehension.

First we must note that middle knowledge [knowledge of the relevant "counterfactuals of freedom"] is not simple *fore*knowledge. . . . For there never was nor will be an actual besieging of Keilah by Saul, nor an actual betrayal of David to Saul by the men of Keilah, to which those propositions might correspond.

Some other grounds that might be suggested for the truth of (1) and (2) are ruled out by the assumption that the actions of Saul and the men of Keilah are and would be free in the relevant sense. The suggestion that Saul's besieging Keilah follows by *logical* necessity from David's staying there is implausible in any case. It would be more plausible to suggest that Saul's besieging Keilah follows by *causal* necessity from David's staying there. . . . But both of these suggestions are inconsistent with the assumption that Saul's action would have been free.

Since necessitation is incompatible with the relevant sort of free will, we might seek non-necessitating grounds for the truth of (1) and (2) in the actual intentions, desires, and character of Saul and the Keilahites. . . .

But the basis thus offered for the truth of (1) and (2) is inadequate precisely because it is not necessitating. A free agent may act out of character, or change his intentions, or fail to act on them. Therefore the propositions which may be true by virtue of correspondence with the intentions, desires, and character of Saul and the men of Keilah are not (1) and (2) but

(5) If David stayed in Keilah, Saul would *probably* besiege the city.
(6) If David stayed in Keilah and Saul besieged the city, the men of Keilah would *probably* surrender David to Saul.

(5) and (6) . . . will not satisfy the partisans of middle knowledge. It is part of their theory that God knows infallibly what definitely would happen, and not just what would probably happen or what free creatures would be likely to do.[22]

Adams is talking about conditional future contingent propositions, but the argument that these cannot be true is similar to the argument that absolute future contingents cannot be true. The point is that there is an alleged tension between the "grounding" and, thus, the truth of both sorts of propositions and their contingency. (Knowledge of conditional future contingent propositions was called "middle knowledge" by the Jesuits because it was supposed to be "in between" God's knowledge of necessary truths and God's knowledge of His own will and those truths that are causally determined by His will.)

It is hard to know how to resolve the controversy between those who deny that future contingents can be true and those who claim that they can be true, and I do not propose to attempt to do this. I do, however, think that the view that such propositions can be true (presently) is not unreasonable. Imagine that Jill plays softball at t_2. It seems to follow that "Jill will play softball at t_2" is true at t_1. As Alfred Freddoso put the point (see note 21), what else could the future tense mean?

But what present facts could "ground" future contingent propositions—conditional or absolute? I am inclined to think that certain present facts about an individual's character could ground the truth of such propositions (without involving causal necessitation). And there is considerable intuitive support for this view. To see the point, consider an example discussed by Robert Adams. It seems that if I were to offer the advertised price to a butcher, he would give me the meat, and he would do so freely. Facts about the character of the butcher—his desires, beliefs, intentions, and so forth—seem to ground the conditional, "If I were to offer to pay the advertised price, the butcher would give me the meat," rather than only the probabilistic conditional, "If I were to offer to pay the advertised price, the butcher would *probably* give me the meat." A proponent of Adams's position must deny that the non-probabilistic conditional is true, given that the butcher would be acting freely.

Consider, also, the conditional, "If John Fischer were offered an endowed chair at Stanford University with a salary of one million dollars a year, he would accept it." It appears to me that facts about my character ground the truth of this conditional, rather than merely the probabilistic conditional, "If John Fischer were offered an endowed chair at Stanford with a salary of one million dollars, he would *probably* accept it." (Of course, the relevant conditional could be strengthened explicitly to, "If John Fischer were offered an endowed chair at Stanford University . . . and he received no comparable offers, then he would accept it," although this is hardly necessary.) Further, it seems to me that the truth of the first (non-probabilistic) conditional is compatible with my accepting the position *freely* (albeit gleefully). Also, there is no reason to deny that similar considerations apply to *absolute* future contingents: facts about character, when conjoined with facts about which circumstances will obtain, seem capable of providing suitable grounding.

Some more support for the claim that future contingent propositions can be presently true comes from an analogy with propositions about the past.[23] It is evident that a proposition such as "John F. Kennedy was assassinated" is now true. But what present conditions "metaphysically ground" its truth? It is tempting to deny that there must be such present conditions, and to claim instead that "John F. Kennedy was assassinated" is now metaphysically grounded insofar as there *were* conditions in the past that metaphysically grounded the proposition, "John F. Kennedy is assassinated." Analogously, one could say that "Jill will play softball tomorrow" is now true if there will be conditions obtaining tomorrow that will metaphysically ground the proposition, "Jill plays softball." Thus, if we believe that propositions about the past can be presently grounded, and if there is an analogy here between past and future, we should also think that propositions about the future can be presently grounded.

Lukasiewicz briefly considered an argument similar to the one just given, and it is interesting that he was willing to "bite the bullet": he accepted the analogy between past and future, but he denied that either is "real" or metaphysically grounded now:

> We should not treat the past differently from the future. . . . Facts whose effects have disappeared altogether, and which even an omniscient mind could not infer from those now occurring, belong to the realm of possibility. One cannot say about them that they took place, but only that they were *possible*. It is well that it should be so. There are hard moments of suffering and still harder ones of guilt in everyone's life. We should be glad to be able to erase them not only from our memory but also from existence.[24]

Remember, also, Stephen Dedalus's lament, "History is a nightmare from which I am trying to awake." Unhappily, I do not think that we can escape from the past in the way suggested by Lukasiewicz—that we can literally banish it from existence. And, given the analogy between past and future, I believe that there is at least some reason to think that future contingents can presently be true.

Also, we should note that, on the picture according to which future contingents cannot be presently true, God's omniscience is significantly attenuated. Although God would know all truths, He would not know about future free actions, and thus He would not be robustly omniscient. This view of God's omniscience, then, has the same problem as Geach's view.

Propositions Are Not True at Times

A final strategy, related to those sketched above, denies the coherence of locutions such as "Proposition p is true at time t." On this approach, one could deny that the proposition, "S will not do X at t_2," is true at t_1, and thus deny that God believed at t_1 that S would not do X at t_2. Clearly, this approach would reject the notion of omniscience that has been employed in the Basic Argument: a person is omniscient just in case at any time t he believes all and only those propositions true *at* t.

Various philosophers have called into question the idea that propositions (or statements) can be true *at particular times*.[25] One might here use the analogy between spatial and temporal location and say that, just as it is inappropriate to think of propositions as being true in certain places, it is inappropriate to think of them as being true at certain times. So, for example, even if there is furniture in the house, it is odd to say that the proposition "There is furniture" is true *in the house*. Also, it is unclear what it would mean to say that the proposition "Two plus two equals four" is true *in Tibet* (or anywhere, for that matter). And just as it is unclear what such locutions mean, one might argue that it is unclear what it means to say that a certain proposition is true at a time.

I am not convinced that it is incoherent to speak of propositions being true at certain times. But I also believe that the Basic Argument can be developed without the assumption that propositions can be true at times. All that seems to be required for the Basic Argument is that at any given time God believes what is true, not that God believes what is true *at that time*.[26] If propositions are "timelessly true," then the pertinent notion of omniscience would be: a person is omniscient just in case at any given time he believes all and only those propositions that are (timelessly) true. This notion of omniscience would generate the Basic Argument, even if propositions could not be true at times. Of course, this notion of omniscience would not generate the Basic Argument if *future contingents* were not timelessly true, but now we have returned essentially to the strategies sketched above. The point I wish to make here is that it is not possible to avoid the thrust of the Basic Argument *simply* by denying that propositions are true at times.

Omniscience and Omnipotence

There is a strategy of response to the Basic Argument that is similar to the strategies discussed in the previous section insofar as it denies to God any beliefs about future contingents, but it is crucially different insofar as it concedes the reality of the future. On this view, future contingents can be true presently, but God cannot know them. Specifically, the claim is that it is "logically impossible" to have knowledge of propositions stating that an agent will freely do something in the future, and because it is logically impossible to know such propositions, it is no real limitation of God that He does not know them. On this view (as on the views discussed above), God can be omniscient without knowing propositions about future free actions. The proponent of this view might claim that there is a close analogy between

God's omnipotence and God's omniscience. Just as it is no limitation of God's power that He cannot perform tasks whose descriptions are logically contradictory, so also it is no limitation of God's knowledge that He cannot know propositions that are logically impossible to know. This position, including the analogy between omnipotence and omniscience, has been defended by Richard Swinburne.[27] This approach provides a distinctive response to the Basic Argument in part because it gives some motivation for a denial that God's existence implies His having beliefs about future free actions.

We can divide Swinburne's claim into two separate parts: (i) it is logically impossible for any individual to have knowledge that someone will freely perform some act in the future, and (ii) it is no limitation of God that He does not have such knowledge. It is not evident why Swinburne takes (i) to be true. Perhaps he is supposing that in order to know that someone will perform some act, one must have infallible evidence that he will perform the act, and that the existence of such evidence is inconsistent with the person's acting freely. But it is unclear that in general we demand infallible evidence for knowledge. And even if we did demand such evidence (or, at least, that God's knowledge be based on infallible evidence), it is not evident why this would rule out acting freely. If acting freely requires freedom to do otherwise, and "infallible evidence" must consist in (or correspond to) facts that, together with the laws of nature, entail that the act in question be performed, then one could claim that infallible evidence rules out acting freely insofar as causal necessitation rules out freedom to do otherwise. This may be the thought that lies behind Swinburne's (i). If so, it is useful first to notice that it seems to deny the idea that certain facts (perhaps about an individual's character) can ground *knowledge* about future action without causally necessitating the future action. (This idea is parallel to the idea mentioned above—that facts about a person's character might ground the *truth* of future contingents, without causally necessitating them.) I am particularly dubious about the claim that only facts that causally necessitate future action can ground knowledge of future action, and thus I am dubious about the claim that knowledge of future free action is logically impossible.

Also, it is not clear that the analogy between omniscience and omnipotence that supports Swinburne's (ii) is a close one. Although I shall not go into this debate here, some philosophers have denied that the analogy is useful.[28]

Finally, as with the strategies that deny the reality of the future, one wonders whether Swinburne's approach provides a sufficiently robust conception of God's omniscience. Because all of the strategies discussed so far seem to retreat from a robust conception of God's omniscience, it will be useful in the next section to consider an approach that embodies a robust conception of God's omniscience—involving genuine foreknowledge.[29]

Ockhamism

Above I introduced a distinction between temporally non-relational and temporally relational facts: the hard fact/soft fact distinction. It is now time to discuss a sort of response to the Basic Argument that exploits this distinction: Ockhamism. The Ockhamist claims that facts such as God's existence and/or God's beliefs are soft facts about the relevant times and thus that it does not follow from the fixity of the past that they are fixed (at later times). The Ockhamist, then, argues that the fixity-of-the-past claims made by the various versions of the Basic Argument are not true, and, thus, that the Basic Argument is not sound. (Another approach—multiple-pasts compatibilism—asserts that the fixity-of-the-past claims are false for a different reason; this strategy will be discussed below.)

In *Predestination, God's Foreknowledge and Future Contingents*, Ockham makes a distinction that corresponds to the distinction between hard and soft facts about times:

Some propositions are about the present as regards both their wording and their subject matter (*secundum vocem et secundum rem*). Where such propositions are concerned, it is universally true that every true proposition about the present has (corresponding to it) a necessary one about the past: e.g., "Socrates is seated," "Socrates is walking," "Socrates is just," and the like.

Other propositions are about the present as regards their wording only and are equivalently about the future, since their truth depends on the truth of propositions about the future. Where such (propositions) are concerned, the rule that every true proposition about the present has corresponding to it a necessary proposition about the past is not true [pp. 46–47].[30]

Ockham's "propositions about the present as regards both their wording and their subject matter" correspond to hard facts, and his claim is that they are fixed at later times. Ockham's "propositions about the present as regards their wording only" correspond to soft facts, and his claim is that they need not be fixed at later times.

In the discussion here of various particular Ockhamistic strategies, I shall want to separate the following questions. (1) Can we give an intuitively adequate account of the distinction between hard and soft facts—an account that at least matches our considered opinions over a wide range of relatively clear cases? (2) Is a fact such as that God believed at t_1 that S would not do X at t_2 a hard fact about t_1? (3) Is a fact such as that God believed at t_1 that S would not do X at t_2 fixed at t_2? This last question raises the issue of the relationship between the distinction between hard and soft facts and the distinction between fixed facts and those facts that are not fixed. Specifically, I want to explore the issue of whether there is good reason to think that some soft facts are fixed (at later times).

The Ockhamist claims that the Basic Argument inappropriately applies the idea of the fixity of the past. The Ockhamist does not deny that some facts about the past are fixed; indeed, he is willing to grant that all hard facts about the past are fixed presently. But the Ockhamist claims that the Basic Argument applies a principle (that of the fixity of the past) to facts to which it is irrelevant: soft facts.

We can distinguish two sorts of Ockhamism. The first sort of Ockhamism might be called "Existence Ockhamism." It claims that God's existence is a soft fact about the past and thus that the fixity-of-the-past principle cannot legitimately be applied to it. The second kind of Ockhamism might be dubbed "Belief Ockhamism." It claims that God's belief at a time is a soft fact about the time and thus that the fixity-of-the-past principle is irrelevant to it.

Marilyn McCord Adams's Approach

I shall begin by considering briefly Existence Ockhamism. This position is represented by Marilyn McCord Adams's essay, "Is the Existence of God a 'Hard' Fact?" (Chapter 3). Adams begins by distinguishing two conceptions of God. Both conceptions employ the term "God" as a "title-term" or "role-indicator" rather than a proper name. On the first conception, "God is essentially everlasting" simply means that it is an analytic truth that whoever is God is everlasting. On the second conception, "God is essentially everlasting" means not only that it is an analytic truth that whoever is God is everlasting, but also that being everlasting is necessary to the personal identity of the individual who is God. So imagine that individual Y is actually God. On the second conception it follows that if some individual were not everlasting, he would not be identical to Y: being everlasting is an essential feature of Y. (This second conception is adopted by Nelson Pike in setting out his version of the Basic Argument in his seminal and classic paper, "Divine Omniscience and Voluntary Action" [Chapter 2]).

Adams also presents an account of the distinction between hard and soft facts by reference to which she argues that on both conceptions of God, God's existence is a soft fact about the relevant time. On the first conception, if G is actually God at time t_1, then Adams argues that "G is God" is a soft fact about t_1. And if this is so, then there is no reason stemming from the fixity of the past to say that one cannot at t_2 so act that G would exist but would not be God at t_1. On the second conception, if G is actually God at t_1, then Adams argues that "G exists" is a soft fact about t_1. And if so, then there is no reason stemming from the fixity of the past to say that one cannot at t_2 so act that G would not have existed at t_1.

Below I shall consider at some length Adams's suggested account of the distinction between hard and soft facts. But here I shall simply claim that Existence Ockhamism is considerably less attractive than Belief Ockhamism. This is because it is theologically implausible to claim that humans can affect the existence of God.[31] That is, God's existence should be construed as "counterfactually independent of possible human action." This assumption was presented above in the development of the Basic Argument. The simple point is that even if God's existence were a soft fact, there would be another reason (different from considerations of the fixity of the past) for the pertinent premise of the Basic Argument. Because of this consideration and because it does not also apply to Belief Ockhamism, I shall focus exclusively on Belief Ockhamism below, and I shall simply refer to this position as "Ockhamism."

Even if Adams's Existence Ockhamism is unattractive, her suggestion for an account of the crucial hard fact/soft fact distinction is important and highly influential. (Obviously, this account might be employed by the Belief Ockhamist as well as the Existence Ockhamist.) For the sake of simplicity, I shall present my own version of Adams's suggestion; it should be kept in mind that this is a simplification and that it differs from the actual form of Adams's suggestion as she presents it. I do not, however, think that my version of the criterion distorts it in any way relevant to my discussion of it. Adams's account of the distinction between hard and soft facts can be presented as follows:

(A) (1) A fact F is about a time t_1 if and only if F's obtaining entails that something occur at t_1; (2) A fact F about t_1 is a soft fact about t_1 if and only if F's obtaining entails that something (contingent) occurs at some later time t_2; (3) A fact F about t_1 is a hard fact about t_1 if and only if it is not a soft fact about t_1.

What exactly is meant by "something's occurring at t_1"? In effect, Adams would say that "something's occurring at t_1" consists in "the happening or not happening, actuality or non-actuality of something at t_1."

Of course, (A) is rather rough, but I believe that it is sufficiently precise to allow us to draw out some implications. On (A) the fact that God believed at t_1 that S would not do X at t_2 is deemed a soft fact about t_1: its obtaining entails that S does not do X at t_2. It is here obvious that (A) embodies an "Entailment Criterion of Soft Facthood": a soft fact about t_1 *entails* that some contingent fact obtains at some later time t_2.

(A) is initially attractive. Also, (A) has the implication that God's belief at a time (about the future) is a soft fact about the time at which it is held, and thus (A) is appealing to an Ockhamist. But I believe that (A) is defective, and I develop some criticisms of (A) in my "Freedom and Foreknowledge" (Chapter 4).[32] It will be useful to set out a fundamental problem with (A) here.

The problem with (A) is that it appears as though (A) must classify all facts as soft. Consider the fact, "Jack is sitting at t_1." This should be classified as a hard fact about t_1. But notice that "Jack is sitting at t_1" entails that it is not the case that Jack sits for the first time at t_2. (And the latter fact entails the "not-happening" of "Jack sits for the first time" at t_2.) Thus, in virtue of (A)'s embodying the Entailment Criterion of Soft Facthood, it must classify "Jack is sitting at t_1" as a *soft* fact about t_1. Because this sort of result is clearly generalizable, it appears as if (A) will classify all facts as soft, and it is therefore evidently unacceptable. One is tempted here to say, with Sergeant Friday, "The facts . . . *just* the facts!"

In their contribution to this volume, Joshua Hoffman and Gary Rosenkrantz (Chapter 7) attempt to refine (A) in part by refining the second component, (A2). Their approach can be understood as providing a more sophisticated Entailment Criterion. On Hoffman and Rosenkrantz's view, it is not sufficient for a fact to be a soft fact that it entail that something contingent occur at a later time; rather, the fact in question must entail that a fact of a *certain sort* obtain at a later time. I shall discuss their proposal below, but here I wish to consider a related strategy.

David Widerker has noted that, whereas a fact such as "Jack is sitting at t_1" does entail the non-occurrence of the event "Jack sits for the first time" at t_2, it does *not* entail that t_2 occur. In other words, "Jack is sitting at t_1" does entail that it is not the case that the event "Jack is sitting for the first time" occurs at t_2, but it does not entail that t_2 occur. The point is that there are two ways in which it might be true that it is not the case that the event "Jack is sitting for the first time" occurs at t_2. In the first way, t_2 occurs but at t_2 either Jack is not sitting at all, or he is sitting and he has sat before. In the second way, the world has gone out of existence and t_2 does not even occur. Obviously, it is a presupposition of this view that it is not logically necessary that time continue: it is presupposed that it is logically and in some sense metaphysically possible that time stop. Presumably, the picture is that time would stop if the world, including all of space (and thus time), went out of existence.[33]

Exploiting Widerker's point, we could slightly modify (A) as follows:

(A') (1') A fact F is about a time t_1 if and only if F's obtaining entails both that t_1 occurs and that something occurs at t_1; (2') A fact F about t_1 is a soft fact about t_1 if and only if F's obtaining entails that some later time t_2 occurs.

The new criterion, (A'), includes (A1'), (A2'), and (A3). (A') appears to remain faithful to the idea of Adams's approach but to avoid the implausible consequence of (A) that all facts about t are considered soft facts about t. Further, (A') has the consequence that "God believed at t_1 that S would (exist but) not do X at t_2" is a soft fact about t_1; this is because God's belief here entails that t_2 occurs.

But I believe that (A') is also inadequate. It will be useful to see exactly why (A') is problematic in part because this will help us better to understand certain features of the accounts of the distinction between hard and soft facts presented in this volume. The problem with (A') is this. On (A'), the fact that God believed at t_1 that S would not do X at t_2 (let us call this fact "F_1") is a soft fact about t_1, as stated above. Now, consider the following fact, which is generated by simply counting all the persons who hold the belief at t_1 that S will not do X at t_2: "Exactly seven persons believed at t_1 that S would not do X at t_2." (Let us call this fact "F_2.") I claim that if F_1 is considered a soft fact about t_1, then F_2 should be considered a soft fact as well. But whereas (A') implies that F_1 is a soft fact about t_1, (A') implies that F_2 is a hard fact about t_1: F_2 does not entail that time continue after t_1. (To see this, remember that the definition of entailment is as follows: p entails q if and only if q is true in all the possible worlds in which p is true. And note that in *some* possible worlds in which F_2 obtains, time stops at t_1; in such worlds, God is not among the seven believers at t_1.)

Insofar as God is one of the seven persons who at t_1 believed that S would not do X at t_2, I claim that, if F_1 is classified as a soft fact about t_1, then F_2 should be so classified as well. But since (A') classifies F_1 but not F_2 as soft, (A') does not capture our intuitive judgments about softness (i.e., about temporal relationality). I believe that this problem in itself shows that (A') is deficient. But I shall now point out why this sort of problem makes it impossible for an Ockhamist to employ (A') in defense of his position. (Of course, the fact that (A') cannot be employed by an Ockhamist does not in itself constitute a reason to think that (A') is inadequate; but this is, nevertheless, an interesting fact.)

Imagine again that S does not do X at t_2 and that both F_1 and F_2 obtain. Suppose also that if S were to do X at t_2, then only God would have had a belief different from His actual belief. That is, assume that if S were to do X at t_2, then everyone but God would have believed at t_1 as he actually believed as regards S's behavior at t_2. Now imagine that S can indeed do X at t_2. It follows that S can so act that F_1 would not have been a fact. This is unproblematic for the Ockhamist who employs (A'), since

(A') implies that F_1 is a soft fact about t_1. But notice that it also follows that S can so act that F_2 would not have been a fact. And F_2 is classified by (A') as a hard fact about t_1. Further, the Ockhamist believes that one cannot at t_2 so act that a hard fact about t_1 would not have been a fact.

The problem for the Ockhamist could be put as follows. On (A') F_1 is classified as soft. But there are circumstances in which the only way an agent can falsify F_1 is to falsify a fact such as F_2. (Further, these circumstances do not seem to affect whether or not S is free.) But F_2 is classified by (A') as a hard fact. When (in certain circumstances) falsifying a soft fact F would require falsifying some hard fact F', I shall say that F is a "hard-core soft fact" (relative to those circumstances). And if one believes that hard facts about the past are presently fixed, one should also believe that hard-core soft facts about the past are currently fixed.[34]

(A') then cannot be employed by the Ockhamist. In circumstances in which the Ockhamist will wish to say that God's prior belief is not fixed, (A') will have the consequence that it is a hard-core soft fact about the past (relative to those circumstances) and thus fixed. I believe that the Ockhamist needs an account of soft facts which allows him to say that F_2 is a soft fact about t_1 insofar as God is one of the believers. One might say that there are different ways in which F_2 could be true, and one wants to be able to take a snapshot of the world to capture the way in which F_2 is actually made true. Thus, one wants a "Snapshot Ockhamism."

A version of Snapshot Ockhamism will presumably say that a fact such as F_2 is a *complex* fact that is "constructed" out of atomic constituents. And since one of its atomic constituents, F_1, is a soft fact, the complex fact is also a soft fact. It is interesting to note that the various accounts of the distinction between hard and soft facts presented by Hoffman and Rosenkrantz, Freddoso, and Hasker (Chapters 7, 8, and 11, respectively) all explicitly employ some such distinction between atomic and complex facts. These accounts thus presuppose some sort of atomism as regards facts (or perhaps states of affairs, propositions, and so forth): the view that we can in some non-arbitrary fashion distinguish between complex and atomic elements. Some sort of atomism is often assumed in order to give an account of the distinction between hard and soft facts that is adequate to Ockhamism, and this atomism appears to issue at least in part from the need to have a Snapshot Ockhamism.

The Pure Present

I now wish to discuss briefly some of the accounts of the distinction between hard and soft facts that are given in this volume. When considering the various accounts, it is important to distinguish the issue of whether the accounts are faithful to our considered judgments about clear cases from whether the accounts are "Ockhamistic"—that is, whether they imply that God's belief about the future is a soft fact. Before I discuss aspects of the particular accounts, I wish to emphasize a feature that they all have in common. As Freddoso puts it in Chapter 8, the Ockhamist believes in the "metaphysical primacy of the pure present." On this view, truths about the past are now true because of what happened in the "pure present" at past times. And truths about the future are now true because of what will happen in the "pure present" at future times. The notion of the "pure present" is the idea of what is "really happening" at a time— of what is happening in a "basic" sense. What is happening in the pure present at any given time can be identified with the temporally non-relational, that is, hard facts about the time. Thus the search for hard facts is the search for the "pure present," which is taken by the Ockhamist (and perhaps any other non-fatalistic philosopher) as metaphysically primary.

Each of the various accounts of hard facts begins with an ingredient meant to capture at least part of the idea of what is happening in the pure present at a time. I shall call this ingredient of each account its "Basic Ingredient." It is interesting to compare the various Basic Ingredients; each account offers a slightly different Basic Ingredient, although some are extremely similar. Further, each account constructs the notion of a hard fact about a time using the Basic Ingredient. Again, it is interesting to compare the various ways in which the different accounts construct hard facts out of the Basic Ingredient. (Some of the constructions explicitly employ the distinction between atomic and complex facts discussed above.)

In my brief presentation of the Basic Ingredients, I shall simplify considerably, because my purpose here is to give the reader the fundamental ideas behind the various approaches and to compare and discuss them in a clear way. In presenting the Basic Ingredients, I shall sometimes depart considerably from the actual presentations by the original authors. Of course, in order to get the full force and subtlety of each of the accounts, it will be necessary to look carefully at the papers in this volume.

Eddy Zemach and David Widerker (Chapter 6) can be understood as employing the idea of a set of facts compatible with the world's ending at t (i.e., there being no times after t) as part of an account of the pure present at t. It is clear, of course, that this Basic Ingredient captures only part of the idea of the pure present at t, because contained in the set of facts compatible with the world's ending at t will be facts about times prior to t. This Basic Ingredient is meant to capture those facts not about the future relative to t; what is happening in the pure present at t, then, will be a *subset* of these facts. Widerker and Zemach then proceed to construct an account of hard facts about t from this Basic Ingredient: the set of facts compatible with the world's ending at t.

Freddoso seeks to articulate the set of facts that are, in Ockham's words, "accidentally necessary" at t. Ockham seems to think of the set of accidentally necessary facts as at least potentially larger than the set of hard facts. Later, I shall be a bit more explicit about the relationship between accidental necessity and hardness, but here I shall simply take Freddoso to be giving an account of the hard facts. To generate the set of hard facts about a time t, Freddoso begins with the set of "present-tense, atomic, and temporally indifferent" facts relative to t. A fact F is temporally indifferent (relative to t) if and only if (roughly) (a) F (and its negation) obtains at t in some possible world in which t is the first moment of time; (b) F (and its negation) obtains at t in some possible world in which t is the last moment of time; and (c) F (and its negation) obtains at t in some possible world in which t is an intermediate moment in time. Freddoso then proceeds to construct an account of hard facts about t from this Basic Ingredient: the set of present tense, atomic, and temporally indifferent facts.

In Chapter 11, Hasker begins with the set of facts that are atomic and "future-indifferent" (with respect to t). He defines the set of atomic propositions that are future-indifferent with respect to t roughly as follows: those atomic propositions that are consistent with there being no times after *t* and also consistent with there being times after *t*. As Hasker puts it, "a future-indifferent proposition must permit, but not require, that the entire universe should disappear and there be nothing at all after [*t*]" (p. 231). As with Widerker and Zemach, it is clear that Hasker's Basic Ingredient is intended to capture *part* of the idea of the pure present: those facts that are not at least partly about the future. Hasker then proceeds to construct an account of the hard facts that employs this Basic Ingredient: the set of atomic, future-indifferent facts.

For Hoffman and Rosenkrantz (Chapter 7), the pure present at *t* is built out of those present-tense facts that obtain at *t*, are "unrestrictedly repeatable," and do not entail unrestrictedly repeatable facts that obtain at times after *t*. Their account is quite subtle and complex, and I shall greatly oversimplify here, in order to provide a clear picture of the thrust of the account. An unrestrictedly repeatable fact is one that "may obtain, then fail to obtain, then obtain again indefinitely many times throughout all of time" (p. 127). For example, "Sam sits" would be an unrestrictedly repeatable fact, whereas "Sam sits at t_1" or "Sam sits for the first time" would not be unrestrictedly repeatable facts. Hoffman and Rosenkrantz then employ their Basic Ingredient— the set of present-tense facts that are unrestrictedly repeatable and do not entail unrestrictedly repeatable facts about future times—to generate the account of the hard facts.

It can now be seen exactly how Hoffman and Rosenkrantz are refining the Entailment Criterion of Soft Facthood. Above I discussed a refinement of Adams's approach, (A'), which embodied a refinement of the Entailment Criterion. Hoffman and Rosenkrantz employ a similar strategy; on their approach, it is not sufficient for a fact to be a soft fact about a time that it entail that some contingent fact obtains at a later time, but the fact must entail that some contingent fact of a certain sort—an unrestrictedly repeatable fact—obtains at a later time.[35]

It is interesting to note that all of the accounts seem to embody some version of the Entailment Criterion of Soft Facthood: the claim that a fact is a soft fact about t_1 if it entails that a certain kind of fact obtains at later times, where the relevant kind of fact might simply be that the world does not go out of existence. The approach of Hoffman and Rosenkrantz explicitly embodies a version of the Entailment Criterion. The other approaches appear implicitly to rely on such a criterion. For instance, Widerker and Zemach employ the notion of a set of facts compatible with the world's ending at t to isolate the hard facts about t. This implies that a soft fact about t is (among other things) incompatible with the world's ending at t. But to say that a fact is incompatible with the world's ending at t is to say that it entails that the world continues at a time after t. (In general, p entails q just in case p is incompatible with not-q.) Similar remarks apply to the other approaches to the distinction between hard and soft facts.

I digress briefly to point out that the distinctions between hard and soft facts and temporally non-relational and temporally relational properties are similar to (or perhaps special cases of) other distinctions that are philosophically important. For instance, one might distinguish between "intrinsic" and "extrinsic" properties of objects. Certain changes involve merely extrinsic properties; Geach called these changes "mere-Cambridge changes."[36] So, for instance, when I take a step farther away from Jane, she acquires a new "extrinsic" property: being located one step farther away from me. Whereas this is a change in Jane, it is only a change in an "extrinsic" property and is thus a mere-Cambridge change. In contrast, when Jane grows an inch taller, she acquires a new intrinsic property: a new height. It is a challenging philosophical project to produce non-circular, illuminating accounts of intrinsic and extrinsic properties. Also, certain predicates seem to pick out "natural kinds"—properties that are referred to in natural laws or perhaps in the best generalizations we can produce in order to predict and explain natural and social phenomena. In contrast, other predicates refer to properties that are in some intuitive sense "artificial" or "contrived."[37] Again, it is difficult to produce a satisfactory account of natural kinds.

I simply conjecture here that some of the machinery developed in the various accounts of the distinction between hard and soft facts presented in this volume may be applicable to the sorts of philosophical projects just mentioned. Of course, this is mere speculation, because I do not know of any attempts to apply this machinery to such projects, but I believe that the enterprise would be interesting and, perhaps, fruitful.

To proceed. Each of the accounts presented in this volume is rigorous, and, I believe, illuminating. It is, however, reasonable to ask about the intuitive motivation that underlies the formal machinery of the various accounts. Specifically, it is useful to consider exactly how one might justify the Entailment Criterion of Soft Facthood, which appears to be the engine driving the various approaches. Why exactly is it that, when a fact about t_1 entails a certain sort of fact about a later time, we say that it is a soft fact about t_1?

Perhaps the Entailment Criterion could be justified as follows. When a fact's obtaining at a time *depends* on a fact's obtaining at some future time, then we think that the first fact is a soft fact about the time at which it obtains; we say that the first fact obtains in virtue of the obtaining of the future fact. And the notion of entailment might be thought to capture the relevant sort of dependence. When p entails q, the truth of p depends on the truth of q.

Whereas this might be the underlying rationale for the Entailment Criterion, it is not evident to me that it is adequate. This is because it is not evident to me that the notion of entailment captures the idea of dependence relevant to soft facthood. To see this point, consider the following example, which I owe to Widerker.[38] Suppose that there were an infallible book, "*IB*." *IB* is infallible in this sense:

(IB) Necessarily, if *IB* contains a sentence, then that sentence is true.

Now let us imagine that at t_1 *IB* contains the sentence,

(R) *S* will not do *X* at t_3.

The fact that the book *IB* contains R at t_1 seems to be a hard fact about t_1. And yet this fact entails that *S* will refrain from doing *X* at t_3. The Entailment Criterion of Soft Facthood is satisfied, but it seems intuitively that the fact that *IB* contains R is a hard fact about t_1.

Widerker defends the intuition behind his claim that the fact that *IB* contains R is a hard fact about t_1 in this way. Suppose that after t_1 (let us say at t_2) *IB* is destroyed. Under such circumstances, it seems that the fact that *IB* contained R at t_1 would be, in Pike's terms, "over-and-done-with and fully accomplished" at t_2. So the fact that *IB* contains R would seem to be a hard fact about t_1, or at least a hard fact about the past relative to t_3, although it is deemed a soft fact by the Entailment Criterion (and thus by any account of the distinction that embodies this criterion).

Widerker's infallible book poses an interesting challenge to the defender of the Entailment Criterion. If the example is as described, then the Entailment Criterion is inadequate. A proponent of the Entailment Criterion might, however, insist that the fact that *IB* contains *R* is a soft fact about t_1. I believe that the plausibility of the Entailment Criterion depends (in part) on the case that can be made that the fact that *IB* contains *R* at t_1 is a soft fact about t_1.

Temporal Relationality and Fixity

I have been considering various accounts of the distinction between hard and soft facts. These accounts embody in various ways the Entailment Criterion of Soft Facthood, and thus they imply that God's belief at t_1 that *S* will not do *X* at t_2 is a soft fact about t_1. I have raised a question about the justification for the Entailment Criterion, and thus I have called into question the claim that God's belief at t_1 is a soft fact about t_1 (at least to the extent that this claim is based on an account that embodies the Entailment Criterion). I now wish to focus on a different question. I wish to explore the question of whether the fact that God believes at t_1 that *S* will not do *X* at t_2 might be *fixed* at t_2, even if it turned out to be a soft fact about t_1. I shall briefly sketch two different strategies that attempt to establish that this fact about God's belief at t_1 is a fixed fact at t_2, even if it is a soft fact about t_1.

Before I develop these strategies, it will be useful to set out some of the relationships between the various sorts of facts. Recall that the distinction between hard and soft facts pertains to the issue of temporal relationality, whereas the distinction between fixed facts and those facts that are not fixed pertains to what it is in an agent's power to "bring about." It is plausible to suppose that all hard facts about past times are fixed, although I shall note below that some philosophers deny this claim. For now, let us assume (with the Ockhamist) that all hard facts about the past are now fixed. Also, whereas some soft facts about the past are now not fixed, other soft facts about the past are now fixed. Presumably, the soft fact about Monday that it was true that I would go to Ithaca on Wednesday is not a fixed fact on Tuesday (or Wednesday) relative to me; it appears that I can so act on Wednesday that it would not have been true on Monday that I would go to Ithaca on Wednesday. But the fact about Monday that it was true that the sun would rise on Wednesday is a soft fact about Monday that is fixed on Tuesday and Wednesday relative to me (and all other human agents). I do not have it in my power on Tuesday or Wednesday so to act that the sun would *not* rise on Wednesday. Thus it is important to keep in mind that there are soft facts about a time that are, nevertheless, fixed at later times (relative to the relevant agent).

Hasker (Chapters 9 and 11) presents one strategy that purports to establish that, although God's belief at t_1 that S will not do X at t_2 is a soft fact about t_1, it is, nevertheless, fixed at t_2. Hasker begins by suggesting that the term "Yahweh" refers to the individual who is actually God—the God of Abraham, Isaac, and Jacob. Further, "Yahweh" does not connote any of the divine attributes. It simply refers to an individual who in fact fills the role of God. Thus, Hasker claims,

(i) Yahweh believed at t_1 that S would not do X at t_2

is a hard fact about t_1 and hence fixed at t_2. Also, Hasker claims,

(ii) If Yahweh exists, Yahweh is God

is metaphysically necessary and thus fixed at t_2: no human can so act that Yahweh would have existed but not have been God. But because it is reasonable to think that fixity is closed under entailment and (i) and (ii) entail

(iii) God believed at t_1 that S would not do X at t_2,

it follows that (iii) is a fixed fact at t_2. (Note that fixity is plausibly taken to be closed under entailment, even if hardness is not. And hardness does not seem to be closed under entailment. For instance, "Smith sits at t_1" entails "$2 + 2 = 4$," and yet the latter fact might not properly be considered a hard fact about t_1. Further, Widerker's Infallible Book might provide counterexamples to the alleged closure of hardness under entailment, although it does not appear to provide counterexamples to the closure of fixity under entailment.) If Hasker's argument is sound, then God's belief at t_1 would be a fixed fact at t_2, even though it was a soft fact about t_1.

I shall now describe a different strategy that might be employed in order to reach the same conclusion. In Chapter 4 I present a reason to think that the fact that Yahweh believed at t_1 that S would not do X at t_2 is a hard fact about t_1, where "Yahweh" refers to an individual who in fact occupies the role of God but is not essentially omniscient, everlasting, and so forth. I call the general reason the "Incompatibilist's Constraint." [39] But this reason might not be applicable to a fact such as "God believed at t_1 that S would not do X at t_2," where "God" refers to an individual who has the divine attributes *essentially*. Thus it might turn out that the latter fact is a soft fact about t_1. Nevertheless, I have argued (elsewhere) that this fact (that God believed at t_1 that S would not do X at t_2) is plausibly thought to be a fixed fact at t_2. [40]

The first step in the argument simply reminds us of the distinction mentioned above between temporally non-relational ("hard") and temporally relational ("soft") properties, which is parallel to the distinction between hard and soft facts. Second, I claim that the reasoning behind the Incompatibilist's Constraint can be employed to show that *believing that p* is a hard property relative to the time at which the belief is held. [41] Third, my claim is that the fact that God believed at t_1 that S would not do X at t_2 is a "hard-type soft fact": it is (if soft at all) a soft fact whose falsification at t_2 would require that some individual (God) would not have had at t_1 some *hard property* that He actually had at t_1. Finally, my claim is that if one thinks that hard facts about t_1 are fixed at t_2, then one ought to think that hard-type soft facts about t_1 are also fixed at t_2. That is, if one thinks that no one can at t_2 so act that some hard fact about t_1 would not have been a fact about t_1, then it seems that one ought also to think that no one can at t_2 so act that some bearer of a hard property at t_1 would not have had that property at t_1. (This reasoning is similar to—although slightly different from—the above claim that if hard facts about t_1 are fixed at t_2, then so also should hard-core soft facts about t_1 be fixed at t_2. The claim here is that if hard facts about t_1 are fixed at t_2, then so also should hard-type soft facts about t_1 be fixed at t_2.) And if hard-type soft facts are fixed at t_2, then even if God's belief at t_1 turned out to be a soft fact about t_1, it would be *fixed* at t_2.

The two strategies sketched above appear to show that even if God's belief at t_1 were a soft fact about t_1, this would not *in itself* vindicate Ockhamism. It is not obvious, however, that the two strategies succeed. Hasker's strategy depends on being able to refer to the individual who is God by some name that does not connote the divine attributes. Further, it depends on saying that the relevant fact (got by referring to the individual who is God by the name) is a hard fact about the time at which the individual has the belief. These points might be denied by an Ockhamist. Further, my strategy depends on claiming that hard-type soft facts about t_1 are fixed at t_2. But an Ockhamist might say that insofar as some soft facts about t_1 are not fixed at t_2, it is possible that some hard-type soft facts about t_1 are not fixed at t_2. An Ockhamist might claim that insofar as one can at t_2 falsify a soft fact about t_1, then one might be able at t_2 so to act that some individual would not have had some hard property that he actually had at t_1. This is a sort of "Bootstrapping Ockhamism," according to which one can "bootstrap" to the ability so to act that an individual would not have possessed some hard property that he actually possessed by falsifying some soft *fact* about the past. Thus, although I would consider the facts in question to be "hard-type soft facts," a Bootstrapping Ockhamist might say that they simply involve "hard properties with soft underbellies."

Accidental Necessity

It is useful to contrast the accounts of the distinction between hard and soft facts with Alvin Plantinga's project in his paper, "On Ockham's Way Out" (Chapter 10). Plantinga does not propose to generate an explicit account of the distinction between hard and soft facts; thus his aim is fundamentally different from that of many of the other authors in this anthology. As regards the issue of temporal relationality, Plantinga employs the basic idea behind the Entailment Criterion of Soft Facthood, but he does not make his criterion explicit. He does claim that God's belief at a time about the future behavior of humans is a soft fact about the time at which it is held.

Above I distinguished between two issues: temporal relationality and fixity. It is helpful also to introduce a third notion: Ockham's idea of "accidental necessity" (already alluded to above). Although accidental necessity is closely related to fixity, it is a different notion, corresponding roughly to "temporally relative fixity." The idea is that, whereas some facts are fixed (in an appropriate sense) at all times (in a given possible world), other facts *become* fixed (in this sense) at a particular point in time. Accidentally necessary facts, then, are facts that are not fixed until a certain time, after which they are forever fixed. Plantinga's goal is to generate an adequate account of accidental necessity.

Here is Plantinga's suggestion:

p is accidentally necessary at t if and only if p is true at t and it is not possible both that p is true at t and that there exist agents $S_1 \ldots , S_n$ and actions $A_1 \ldots , A_n$ such that (1) A_i is basic for S_i, (2) S_i has the power at t or later to perform A_i, and (3) necessarily, if every S_i were to perform A_i at t or later, then p would have been false. [p. 209]

Notice that the definition of accidental necessity is in terms of the powers of agents and that the pertinent notion of fixity is "stronger" than the notion I have been employing above. (That is, (3) implicitly embodies entailment rather than the subjunctive conditional I have been employing in my account of "fixity.") Note also that one could not similarly define hardness (in terms of the powers of agents) if the notion of hardness is expected to play its normal role in argumentation concerning God's foreknowledge and human freedom. This is because it is normally supposed that we can generate an account of hardness that is *independent* of judgments about the powers of agents, and then apply this account to God's prior beliefs in order to help to settle the question of whether human agents have power over these beliefs. It would appear to introduce an unacceptable circularity first to define hardness in terms of powers of human agents and then to apply this definition to settle the question of whether God's prior beliefs are fixed. (Of course, Plantinga is not guilty of this sort of circularity, because his project is to generate an account of accidental necessity, not hardness.) Finally, notice that the definition of accidental necessity in itself will not help to resolve the question of whether an agent can at a time so act that God would have held a different belief (in the past) from what He actually held; the definition of accidental necessity presupposes a prior answer to this question.

Thomism

Another way of blocking the Basic Argument is to deny another one of its assumptions: the temporal interpretation of God's eternality. On this view, God does not exist within the temporal framework in which human beings exist. Thus God's omniscience is not *foreknowledge*. On this approach, God's beliefs are not in the past, and thus it appears that a human agent could have the power to do otherwise without thereby having the power so to act that the past would have been different from what it actually was. This approach, then, is promising insofar as it seems to allow one to accept the Principle of the Fixity of the Past along with the view that human agents are sometimes free to do otherwise. This strategy is associated with St. Thomas Aquinas.[42] It is also widely believed that Boethius employs this approach to denying the conclusion of the Basic Argument.[43] I shall call the position which denies that God exists in the temporal framework in which humans exist, "Thomism."

On the Thomistic approach, the content of God's knowledge may include temporal features. That is, God knows that John F. Kennedy was assassinated in 1963, that Reagan was president after Carter, and so forth. But whereas the content of God's beliefs includes temporal components, God's beliefs *themselves* are not in the human temporal framework. If one accepts Thomism, it appears as though one can block the claim made by the Basic Argument that if one is free at a time to do otherwise, then one is free so to act that the past would have been different from what it actually was. God's beliefs are not in our past, and thus one might be free without having the problematic power concerning the past.

Notice that it might be thought that a God who is outside the human temporal framework cannot know certain things. For instance, such a God cannot know what time it is now (in human time). Some philosophers take this to be a serious defect in the atemporal conception of God's eternality because it seems to imply that God is not omniscient (in a sufficiently robust sense). They claim that any being who does not know such truths as what time it is now (in human time) cannot be truly omniscient (and thus the Supreme Being). Although a God who is outside human time might know all that such a being could know, this sort of God, according to some, would not know *enough* to be properly considered omniscient.

But it is unclear that this sort of worry is well-formulated. The problem is that such locutions as "The time is now eight o'clock" do not denote propositions at all. Rather, because they contain the "indexical" component, "now," they pick out different propositions on different occasions of utterance. Further, if it is eight o'clock, then the utterance "It is now eight o'clock" picks out the proposition "It is eight o'clock at eight o'clock." And this is a proposition that even an atemporal God can truly believe. Thus it seems that even a God outside human time can know all the *truths* there are. Of course, such a God will not "have access to" those truths *via* such phrases (and the associated concepts) as "It is now (in human time) eight o'clock." But, nevertheless, this sort of God would still be omniscient in a rather robust sense: He would timelessly know all the truths there are, including truths about future contingents.[44]

We might distinguish two different versions of Thomism. On one version, "Thomism One," God does not exist in time at all: He exists in *no* temporal framework. On another version, "Thomism Two," God exists within His own temporal framework, which is different from the human temporal sequence.

Let us begin by discussing Thomism Two. If we accept this form of Thomism and thus say that God is outside human time but within His own temporal framework, we can say that God's existence has both duration and succession; we thus avoid the puzzling claim that God's existence can be thought of as possessing duration without succession.[45]

This form of Thomism, then, is attractive. It seems to preserve the ideas that God is omniscient and also that His existence possesses both duration and succession compatibly with avoiding the thrust of the Basic Argument. It is interesting, however, to note that Thomism Two is crucially different from Thomism One. Thomism Two is susceptible to the claim that God is not himself free. That is, if God is in His own temporal sequence, one can construct an argument parallel to the Basic Argument that would purport to show that God himself is not free to do otherwise after the first instant of God's time, if there is one. I shall briefly sketch such an argument here. My aim is to contrast the two forms of Thomism. But it should also be evident that the sort of argument discussed here could be constructed to show that if God does in fact share our temporal framework, then *He* is not free to do otherwise after the first instant of time, if there was one.[46] Indeed, I believe that if one accepts the conclusion of the Basic Argument, then one ought also to accept the conclusion of the similar argument: if God exists, then *He* is not free to do otherwise after the first instant of time, if there was one. This similar argument may be even more troubling than the Basic Argument insofar as it seems to point to a possible incoherence in the very idea of God. But let us here focus on the distinction between the two forms of Thomism.

Suppose that Thomism Two is true and thus that God exists outside of our time but within His own time sequence. Since God is omniscient, He knows *in advance* (with respect to His time) what He will do. But if this is so, then (for reasons developed in the Basic Argument) His own freedom to do otherwise (at any time after the first instant of God's time, if there is one) would require that He have the power so to act that the past (within God's temporal sequence) would have been different from what it actually was. Further, it is plausible to think that if one accepts the Principle of the Fixity of the Past, one should accept a similar principle applicable to God (and His temporal framework). I do not see any reason to distinguish our past from God's past, with regard to considerations of fixity. Thus, on Thomism Two, God's own freedom is called into question, at least at any time after the first instant of God's time, if there is one. This result is problematic insofar as one believes that God does not make all his decisions at the first instant of God's time. Also, it is problematic if one does not believe that there is a first instant of God's time.

According to Thomism One, God is *completely* atemporal. Thomism One would appear to enjoy some of the advantages of Thomism Two (for example, the advantage of avoiding the thrust of the Basic Argument) without the disadvantage of being susceptible to the worry that it implies that God himself is not free to do otherwise. If, however, one wishes to maintain that God's existence is durational (perhaps because of the view that God is Supreme), then there is this cost of adopting Thomism One: God's existence is construed as durational but not successive. We saw above that one way to avoid the puzzling claim that God's existence is durational but not successive would be to adopt Thomism Two and thus to claim that God's existence possesses *both* duration and succession. Another way to avoid the puzzling claim would be to say that God's existence possesses *neither* duration nor succession. This would involve adopting a "pointlike" conception of God's atemporal existence. (This conception is certainly compatible with Thomism One.)

Does Thomism One allow a compatibilist to avoid the thrust of the Basic Argument? Some philosophers have argued that it does not, and it will be useful to consider their position. Plantinga puts the point roughly as follows. Even on Thomism One, it would seem that a proposition such as "God timelessly believes that S will not do X at t_2" is true at all times, including t_1. But then if S is free at t_2 to do X at t_2, then he is free at t_2 so to act that a fact about the past—that God timelessly believes that S will not do X at t_2—would not be a fact about the past. Thus, Plantinga's claim is that Thomism does not allow one to sidestep the Basic Argument.[47]

I believe that this particular objection to Thomism is unconvincing. Surely the Thomist should appeal here to the distinction (employed by the Ockhamist and indeed by any nonfatalistic philosopher) between hard facts about the past and facts that are not hard facts about the past. Certainly, the fact that it was true at t_1 that God timelessly believes that S will not do X at t_2 is not a hard fact about t_1: it does not seem to imply that anything happen in the "basic sense" at t_1.

Perhaps it is useful here to be reminded that there are two components of hardness: "genuineness" and "strictness" (Plantinga, p. 192). Some facts that fail to be hard facts about t_1 are genuinely about t_1 but not *strictly* about t_1: for example, the fact that Sally wakes up four hours prior to eating lunch. Further, it should now be evident that there are two different ways in which a fact could fail even to be *genuinely* about a time t_1. First, it could be genuinely about some other time: for example, the fact that (at t_1) it is true that at t_2 Joan eats dinner. Second, it could be genuinely about God's atemporal sphere: at t_1 God timelessly believes that S will not do X at t_2.

I believe, then, that Thomism can be defended from this particular objection. There may, of course, be other objections to Thomism (even similar ones), and it should be conceded that it is not altogether obvious that it is coherent to conceive of an atemporal entity that can have temporal effects of the sort God can allegedly have.[48]

Some philosophers have been unsatisfied with an aspect of St. Thomas Aquinas' theory. As we have seen, Aquinas put God outside of human time, and thus God's omniscience is not the sort of foreknowledge that constitutes a threat to human freedom (at least in virtue of the fixity of the past). But Aquinas also believed that God *causes* all human behavior, and some philosophers worry that this causal activity of God is inconsistent with human freedom to do otherwise. Thus these philosophers think that the benefits of adopting an atemporal conception of God are negated by the causal component of Aquinas' theory.

I do not have a proof that God's causal activity is compatible with human freedom to do otherwise. But it is interesting to note that the argument presented above that causal determinism is incompatible with human freedom to do otherwise *reduces* the problem posed by causation to the problem of the fixity of the past. In other words, causal determinism was thought to threaten freedom in part because of the fixity of the past. But if one combines the doctrine of God's causal activity with an atemporal conception of God's existence, then one prescinds the issue of whether God's causation rules out human freedom from considerations pertaining to the fixity of the past. Thus, one could combine a strong notion of God's providential activity (according to which this implies *causation*) with an atemporal conception of God's eternality; this would be a way of preserving a strong conception of God's providence compatibly with avoiding the thrust of the Basic Argument.[49] Of course, there might be some other reason why God's causation threatens human freedom, but, if so, it will not be the reason embodied in this argument for the incompatibility of causal determinism and human freedom to do otherwise.

Multiple-Pasts Compatibilism

The Principle of the Fixity of the Past claims that all hard facts about the past are presently fixed. We have seen, however, that the Ockhamist denies that God's prior beliefs are currently fixed.

The Ockhamist's approach is to accept the Principle of the Fixity of the Past, but to deny that God's beliefs are hard facts about the past.

There is another strategy that results in a denial that God's prior beliefs are currently fixed. In this approach, one concedes that God's beliefs are hard facts about the times at which they are held, but one denies the Principle of the Fixity of the Past. This position is developed by Martin Davies in his essay, "Boethius and Others on Divine Foreknowledge" (Chapter 13). This sort of compatibilism is parallel to a certain kind of compatibilism about causal determinism and freedom to do otherwise. As noted above, there is an argument for the incompatibility of causal determinism and freedom to do otherwise that is parallel to the Basic Argument. Both arguments employ (among other ingredients) the Principle of the Fixity of the Past. If the Ockhamist is correct and God's beliefs are not hard facts about the past, then the fixity-of-the-past claim in the argument from causal determinism is different from (and more plausible than) that made in the argument from God's foreknowledge. However, if God's beliefs are hard facts, then the fixity-of-the-past claims are on a par. Further, whereas the incompatibilist asserts that both claims are persuasive, the multiple-pasts compatibilist insists that both fixity-of-the-past claims are unacceptable.[50]

"Can"

At the beginning of this Introduction, I formulated the Principle of the Fixity of the Past:

(FP) For any action Y, agent S, and time t, if it is true that if S were to do Y at t, then some hard fact about the past (relative to t) would not have been a fact, then S cannot do Y at t.

We have seen that certain compatibilists are willing to accept (FP) but deny its relevance to God's beliefs. Other compatibilists—multiple-pasts compatibilists—deny (FP), claiming that one can sometimes so act that a hard fact about the past would not have been a fact.

Consider the debate between the incompatibilist and the multiple-pasts compatibilist concerning (FP). It appears as though they have a genuine disagreement. But both William

Alston (Chapter 12) and William Hasker (Chapter 11) suggest that they are "talking past each other." Alston argues that the compatibilist is adopting one sense of "can," whereas the incompatibilist is presupposing a different sense of "can." Given this situation, Alston claims that they are not really disagreeing about (FP) but that they are tacitly discussing different principles. These principles are generated by employing the different senses of "can" (and thus "cannot").

I am not convinced by the suggestion that the compatibilist (of a certain sort) and the incompatibilist are talking past each other. Rather than construing the dialectical situation as Alston does, one might understand it as follows. We all (compatibilists and incompatibilists and agnostics) start with the same intuitive idea of "can" (or freedom). We then try to articulate this idea, and in so doing, there is a disagreement. More specifically, there is a disagreement about one of the constraints on any adequate understanding of our shared (but inchoate) sense of "can." This constraint is formulated by (FP).

Alston's claim is that there are two senses of "can." The alternative supposition is that there is a disagreement about the proper constraints on an analysis of the single (relevant) notion of "can." Now I do not claim that the alternative supposition is clearly preferable to Alston's. My point is simply that I do not see an argument in Alston that his way of construing the situation is preferable to the alternative way.

Why, one might ask, is the situation with respect to "can" different from the situation with respect to "knows"? Presumably, the different proposals for an analysis of knowledge—causal theories, defeasibility theories, and so forth—are different ways of attempting to crystallize our shared, underlying concept of knowledge. One could, I suppose, claim that there is a different sense of "knowledge" corresponding to each proposed analysis, but this sort of move does not seem to be plausible or illuminating. And if the "proliferation-of-senses" strategy is unappealing in epistemology, why should it be more promising with regard to "can"?[51]

In conclusion, I wish to sketch a brief explanation of the order of presentation of some of the essays in this volume. In Chapter 2, Pike sets out a version of the Basic Argument for the incompatibility of God's foreknowledge and human freedom to do otherwise. As I said above, most of the articles in this book focus on the "Ockhamistic" response to this argument. In Chapter 3 Adams sets out an influential account of the distinction between hard facts and soft facts. In Chapter 4, I criticize this account and offer a reason to think that any adequate account of this distinction should imply that God's beliefs are hard facts about the times at which they are held (on the assumption that the individual who is God is not necessarily God). In Chapter 6, Zemach and Widerker argue against my claim that any adequate account will imply that God's beliefs will be hard fact, and they provide an account of the distinction that has the result congenial to Ockhamism—that God's beliefs are soft facts about the times at which they are held.

Hoffman and Rosenkrantz (Chapter 7), Freddoso (Chapter 8), and Hasker (Chapter 11) present accounts of the distinction between hard and soft facts; these accounts, they argue, avoid the kinds of objections that plague Adams's account. (As pointed out above, however, Hasker argues that whereas God's beliefs are soft facts about the relevant times, there is reason to suppose that they are *fixed* at later times.)

One goal of this anthology is to provide the reader with an understanding of how the more sophisticated accounts of the distinction between hard and soft facts arise as reactions to the inadequacies of simpler approaches. Also, the reader should get a sense of how compatibilistic strategies that exploit the distinction between hard and soft facts fit into the larger context of the debate about God and foreknowledge.

CHAPTER TWO

Divine Omniscience and Voluntary Action

Nelson Pike

In Book V, sec. 3 of his *Consolatio Philosophiae*, Boethius enter-
tained (though he later rejected) the claim that if God is omniscient, no human action is voluntary. This claim seems intuitively
false. Surely, given only a doctrine describing God's *knowledge*,
nothing about the voluntary status of human actions will follow.
Perhaps such a conclusion would follow from a doctrine of divine omnipotence or divine providence, but what connection
could there be between the claim that God is *omniscient* and the
claim that human actions are determined? Yet Boethius thought
he saw a problem here. He thought that if one collected together
just the right assumptions and principles regarding God's knowledge, one could derive the conclusion that if God exists, no human action is voluntary. Of course, Boethius did not think that
all the assumptions and principles required to reach this conclusion are true (quite the contrary), but he thought it important to
draw attention to them nonetheless. If a theologian is to construct a doctrine of God's knowledge which does not commit him
to determinism, he must first understand that there is a way of
thinking about God's knowledge which would so commit him.

In this paper, I shall argue that although his claim has a sharp
counterintuitive ring, Boethius was right in thinking that there
is a selection from among the various doctrines and principles
clustering about the notions of knowledge, omniscience, and

Reprinted by permission from *The Philosophical Review*, 74 (1965): 27–46.

God which, when brought together, demand the conclusion that if God exists, no human action is voluntary. Boethius, I think, did not succeed in making explicit all of the ingredients in the problem. His suspicions were sound, but his discussion was incomplete. His argument needs to be developed. This is the task I shall undertake in the pages to follow. I should like to make clear at the outset that my purpose in rearguing this thesis is not to show that determinism is true, nor to show that God does not exist, nor to show that either determinism is true or God does not exist. Following Boethius, I shall not claim that the items needed to generate the problem are either philosophically or theologically adequate. I want to concentrate attention on the implications of a certain set of assumptions. Whether the assumptions are themselves acceptable is a question I shall not consider.

I

A. Many philosophers have held that if a statement of the form "A knows X" is true, then "A believes X" is true and "X" is true. As a first assumption, I shall take this partial analysis of "A knows X" to be correct. And I shall suppose that since this analysis holds for all knowledge claims, it will hold when speaking of God's knowledge. "God knows X" entails "God believes X" and "'X' is true."

Secondly, Boethius said that with respect to the matter of knowledge, God "cannot in anything be mistaken."[1] I shall understand this doctrine as follows. Omniscient beings hold no false beliefs. Part of what is meant when we say that a person is omniscient is that the person in question believes nothing that is false. But, further, it is part of the "essence" of God to be omniscient. This is to say that any person who is not omniscient could not be the person we usually mean to be referring to when using the name "God." To put this last point a little differently: if the person we usually mean to be referring to when using the name "God" were suddenly to lose the quality of omniscience (suppose, for example, He came to believe something false), the resulting person would no longer be God. Although we might call this second person "God" (I might call my cat "God"), the absence of the quality of omniscience would be sufficient to guarantee that the person referred to was not the same as the person formerly called by that name. From this last doctine it follows that the statement "If a given person is God, that person is omniscient" is an a priori truth. From this we may conclude that the statement "If a given person is God, that person holds no false beliefs" is also an a priori truth. It would be conceptually impossible for God to hold a false belief. "'X' is true" follows from "God believes X." These are all ways of expressing the same principle—the principle expressed by Boethius in the formula "God cannot in anything be mistaken."

A second principle usually associated with the notion of divine omniscience has to do with the scope or range of God's intellectual gaze. To say that a being is omniscient is to say that he knows everything. "Everything" in this statement is usually taken to cover future, as well as present and past, events and circumstances. In fact, God is usually said to have had foreknowledge of everything that has ever happened. With respect to anything that was, is, or will be the case, God knew, *from eternity*, that it would be the case.

The doctrine of God's knowing everything from eternity is very obscure. One particularly difficult question concerning this doctrine is whether it entails that with respect to everything that was, is, or will be the case, God knew *in advance* that it would be the case. In some traditional theological texts, we are told that God is *eternal* in the sense that He exists "outside of time," that is, in the sense that He bears no temporal relations to the events or circumstances of the natural world.[2] In a theology of this sort, God could not be said to have known that a given natural event was going to happen before it happened. If God knew that a given natural event was going to occur *before* it occurred, at least one of God's cognitions would then have occurred before some natural event. This, surely, would violate the idea that God bears no temporal relations to natural events.[3] On the other hand, in a considerable number of theological sources, we are told that God *has always* existed—that He existed long *before* the occurrence of any natural event. In a theology of this sort, to say that God is eternal is not to say that God exists "outside of time" (bears no temporal relations to natural events); it is to say, instead, God has existed (and will continue to exist) at each moment.[4] The doctrine of omniscience which goes with this second understanding of the notion of eternity is one in which it is affirmed that God *has always* known what was going to happen in the natural world. John Calvin wrote as follows:

> When we attribute foreknowledge to God, we mean that all things have ever been and perpetually remain before, his eyes, so that to his knowledge nothing is future or past, but all things are present; and present in such manner, that he does not merely conceive of them from ideas formed in his mind, as things remembered by us appear to our minds, but really he holds and sees them as if (*tanquam*) actually placed before him.[5]

All things are "present" to God in the sense that He "sees" them as if (*tanquam*) they were actually before Him. Further, with respect to any given natural event, not only is that event "present" to God in the sense indicated, it has *ever been and has perpetually remained* "present" to Him in that sense. This latter is the point of special interest. Whatever one thinks of the idea that God "sees" things as if "actually placed before him," Calvin would appear to be committed to the idea that God has *always known* what was going to happen in the natural world. Choose an event (E) and a time (t_2) at which E occurred. For any time (t_1) prior to t_2 (say, five thousand, six hundred, or eighty years prior to t_2), God knew at t_1 that E would occur at t_2. It will follow from this doctrine, of course, that with respect to any human action, God knew well in advance of its performance that the action would be performed. Calvin says, "when God created man, He foresaw what would happen concerning him." He adds, "little more than five thousand years have elapsed since the creation of the world."[6] Calvin seems to have thought that God foresaw the outcome of every human action well over five thousand years ago.

In the discussion to follow, I shall work only with this second interpretation of God's knowing everything *from eternity*. I shall assume that if a person is omniscient, that person has always known what was going to happen in the natural world—and, in particular, has always known what human actions were going to be performed. Thus, as above, assuming that the attribute of omniscience is part of the "essence" of God, the statement "For any natural event (including human actions), if a given person is God, that person would always have known that that event was going to occur at the time it occurred" must be treated as an a priori truth. This is just another way of stating a point admirably put by St. Augustine when he said: "For to confess that God exists and at the same time to deny that He has foreknowledge of future things is the most manifest folly. . . . One who is not prescient of all future things is not God."[7]

B. Last Saturday afternoon, Jones mowed his lawn. Assuming that God exists and is (essentially) omniscient in the sense outlined above, it follows that (let us say) eighty years prior to last Saturday afternoon, God knew (and thus believed) that Jones would mow his lawn at that time. But from this it follows, I think, that at the time of action (last Saturday afternoon) Jones was not *able*—that is, it was not *within Jones's power*—to refrain from mowing his lawn.[8] If at the time of action, Jones had been able to refrain from mowing his lawn, then (the most obvious conclusion would seem to be) at the time of action, Jones was able to do something which would have brought it about that God held a false belief eighty years earlier. But God cannot in anything be mistaken. It is not possible that some belief of His was false. Thus, last Saturday afternoon, Jones was not able to do something which would have brought it about that God held a false belief eighty years ago. To suppose that it was would be to suppose that, at the time of action, Jones was able to do something having a conceptually incoherent description, namely something that would have brought it about that one of God's beliefs was false. Hence, given that God believed eighty years ago that Jones would mow his lawn on Saturday, if we are to assign Jones the power on Saturday to refrain from mowing his lawn, this power must not be described as the power to do something that would have rendered one of God's beliefs false. How then should we describe it vis-à-vis God and His belief? So far as I can see, there are only two other alternatives. First, we might try describing it as the power to do something that would have brought it about that God believed otherwise than He did eighty years ago; or, secondly, we might try describing it as the power to do something that would have brought it about that God (Who, by hypothesis, existed eighty years earlier) did not exist eighty years earlier—that is, as the power to do something that would have brought it about that any person who believed eighty years ago that Jones would mow his lawn on Saturday (one of whom was, by hypothesis, God) held a false belief, and thus was not God. But again, neither of these latter can be accepted. Last Saturday afternoon, Jones was not able to do something that would have brought it about that God believed otherwise than He did eighty years ago. Even if we suppose (as was suggested by Calvin) that eighty years ago God knew Jones would mow his lawn on Saturday in the sense that He "saw" Jones mowing his lawn as if this action were occurring before Him, the fact remains that God knew (and thus believed) eighty years prior to Saturday that Jones would mow his lawn. And if God held such a belief eighty years prior to Saturday, Jones did not have the power on Saturday to do something that would have made it the case that God did not hold this belief eighty years earlier. No action performed at a given time can alter the fact that a given person held a certain belief at a time prior to the time in question. This last seems to be an a priori truth. For similar reasons, the last of the above alternatives must also be rejected. On the assumption that God existed eighty years prior to Saturday, Jones on Saturday was not able to do something that would have brought it about that God did not exist eighty years prior to that time. No action performed at a given time can alter the fact that a certain person existed at a time prior to the time in question. This, too, seems to me to be an a priori truth. But if these observations are correct, then, given that Jones mowed his lawn on Saturday, and given that God exists and is (essentially) omniscient, it seems to follow that at the time of action, Jones did not have the power to refrain from mowing his lawn. The upshot of these reflections would appear to be that Jones's mowing his lawn last Saturday cannot be counted as a voluntary action. Although I do not have an analysis of what it is for an action to be *voluntary*, it seems to me that a situation in which it would be wrong to assign Jones the *ability* or *power* to do *other* than he did would be a situation in which it would also be wrong to speak of his action as voluntary. As a general remark, if God exists and is (essentially) omniscient in the sense specified above, no human action is voluntary.[9]

As the argument just presented is somewhat complex, perhaps the following schematic representation of it will be of some use.

1. "God existed at t_1" entails "If Jones did X at t_2, God believed at t_1 that Jones would do X at t_2.
2. "God believes X" entails "'X' is true."
3. It is not within one's power at a given time to do something having a description that is logically contradictory.
4. It is not within one's power at a given time to do something that would bring it about that someone who held a certain belief at a time prior to the time in question did not hold that belief at the time prior to the time in question.
5. It is not within one's power at a given time to do something that would bring it about that a person who existed at an earlier time did not exist at that earlier time.
6. If God existed at t_1 and if God believed at t_1 that Jones would do X at t_2, then if it was within Jones's power at t_2 to refrain from doing X, then (1) it was within Jones's power at t_2 to do something that would have brought it about that God held a false belief at t_1, or (2) it was within Jones's power at t_2 to do something which would have brought it about that God did not hold the belief He held at t_1, or (3) it was within Jones's power at t_2 to do something that would have brought it about that any person who believed at t_1 that Jones would do X at t_2 (one of whom was, by hypothesis, God) held a false belief and thus was not God—that is, that God (who by hypothesis existed at t_1) did not exist at t_1.
7. Alternative 1 in the consequent of item 6 is false. (from 2 and 3)
8. Alternative 2 in the consequent of item 6 is false. (from 4)
9. Alternative 3 in the consequent of item 6 is false. (from 5)
10. Therefore, if God existed at t_1 and if God believed at t_1 that Jones would do X at t_2, then it was not within Jones's power at t_2 to refrain from doing X. (from 6 through 9)
11. Therefore, if God existed at t_1, and if Jones did X at t_2, it was not within Jones's power at t_2 to refrain from doing X. (from 1 and 10)

In this argument, items 1 and 2 make explicit the doctrine of God's (essential) omniscience with which I am working. Items 3, 4, and 5 express what I take to be part of the logic of the concept of ability or power as it applies to human beings. Item 6 is offered as an analytic truth. If one assigns Jones the power to refrain from doing X at t_2 (given that God believed at t_1 that he would do X at t_2), so far as I can see, one would have to describe this power in one of the three ways listed in the consequent of item 6. I do not know how to argue that these are the only alternatives, but I have been unable to find another. Item 11, when generalized for all agents and actions, and when taken together with what seems to me to be a minimal condition for the application of "voluntary action," yields the conclusion that if God exists (and is essentially omniscient in the way I have described) no human action is voluntary.

C. It is important to notice that the argument given in the preceding paragraphs avoids use of two concepts that are often prominent in discussions of determinism.

In the first place, the argument makes no mention of the *causes* of Jones's action. Say (for example, with St. Thomas)[10] that God's foreknowledge of Jones's action was, itself, the cause of the action (though I am really not sure what this means). Say, instead, that natural events or circumstances caused Jones to act. Even say that Jones's action had no cause at all. The argument outlined above remains unaffected. If eighty years prior to Saturday, God believed that Jones would mow his lawn at that time, it was not within Jones's power at the time of action to refrain from mowing his lawn. The reasoning that justifies this assertion makes no mention of a causal series preceding Jones's action.

Secondly, consider the following line of thinking. Suppose Jones mowed his lawn last Saturday. It was then *true* eighty years ago that Jones would mow his lawn at that time. Hence, on Saturday, Jones was not able to refrain from mowing his lawn. To suppose that he was would be to suppose that he was able on Saturday to do something that would have made false a proposition that was *already true* eighty years earlier. This general kind of argument for determinism is usually associated with Leibniz, although it was anticipated in chapter ix of Aristotle's *De Interpretatione*. It has been used since, with some modification, in Richard Taylor's article, "Fatalism."[11] This argument, like the one I have offered above, makes no use of the notion of causation. It turns, instead, on the notion of its being *true eighty years ago* that Jones would mow his lawn on Saturday.

I must confess that I share the misgivings of those contemporary philosophers who have wondered what (if any) sense can be attached to a statement of the form "It was true at t_1 that E would occur at t_2."[12] Does this statement mean that had someone believed, guessed, or asserted at t_1 that E would occur at t_2, he would have been right?[13] (I shall have something to say about this form of determinism later in this paper.) Perhaps it means that at t_1 there was sufficient evidence upon which to predict that E would occur at t_2.[14] Maybe it means neither of these. Maybe it means nothing at all.[15] The argument presented above presupposes that it makes straightforward sense to suppose that God (or just anyone) held a true belief eighty years prior to Saturday. But this is not to suppose that *what* God believed *was true eighty years prior to Saturday*. Whether (or in what sense) it was true eighty years ago that Jones would mow his lawn on Saturday is a question I shall not discuss. As far as I can see, the argument in which I am interested requires nothing in the way of a decision on this issue.

II

I now want to consider three comments on the problem of divine foreknowledge which seem to be instructively incorrect.

A. Leibniz analyzed the problem as follows:

They say that what is foreseen cannot fail to exist and they say so truly; but it follows not that what is foreseen is necessary. For necessary truth is that whereof the contrary is impossible or implies a contradiction. Now the truth which states that I shall write tomorrow is not of that nature, it is not necessary. Yet, supposing that God foresees it, it is necessary that it come to pass, that is, the consequence is necessary, namely that it exist, since it has been foreseen; for God is infallible. This is what is termed a *hypothetical necessity*. But our concern is not this necessity; it is an *absolute* necessity that is required, to be able to say that an action is necessary, that it is not contingent, that it is not the effect of free choice.[16]

The statement "God believed at t_1 that Jones would do X at t_2" (where the interval between t_1 and t_2 is, for example, eighty years) does not entail "'Jones did X at t_2' is necessary." Leibniz is surely right about this. All that will follow from the first of these statements concerning "Jones did X at t_2" is that the latter is *true*, not that it is *necessarily true*. But this observation has no real bearing on the issue at hand. The following passage from St. Augustine's formulation of the problem may help to make this point clear.

Your trouble is this. You wonder how it can be that these two propositions are not contradictory and incompatible, namely that God has foreknowledge of all future events, and that we sin voluntarily and not by necessity. For if, you say, God foreknows that a man will sin, he must necessarily sin. But if there is necessity there is no voluntary choice of sinning, but rather fixed and unavoidable necessity.[17]

In this passage, the term "necessity" (or the phrase "by necessity") is not used to express a modal-logical concept. The term "necessity" is here used in contrast with the term "voluntary," not (as in Leibniz) in contrast with the term "contingent." If one's action is necessary (or by necessity), this is to say that one's action is not voluntary. Augustine says that if God has foreknowledge of human actions, the actions are necessary. But the form of this conditional is "p implies q," not "p implies n (q)." "q" in the consequent of this conditional is the claim that human actions are not voluntary—that is, that one is not able, or does not have the power, to do other than he does.

Perhaps I can make this point clearer by reformulating the original problem in such a way as to make explicit the modal operators working within it. Let it be *contingently* true that Jones did X at t_2. Since God holds a belief about the outcome of each human action well in advance of its performance, it is then *contingently* true that God believed at t_1 that Jones would do X at t_2. But it follows from this that it is *contingently* true that at t_2 Jones was not able to refrain from doing X. Had he been (contingently) able to refrain from doing X at t_2, then either he was (contingently) able to do something at t_2 that would have brought it about that God held a false belief at t_1, or he was (contingently) able to do something at t_2 that would have brought it about that God believed otherwise than He did at t_1, or he was (contingently) able to do something at t_2 that would have brought it about that God did not exist at t_1. None of these latter is an acceptable alternative.

B. In *Concordia Liberi Arbitrii*, Luis de Molina wrote as follows:

It was not that since He foreknew what would happen from those things which depend on the created will that it would happen; but, on the contrary, it was because such things would happen through the freedom of the will, that He foreknew it; and that He would foreknow the opposite if the opposite was to happen.[18]

Remarks similar to this one can be found in a great many traditional and contemporary theological texts. In fact, Molina assures us that the view expressed in this passage has always been "above controversy"—a matter of "common opinion" and "unanimous consent"—not only among the Church fathers, but also, as he says, "among all catholic men."

One claim made in the above passage seems to me to be truly "above controversy." With respect to any given action foreknown by God, God would have foreknown the opposite if the opposite was to happen. If we assume the notion of omniscience outlined in the first section of this paper, and if we agree that omniscience is part of the "essence" of God, this statement is a conceptual truth. I doubt if anyone would be inclined to dispute it. Also involved in this passage, however, is at least the suggestion of a doctrine that cannot be taken as an item of "common opinion" among *all* catholic men. Molina says it is not because God foreknows what He foreknows that men act as they do: it is because men act as they do that God foreknows what He foreknows. Some theologians have rejected this claim. It seems to entail that men's actions determine God's cognitions. And this latter, I think, has been taken by some theologians to be a violation of the notion of God as self-sufficient and incapable of being affected by events of the natural world.[19] But I shall not develop this point further. Where the view put forward in the above passage seems to me to go wrong in an interesting and important way is in Molina's claim that God can have foreknowledge of things that will happen "through the freedom of the will." It is this claim that I here want to examine with care.

What exactly are we saying when we say that God can know in advance what will happen *through the freedom of the will*? I think that what Molina has in mind is this. God can know in advance that a given man is going to *choose* to perform a certain action sometime in the future. With respect to the case of Jones mowing his lawn, God knew at t_1 that Jones would *freely decide* to mow his lawn at t_2. Not only did God know at t_1 that Jones would mow his lawn at t_2, He also knew at t_1 that this action would be performed *freely*. In the words of Emil Brunner, "God knows that which will take place in freedom in the future as something which happens in freedom."[20] What God knew at t_1 is that Jones would *freely* mow his lawn at t_2.

I think that this doctrine is incoherent. If God knew (and thus believed) at t_1 that Jones would *do* X at t_2,[21] I think it follows that Jones was not able to do other than X at t_2 (for reasons already given). Thus, if God knew (and thus believed) at t_1 that Jones would *do* X at t_2, it would follow that Jones did X at t_2, but *not freely*. It does not seem to be possible that God could have believed at t_1 that Jones would freely do X at t_2. If God believed at t_1 that Jones would do X at t_2, Jones's action at t_2 was not free; and if God *also* believed at t_1 that Jones would freely act at t_2, it follows that God held a false belief at t_1—which is absurd.

C. Frederich Schleiermacher commented on the problem of divine foreknowledge as follows:

In the same way, we estimate the intimacy between two persons by the foreknowledge one has of the actions of the other, without supposing that in either case, the one or the other's freedom is thereby endangered. So even the divine foreknowledge cannot endanger freedom.[22]

St. Augustine made this same point in *De Libero Arbitrio*. He said:

Unless I am mistaken, you would not directly compel the man to sin, though you knew beforehand that he was going to sin. Nor does your prescience in itself compel him to sin even though he was certainly going to sin, as we must assume if you have real prescience. So there is no contradiction here. Simply you know beforehand what another is going to do with his own will. Similarly God compels no man to sin, though he sees beforehand those who are going to sin by their own will.[23]

If we suppose (with Schleiermacher and Augustine) that the case of an intimate friend having foreknowledge of another's action has the same implications for determinism as the case of God's foreknowledge of human actions, I can imagine two positions which might then be taken. First, one might hold (with Schleiermacher and Augustine) that God's foreknowledge of human actions cannot entail determinism—since it is clear that an intimate friend can have foreknowledge of another's voluntary actions. Or, secondly, one might hold that an intimate friend cannot have foreknowledge of another's voluntary actions—since it is clear that God cannot have foreknowledge of such actions. This second position could take either of two forms. One might hold that since an intimate friend *can* have foreknowledge of another's actions, the actions in question cannot be voluntary. Or, alternatively, one might hold that since the other's actions *are* voluntary, the intimate friend cannot have foreknowledge of them.[24] But what I propose to argue in the remaining pages of this paper is that Schleiermacher and Augustine were mistaken in supposing that the case of an intimate friend having foreknowledge of another's actions has the same implications for determinism as the case of God's foreknowledge of human actions. What I want to suggest is that the argument I used above to show that God cannot have foreknowledge of voluntary actions cannot be used to show that an intimate friend cannot have foreknowledge of another's actions. Even if one holds that an intimate friend *can* have foreknowledge of another's voluntary actions, one ought not to think that the case is the same when dealing with the problem of divine foreknowledge.

Let Smith be an ordinary man and an intimate friend of Jones. Now, let us start by supposing that Smith believed at t_1 that Jones would do X at t_2. We make no assumption concerning the truth or falsity of Smith's belief, but assume only that Smith held it. Given only this much, there appears to be no difficulty in supposing that at t_2 Jones was able to do X and that at t_2 Jones was able to do not-X. So far as the above description of the case is concerned, it might well have been within Jones's power at t_2 to do something (namely, X) which would have brought it about that Smith held a true belief at t_1, and it might well have been within Jones's power at t_2 to do something (namely, not-X) which would have brought it about that Smith held a false belief at t_1. So much seems apparent.

Now let us suppose that Smith *knew* at t_1 that Jones would do X at t_2. This is to suppose that Smith correctly believed (with evidence) at t_1 that Jones would do X at t_2. It follows, to be sure, that Jones *did* X at t_2. But now let us inquire about what Jones was *able* to do at t_2. I submit that there is nothing in the description of this case that requires the conclusion that it was not within Jones's power at t_2 to refrain from doing X. By hypothesis, the belief held by Smith at t_1 was true. Thus, by hypothesis, Jones did X at t_2. But even if we assume that the belief held by Smith at t_1 was *in fact* true, we can add that the belief held by Smith at t_1 *might have* turned out to be false.[25] Thus, even if we say that Jones *in fact* did X at t_2, we can add that Jones *might not* have done X at t_2—meaning by this that it was within Jones's power at t_2 to refrain from doing X. Smith held a true belief which might have turned out to be false, and, correspondingly, Jones performed an action which he was able to refrain from performing. Given that Smith correctly believed at t_1 that Jones would do X at t_2, we can still assign Jones the *power* at t_2 to refrain from doing X. All we need add is that the power in question is one which Jones *did not exercise*.

These last reflections have no application, however, when dealing with God's foreknowledge. Assume that God (being essentially omniscient) existed at t_1, and assume that He believed at t_1 that Jones would do X at t_2. It follows, again, that Jones did X at t_2. God's beliefs are true. But now, as above, let us inquire into what Jones was *able* to do at t_2. We cannot claim now, as in the Smith case, that the belief held by God at t_1 was *in fact* true but *might have* turned out to be false. No sense of "might have" has application here. It is a conceptual truth that God's beliefs are true. Thus, we cannot claim, as in the Smith case, that Jones *in fact* acted in accordance with God's beliefs but had the *ability* to refrain from so doing. The ability to refrain from acting in accordance with one of God's beliefs would be the ability to do something that would bring it about that one of God's beliefs was false. And no one could have an ability of this description. Thus, in the case of God's foreknowledge of Jones's action at t_2, if we are to assign Jones the ability at t_2 to refrain from doing X, we must understand this ability in some way other than the way we understood it when dealing with Smith's foreknowledge. In this case, either we must say that it was the ability at t_2 to bring it about that God believed otherwise than He did at t_1; or we must say that it was the ability at t_2 to bring it about that any person who believed at t_1 that Jones would do X at t_2 (one of whom was, by hypothesis, God) held a false belief and thus was not God. But, as pointed out earlier, neither of these last alternatives can be accepted.

The important thing to be learned from the study of Smith's foreknowledge of Jones's action is that the problem of divine foreknowledge has as one of its pillars the claim that truth is *analytically* connected with God's *beliefs*. No problem of determinism arises when dealing with human knowledge of future actions. This is because truth is not analytically connected with human belief even when (as in the case of human knowledge) truth is contingently conjoined to belief. If we suppose that Smith knows at t_1 that Jones will do X at t_2, what we are supposing is that Smith believes at t_1 that Jones will do X at t_2 and (as an additional, contingent, fact) that the belief in question is true. Thus having supposed that Smith knows at t_1 that Jones will do X at t_2, when we turn to a consideration of the situation of t_2 we can infer (1) that Jones *will* do X at t_2 (since Smith's belief is true), and (2) that Jones does not have the power at t_2 to do something that would bring it about that Smith did not *believe* as he did at t_1. But paradoxical though it may seem (and it seems paradoxical only at first sight), Jones can have the power at t_2 to do something that would bring it about that Smith did not have *knowledge* at t_1. This is simply to say that Jones can have the *power* at t_2 to do something that would bring it about that the belief held by Smith at t_1 (which was, in fact, true) was (instead) false. We are required only to add that since Smith's belief was in fact true (that is, was knowledge) Jones *did not* (in fact) *exercise* that power. But when we turn to a consideration of God's fore-knowledge of Jones's action at t_2 the elbowroom between belief and truth disappears and, with it, the possibility of assigning Jones even the *power* of doing other than he does at t_2. We begin by supposing that God *knows* at t_1 that Jones will do X at t_2. As above, this is to suppose that God believes at t_1 that Jones will do X at t_2, and it is to suppose that this belief is true. But it is *not* an additional, contingent fact that the belief held by God is true. "God believes X" entails "X is true." Thus, having supposed that God knows (and thus believes) at t_1 that Jones will do X at t_2, we can infer (1) that Jones *will do* X at t_2 (since God's belief is true); (2) that Jones does not have the power at t_2 to do something that would bring it about that God did not hold the belief He held at t_1, and (3) that Jones does not have the power at t_2 to do something that would bring it about that the belief held by God at t_1 was false. This last is what we could *not* infer when truth and belief were only factually connected—as in the case of Smith's knowledge. To be sure, "Smith knows at t_1 that Jones will do X at t_2" and "God knows at t_1 that Jones will do X at t_2" both entail "Jones will do X at t_2" ("A knows X" entails "'X' is true"). But this similarity between "Smith knows X" and "God knows X" is not a point of any special interest in the present discussion. As Schleiermacher and Augustine rightly insisted (and as we discovered in our study of Smith's foreknowledge), the mere fact that someone knows in advance how another will act in the future is not enough to yield a problem of the sort we have been discussing. We begin to get a glimmer of the knot involved in the problem of divine foreknowledge when we shift attention away from the *similarities* between "Smith knows X" and "God knows X" (in particular, that they both entail "'X' is true") and concentrate instead on the logical *differences* which obtain between Smith's knowledge and God's knowledge. We get to the difference which makes the difference when, after analyzing the notion of knowledge as true belief (supported by evidence) we discover the radically dissimilar relations between truth and belief in the two cases. When truth is only factually connected with belief (as in Smith's knowledge) one can have the power (though, by hypothesis, one will not exercise it) to do something that would make the belief false. But when truth is analytically connected with belief (as in God's belief) no one can have the power to do something which would render the belief false.

To conclude: I have assumed that any statement of the form "A knows X" entails a statement of the form "A believes X" as well as a statement of the form "'X' is true." I have then supposed (as an analytic truth) that if a given person is omniscient, that person (1) holds no false beliefs, and (2) holds beliefs about the outcome of human actions in advance of their performance. In addition, I have assumed that the statement "If a given person is God that person is omniscient" is an a priori statement. (This last I have labeled the doctrine of God's essential omniscience.) Given these items (plus some premises concerning what is and what is not within one's power), I have argued that if God exists, it is not within one's power to do other than he does. I have inferred from this that if God exists, no human action is voluntary.

As emphasized earlier, I do not want to claim that the assumptions underpinning the argument are acceptable. In fact, it seems to me that a theologian interested in claiming both that God is omniscient and that men have free will could deny any one (or more) of them. For example, a theologian might deny that a statement of the form "A knows X" entails a statement of the form "*A* believes *X*" (some contemporary philosophers have denied this) or, alternatively, he might claim that this entailment holds in the case of human knowledge but fails in the case of God's knowledge. This latter would be to claim that when knowledge is attributed to God, the term "knowledge" bears a sense other than the one it has when knowledge is attributed to human beings. Then again, a theologian might object to the analysis of "omniscience" with which I have been working. Although I doubt if any Christian theologian would allow that an omniscient being could believe something false, he might claim that a given person could be omniscient although he did not hold beliefs about the outcome of human actions *in advance* of their performance. (This latter is the way Boethius escaped the problem.) Still again, a theologian might deny the doctrine of God's essential omniscience. He might admit that if a given person is God that person is omniscient, but he might deny that this statement formulates an a priori truth. This would be to say that although God is omniscient, He is not *essentially* omniscient. So far as I can see, within the conceptual framework of theology employing any one of these adjustments, the problem of divine foreknowledge outlined in this paper could not be formulated. There thus appears to be a rather wide range of alternatives open to the theologian at this point. It would be a mistake to think that commitment to determinism is an unavoidable implication of the Christian concept of divine omniscience.

But having arrived at this understanding, the importance of the preceding deliberations ought not to be overlooked. There is a pitfall in the doctrine of divine omniscience. That knowing involves believing (truly) is surely a tempting philosophical view (witness the many contemporary philosophers who have affirmed it). And the idea that God's attributes (including omniscience) are essentially connected to His nature, together with the idea that an omniscient being would hold no false beliefs and would hold beliefs about the outcome of human actions in advance of their performance, might be taken by some theologians as obvious candidates for inclusion in a finished Christian theology. Yet the theologian must approach these items critically. If they are embraced together, then if one affirms the existence of God, one is committed to the view that no human action is voluntary.

CHAPTER THREE

Is the Existence of God a 'Hard' Fact?

Marilyn McCord Adams

Nelson Pike, in his article, "Divine Omniscience and Voluntary Action" [Chapter 2 in this volume], argues that if an essentially omniscient and everlasting God exists, no human action is voluntary. Pike's argument depends upon the following two claims:

4. It is not within one's power at a given time to do something that would bring it about that someone who held a certain belief at a time prior to the time in question did not hold that belief at the time prior to the time in question.

5. It is not within one's power at a given time to do something that would bring it about that a person who existed at an earlier time did not exist at an earlier time. [p. 63]

In "Of God and Freedom,"[1] Professor Saunders evidently intends to discount these claims by arguing that the following statement

(A) One does not have the power (at a given time) so to act that the past (relative to that time) would be other than it was.

is false. Pike points out in the first part of his reply to Saunders that (A) has unrestricted application to all facts about the past.[2]

Reprinted by permission from *The Philosophical Review*, 76 (1967): 492–503. I wish to thank Professor Nelson Pike for his encouragement and comments in the preparation of this paper. I am also indebted to my husband, Robert Merrihew Adams, and to Professor Keith Donnellan for helpful discussions and suggestions. Needless to say, however, none of these persons necessarily agrees with everything I say here.

He distinguishes "hard" from "soft" facts about the past (see Section I below) and claims that premises (4) and (5) are about restricted classes of "hard" facts: namely, facts about the beliefs and existence of persons respectively. But, Pike says, Saunders has argued only that (A) is false as applied to "soft" facts and has given no reason to think that (A) is false as applied to these restricted classes of "hard" facts as well. Elsewhere in his rejoinder, Pike indicates that in the original paper he had intended "belief" and "person" to occur in their ordinary senses in premises (4) and (5) respectively.[3] So understood, premises (4) and (5) seem to me to be true statements about "hard" facts. Pike seems also to concede that Saunders is right in claiming that (A) is false as applied to "soft" facts.

In this paper I shall assume that Saunders and Pike are correct at least in thinking that (A) is not generally true as applied to "soft" facts about the past. I shall argue, however, that the existence of an essentially omniscient and everlasting God is not a "hard" fact, and that as a consequence the argument of Pike's original paper fails. By arguing in this way, I shall be insisting on a position Pike considers in the second part of his reply to Saunders.

I

It is useful before proceeding with the argument briefly to examine the distinction between "hard" and "soft" facts. Pike makes the distinction between "hard" and "soft" facts about the past by contrasting facts which were "fully accomplished" or "over-and-done-with" at a given past time with those which were not.[4] I think that the distinction Pike has in mind can also be drawn in terms of a statement's being about a given time. This alternative explanation is no less intuitive (it relies on an intuitive understanding of "happening" and "actual"), but it will be more convenient for my purposes.[5] Consider the following:

(B) "Statement p is at least in part about a time t" = df. "The happening or not happening, actuality or non-actuality of something at t is a necessary condition of the truth of p."

Thus the statement "Caesar died 2,009 years before Saunders wrote his paper" is at least in part about 44 B.C., since Caesar's death at that time is a necessary condition of the truth of that statement. It is also at least in part about A.D. 1965 since Saunders's writing his paper in A.D. 1965 is also a necessary condition of the truth of that statement. Given (B) the notion of a "hard" fact may be explained as follows.

(C) "Statement p expresses a 'hard' fact about a time t" = df. "p is not at least in part about any time future relative to t."

Hence the statement "Caesar died in 44 B.C." expresses a "hard" fact about 44 B.C. But the statement "Caesar died 2,009 years before Saunders wrote his paper" does not, since it is at least in part about A.D. 1965.

It should be clear from the above examples that the tense of the verb of the sentence used to express the statement in question is no indication of the times which the statement is in part about. A sentence with a past-tense verb may express a statement which is in part about the present and future; with a present-tense verb, the past and future; and with a future-tense verb, the present and past.

II

The two features of the concept of God which are important for Pike's argument and with which I shall be concerned are *essential* everlastingness and *essential* omniscience.

The doctrine that God is everlasting can be summarized in two claims. The first is that God is the kind of thing to which temporal predicates apply—that is to say, God has time location. Thus, according to this doctrine, it would not be a category mistake to say that God exists *now*, or that he existed *before* Saunders wrote his paper and *after* the death of Caesar. The second is that if God exists at any time, then He exists at all times.

To say that God is omniscient is also to make two claims about Him. The first is that God holds no false beliefs—that is, if God believes that p, then p. The second is that God's knowledge is complete; and therefore, if p, then God believes that p. Thus God is said to know everything that happens in the created world. Further, if God is said to be everlasting as well as omniscient, it is said that God has *always* known everything that happens, has happened, or will happen in the created world. Thus for everything that happens, has happened, or will happen, it is true to say that God knew it was going to happen *before* it happened.

What further is meant by saying not just that God is everlasting and omniscient, but also that He is *essentially* everlasting and *essentially* omniscient? I shall consider two answers to this question. The first is that the statements "God is everlasting" and "God is omniscient" are analytic (more formally, "x is God" entails "x is everlasting"; and "x is God" entails "x is omniscient"). The second (the answer which Pike gives) is to claim not just that the statements "God is everlasting" and "God is omniscient" are analytic, but in addition that the person x who is God would not be the individual person he is if he failed either to be everlasting or to be omniscient.

In what follows I shall begin by interpreting the doctrines of essential everlastingness and essential omniscience in the first way and argue from each of these doctrines in turn that the existence of an essentially omniscient and everlasting God is not a "hard" fact. In addition, I shall try to show how Pike's argument would fail if he had interpreted these doctrines in the first way. In the remainder of the paper, I shall maintain that these results are damaging to Pike's original argument even if one interprets the doctrines of essential everlastingness and essential omniscience as Pike does.

III

Consider the doctrine of God according to which the statements "God is everlasting" and "God is omniscient" are analytic.

1. The following is an argument from the doctrine of essential everlastingness alone that the existence of God is not a "hard" fact.

(D) "God is everlasting" is analytic (that is, "x is God" entails "x is everlasting").

(E) "x is everlasting" = df. "If $(\exists t)$ (x exists at t), then (t) (x exists at t)."

Therefore

(F) "x is God" entails "If $(\exists t)$ (x exists at t), then (t) (x exists at t)."

And therefore

(G) "x is God and $(\exists t)$ (x exists at t)" entails "(t) (x exists at t)."

What (G) says is that it is a necessary condition of the truth of the claim that some extant individual x is God, that that individual exist at all times whatever. But the statement that an individual x exists at all times whatever is a statement which is in part about the future (future relative to any time t for which there is a t' later than t). Hence the statement that some extant individual x is God is a statement which is at least in part about the future. Therefore, the statement that some extant individual x (for whatever extant x you choose) is God does not state a "hard" fact about any time t for which there is a time t' later than t.

Therefore, it follows merely from the claim that the statement "God is everlasting" is analytic that the existence of an essentially omniscient and everlasting God is not a "hard" fact about any time t for which there is a t' later than t. Hence, assuming that (A) is at least not generally true as applied to "soft" facts about the past, one cannot conclude by reference to (A) alone that it is not within someone's power at a time t' so to act that God would not have existed at an earlier time t even though He did exist at t. In particular, one cannot conclude by reference to (A) alone, that if an individual x is God at t (and hence in fact exists at all times whatever), no one can have the power at a time t' later than t so to act that x not exist at that *later* time (although if x is God at t, no one will in fact exercise such a power at t').

I think the result just derived, if correct, indicates that Pike's argument would be invalid if he interpreted the doctrine of essential everlastingness in the first way. Pike claims to show that if an essentially omniscient and everlasting God exists, then Jones who mowed his lawn at t_2 did not have the power at t_2 to refrain from mowing his lawn. He proceeds by offering three (supposedly exhaustive) alternative descriptions of Jones's alleged power at t_2 to refrain from mowing his lawn—namely, "the power at t_2 to do something that would have brought it about that God held a false belief at t_1," "the power at t_2 to do something which would have brought it about that God did not hold the belief he held at t_1," and "the power at t_2 to bring it about that God did not exist at t_1"—and by eliminating each on the grounds that it is conceptually impossible that a human being have such a power (see steps 6–9 of Pike's original argument). Pike cites premise (5) as a warrant for step (9), the step in which he rejects the last of those descriptions. But if "person" occurs in its ordinary sense in premise (5), then premise (5) is a conceptual truth about what is within the power of human beings as regards a restricted class of "*hard*" facts. No reason has yet been given for supposing that it follows from the claim that it is conceptually impossible that a human being so act at t_2 that a certain "*hard*" fact—namely, the existence of a particular person—about t_1 would be other than it was, that it is conceptually impossible that a human being so act at t_2 that a certain "*soft*" fact—namely, the existence of God—about t_1 would be other than it was.

Therefore, if Pike had interpreted the doctrine of essential everlastingness in the first way, his inference of (9) from (5) would be invalid. Hence his argument would not provide sufficient reason for denying to Jones who mowed his lawn at t_2 the power at t_2 to refrain from mowing his lawn.

2. The following argument from the doctrine of essential omniscience may be used to establish the same conclusions. If

(H) "x is God" entails "If p, then x believes p,"

then

(I) "p" entails "If x is God, then x believes p."

And if

(J) "x is God" entails "If x believes p, then p,"

then

(K) "x believes p" entails "If x is God, then p."

Either the individual x holds beliefs about the future or x does not hold beliefs about the future. If x holds no beliefs about the future, then by (I) x is not God, since there are true statements about the future. But, applying (K), if x holds beliefs about the future, it is a necessary condition of individual x's being God that those beliefs about the future are true. Hence, that certain things happen (or do not happen) or obtain (or fail to obtain) in the future is a necessary condition of any individual x who holds beliefs about the future, being God. But since at any time t for which there is a t' later than t only individuals who hold beliefs about the future can be God, it is a necessary condition of any individual x's being God that certain things happen (or do not happen) or obtain (or fail to obtain) in the future. In that case, the statement that an individual x is God is a statement which does not express a "hard" fact about any time t for which there is a t' later than t.

Therefore, that the existence of God is not a "hard" fact about any time t for which there is a t' later than t follows also merely from the claim that "God is omniscient" is analytic. Since (A) is not generally true as regards "soft" facts about the past, one cannot conclude by reference to (A) alone that it is not within someone's power at t' so to act that the belief that p held at t by the individual x who is in fact God would be false.

In particular, one could not conclude by reference to (A) alone that Jones does not have the power at t_2 so to act that God would not have existed at t_1 in virtue of his having the power at t_2 to refrain from mowing his lawn. Consider the following. For any x whatever, the statement "x is God" does not express a "hard" fact about t_1 (since *ex hypothesi* there is a time t_2 later than t_1). Suppose an individual x believes at t_1 that Jones will mow his lawn at t_2. No reason has been given to suppose that Jones may not have the power at t_2 so to act that the belief of x at t_1 would be false even though the belief of x at t_1 was in fact true: namely, the power at t_2 to refrain from mowing his lawn. But by the argument from the doctrine of essential omniscience just presented, that power of Jones would be the power at t_2 so to act that an individual x who believed at t_1 that Jones would mow his lawn at t_2 was not God. If a certain individual x is God, then he must have believed at t_1 that Jones would mow his lawn at t_2 since Jones did mow his lawn at t_2. Further, assuming that x is the sole possessor of some of the other attributes of God,[6] no individual who did not believe at t_1 that Jones would mow his lawn at t_2 was God. Hence, assuming that x is the sole possessor of some of the other essential attributes of God, Jones's power at t_2 to refrain from mowing his lawn would be the power at t_2 so to act that God would not have existed at t_1 even though He did exist at t_1. Therefore, one could not conclude by reference to (A) alone that Jones does not have the power at t_2 so to act that God would not have existed at t_1 in virtue of his having the power at t_2 to refrain from mowing his lawn.

As discussed above in connection with the argument from essential everlastingness, Pike cites premise (5) as his warrant for denying to Jones the power at t_2 so to act that God would not have existed at t_1. But again, if "person" occurs in its ordinary sense in premise (5), then premise (5) is a conceptual truth about what is within the power of human beings as regards a restricted class of "*hard*" facts. No reason has yet been given for supposing that it follows from the claim that it is conceptually impossible that a human being so act at t_2 that a certain "*hard*" fact— namely, the existence of a particular person—about t_1 would be other than it was, that it is conceptually impossible that a human being so act at t_2 that a certain "*soft*" fact—namely, the existence of God—about t_1 would be other than it was.

Therefore, if Pike had interpreted either the doctrine of essential everlastingness or the doctrine of essential omniscience in the first way, his inference of (9) from (5) would be invalid. Hence his argument would not provide a sufficient reason for denying to Jones who mowed his lawn at t_2 the power at t_2 to refrain from mowing his lawn.

IV

The arguments in Section III explicitly presuppose analyses of essential everlastingness and essential omniscience different from those Pike employs in his argument. Pike agrees that the doctrines of essential everlastingness and essential omniscience imply that "God is everlasting" and "God is omniscient" are analytic. But he thinks that these doctrines also imply that everlastingness and omniscience are connected in a special way with the personal identity of the individual who is God: that is, if the individual x who is God failed either to be everlasting or to be omniscient, not only would x fail to be God but also x would fail to be the individual person x is.

I think, however, that this way of analyzing essential everlastingness and essential omniscience is in conflict with the criteria of identity for our ordinary concept "person." In the remainder of the paper I shall try to show that in view of this difficulty the reasoning offered in Section III above is telling against Pike's argument even if one interprets the doctrines of essential everlastingness and essential omniscience as Pike does.

As noted at the outset, Pike indicated in his original paper that he understood the concept "person" involved to be the ordinary concept "person." Further, it is clear that he thinks that an extant individual x's being a person and being the individual person he is are "hard" facts. For he seems to grant to Saunders that (A) is false as applied to "soft" facts, but denies that this concession damages premises (4) and (5).

If Pike were right in supposing that, say, omniscience can be tied to the conditions of personal identity (in the ordinary sense), it would be apparent why he thought he could infer from (5) that it was not within Jones's power at t_2 so to act that God would not have existed at t_1 even though He did exist at t_1 (step 9 of Pike's original argument). For on Pike's analysis, the individual x who is God must be such that if x failed to be omniscient and so failed to be God, x would be a different individual person from the person he in fact is. Therefore, if someone had the power at t_2 so to act that x would not have been omniscient at t_1 and hence not God at t_1 even though x was omniscient at t_1 and was God at t_1, he would have the power so to act that x would not have been the individual person he in fact was. But premise (5) says that it is impossible that any human being should have that power. Thus if omniscience could be tied to personal identity (in the ordinary sense) in the way Pike's analysis presupposes, it would be impossible that Jones should have the power at t_2 so to act that the person x who is God would not have been omniscient at t_1 and hence not God at t_1, so that his inference of (9) from (5) would be legitimate.

If, however, the ordinary concept of person is such that to be a person in the ordinary sense is a "hard" fact, and if the criteria of identity for the ordinary concept of person are such that to be the individual person one is is a "hard" fact, then being omniscient (or everlasting) can be a necessary condition neither of an individual x's being a person in the ordinary sense nor of x's being the individual person x is. For the arguments in Section III show that "x is everlasting" and "x is omniscient" express "soft" facts about any time t for which there is a time t' later than t. And if x's being a person in the ordinary sense, or x's being the individual person (in the ordinary sense) that x is, depended on x's being omniscient or everlasting, then x's being a person in the ordinary sense, or being the individual person (in the ordinary sense) that x is, would be "soft" facts—which they are not. It seems, therefore, that Pike's analysis of essential omniscience cannot be correct if it is assumed that the concept involved is the ordinary concept of person.

It is possible, of course, to construct an extraordinary concept of person—"person$_2$"—such that an individual x would not be the individual person$_2$ x is if x failed to have any one of the attributes traditionally assigned to God. Might not Pike repair his inference of (9) from (5) by replacing "person" (in the ordinary sense) in (5) with "person$_2$"? I think not. For x's being the individual person$_2$ x is will not be a "hard" fact about any time t for which there is a t' later than t. Hence, since (A) is not generally true as applied to "soft" facts about the past, one cannot conclude from (A) alone that it is conceptually impossible that a human being have the power at t' so to act that a given person$_2$ would not have existed at an earlier time t even though that person$_2$ did exist at t. No reason has been given for supposing that the statement obtained by replacing "person" (in the ordinary sense) in (5) by "person$_2$" is true. Hence there is no reason to suppose that the inference of (9) from (5) (where "person" in (5) is replaced by "person$_2$") is sound.

Therefore, there is no adequate reason to suppose that Pike's inference of (9) from (5) holds good even if one employs a doctrine of God according to which "God is a person$_2$" is analytic.

V

When considering objections similar to the ones I have raised in Section IV, Pike expresses doubts as to whether or not they hold good but makes the following remarks as regards the consequences if they do hold good:

[I]f the stipulation that God is essentially omniscient constitutes a modification of the ordinary concept of *person* and if this modification is sufficient to falsify principle (5), then we can no longer claim that God is a *person*. Again, what sense would it make to claim that God is a person and then to add that He is a person of such a sort that it would be within someone's power at a given time so to act that a person (of that sort) who existed at an earlier time would not have existed at an earlier time? This would simply be to say that the (so-called) person named "God" was not a *person* at all.[7]

I think that Pike here misreads the upshot of the above objections to his argument. Neither the claim that the statement "x is God" does not express a "hard" fact about any time t for which there is a time t' later than t, nor the claim that the statement "God is a person$_2$" is analytic, is inconsistent with the claim that the statement "God is a person (in the ordinary sense)" is analytic. For to insist on all three of these claims is in effect to assert (i) that the individual x who is God falls under three concepts— "God," "person$_2$," and the ordinary concept "person"—the criteria of identity for each of which are different from the criteria of identity for each of the other two; and (ii) that it is a necessary condition for an individual x's falling under one of these concepts (that is, the concept "God") that that individual x fall under each of the other two concepts (that is, the concept "person$_2$" and the ordinary concept "person") where the criteria of identity for the concept "person$_2$" are different from the criteria of identity for the ordinary concept "person." But I can see no logical difficulty with (i), with (ii), or with their conjunction; and in any case no reason has been given by Pike to suppose that there is such a difficulty. Therefore, no reason has been given why one cannot say that it is a necessary condition of an individual x's being God that x be a person (in the ordinary sense), even if one admits that x would be the same individual person (in the ordinary sense) that x is even if x were not God, and claims that x would not be the same person$_2$ that x is if x were not God.

What is self-contradictory, assuming that my argument in Section IV is correct, is the claim that x's having any and/or all of the attributes traditionally assigned to God is a necessary condition of x's being the individual person (in the ordinary sense) that x is. But so far as I can see, one can still claim that God is a person in the ordinary sense and further that the statement "God is a person (in the ordinary sense)" is analytic. And this is true even if it be granted that "God is a person$_2$" is analytic.

VI

In sum, I have argued that the existence of an essentially omniscient and everlasting God is not a "hard" fact and consequently that there is no adequate reason to suppose that Pike's
inference of (9) from (5) in his original argument is legitimate.
The claim that the existence of an essentially omniscient and
everlasting God is inconsistent with the voluntary character of
some human actions has yet to be made out.

CHAPTER FOUR

Freedom and Foreknowledge

John Martin Fischer

A powerful argument can be made that God's omniscience is incompatible with human freedom.[1] If God is eternal and omniscient, then it might seem that my freedom now to do other than what I am doing must be the freedom so to act that a fact about the past (God's prior belief about my present activity) would not be a fact about the past. But since the past is "fixed," it seems that if God exists, then I am now not free to do other than what I am doing.

Many philosophers have been attracted to an Ockhamist response to this argument.[2] Both the Ockhamist and the incompatibilist can distinguish between "hard" and "soft" facts about the past; the hard facts are fixed while the soft facts need not be fixed. But the Ockhamist claims that God's prior belief about my present activity is a soft fact about the past and hence not fixed; my freedom is thus preserved. Some Ockhamists even claim that the very existence of God is also a soft fact about the past.

I shall argue that a very attractive presentation of the Ockhamist approach, one explicitly formulated by Marilyn Adams, is inadequate.[3] There are significant problems with Adams's attempt to characterize the hard fact/soft fact distinction. Further,

Reprinted by permission from *The Philosophical Review*, 92 (1983): 67–79. I have benefited from comments by Carl Ginet, Norman Kretzmann, T. H. Irwin, and Judith Jarvis Thomson. I am especially indebted to Robert Stalnaker, many of whose suggestions have been incorporated in this paper.

I shall present a general challenge to *any* sort of Ockhamist attempt to explain this distinction.

I. Pike's Argument

Nelson Pike claims to exhibit the incompatibility of human freedom and divine foreknowledge, relative to certain plausible assumptions about God's nature.[4] These assumptions reflect central features of the standard Judeo-Christian conception of God. Pike explicitly adopts the assumption that if God exists, then God is essentially omniscient and God is eternal. On Pike's account, God is omniscient if and only if God believes all and only true propositions, and we might say that God is essentially omniscient if and only if God is omniscient in all possible worlds in which God exists. Pike says that God is eternal if and only if God has always existed and always will.[5]

Following Pike's presentation in a different article, I assume that the term "God" is a descriptive expression used to mark a certain *role*, rather than a proper name.[6] Whoever occupies the role of God is omniscient, omnipotent, eternal, etc. In contrast, the term "Yahweh" is a proper name; it refers to the person who actually occupies the role of God (if God exists). It is not necessarily true that Yahweh is omniscient, omnipotent, eternal, etc.; it is logically possible that some other person has been God.[7]

Since "God" is being used here as a non-rigid designator, there is some ambiguity in the assumptions about God's attributes. "God is essentially omniscient" does not mean that the person who is in fact God is essentially omniscient, but rather, that necessarily, whoever is God is omniscient. In terms of possible worlds, God is essentially omniscient just in case for any possible world in which there is a person who is God, that person is omniscient. (One can assume that if God is eternal in a particular world, then it follows that there is one and the same person who is God at all times in that world. Pike need not accept this particular assumption, as it is not crucial to his argument.)

Though this is the approach to the term "God" that Pike appears to adopt, it might seem to be an unusual and unappealing position. I shall follow Pike in adopting this interpretation, but it is important to note that Pike could just as easily embrace the stronger interpretation according to which the person who is in fact God is essentially God. Nothing in Pike's proof, or in my criticism of Adams's Ockhamism, rests on adopting the weaker rather than the stronger interpretation of God's attributes.

In effect, Pike also appears to adopt what might be called the "fixed past" constraint on power attributions:

(FPC) It is never in any person's power at a time t so to act that the past (relative to t) would have been different from what it actually was.

Pike's view about the fixity of the past implies not only that one cannot causally influence the past; it implies that no person is free to do something which is such that, were he to do it, the past would have been different from what it actually was.

Pike's argument is essentially as follows. Suppose Jones did X at time t_2 and God exists. Since God exists, it follows from God's eternality that He existed at t_1 (a time prior to t_2). Let us call the person who was God at t_1, "Y." Since Jones did X at t_2, it follows from God's omniscience that He believed at t_1 that Jones would do X at t_2. Now if it was within Jones's power at t_2 to refrain from doing X, then (1) it was in Jones's power at t_2 to act in such a way that Y would have been God and would have held a false belief at t_1, or (2) it was in Jones's power at t_2 to act in such a way that Y would have been God but would not have held the belief He held at t_1, or (3) it was in Jones's power at t_2 to act in such a way that Y would not have been God at t_1.

But (1) is ruled out by God's essential omniscience, and (2) and (3) are ruled out by (FPC). Hence it was not in Jones's power at t_2 to refrain from doing X. If the argument is sound, it can easily be generalized to show that God's eternality and essential omniscience are incompatible with any human agent's being free at any time.

It should be pointed out that incompatibilism about divine foreknowledge and human freedom need not entail incompatibilism about human foreknowledge and human freedom. The problem is deeper with divine foreknowledge because of God's essential omniscience; perhaps it was in Jones's power at t_2 so to act that Smith (who actually held only correct beliefs) would have held a false belief at t_1. Pike wants to insist on an *asymmetry* between divine and human foreknowledge.[8]

II. Hard and Soft Facts

It is sometimes in one's power so to act that facts about the past *would not* be facts. John Turk Saunders discusses such a fact:

Although it is true that if I had refrained from writing this paper in 1965, Caesar's assassination would have been other than it is in that it would not have preceded by 2,009 years my writing this paper, it would be absurd to argue that I therefore did not have it in my power to refrain from writing this paper in 1965.[9]

It is obvious that the mere fact that if Saunders had refrained from writing his paper, then Caesar's assassination would not have preceded Saunders's writing his paper by 2,009 years did not render Saunders incapable of refraining; relative to 1965, "Caesar died 2,009 years prior to Saunders's writing his paper" expresses a soft fact about the past. Of course, it was not in Saunders's power so to act that Caesar would not have died on the steps of the Senate. Relative to Saunders's lifetime, the fact that Caesar died on the steps of the Senate is a hard fact about the past.

Pike agrees with the Ockhamist that there are both hard and soft facts about the past.[10] It is not easy to provide a precise characterization of the hard fact/soft fact distinction. Pike himself provides no such account, though he claims we can recognize clear examples of each sort.[11] The disagreement between Pike and the Ockhamist is about where to draw the line. Pike's position is that if the ordinary notions of belief and existence are applied to God, then God's belief at t_1 and God's existence at t_1 (including the fact that Y was God at t_1) are hard facts about the past relative to t_2. And if they were soft facts about the past relative to t_2, this would show that we were ascribing beliefs and existence to God in a special, nonstandard way.

Given the hard fact/soft fact distinction, the appropriate interpretation of Pike's claim about the fixity of the past should be made explicit:

(FPC*) It is never in any person's power at a time *t* so to act that any hard fact about the past (relative to *t*) would have been different from what it actually was.[12]

Marilyn Adams presents an account of the distinction which she believes supports compatibilism against Pike's attack. It will be useful to consider Adams's attempt at giving an account of the distinction:

(B) "Statement p is at least in part about a time t'' = df. "The happening or not happening, actuality or non-actuality of something at t is a necessary condition of the truth of p."

Thus the statement, "Caesar died 2,009 years before Saunders wrote his paper" is at least in part about 44 B.C., since Caesar's death at that time is a necessary condition of the truth of that statement. It is also at least in part about A.D. 1965 since Saunders's writing his paper in A.D. 1965 is also a necessary condition of the truth of that statement. Given (B) the notion of a "hard" fact may be explained as follows.

(C) "Statement p expresses a 'hard' fact about a time t'' = df. "p is not at least in part about any time future relative to t."[13]

Adams uses this account to present an Ockhamist response to Pike's argument. On her account, God's belief at t_1 and the fact that Y was God at t_1 are deemed soft facts about t_1.

Adams claims that her account shows why "Caesar died 2,009 years before Saunders wrote his paper" does not express a hard fact about 44 B.C. But her account does *not* explain this unless it is interpreted to imply that *no* sentence expresses a hard fact. Adams says that "Caesar died 2,009 years before Saunders wrote his paper" is at least in part about 1965, since Saunders's writing his paper in 1965 is a necessary condition of the truth of that statement. But this seems plainly false; the statement entails that Caesar's death and Saunders's writing his paper be separated by 2,009 years, but it does not entail any two particular dates for the two events. The statement entails that the two events stand in a certain temporal *relation*, but it does not entail that they occur on any specific dates. Hence, Saunders's writing his paper in 1965 is *not* a necessary condition of Caesar's death being 2,009 years prior to Saunders's writing his paper, if we interpret "q is a necessary condition for p" as "p entails q."

One might reply that since it is true that Saunders wrote his paper in 1965, "Saunders wrote his paper in 1965" is *materially implied* by "Caesar died 2,009 years prior to Saunders's writing his paper." So if we interpret "q is a necessary condition for p" as "p materially implies q," Saunders's writing his paper in 1965 is a necessary condition of the truth of "Caesar died 2,009 years prior to Saunders's writing his paper." But it is obvious that if this sense of "necessary condition" is adopted, then *no* sentence will express a hard fact about 44 B.C. So Adams's account of Pike's intuitive distinction is inadequate as it stands. Adams gives no explication of the notion of a necessary condition by reference to which she can say that "Caesar died 2,009 years prior to Saunders's writing his paper" does not express a hard fact about 44 B.C.

Consider also the statement, "John F. Kennedy was assassinated." Given the entailment interpretation, this statement expresses a hard fact about 1961, since it does not *entail* the occurrence of anything subsequent to 1961. Of course, there are logically possible worlds in which Kennedy was assassinated in 1961. But we want to say that in 1962 (and in 1963, until November 22), it was within Oswald's power so to have acted that Kennedy would not have been assassinated. And again, it is obvious that the material implication interpretation of "necessary condition" is inadequate.

Complex statements further illustrate the inadequacy of the entailment account of "necessary condition." If Jones did not believe at t_1 that he would do X at t_2, then "Either Smith knew at t_1 that Jones would do X at t_2 or Jones believed at t_1 that Jones would do X at t_2" should *not* express a hard fact about t_1; the Ockhamist would say that Jones might have been able so to act at t_2 that this disjunctive statement would be false. Yet on Adams's account, the statement expresses a *hard* fact about t_1, since its truth does not entail that anything happens after t_1; the truth of the disjunction does not entail that anything happens (or fails to happen, etc.) after t_1.

In defense of Adams's approach, one might offer the following account of a necessary condition: q is a necessary condition for p if and only if p would not be true (or have been true) if q were not true (or had not been true). Let us call this interpretation the "counterfactual" account of a necessary condition. It *is* plausible to say that if Saunders had not written his paper in 1965, then it *would not* have been the case that Caesar died 2,009 years prior to Saunders's writing his paper. Thus, Adams could say, on the counterfactual account, that "Saunders wrote his paper in 1965" is a necessary condition of "Caesar died 2,009 years prior to Saunders's writing his paper." Also, it is perhaps reasonable to say (though I am not sure) that if Oswald had not shot Kennedy in 1963, then Kennedy would not have been assassinated. If this is so, then Adams could say that "Oswald shot Kennedy in 1963" is a necessary condition of "John F. Kennedy was assassinated." Similarly, if Jones had not done X at t_2, then it would have been false that either Smith knew at t_1 that Jones would do X at t_2 or Jones believed at t_1 that Jones would do X at t_2. Thus, Adams could say that "Jones did X at t_2" is a necessary condition of the disjunction.

But there is another sort of problem which afflicts both plausible accounts—both the counterfactual and entailment interpretations of "necessary condition." Suppose "Smith existed at t_1" is true. It is a necessary condition of the truth of this statement (on both the counterfactual and entailment accounts) that it is not the case that Smith existed for the first time at t_2. It is obvious that Smith's existing at t_1 entails that he does not exist for the first time at t_2. And if Smith had existed for the first time at t_2, then he would not have existed at t_1, so the counterfactual account fares no better than the entailment account. Thus, by (B), the statement "Smith existed at t_1" is at least in part about t_2; by (C) the statement *fails* to express a hard fact about t_1. But since Smith need not be eternal (or essentially omniscient), this is a disastrous result for Adams's account. The same sort of argument shows that Adams must say that "Jones believed at t_1 that Jones would do X at t_2" does not express a hard fact about t_1. This is because "It is not the case that Jones believed for the first time at t_2 that he would do X at t_2" is a necessary condition of "Jones believed at t_1 that he would do X at t_2."

Also, it is a necessary condition (on both interpretations) of the truth of the statement, "Piece of salt S dissolved at t_1," that S did not dissolve at t_2. One wants to say that this statement expresses a hard fact about t_1, but Adams's account does not capture this intuition (since the statement is at least in part about t_2).

It is not easy to see how Adams could provide an account of "necessary condition" which would avoid all the problems raised above. Without such an account, she has not presented an adequate explanation of the distinction between hard and soft facts.

III. The Incompatibilist's Constraint

Various contemporary Ockhamists have argued that on any acceptable account of the distinction between hard and soft facts, God's prior belief will be a soft fact about the past. I shall not here further discuss particular compatibilist accounts of the distinction; rather, I shall sketch a constraint on the account of the distinction which an incompatibilist might use to defeat *any* compatibilist characterization of the distinction. That is, I shall develop an explanation of the claim that God's prior belief is a hard fact about the past; this explanation will *not* imply that *human* foreknowledge is also a hard fact about the past. This might provide a way in which Pike could defend both his incompatibility claim and the asymmetry thesis—the thesis that God's foreknowledge undermines human freedom in a way in which human foreknowledge does not.

Consider the fact that Caesar died 2,009 years prior to Saunders's writing his paper. What lies behind our view that this fact is not a hard fact about 44 B.C.? We might say that it is a soft fact about 44 B.C. because one and the same physical process would have counted as Caesar's dying 2,009 years prior to Saunders's writing his paper, if Saunders wrote his paper in 1965, and would *not* have counted as Caesar's dying 2,009 years prior to Saunders's writing his paper, if Saunders had not written his paper in 1965. This captures the "future dependence" of soft facts; a soft fact is a fact *in virtue* of events which occur in the future.

Similarly, suppose that Smith knew at t_1 that Jones would do X at t_2. Smith's knowledge is a soft fact about t_1 because one and the same state of Smith's mind (at t_1) would count as knowledge if Jones did X at t_2, and would not count as knowledge if Jones did not do X at t_2. Exactly the same sort of future dependence explains why both facts—the fact about Caesar's death and the fact about Smith's knowledge—are soft facts.

Thus an incompatibilist might insist on the following sort of constraint on an account of the hard fact/soft fact distinction: the only way in which God's belief at t_1 about Jones at t_2 could be a soft fact about the past relative to t_2 would be if one and the same state of the mind of the person who was God at t_1 would count as one belief if Jones did X at t_2, but a different belief (or not a belief at all) if Jones did not do X at t_2. But it is implausible to suppose that one and the same state of the mind of the person who was God at t_1 would count as different beliefs given different behavior by Jones at t_2.

Suppose again that Jones did X at t_2. Y (being God) believed at t_1 that Jones would do X at t_2. Let us say that Y's mind was in state s at t_1; this constituted His believing that Jones would do X at t_2. Now if Y's mind were in state s and Jones did *not* do X, Y's mind being in s would still count as a belief that Jones would do X. (In this case, Y would not be God, since he would have a false belief.) Hence, Y's mind being in s at t_1 would *not* count as one belief if Jones did X at t_2 and another belief (or not a belief at all) if Jones did not do X at t_2.

Someone might agree that the incompatibilist's constraint is appropriate but disagree with what I have said about its application. That is, one might argue that if Jones had not done X at t_2, then the state of God's mind that actually constituted His believing that Jones would do X would not have constituted that belief. This position might be supported by extending Putnam's point that meanings and beliefs ain't in the head.[14] According to Putnam, my belief that water is wet—the state of my mind that constitutes in fact, my believing that—would have been a different belief—the belief that XYZ is wet—if lakes and oceans on earth had been filled with XYZ rather than water. On this approach, the state of God's mind at t_1 that counts as His belief that Jones will do X at t_2 counts as that belief partly in virtue of the fact that Jones does in fact do X at t_2.

But this picture of God's omniscience is highly implausible. God's omniscience would be seriously attenuated if the same state of God's mind at t_1 would constitute different beliefs about Jones, depending on Jones's behavior at t_2. The following is a more appealing picture of God's omniscience. An Ockhamist might deny the appropriateness of the constraint, claiming that while it is not true that one and the same state of God's mind at t_1 would constitute different beliefs, depending on Jones's behavior at t_2, it is true that God's mind would have been in a *different* state at t_1 (from the one it was actually in), if Jones had not done X at t_2. Whereas Y's mind was actually in state s at t_1, it would not have been in s had Jones not done X at t_2.

If the Ockhamist makes this move, however, he weakens his argument to the conclusion that God's belief at t_1 is a soft fact about t_1. There is now an *asymmetry* between soft facts such as Caesar's dying 2,009 years prior to Saunders's writing his paper and Smith's knowing at t_1 that Jones will do X at t_2, on the one hand, and God's belief at t_1 that Jones will do X at t_2, on the other. But it was the assimilation of these sorts of facts that was the ground for claiming that God's belief at t_1 is a soft fact about t_1.

The incompatibilist can agree with the Ockhamist that the facts discussed above about Caesar's death and Smith's knowledge are "spurious" facts about the relevant times. They are temporal analogues of facts involving "mere Cambridge" spatial properties, such as the property of being ten miles south of a burning barn. But if the incompatibilist's constraint is rejected, then it is open to him to argue that God's prior belief is a *genuine* fact about the past.

The constraint I have proposed captures the incompatibilist's notion of the fixity of the past. If this constraint is acceptable, then Pike could defend both his incompatibility claim and the asymmetry thesis.

There is, however, one form of Ockhamism that is not defeated by the proposed constraint. Consider again, "If it was within Jones's power at t_2 to refrain from doing X, then (3) it was in Jones's power at t_2 to act in such a way that Y would not have been God at t_1." There are two ways in which it might be true that it was in Jones's power at t_2 so to act that Y would not have been God at t_1. First, Jones could have had it in his power at t_2 so to act that Y would not have existed at t_1. Second, Jones could have been free at t_2 to act in such a way that Y (though existing) would not have filled the role of God at t_1. The Ockhamist might agree with Pike that the existence of a particular person is a hard fact about a time, but he might insist that the fact that the person is God is *not* a hard fact about a time.

Thus, the Ockhamist might claim (following Adams) that the fact that Y had the property of being God at t_1 is a soft fact about t_1. This is because the fact that Y was God at t_1 depends on the truth of Y's beliefs about future contingent events; indeed, since God is eternal, the fact that Y was God at t_1 depends on the fact that Y existed at t_2.

But the incompatibilist should point out that from the claim that Y's occupying the role of God at t_1 is a soft fact about t_1 it does *not* follow that Jones could have at t_2 so acted that Y would not have been God at t_1. There are soft facts about the past which are such that one cannot now so act that they would not have been facts. For instance, on Tuesday it was a soft fact about the past that on Monday it was the case that the sun would rise on Wednesday morning.[15] But on Tuesday, one could not have acted in such a way that it would not have been the case that on Monday it was true that the sun would rise on Wednesday.

Thus, even if the fact that Y was God at t_1 is a soft fact about t_1, this does not *suffice* to establish that Jones could have so acted at t_2 that Y would not have been God at t_1. Further, it is theologically implausible to suppose that any human agent is free so to act that the person who is actually God would not be God. This would make the identity of God dependent on human actions in an unacceptable way; such a God would hardly be worthy of worship. So, whereas the fact that Y was God at t_1 might be a soft fact about t_1, an Ockhamist who claims that one could have at t_2 so acted that Y would not have been God at t_1 would posit an unacceptable view of God. Incompatibilism can be defended even if Pike's claim that the fact that Y was God at t_1 is a hard fact about t_1 were false.

IV. Conclusion

Adams's formulation of Ockhamism is inadequate. I have not here argued that *no* account of the hard fact/soft fact distinction can be given which captures the Ockhamist intuition. Rather, I have posed a challenge to Adams's Ockhamism and have presented the incompatibilist's motivation for thinking that any Ockhamist account will be unacceptable. I have thus issued a twofold challenge to the Ockhamist: first, to formulate the hard fact/soft fact distinction in a way which yields Ockhamism, and second, to explain why the incompatibilist's constraint is inappropriate.

CHAPTER FIVE

Two Forms of Fatalism

David Widerker

There is a well-known fatalistic argument which purports to show that, since every proposition about the future entails a proposition about the past, and since the past is fixed and un-alterable, no human action is ever free.[1] This argument has a close sibling in the theological argument against freedom from divine foreknowledge.[2] In this article, I wish to examine these two arguments carefully. I shall try to show that of the two it is only the theological argument that poses a real threat to human freedom. The non-theological argument, I argue, can be rejected by taking account of the fact that it involves an incorrect applica-tion of the principle of the fixity of the past.

I

Let us start our discussion by considering a special case of the non-theological argument for fatalism.

(NTF) Suppose that at a certain moment, t_{10}, Jack pulls the trigger. It was therefore true at t_0 that Jack would pull the trigger at t_{10}. In-deed, it was always true that Jack would pull the trigger at t_{10}. But if it was always true that Jack would pull the trigger at t_{10}, it was not

I am indebted to Carl Ginet, Eddy Zemach, Bill Rowe, Phil Quinn, Alvin Plantinga, Norman Kretzmann, Harry Friedman, Dale Gottlieb, Fred Freddoso, and John Fischer for some excellent discussions and comments on earlier ver-sions of this paper.

within Jack's power not to do so. To suppose otherwise, would be to suggest that Jack had power over the past.

That is, the fatalist argues that by attributing to Jack, say, at t_9, the power not to pull the trigger at t_{10}, one is committed to holding that at t_9 Jack had the power to bring it about that it was not true at t_0 that he would pull the trigger at t_{10}. And this, he claims, is to have power over the past.

This type of argument for philosophical fatalism has been dealt with in various ways in the recent philosophical literature. Some philosophers have tried to block it by contending that such tensed ascriptions of truth as

(X1) It is true at t_0 that Jack will pull the trigger at t_{10}

do not make sense.[3] Others have suggested that we give up the law of bivalence for future tensed propositions, claiming that such propositions are neither true nor false.[4] Still others have questioned the assumption that 'it will be the case that p' entails 'it was always the case that it will be the case that p'.[5] And, there have also been those who have objected to the move from

(1) It was within Jack's power at t_9 to bring it about that he does not pull the trigger at t_{10}

to

(2) It was within Jack's power at t_9 to bring it about that it was not true at t_0 that Jack will pull the trigger at t_{10},

arguing that the Power Entailment Principle underlying this inference is fallacious. This principle is:

(PR) If q is a logically necessary condition for p, then an agent has it within his power at t to bring it about that p only if he has it within his power at t to bring it about that q,

or formally

$$\Box(p \supset q) \supset [P^*_{a,t}(p) \supset P^*_{a,t}(q)]^6$$

(Here 'p' and 'q' are sentence letters to be replaced by sentences denoting dated states of affairs, '$\Box$' denotes broadly logical necessity, and '$P^*_{a,t}$' is short for 'it is within a's power at t to bring it about that'.) So, for example, I may have the power at t_9 to bring it about that Sam's mother will be very angry at me at t_{10}. But this does not imply that I have the power to bring it about that Sam exists (or did exist), that he has a mother, that his mother is alive at t_{10}, etc. Similarly, I may have the power now to smoke a cigarette for the first time in my life. But obviously I do not have the power now to bring it about that I did not smoke a cigarette in the past.

In my view, all these lines of response to (NTF) are unconvincing. The complaint that a locution such as (X1) is improper is unfounded. This locution can be explicated unproblematically in the following way:

(X1′) Had someone uttered at t_0 the sentence 'Jack will pull the trigger at t_{10}', he would have expressed a proposition that is true.[7]

The trouble with the other two responses is that they provide what one may call "only a formal solution" to the problem posed by (NTF). I say "formal solution" because their proponents, though urging us to reject some of the basic assumptions (NTF) is based on, leave us completely in the dark as to what precisely is wrong with these assumptions, except being part of a piece of reasoning that leads to a paradoxical conclusion. It seems to me that adopting these two responses *merely* for the sake of blocking (NTF) is already to concede too much to the fatalist.[8] As for the attempt to dispose of (NTF) by rejecting the inference from (1) to (2), it can be countered by devising a more satisfactory Power Entailment Principle than (PR). The fallacy underlying (PR) may be diagnosed as follows: the fact that q is a logically necessary condition for p does not imply that my power to bring it about that p is contingent on my power to bring it about that q. As the above counterexamples to (PR) indicate, I may have the power to bring it about that p, even if I lack the power to bring it about that q in situations where q is already in existence, or will be in existence independent of which power of mine I may actualize. This observation suggests an easy way of modifying (PR), that is:

(PRW) If q is a logically necessary condition for p, and q is lacking, then an agent has it within his power at t to bring it about that p only if he has it within his power at t to bring it about that q.

$$[\Box(p \supset q) \cdot \sim q] \supset [P_{a,t}^*(p) \supset P_{a,t}^*(q)]$$

The plausibility of (PRW) may also be grasped by noting that it is logically equivalent to the following principle, which seems intuitive:

(TW) No agent has it within his power to bring about a state of affairs, if there is lacking at the same or any other time some condition logically (or causally) necessary for the obtaining of that state of affairs, provided that the agent does not have the power to prevent the lack of that condition.[9] That is:

$$[\Box(p \supset q) \cdot \sim q \cdot \sim P^*_{a,t}(q)] \supset \sim P^*_{a,t}(p)$$

II

To see exactly what is wrong with (NTF), let us examine more closely an assumption crucial to it, namely, the principle of the fixity of the past. There are various ways of stating this principle. For present purposes, let us consider the following version of it:

(PST1) No one has it within his power after a certain event occurred to bring about the non-occurrence of that event,[10]

or, more formally put,

$$O(e,t) \supset \sim(\exists a)(\exists t')[t'>t \cdot P^*_{a,t'}(\sim O(e,t))]$$

(where 'e', 't', and 'a' range over events, times, and agents, respectively, and 'O' and '$P^*_{a,t}$' are short for 'occurred' and 'it is within a's power at t to bring it about that'). Notice that even though we do not have the power to bring about the non-occurrence of any given past event e, we do sometimes have the power to bring it about that it does or does not exemplify certain relational properties—that is, those properties it exemplifies *in virtue of* events occurring in the future. So, for example, if on January 1, 1985, Smith told his partners that he thinks Jack will sign the contract on January 3, Jack does not have it within his power after January 1 to bring about the non-occurrence of events such as

E1: Smith's uttering on January 1 the sentence 'Jack will sign the contract on January 3';

E2: Smith's expressing on January 1 his belief that Jack will sign the contract on January 3.

However, given that Jack is free with respect to signing the contract, it is within his power to bring it about that E1 and E2 do or do not exemplify properties like

P1: occurring two days before Jack's signing the contract on January 3;

P2: being an uttering of the true (false) sentence 'Jack will sign the contract on January 3';

P3: being an expression of the true (false) belief that Jack will sign the contract on January 3.

Once having drawn the distinction between

(i) having the power to bring about the non-occurrence of a certain past event

and

(ii) having the power to bring it about that a past event does or does not exemplify a certain relational property,

we are in a position to provide an adequate answer to the fatalist. Our answer is this: we grant the fatalist that by attributing to Jack at t_9 the power not to pull the trigger at t_{10}, we are committed to holding that

(2) It was within Jack's power at t_9 to bring it about that it was not true at t_0 that Jack will pull the trigger at t_{10}.

However, we deny that this power is a power to bring about the non-occurrence of a past event. To see this, let us recall that to say that

(X1) It was true at t_0 that Jack will pull the trigger at t_{10}

is tantamount to saying that

(X1') Had someone uttered at t_0 the sentence 'Jack will pull the trigger at t_{10}', he would have expressed a proposition that is true.

Thus (X1) may be understood as attributing to the time-moment t_0 the following property

P4: being a moment such that had someone uttered at it the sentence 'Jack will pull the trigger at t_{10}', he would have expressed a true proposition.

Whether or not t_0 has this property depends, of course, on the truth-value of the proposition expressed by 'Jack will pull the trigger at t_{10}', which in turn depends on what *Jack* does at t_{10}. And now it is obvious that, in order to accept (2), we do not have to give up (PST1). All we need to claim is that it was within Jack's power at t_9 to bring it about that the time-moment t_0 does not have the property P4. A determined defender of (NTF) might argue at this point that (PST1) is not the only way in which the principle of the fixity of the past may be stated. Another way of stating it, which perhaps in the context of our discussion might be more appropriate, is the following:

(PST2) If an object x exemplifies a property F at a given time t, then it is not within anyone's power at a time later than t to bring it about that x did not exemplify F at t,

or, assuming universal closure:

$$[F(x,t) \cdot t'{>}t] \supset {\sim}P^*_{a,t'}({\sim}F(x,t))$$

(where 'x', 'F', 't', and 'a' range over objects, properties, times, and persons, respectively).

Furthermore, viewing (X1) as a case of an object having a certain property in the past (relative to t_9), the adherent of (NTF) might contend that the acceptance of (2) constitutes a violation of (PST2). The object and the property in question would be the sentence

(S) Jack will pull the trigger at t_{10}

and the property of

(TR) being *true* (as applied to sentences.)[11]

To expose the fallacy underlying this reasoning, let us first distinguish between two sorts of property an object x might exemplify at a given time t:

(a) A property x might exemplify at t such that its having that property is partly contingent upon some object y exemplifying some property at a time later than t. Call such a property "a future contingent property of x, relative to t."
(b) A property x might exemplify at t, such that its having that property is not contingent in the sense specified above.

The following are examples of future contingent properties of Smith, relative to January 1, 1985:

F1: talking to his friends two days before Jack's signing the contract,
F2: correctly believing that Jack will sign the contract on January 3, and
F3: uttering the true sentence 'Jack will sign the contract on January 3';

whereas properties like

F4: uttering a sentence,
F5: talking to his friends, and
F6: weighing 80 kg

would count as properties of Smith that are not future contingent, relative to January 1, 1985. More precisely, we may say that

(FCP) F is a future contingent property of an object x, relative to a time t if
  (a) x has F at t
  (b) the exemplification of a property by some object at a time later than t is a logically necessary condition for x having F at t;

That is,

$$\Box\{F(x,t) \supset (\exists y)(\exists G)(\exists t')[t'>t \cdot G(y,t')]\}^{12}$$

(where 'y' and 'G' range over objects and properties, respectively).

This account of the notion of a future contingent property of an object may be strengthened by replacing 'logically necessary condition' with 'counterfactually necessary condition', that is:

$$(\exists y)(\exists G)(\exists t')\{t'>t \cdot G(y,t') \cdot (\sim[G(y,t')] > \sim[F(x,t)])\}$$

(where '$>$' is the counterfactual connective). This is an amendment that might also enable us to assimilate to the class of future contingent properties of Smith, relative to January 1, 1985, such properties as

F7: correctly believing that it is not the case that Jack will sign the contract on January 2, or
F8: correctly believing that John F. Kennedy died in 1963 or Jack will sign the contract on January 3.

Given the above distinction between future contingent and future non-contingent properties of objects, let us now re-examine (PST2). Whatever its plausibility, there seems to be no reason to suppose that this principle holds in general for those cases in which F is a future contingent property of an object x relative to t. For if x has F at t in virtue of some object y exemplifying some property G at a time t' later than t, then to the extent that an agent has the power to bring about y's not having G at t', he also has the power to bring about x's not having F at t. This observation applies in particular to (X1), which in the way it is analyzed by the fatalist—that is, as (S) having the property (TR) at t_0—can be seen to involve the instantiation of a future contingent property of (S), relative to t_0, had by (S) in virtue of Jack's pulling the trigger at t_{10}.

The strategy suggested here for countering (NTF) based on the distinction between future contingent and future non-contingent properties of objects, relative to a given time, may seem open to an objection raised by John Fischer in connection with his criticism of a parallel distinction suggested by Marilyn Adams: that between soft facts and hard facts about the past.[13] On Adams's account:

(C) "Statement p expresses a 'hard' fact about a time t'' = df. "p is not at least in part about any time future relative to t,"

where 'p is at least in part about time t' is defined by her as follows:

(B) "Statement p is at least in part about time t'' = df. "The happening or not happening, actuality or non-actuality of something at t is a necessary condition of the truth of p."

By contrast, a statement p expresses a soft fact about a time t, if and only if p is at least in part about some time future realtive to t. Fischer argues against this account by pointing out that a statement such as

(S1) Jack pulls the trigger at t_1,

which intuitively expresses a hard fact about t_1, fails to do so, on Adams's theory. For (S1) has as a logically necessary condition of its truth that

(S2) It is not the case that Jack pulls the trigger for the first time at t_3.

Hence, being at least in part about t_3, (S1) expresses merely a *soft* fact about t_1. This is counterintuitive. One might think that Fischer's counterexample equally applies to (FCP), showing that the property of pulling the trigger is a future contingent property of Jack, relative to t_1. But a close examination of his objection proves that this is not the case. Notice that although (S1) entails (S2), (S1) does not entail, as is required by (FCP), the existence of times after t_1.[14] Nor does it entail that Jack exists after t_1. That is, the truth of (S1) and (S2) is perfectly compatible with there being no times after t_1, or with the non-existence of Jack after t_1.[15] This point may be grasped more clearly by rendering (S2) formally as follows:

$$\sim\{P(j,t_3) \cdot (t)(t<t_3) \supset \sim P(j,t)\}$$

where 'P' stands for 'pulls the trigger'.

Summing up our discussion so far, we can say that the error committed by the fatalist in (NTF) consists in his incorrect application of the principle of the fixity of the past. Given the fact that Jack pulls the trigger at t_{10}, we may perfectly agree with the fatalist that it was always true that he would do so. But this does not mean that it was not within Jack's power to do otherwise. On the contrary. What our discussion of (NTF) has shown is that it was *Jack* who, by acting in the way he did, brought that state of affairs about. To the extent that it was within his power not to pull the trigger at t_{10}, it also was within his power to bring it about that it was not always true that he would do so. The sense in which Jack might be said as a result to have power over the past is, as we have seen, a completely innocuous one.[16]

III

We may now turn to the comparison of (NTF) with what may be considered its theological counterpart—that is, the argument against freedom from divine foreknowledge.[17] An instance of the latter (henceforth (TF)) may be obtained from (NTF) by replacing 'it was true' with 'God believed'. In a more perspicuous say, (TF) may be rendered as follows:

(TF) (1) 'Qt_{10}' and 'P^*_{j,t_9}' abbreviate respectively, 'Jack will pull the trigger at t_{10}' and 'it was within Jack's power at t_9 to bring it about that'. 'God' is a proper name. God is essentially omniscient.

(2) $Qt_{10} \cdot P^*_{j,t_9}(\sim Qt_{10})$. (assumption)

(G) God believed at t_0 that Qt_{10}. (by (1))

(PRW) $[\Box(p \supset q) \cdot \sim q] \supset [P^*_{a,t}(p) \supset P^*_{a,t}(q)]$. (assumption)

(3) $\Box(\sim Qt_{10} \supset$ God did not believe at t_0 that $Qt_{10})$. (by (1))

(4) P^*_{j,t_9} (God did not believe at t_0 that Qt_{10}). (by (2), (3), and (PRW))

(5) However, (4) contradicts the principle of the fixity of the past.[18]

Can we rebut (TF) in the same way we rebutted (NTF)? The crucial problem here is how to avoid the objection that the acceptance of (4) violates the principle of the fixity of the past in the sense of (PST1). For on the face of it, (4) seems to imply that

(6) It was within Jack's power at t_9 to bring about the non-occurrence of some past event (state), i.e. E_G: God's believing at t_0 that Qt_{10}.

In view of our discussion of (NTF), we know that in order to counter this objection we would have to argue that (4), rather than entailing (6), commits us merely to

(6') It was within Jack's power at t_9 to bring about that E_G would not exemplify a certain relational property, which it exemplifies in virtue of events occurring in the future relative to t_9.

But would such a reply be adequate? One main difficulty with it is that (a) the only plausible candidate for the kind of property that would not be exemplified by E_G, if God were not to believe at t_0 that Qt_{10} is

P_G: being an event of believing that Qt_{10},

which does not seem to be a relational property.

If P_G were a relational property involving reference to the event of Jack's pulling the trigger at t_{10}—that is, a property denoted by a predicate of the form '$R($,Jack's pulling the trigger at $t_{10})$'—it would follow that no one could *falsely* believe that Qt_{10}. This consequence seems strongly counterintuitive, since one can clearly be mistaken in holding such a belief.

There is, however, a further consideration that counts strongly against the acceptance of (4). Notice that if, indeed, Jack had the power attributed to him in (4), he would have that power only to the extent that he would have the power at t_9 not to pull the trigger at t_{10}. However, as the following two arguments show, (b) the assumption of his having that power leads to the conclusion that he would have the power to bring about the non-occurrence of a past event. The first argument involves an example of what may be called "a future contingent causal chain":

Suppose that God believes at t_0 that Jack will pull the trigger at t_{10}, with the intention of killing Smith. Suppose further that wanting to save Smith, God reveals this fact to Smith at t_3, in which case Smith when meeting with Jack wears a bulletproof vest that saves his life. It seems plausible to suppose that were Jack not to pull the trigger at t_{10}, God would not have believed so, and hence would not have told Smith about this. Hence, if it were within Jack's power at t_9 not to pull the trigger at t_{10}, it would be within his power to bring about the non-occurrence of a causally necessary condition of the event of Smith's coming to believe at t_3 that Jack will attempt to kill him, and by implication to bring about the non-occurrence of that past event itself.[19]

In response to this argument it might be argued that if God, on the basis of his knowledge of Jack's future action, intervenes in the course of events before that action takes place, then the said action cannot be deemed a free one. This reply does not seem to me to be a convincing one, for I do not see any relevant difference in the status of Jack's action at t_{10} as a free action between a situation in which God reveals a certain fact to Smith at t_3 and one in which he is merely aware of this fact. Nor would it be sufficient to reply that *as a matter of fact* God never intervenes in the course of events on the basis of his knowledge of the future. For all that is required by the above argument is that the situation described in it is *possible*.

The second argument in favor of (b) is this:

Consider, for a moment, what would have happened had Jack not pulled the trigger at t_{10}. In that case God, being infallible, would not have believed at t_0 that Qt_{10}. Moreover, being essentially all-knowing, God would have believed at t_0 that $\sim Qt_{10}$. But then, since the *propositional content* of his belief would have been different, God would have held at t_0 a *different* belief, and hence would have been in a *different* mental state from the one he actually was in. Consequently, had it been within Jack's power at t_9 not to pull the trigger at t_{10}, it would have been within his power to bring about the non-occurrence of a past event, i.e., E_G.[20]

Note that one cannot apply this type of argument to the case of Smith's correctly believing at t_0 that Qt_{10}. If Jack had not pulled the trigger at t_{10}, the content of Smith's belief would have remained the same. What would have changed would be only the truth-value of his belief.

If the arguments adduced in favor of (a) and (b) are sound, they can be also used to explain why, even though believing that Qt_{10} is a future contingent property of God, relative to t_0, it is not within anyone's power after t_0 to alter the fact that

(G) God believed at t_0 that Qt_{10}.

The reason is simple. An agent could be said to have the power to alter (G), only to the extent that he would have the power to bring it about that Jack does not pull the trigger at t_{10}. But as we have seen, his having such a power leads to a violation of (PST1).

The conclusion that emerges on the basis of the above considerations is that there does seem to be a fundamental difference between the theological and the non-theological arguments for fatalism. The former, as we have seen, cannot be refuted by accusing its proponent of having confused two different notions of bringing about the past. Hence it is only the theological argument that poses a real threat to our freedom of choice. Our discussion has also shown what the theological compatibilist would have to provide in order to defend the claim that the conclusion of (TF) does not violate (PST1). He would have to opt for an account of God's prior knowledge about a human free action, according to which such knowledge could be viewed as involving a *relation* of some sort obtaining between God's mental state and that action.[21] What the nature of such a relation might be, however, and whether such an account of God's knowledge can be at all successful, are questions that lie outside the scope of this paper.

Appendix

In his article "Hard-Type Soft Facts,"[22] John Fischer has also made an attempt to explain the special unalterability of (G). Assuming the theoretical framework of the soft/hard fact distinction, Fischer argues that (G), although being a soft fact about t_0, is a special type of soft fact, what he calls a "hard-type soft fact" about t_0. By this he means a soft fact whose constitutive property, the property of believing that Qt_{10}, is a "hard property" relative to t_0. He sharply distinguishes (G) from such standard soft facts as "Smith wakes up at t_0 four hours prior to eating lunch" or "Smith correctly believes at t_0 that Qt_{10}." These are facts whose constitutive property is merely a "soft property" relative to t_0. By a soft property, relative to a time t, Fischer understands a property p such that if *anything* were to have that property at t, it would necessarily follow that some immediate fact obtains after t, in any plausible sense of 'immediate'. And by a hard property, relative to t, he understands one that is not soft, relative to that time. So, for instance, relational properties such as "correctly believing that Qt_{10}," "waking up four hours prior to eating lunch," or "uttering the true sentence 'Jack will sign the contract on Janaury 3'" are, according to Fischer, examples of soft properties (relative to the pertinent times), whereas "believing that Qt_{10}," "waking up," or "eating lunch" count as hard properties (relative to the pertinent times). The leading idea underlying this distinction between the two sorts of property is to stress the resemblance between (G) and regular hard facts about t_0—such as that Jack wakes up at t_0—which also have as their constitutive property a hard property. Moreover, Fischer assumes that no one has it within his power at a time later than t so to act that what is a bearer of a hard property relative to t would not have possessed that property at t. Consequently, a hard-type soft fact such as (G), similar to a regular hard fact about t_0, is in his view fixed and unalterable at times later than t_0. Although I am sympathetic to this strategy by Fischer of trying to bring out the unique unalterability of (G), I nevertheless think that his account of the notion of a hard property faces some serious difficulties and is in this sense incomplete. To see this, consider a standard soft fact such as

(Y1) The sentence 'Jack will pull the trigger at t_{10}' is *true* at t_0.

On Fischer's analysis, (Y1) may be viewed as a fact about t_0, whose constitutive elements are: the sentence 'Jack will pull the trigger at t_{10}', the property of being *true*, and the time t_0. But now notice that on his account, the property of being *true* is a hard property, relative to t_0. Clearly, it is not the case that if *anything* were to have that property at t_0, it would necessarily follow that some immediate fact obtains after t_0. (For example, if Jack raises his arm at t_0, then 'Jack raises his arm at t_0' has the property of being *true* at t_0. But this does not entail that some immediate fact obtains at some time after t_0.) Hence, (Y1) would have to be treated by Fischer as a hard-type soft fact about t_0, which is counterintuitive. A further problem for Fischer's account is posed by properties such as: correctly believing that it is not the case that Jack will sign the contract on January 2; correctly believing that either Smith weighs 50 kg on January 1 or Jack will sign the contract on January 3 (where the first disjunct is false). These properties turn out, on his definition, to be hard properties relative to, say, January 1. But their exemplification by some individual on January 1 may easily yield soft facts of the standard type. The moral to be drawn from all this is that in order to give us an acceptable account of the notion of a hard property, Fischer must base it on richer metaphysical notions than that of entailment.

CHAPTER SIX

Facts, Freedom, and Foreknowledge

Eddy Zemach and David Widerker

Is God's foreknowledge compatible with human freedom? One of the most attractive attempts to reconcile the two is the Ockhamistic view, which subscribes not only to human freedom and divine omniscience, but retains our most fundamental intuitions concerning God and time: that the past is immutable, that God exists and acts in time, and that there is no backward causation. In order to achieve all that, Ockhamists (1) distinguish 'hard facts' about the past which cannot possibly be altered from 'soft facts' about the past which are alterable, and (2) argue that God's prior beliefs about human actions are soft facts about the past.[1]

John M. Fischer[2] thinks, however, that neither thesis has yet been adequately defended by any Ockhamist. He challenges the Ockhamist, on the one hand, to provide an adequate explication of the hard/soft fact distinction. On the other hand, he objects to any attempt to apply this distinction to God's prior beliefs concerning human actions. This paper intends to meet these challenges, working out a tenable Ockhamistic position.

The discussion to follow is divided into four parts: In Section I, we give a brief account of the Ockhamistic approach to the problem of divine foreknowledge and human freedom. In Section II,

Reprinted by permission from *Religious Studies*, 23 (1988): 19–28. We are indebted to Charlotte Katzoff, Dale Gottlieb, Alex Blum, Yehudah Gellman, and Harry Friedman for some good discussions on the problem of God's foreknowledge.

we suggest a novel account of the hard /soft fact distinction, thus responding to Fischer's first challenge. In Section III, we take up Fischer's second objection and argue that it is unfounded. Finally, in Section IV, we present what seems to us the strongest objection to the Ockhamistic position and argue that it too can be adequately met.

I. The Ockhamistic Position

Consider the following *reductio* argument against the compatibility of God's foreknowledge and human freedom.

Let 'Qt_{10}' abbreviate 'Jones will raise his arm at t_{10}', and let '↔' symbolize the relation of logical equivalence, and let α and β be any two contingent statements. Now suppose that,

(1) God believed at t_0 that Qt_{10},
(2) it was within Jones's power at t_9 to bring it about that $\sim Qt_{10}$.

Suppose further that we accept the following intuitive assumption concerning the notion of being within one's power:

(3) If $\alpha \leftrightarrow \beta$, and $\ulcorner$ it is within an agent's power to bring about that $\alpha \urcorner$ is true, then $\ulcorner$ it is within that agent's power to bring about that $\beta \urcorner$ is true.

By the omniscience of God we have that,

(4) $\ulcorner \sim Qt_{10} \urcorner \leftrightarrow \ulcorner$ God does not believe that $Qt_{10}. \urcorner$

Now we get, on the basis of (2), (3), and (4):

(5) It was within the power of Jones at t_9 to bring it about that God did not believe at t_0 that Qt_{10}.

However, (5) contradicts the fairly intuitive assumption:

(N) It is not within our power to alter the past,

since by (1) God's belief at t_0 that Qt_{10} is a fact about the past relative to t_9.[3]

The Ockhamist answer to the above argument is to qualify (N). (N), says the Ockhamist, holds only for what may be called 'hard facts about the past' as opposed to 'soft facts about the past'. That is, what the Ockhamist is ready to accept is not (N), but the weaker:

(NN) It is not within our power to alter hard facts about the past.

It is his contention that a fact like

(G) God believed at t_0 that Qt_{10}

is a soft fact about the past relative to t_9 and hence alterable. Intuitively speaking, a soft fact about the past is a past fact, the obtaining of which is contingent upon certain future events. Thus, the following are examples of soft facts about the past (relative to, say, 1975):

(a) Nixon resigned in 1974, three years before Sadat's visit to Jerusalem in 1977.
(b) John *correctly* believed in 1974 that Carter will be elected president in 1976.
(c) John uttered in 1974 the *true* sentence 'Carter will be elected president in 1976'.
(d) Kennedy died in 1963 and Sadat will die in 1981.

Whereas

(e) Nixon resigned in 1974.
(f) John believed in 1974 that Carter will be elected president in 1976.
(g) John uttered in 1974 the sentence 'Carter will be elected president in 1976'.
(h) Kennedy died in 1963 or Sadat will die in 1981.

are examples of hard facts about the past (relative to 1975).

Fischer's first challenge is to demand a precise formulation of the hard/soft fact distinction. He argues, and we think correctly, that the only sufficiently detailed attempt to do so, the one suggested by Marilyn McCord Adams, is inadequate.[4] We believe, however, that an adequate account of the hard/soft fact distinction can be worked out.

II. Soft Facts and Hard Facts

We begin with the following set of definitions:

1. Let w be a given possible world and TRUEw the set of all propositions true in w.

2. Let t be a given time and let ANHt be the following assumption:

ANHt: There are no times after t (i.e., the world ceases to exist at t).

3. Let PAST(t,w) be the set of all propositions belonging to TRUEw which are compossible with ANHt; that is,

PAST(t,w) = {p:p $\in$ TRUEw and p is compossible with ANHt}.

4. Let C(w,t) be the set of all possible worlds w^* such that (i) w^* share the same ontology with w, and (ii) PAST(t,w^*) = PAST(t,w).[5]

Intuitively speaking, C(w,t) may be viewed as the set of all possible worlds whose 'past prior to t' is identical with that of w.

Suppose that t is the year 1975 and w is the real world. Then, among the members of PAST(t,w) are propositions such as those expressed by 'John F. Kennedy was killed in 1963', 'The First World War ended in 1918', 'Hitler attacked Russia in 1941, seven years before the establishment of Israel', etc. On the other hand, PAST(t,w) does not include propositions like 'The Olympic games will open in Moscow in 1980,' 'Reagan was elected president in 1980', etc. Note that a negative proposition such as:

(k) It is not the case that Carter will be re-elected in 1980

is also not an element of PAST (t,w). For, given the truth of ANHt, '1980' fails of reference, and therefore (k) is truth-valueless. In general, we assume that any proposition expressed by a sentence which contains a non-denoting singular term is truth-valueless, unless that singular term falls within the scope of a propositional attitude operator. Also, we shall assume that a truth-functional compound involving components which are truth-valueless is also truth-valueless.[6] As a result, a proposition like that expressed by 'Kennedy died in 1963 or Begin will resign in 1983' is also not an element of PAST(t,w).

Given the above definitions, we provide the following account of the notions *future contingency, future necessity, soft fact,* and *hard fact*.

(FC) A proposition S is *future contingent* in w relative to a given time t iff there is a world $w^* \in$ C(w,t) such that the truth-value of S in w^* differs from its truth-value in w; i.e. ($\exists w^*$) [$w^* \in$ C(w,t) $\cdot$ V(S,w^*) $\neq$ V(S,w)].

(FN) A proposition S is *future necessary* in w relative to a given time t iff (w^*) [$w^* \in$ C(w,t) $\supset$ V(S,w^*) = V(S,w)].

(SF) A true proposition S expresses a *soft fact* about the past in w, relative to a given time t, iff S is of the form αt_i, $t_i < t$, and S is future contingent.

(HF) A true proposition S expresses a *hard fact* about the past in w relative to a given time t iff S is of the form αt_i, $t_i < t$, and S is future necessary.

Definitions (SF) and (HF) capture the Ockhamistic notions of *soft fact* and *hard fact* about the past, as evidenced by the examples (a)–(d) and (e)–(h) above. Note that even though

(i) Kennedy died in 1963 or Begin will resign in 1983

does not belong to PAST(1975, w), it nevertheless expresses a hard fact about the past, relative to 1975, because it is true in every possible world $w^* \in C(1975, w)$.

Any quantified sentence involves a tacit reference to an understood domain of quantification. For example, the sentence 'All As are Bs' says that every object *in the intended domain* which is an A, is a B. Therefore, no proposition expressed by a quantified sentence true of a world w, in which there are times later than t, is a member of PAST(t,w), since it is incompatible with ANHt. By ANHt, some time moments, which are in the domain intended by the interpretation of any quantified sentence purportedly about w, do not exist. Hence the proposition, expressed by the said sentence under the said interpretation, has no truth value. For example, the proposition expressed by

(j) ($\forall t$) ($t < 1974 \supset$ Carter is not re-elected at t),

whose intended domain is that of the real world, is *not* compatible with ANH_{1975} and therefore is not a member of PAST(t,w). Yet the proposition (j) expresses is *true* in all members of C(w,t), and is, thus, future necessary. Therefore it does express a hard fact about the past (relative to 1975). On the other hand, the proposition expressed (under the intended interpretation) by

(k) ($\forall t$) ($t > 1974 \supset$ Carter is not re-elected at t)

is future contingent, and, since it tacitly refers to times before 1975, it expresses a soft fact about the past.

Another bonus of our treatment is that

(G) God believed at t_0 that Jones will raise his arm at t_{10}.

comes out as expressing a soft fact about the past, relative to t_9:
(G) does not belong to $\text{PAST}(t,w)$, because it is inconsistent with
$\text{ANH}t_9$ and it is false in some $w^* \in C(t_9,w)$. In addition, (HF)
and (SF) enable us to cope adequately with all of Fischer's 'difficult cases', i.e.,

(m1) Smith existed at t_1.
(m2) It is not the case that Smith existed for the first time at t_3.
(n1) A piece of salt S dissolved at t_1.
(n2) S did not dissolve at t_3.

On our account, as opposed to that provided by Adams,[7] (m1)
and (n1) both describe hard facts about the past, relative to t_2,
while (m2) and (n2) are both future necessary, relative to t_2.
(m2) and (n2) are not about the past at all; but we saw earlier that
a proposition need not express a hard fact about the past in order
to count as future necessary. In "Accidental Necessity and Logical Determinism" [Chapter 8 in this volume], Alfred Freddoso
has offered an alternative account of the hard/soft fact distinction. Freddoso makes use of the concept of an *immediate proposition*, which is an unquantified proposition whose truth or falsity
is logically independent of anything that happens at any moment prior, or subsequent, to the immediate present. It seems to
us, however, that Freddoso's account is unsuccessful, because
no proposition known to us is immediate, in Freddoso's sense.
Consider, for example, Freddoso's own example of an immediate proposition, 'David is sitting'. Surely the truth of that
proposition logically depends on the truth of propositions about
David's positions at instants prior to (and subsequent to) the
present instant? If David is falling from the attic, hitting the chair
on his way down, he may assume for an instant a posture indistinguishable from that of a sitting person, yet surely he is *not*
sitting. Freddoso requires that any proposition, the truth conditions of which are partially dependent on past or future states of
the world, is a truth function of elementary propositions, some
of which are exclusively immediate. For example, '*S* truly believes that p will be the case' is a conjunction of 'Future $(p) \cdot q$'.
As a general requirement, however, this constraint is absurd.
'David is human,' e.g., implies 'David was born' (and similar
propositions) by virtue of meaning postulates. What analysis
can separate the purely present-tense propositions which al-

legedly go into this 'complex' proposition? The same goes for 'David is a methodist', 'David is Dutch', 'David is brave', etc. In fact, the simpler the predicate, the more absurd the task seems to be. Think, for example, about 'x moves', 'x has an angular momentum', 'x is made of wood', 'x is red', 'it is 6 A.M.'. Apart from this essential flaw, Freddoso's theory is encumbered with other, more technical difficulties. For instance, in his account quantified propositions ought to be reduced to conjunctions and disjunctions of atomic sentences. But this is mathematically impossible in domains of certain orders of magnitude.

III. Fischer's Second Objection

Fischer's strategy in stating his second objection is to argue that on an intuitive understanding of the notion of a soft fact about the past, God's prior beliefs about human activity cannot plausibly be treated as soft facts about the past. He argues as follows:

Consider the fact that Caesar died 2,009 years prior to Saunders's writing his paper. What lies behind our view that this fact is not a hard fact about 44 B.C.? We might say that it is a soft fact about 44 B.C. because one and the same physical process would have counted as Caesar's dying 2,009 years prior to Saunders's writing his paper, if Saunders wrote his paper in 1965, and would *not* have counted as Caesar's dying 2,009 years prior to Saunders's writing his paper if Saunders had not written his paper in 1965. This captures the "future dependence" of soft facts; a soft fact is a fact *in virtue* of events which occur in the future. . . . Thus an incompatibilist might insist on the following sort of constraint on an account of the hard fact/soft fact distinction: the only way in which God's belief at t_1 about Jones at $[t_3]$ could be a soft fact about the past relative to $[t_3]$ would be if one and the same state of the mind of the person who was God at t_1 would count as one belief if Jones did X at $[t_3]$, but a different belief (or not a belief at all) if Jones did not do X at $[t_3]$. But it is implausible to suppose that one and the same state of the mind of the person who was God at t_1 would count as different beliefs given different behavior by Jones at $[t_3]$. [pp. 93–94 in this volume].

The conclusion is a *non-sequitur*. Fischer claims that the view that

(F) One and the same mental state of God at t_1 can count as different beliefs, given different behavior by Jones at t_3

is implausible. We do not think that it is (this shall be discussed later on). For present purposes, however, note that what follows from Fischer's account of soft facts as applied to God's beliefs is not (F) but, rather,

(FF) One and the same mental state of God can count as a belief that Jones would do X at t_3, if Jones would do X at t_3, and would not count as such belief, if Jones would not do X at t_3.

That is, one and the same mental state of God would have the property of being a belief that Jones would do X at t_3, if Jones would do X at t_3, and would not have that property if Jones would not do X at t_3.

But (FF) is not implausible at all. (FF) is unacceptable only on the following essentialist assumption:

(E) If some state m has the property of being a belief that p, it has that property *essentially* (i.e., in all possible worlds).

(E), however, need not be granted by the Ockhamist. We shall show that being a belief that p can be a property which a mental state m of God has at some possible worlds only, viz. those worlds in which it is the case that p. Moreover, in each world in which it is *not* the case that p, either m itself, or some other state of God n, has the property of being a belief that not-p.

Fischer pays surprisingly little attention to the functionalist account of the mental (cf. his discussion of Putman's Earth / Twin Earth example). Functionalists, however (e.g., Dennett, Fodor, Lewis, and yester-year Putnam), say that what we know as the mental content of an item *is* its function in a certain kind of system. Therefore, for the functionalist, the same state or item can *be* different mental states if lodged in different socio-logical or biological systems. Thus a certain state m which in fact is a belief that p, may have realized, in different surroundings, a different propositional content (e.g., that q instead of that p), a different propositional force (e.g., a wish instead of a belief), or it might have lacked both. If this is so, then, for all we know, the fact that p may be such an environmental necessary condition for the internal state of God, m, to count as a belief that p. It may be that m is God's belief that p only if p is the case, and thus he who is able to bring it about that not-p is able to bring it about that m is not a belief that p.

There is no need, however, to endorse functionalism in order to construe beliefs relationally. *Our* beliefs consist in our using some symbols (words, pictures, etc.) to stand for certain states of affairs which we take to exist. If God's beliefs are fashioned in a *radically* different way, we cannot say that he has *beliefs*. To have beliefs *about* something, He must use some symbols to represent that something.

But whence the meaningfulness of those symbols? If I happen to form a sequence of symbols in my mind which in some to me unknown language stands for 'it is raining', I have not said 'it is raining' in my heart. To mean is to have a definite use, and it is because I am a member of *this* community that *its* use of the symbols in question determines their correct interpretation. God, however, is not a member of any linguistic community. How, then, can the mental items he uses have this or that definite meaning?

We suggest that the item in virtue of which some state of God's means that p, is the fact that p. The way the word 'cat' is used in my society does not *cause* my token of this word to mean what it means; rather, it is *in virtue of* that use that it has that meaning. The fact that p, likewise, does not *cause* God's mental state m to mean 'p'; rather it is *in virtue of* its being the case that p, that God's mental state m means 'p'. Thus, the property *is a belief that p* is a relational property m has in virtue of its relation to the fact that p. Therefore, 'God's belief that p' is a non-rigid designator which picks out m in some worlds only.

Thus, if one is able to bring it about that p, one is able to bring it about that the world at which 'God's belief that p' is evaluated is (or is not) a p world. Hence, one can bring it about that one's token of 'God's belief that p' will (or will not) refer to God's state m in one's world. Thus it can be seen that 'God's believing that p' *can* be construed as a soft fact about the past, in the full Ockhamist sense of the term.

'But does not God *know*, at t_0, whether he does or does not believe that Qt_{10}?' This, apparently naïve, question makes in fact a highly dubitable metaphysical assumption: it tacitly presupposes that a certain state of God, m, is describable *in itself*, i.e., non-relationally as a belief that p. We do not think that such a strong assumption is justified. For our argument, all that is needed is that it is possible to describe it relationally as a belief, i.e., that its description as a belief is a relational one.

An example may help. Suppose that an anthropologist behaves in some way n which tribe a describes as polite and tribe b describes as rude. It is analytic that rude behavior is not polite, and vice versa. Must there be an answer to the question whether n is truly polite, or rude? Of course not. The anthropologist himself, however, who is a member of neither society, can describe n in neither way, i.e., only as it is in itself, although he is well aware of the fact that in one society it is correct to regard this action as polite, and in the other it is correct to regard it as rude.

There is a very old tension in theology between the view that all of God's properties are necessary—i.e., that what God is cannot be a matter of some merely contingent fact—and the view that God responds differentially to different circumstances. The first view implies that God has the same properties in every possible world; the second view implies that He may have different properties in different possible worlds. It seems that the only model which can resolve that tension is the Ockhamistic model we suggest: what is in itself, intrinsically the very same state, may have very different relational descriptions in different possible worlds.

In refusing to describe a state of God's as it is *in itself*, in all possible worlds, we side with the traditional 'negative' theologians who allow us to describe God by His relational properties only. Yet, if God's belief that p is construed as a *relation* between m and the fact that p (which exists in some possible worlds), we may also say, with the naïve believer, that God has foreknowledge that p (i.e., in every p world, m is truly describable as a belief that p).

In view of the above considerations, it seems clear that one needs an independent argument in order to maintain (E). Since Fischer has not provided such an argument, he has not given us a good reason for rejecting the Ockhamistic solution to the problem of divine foreknowledge and human freedom.

IV. Stronger Objections

The above response to Fischer's second objection gives us a clue on how to meet other, more sophisticated criticisms of the Ockhamistic position. Consider, first, the following objection designed to show that (G) does not express a soft fact about the past. Suppose that, contrary to fact, Jones had not raised his arm at t_{10}. In that case God, being infallible, would not have believed that Qt_{10}. Moreover, being all-knowing, God would have believed that $\sim Qt_{10}$. But then God would have been in a *different* mental state from the one he actually was in. It thus follows that, had it been within Jones's power not to raise his arm, he would have had the power to bring about the non-occurrence of a certain event in the past, i.e., God's believing at t_0 that Qt_{10}. However, neither Jones nor anyone else has the power to bring about the non-occurrence of events in the past.

There is, the incompatibilist may argue, an important asymmetry between (G) and its human analogue,

(B) Smith correctly believed at t_0 that Qt_{10}.

(B), he might argue, is a soft fact, for had Jones not raised his arm at t_{10}, the event of Smith's believing that Qt_{10} would have nevertheless occurred. It would just be deprived of the property of being correct. But the event described in (G) would not have occurred at all. Jones would have it within his power to annihilate a past event. But this is impossible.

The answer is simple. It is not that through our action we can bring about the non-occurrence of an event in the past. Rather, through our action we can deprive a past event from having a certain relational property, a property which accrues to it by virtue of the occurrence of a certain future event over which we have control. Since, as argued above, God's belief that Qt_{10} is a relation obtaining between a certain mental state of God m and the fact that Qt_{10}, we can, by exercising our control over the latter, bring it about that the mental state, would, or would not, count as a belief that Qt_{10}.

The strongest objection the incompatibilist may have at this point to our view is the following. He may grant that

(G) God believed at t_0 that Qt_{10}

is a soft fact about the past relative to t_9, and yet argue that *it is not a soft fact which we have the power to alter*. For surely not all soft facts about the past are such that it is within our power to alter them? Consider, e.g., the soft fact described in (q) below,

(q) Smith correctly believed at t_0 that the sun will shine at t_{10},

which is not alterable by creatures unable to alter the motions of heavenly bodies.[8] The reason for the non-alterability of (G) is that, were soft facts like the one described in (G) within our control, we would have it within our power to determine God's beliefs. This, however, may seem problematic, or even blasphemous.

The answer, we think, is that it is indeed sometimes within our power to determine what God believes. We do not thereby cause any changes in God, nor limit His omniscience, for it is neither change nor limitation in God that some of His states count as beliefs of what we do in virtue of our doing those very things. "A thing will happen in the future not because God knows it will happen, but because it is going to happen, therefore it is known by God before it does happen," as Origen said.[9] This is, perhaps, what God's foreknowledge is all about.

CHAPTER SEVEN

Hard and Soft Facts

Joshua Hoffman and Gary Rosenkrantz

One of the traditional problems of philosophical theology is reconciling divine foreknowledge and human freedom. By being eternally omniscient God foreknows our choices and actions. If we now have it in our power to do other than we actually do, then do we not have it in our power so to act that a fact about the past, viz., God's having known that we would now be performing certain actions, would not be a fact about the past? But it may appear that past facts are "fixed" in a way that precludes our having such a power. Hence, it seems that God's foreknowledge is incompatible with its being in our power to do other than we actually do—a condition widely held to be necessary for human freedom. The Ockhamist reply to this alleged incompatibility is to distinguish "hard" and "soft" facts about the past and to claim that while hard facts about the past are indeed fixed in the. intended sense, this is not always true of soft facts about the past. Since the Ockhamist thinks that God's foreknowings of present and future human actions are soft facts about the past which are not fixed, the Ockhamist believes that he can allow for human freedom.

One of the more widely discussed recent defenses of ths Ockhamist position is that of Marilyn Adams [Chapter 3 in this

Reprinted by permission from *The Philosophical Review*, 93 (1984): 419–34. We would like to thank the editors of *The Philosophical Review* for their helpful comments on earlier versions of this paper. Thanks are also due to John Fischer for his comments on an earlier draft of this paper.

volume]. She offers an analysis of the crucial hard fact/soft fact distinction. More recently, John Fischer has persuasively argued that Adams's analysis is faulty [Chapter 4 in this volume]. Our goal is to provide an analysis of the hard fact/soft fact distinction which is correct and thus avoids all of the difficulties raised by Fischer. In the light of the controversy over the distinction, such an analysis is required if there is to be adequate support for the compatibilist position.

A useful way to begin is by examining Marilyn Adams's analysis of the hard fact/soft fact distinction. She first offers the following definition [pp. 75–76]:

(B) "Statement p is at least in part about time t" = df. "The happening or not happening, actuality or non-actuality of something at t is a necessary condition of the truth of p."

Based on (B), she tries to capture the idea of a hard fact as follows:

(C) "Statement p expresses a 'hard' fact about a time t" = df. "p is not at least in part about any time future relative to t."

The basic idea of Adams's account is that a hard fact about a time t does not entail anything about the future relative to t, while a soft fact about t does. In other words, a soft fact about a time t is not a fact which is just about t (or some earlier time) but also about some time later than t. For example, suppose that it is a fact that in 44 B.C. God knew that you would be reading this paper today. This is not a hard fact about 44 B.C. because a necessary condition of its truth is that you read this paper today, which is at a time which is future relative to 44 B.C. By (B), this makes the fact in question at least in part about today. Thus by (C), it is not a hard fact about 44 B.C., and hence it is a soft fact about 44 B.C. Consequently, generally speaking God's foreknowings are soft facts relative to their (past) times of occurrence. This leaves the way open for a further argument that some of God's foreknowings are the sorts of soft facts such that at certain times it is in our power so to act that they would never have been facts at all.

Unfortunately, as Fischer has demonstrated, Adams's analysis is fatally flawed. As Fischer has noted, in order to evaluate Adams's analysis one must first interpret what is meant by a necessary condition in (B). Following Fischer, we may distinguish three such interpretations. First, 'q is a necessary condition of the truth of p' may mean "$p \rightarrow q$" or "p materially implies q." Secondly, it may mean "necessarily $(p \rightarrow q)$," where the modal term expresses broadly logical or metaphysical necessity. Finally, it may mean "if q were not or had not been true, then p would not be or would not have been true."[1]

On the first two of these interpretations of Adams's (B) and (C), there seems to be the following serious problem. If there are necessary "actualities," that is, existents which must exist at every time, then their existence at any time t is a necessary condition of the truth of any statement whatsoever. This implies that for any statement p, and any time t, p is at least in part about t. Then by (C), p does not express a hard fact about t; that is, no statement is a hard fact about any time t. But this makes the hard fact/soft fact distinction an empty one. But are there any such necessary actualities? Since Adams's paper attempts to show that the existence of God is not a hard fact, in the context of her paper she should concede, given the traditional concept of God, that there is at least one necessary actuality, viz., God. And, of course, it is arguable that there are many other necessary actualities; for example, properties, numbers, propositions, and so on. The existence of even one such necessary actuality is enough to refute Adams's analysis. Furthermore, if the counterfactual conditional used in the third interpretation of Adams's (B) and (C) is of a sort which must be true if it has an impossible antecedent, then this refutation also applies to the third interpretation of Adams's analysis.

In any case, Fischer has developed another major problem with Adams's analysis which appears to hold on any of the three interpretations of her (B) and (C). Intuitively, the statement "Columbus walks in 1492" expresses a hard fact about 1492. But this statement has as a necessary condition of its truth that Columbus does not walk for the first time in 1983. Thus, by (B) the former statement is at least in part about 1983, and so by (C) it is not a hard fact about 1492. This strategy can be employed to show that on Adams's analysis any purported hard fact turns out to be a soft one, and once again the distinction between them collapses.[2]

In light of these serious problems for Adams's analysis, if

Ockhamism is to be fully defended, then an alternative analysis is needed. We now propose to provide such an analysis, one which adequately meets the challenge issued by incompatibilists like Fischer [p. 96 in this volume].

Intuitively, a hard fact about a time t is one which is only about a past time t or which consists of the occurring or obtaining of a state of affairs at such a time t, in the basic sense of 'occurring or obtaining at t'. For example, the fact that Socrates walks at a past time t_1 is intuitively a hard fact about t_1, while the fact that in 400 B.C. it is true that in 1983 Reagan is president, is not intuitively a hard fact about either 400 B.C. or 1983. This is because the latter fact does not consist of a state of affairs which occurs in the fundamental sense either in 400 B.C. or in 1983, but one which in some sense occurs at both times, or which is about both times. Clearly, such an informal characterization of the idea of a hard fact stands in need of clarification in terms of an analysis. This is what we intend to provide in the following discussion.

We shall employ the notion of a *state of affairs*, which we understand to be the notion of a propositional entity. Facts, whether hard or soft, we take to be states of affairs which occur or obtain. Hence, facts or states of affairs, like propositions, may entail one another, and have modal characteristics such as being possible, impossible, necessary, or contingent. Entities of this sort can obtain at a given time or fail to obtain at a given time. For instance, if Socrates is walking at t, then the state of affairs, *Socrates is walking*, obtains at t. And if Socrates is not walking at t, then the state of affairs, *Socrates is walking*, fails to obtain at t. However, the ontological status of facts is a matter of some controversy. Unlike us, some philosophers regard facts as concrete occurrences or happenings. We could accommodate this view provided that such concrete facts or events instantiate, satisfy, or are tokens of states of affairs. Although we will formulate our analysis of a hard fact in terms of states of affairs, if one were to reject these altogether, our analysis could be reformulated in terms of sentences or statements, where these are understood to be linguistic or quasi-linguistic entities having truth values, entailment relations, and modal characteristics. Analogues to the key notions which our analysis involves can be expressed in a straightforward way in these alternative theoretical vocabularies.

We accept the following implication of the timeless theory of truth: a dated state of affairs, for example, *Socrates is walking at t*, is necessarily such that if it obtains, then it obtains for all of time. Call such a state of affairs an *eternal* one, which we define as follows:

s is eternal = df. s is a state of affairs such that: $\sim \Diamond$ (Et) (Et') (t ≠ t' & s obtains at time t & s does not obtain at time t').

Other examples of eternal states of affairs are 2 + 2 = 4, and *it never rains on the plains of Spain*. However, other states of affairs possess a contrary property, *being unrestrictedly repeatable*. This property is at the other extreme from eternality. While an eternal state of affairs must either always obtain or always fail to obtain, an unrestrictedly repeatable state of affairs may obtain, then fail to obtain, then obtain again, indefinitely many times *throughout all of time*.[3] An example of such a state of affairs is *Socrates walks* or *Socrates is walking*. We define the concept of a state of affairs being unrestrictedly repeatable in the following two definitions.

(I) The period of time *t* has the *minimal duration* of *s* = df. *s* is a state of affairs such that: (i) it is possible that *s* obtains at a time period which has the duration of *t*, and (ii) *s* is necessarily such that if it obtains, then it obtains at a time period which has at least the length of the period of time *t*.

For instance, every period of time which is one instant in length has the minimal duration of the state of affairs that Mount St. Helens comes into existence, every period of time which is one minute in length has the minimal duration of the state of affairs that Mount St. Helens is erupting for one minute, and so forth. Generally speaking, a state of affairs of the form *xϕ's for n units of time u* cannot obtain at a time period which has a length of less than the product of *n* times *u*.

(II) *s* is *unrestrictedly repeatable (UR)* = df. *s* is a state of affairs such that: (i) *s* is not eternal, and (ii) (n) (t_1) (t_2) (t_3) . . . (t_n) $([t_1 < t_2 < t_3 . . . t_n$ are periods of time which have the minimal duration of s] $\rightarrow$ s is possibly such that: (s obtains at t_1, s does not obtain at t_2, s obtains at t_3, . . . s obtains at $t_n \equiv n$ is odd)).[4]

Examples of *UR* states of affairs are *Mount St. Helens comes into existence*, *Socrates is walking*, and *Mount St. Helens is erupting*.[5]

There is a dispute over the nature of these and similar states of affairs: are they "present-tense" states of affairs or "timeless," that is, tenseless states of affairs?[6] Our analysis will be formulated so as to remain neutral on this question. We only assume what seems evident, namely, that one or the other of these views is correct.

As we said before, a hard fact about a past time t is one which intuitively is only about t. This notion can be captured if we can, first, pick out a class of states of affairs which are not about any specific time at all, and then index these to t. Such a class of states of affairs can be identified by employing the notion of a state of affairs which is unrestrictedly repeatable, the distinction between complex and simple states of affairs, and a particular conception of a state of affairs being present tense or tenseless. Thus, our definition of a hard fact may be developed as follows.

(III) s is a URP state of affairs = df. (i) s is UR, and (ii) s is present tense or tenseless.

The conception of a present-tense or tenseless state of affairs we are employing here is a technical one, and it may be explicated in terms of the following examples. UR states of affairs like *Jones walks* and *Jones is seated* are present tense or tenseless and thus URP. Furthermore, notice that states of affairs of this sort are expressed by sentences which employ no expression for tense except for the present tense. However, some URP states of affairs are expressed by sentences which employ tenses other than the present; for example, *Smith believes that Jones will walk*. In an example of this kind an expression for future tense or past tense is employed just within the scope of a verb of psychological attitude. The result is that the whole state of affairs expressed by a sentence is neither future tense nor past tense. On the other hand, the states of affairs expressed by sentences like 'Jones will walk tomorrow', 'Jones walked', 'One day after today Jones walks', and 'One day later Jones walks', are not present tense or tenseless. This is true despite the fact that some of these sentences do not employ a future-tense or past-tense verb. The intuition at work here is that sentences like these employ in a non-psychological context either a future-tense (past-tense) verb or another sort of temporal expression whose use is either tantamount to or an eliminative analysis of the use of such a tensed verb.

(IV) A state of affairs *r* is a *hard fact about a time t* = df. (1) *r* is the state of affairs, *s at (in) t*; (2) *s* is a *URP* state of affairs; (3) *s* obtains throughout (throughout some part of) *t*; (4) either *s* is a simple state of affairs, or if it is complex, then all of its parts are *URP*; (5) neither *r* nor *s* nor any of *s*'s parts entails either a simple *URP* state of affairs indexed to a time which does not overlap with *t*, or a complex *URP* state of affairs all of whose parts are *URP* and which is indexed to a time which does not overlap with *t*; and (6) *t* is a past time.

(IV) requires some further explanation. By a time *t* we mean either a moment or an interval. We remind the reader that the occurrence of some states of affairs requires a certain minimal duration of time. When we say that the state of affairs *r* is the state of affairs *s at (in) t*, we imply that *r* is constructed by indexing *s* to *t*, where *t* is a moment or period of time having a length at least the minimal duration of *s*. In general, when a state of affairs *s* is indexed to *t*, this operation yields a state of affairs *s at t (s in t)*. If *r* is the state of affairs *s at (in) t*, then *r* consists of a *kernel* state of affairs, *s*, and a temporal suffix or prefix, *at t (in t)*, which indexes *s*. For example, if the state of affairs *Socrates is walking* is indexed to *t*, this yields the state of affairs *Socrates is walking at (in) t*, whose kernel is the state of affairs *Socrates is walking*. In clause (3) of (IV), the term 'throughout *t*' applies just when *s* is indexed by *at t*, and the term 'throughout some part of *t*' applies just in case *s* is indexed by *in t*. When we say that a state of affairs *s* entails a state of affairs *r*, we mean that necessarily ($s \rightarrow r$). Finally, there are two approaches to explicating the distinction between *simple* or *atomic* states of affairs and *complex* ones. The first involves taking the notion of a simple state of affairs as primitive and defining a complex state of affairs as one which is not simple. On this approach the distinction would have to be supported solely by examples, such as the state of affairs *Socrates is wise*, which is simple, and the state of affairs *Socrates is wise and Socrates is ugly*, which is complex. The second and more forthcoming approach is to say that a complex state of affairs is any state of affairs which is either constructable out of other states of affairs by use of the logical apparatus of first-order quantification theory enriched with whatever modalities one chooses to employ, or else analyzable into a state of affairs which is so constructable. Accordingly, a simple state of affairs is one which is not complex, and a *part* of a complex state of affairs s is one of those states of affairs out of which s, or s's analysis, is constructable. For example, the state of affairs *Socrates is wise and Socrates is ugly* is complex because constructable out of the states of affairs *Socrates is wise* and *Socrates is ugly*, which are therefore its (conjunctive) parts. This second account of the simple/complex distinction either presupposes or makes use of the concepts of the identity and the analysis of states of affairs. For a given state of affairs, p, to be an *analysis* of a state of affairs, q, it is necessary but not sufficient that $\Box \, (p \equiv q)$. For example, take a case where p is identical with q, such as $\Box \, (S \text{ knows } r \equiv S \text{ knows } r)$. Obviously, this is an uninformative tautology and hence no analysis. An analysis would be informative and in this case give us some sort of insight into or understanding of the nature of knowledge, knowledge being a constituent of the sort of state of affairs in the example. On the traditional view, for instance, such a state of affairs would be analyzable into a complex state of affairs, *r is true and S believes r and r is justified for S*. Achieving some such insight into the nature of a state of affairs is a requirement of an analysis in the philosophical sense we are employing. Furthermore, the *identity* of p and q requires more than $\Box \, (p \equiv q)$. For example, $\Box \, (2 + 2 = 4 \equiv 7 + 5 = 12)$, but these are not the same state of affairs. The identity of p and q has in addition some condition which guarantees that p and q have the same cognitive content. For instance, it is plausible that the state of affairs *Socrates is ugly and wise* and the state of affairs *Socrates is wise and Socrates is ugly* have the same cognitive content, and hence are one and the same state of affairs. Because the latter state of affairs is complex, so is the former one. Since the question of the nature of the analysis and identity of states of affairs raises issues about the criteria of informativeness and cognitive synonymy which we do not resolve here, we do not insist that the simple/complex distinction we employ has been ideally explicated, but it is serviceable nonetheless.[7]

Now that we have explained our analysis, we will show how it classifies various sorts of states of affairs in terms of the hard fact/soft fact distinction. God's knowledge of the future is for the Ockhamist a paradigm case of a soft fact about a time. For example, let r in (IV) be the state of affairs *at t_1, God knows that Jones walks at t_2,* where $t_1 < t_2$. We may suppose that this state of affairs (call it r_1) satisfies conditions (1), (3), (4), and (6) of (IV).[8] However, because God has necessary existence and is essentially omniscient, the state of affairs which is the kernel of r_1, viz., *God knows that Jones walks at t_2* (which corresponds to s in (IV)), is not *URP*: it is an eternal state of affairs. Hence, r_1 fails to satisfy condition (2) of (IV) and is a soft fact about t_1. Furthermore, r_1 entails that Jones exists at t_2, that Jones walks at t_2, etc.—which are the simple *URP* states of affairs, *Jones exists*, *Jones walks*, etc., indexed to a time later than t_1, viz., t_2.[9] Consequently, r_1 fails to satisfy condition (5) of (IV). Therefore, for this reason as well, r_1 is not a hard fact about t_1.

On the other hand, take the state of affairs *Socrates walks at t_1.* This should turn out to be a hard fact about t_1. Call this state of affairs r_2, and call the state of affairs *Socrates walks,* s_2. We may assume that r_2 satisfies conditions (1), (3), and (6) of (IV). Because s_2 is *URP* and simple, r_2 satisfies conditions (2) and (4) of (IV). Furthermore, unlike r_1, r_2 satisfies condition (5) of (IV). Thus r_2 meets all the conditions in (IV) and is a hard fact about t_1. As we noted in our discussion of Adams's analysis, a state of affairs like r_2 does entail the state of affairs $\sim$ *(Socrates walks for the first time) at t_2,* where $t_2 > t_1$. This entailment was one of the bases for Fischer's refutation of Adams. But observe that the kernel of the entailed state of affairs is not *UR*. It may obtain (because Socrates has never walked), then fail to obtain (because Socrates takes his first walk), and then obtain again (he stops walking), but then it must obtain forever after. Consequently, the fact that r_2 has this entailment does not prevent it from satisfying condition (5) of (IV). Thus on our view it is not enough merely for a state of affairs about a time t to entail a state of affairs about a later time to prevent it from being a hard fact; it must entail the right sort of state of affairs. For the same reasons the fact that r_2 entails certain necessary actualities such as the state of affairs $2 + 2 = 4$ *at t_2,* or the state of affairs *God exists at t_2,* does not prevent r_2 from satisfying condition (5) of (IV), inasmuch as the kernel state of affairs in each case is eternal and thus not *UR*. Thus both of the kinds of objections which were fatal to Adams's analysis pose no problem for ours.

The preceding discussion showed that while r_2 entails certain states of affairs indexed to a time later than t_1, the kernels of these indexed states of affairs are not UR. In one case, the kernel could obtain, fail to obtain, and obtain again (i.e., was *repeatable*) but was not UR. In the other case, the kernel was eternal. Why then did we not simply state condition (5) of (IV) by saying that r does not entail a state of affairs which could obtain, fail to obtain, obtain again, and fail to obtain again (which may undergo three changes of truth value rather than two)? The answer derives from the existence of certain peculiar states of affairs which are intuitively hard facts about some time, but which entail a kernel state of affairs indexed to later time, such that for any given natural number, the kernel of this state of affairs may undergo that number of changes of truth value. For example, take the state of affairs *(Socrates walks and Plato walks) at t_1*. Call this state of affairs r_3. r_3 entails the state of affairs [~*(Socrates walks for the first time) and ~(Plato walks for the first time)*] at t_2, where $t_2 > t_1$. The kernel of the latter state of affairs may obtain (neither Plato nor Socrates ever walked), and then fail to obtain (Socrates walks for the first time), then obtain again (Socrates stops walking), and then fail to obtain again (Plato takes his first walk), and then obtain a third time (Plato stops walking). Once it has obtained this third time, the kernel in question obtains forever after. r_3 is clearly a hard fact about t_1, yet it entails a complex state of affairs indexed to a later time whose kernel is more than repeatable. Furthermore, each time a new conjunct is added to r_3 (for example, *(Socrates walks and Plato walks and Aristotle walks) at t_1*), we get a state of affairs which entails a kernel state of affairs indexed to a time later than t_1 and which may undergo two more changes of truth value. If we start with an infinite conjunction of this sort it will entail a UR state of affairs indexed to a time later than t_1. Hence, if it were only required in condition (5) of (IV) that r not entail a more than repeatable state of affairs indexed to a time later than t, then any conjunction of the sort cited above would turn out to be a soft fact about t. And for any natural number n, it would not help to require that r not entail a kernel state of affairs indexed to a time later than t where this kernel may change its truth value n number of times. Finally, if some conjunctive states of affairs like the ones above have infinitely many conjuncts—and since we are taking seriously the possibility of an omniscient God, it would be odd to rule out that such infinite states of affairs are objects of divine thought—then even if condition (5) of (IV) were to require that r not entail any UR state of affairs indexed to a time later than t, then (IV) would have the unhappy consequence of implying that those infinite conjunctions are soft facts about t. As we actually state condition (5), however, all of these conjunctions, even the infinite ones, are hard facts about t, because while each of them entails a complex repeatable state of affairs indexed to a time later than t, for any such complex state of affairs, some of its parts are *not UR*.

According to Fischer, some facts which an Ockhamist would classify as soft are misclassified as hard by Adams's analysis; for example, a fact such as *at t_1 (either Smith knows that Jones walks at t_2 or Jones believes that Jones walks at t_2)*, where the second disjunct is false.[10] Call the whole state of affairs we have here r_4. An Ockhamist would say that r_4 is a soft fact about t_1, since Jones might have been able so to act at t_2 that r_4 would never have been a fact at all. This Ockhamist intuition is confirmed by our analysis of the notion of a hard fact, since as the following discussion shows, r_4 does not satisfy this analysis. To start with, notice that r_4 *does* satisfy conditions (1), (2), (3), and (6) of (IV). And if the concept of knowledge is simple and unanalyzable, then r_4 also satisfies condition (4) (otherwise r_4 fails to satisfy (4)).[11] But in any case, the following two observations show that r_4 does not satisfy condition (5). First, the kernel of r_4 is a complex state of affairs with two disjunctive parts. Secondly, the first disjunct entails that Jones exists at t_2, that Jones walks at t_2, etc.—which are the simple URP states of affairs, *Jones exists, Jones walks*, etc., indexed to a time later than t_1, viz., t_2.

Some further inplications of our analysis should be brought to light. First, any necessary state of affairs indexed to a time is a soft fact about that time because of condition (2) of (IV). Since a necessary state of affairs is eternal it does not seem to be *only about* any moment or finite period of time to which it may be indexed—a feature which intuitively disqualifies it as being a hard fact about any such time. If it is about any time it is about eternity. But if a state of affairs is about eternity, then it is not a hard fact even about eternity. The concept of a hard fact about a time t is a concept of a fact which is *past*, over and done with, and for that reason beyond anyone's power so to act that it would never have been a fact at all. Necessary states of affairs are never over and done with (assuming they are always about eternity), so that they are not hard facts. Hence, on our view, the necessary state of affairs, *God exists*, is a soft fact about any time *t* to which it is indexed.[12]

At this point, we emphasize that the distinction between hard facts and soft facts as we have drawn it is *not* the distinction between those facts about the past which are such that it is *beyond* our power so to act that they would not have occurred at all, and those facts about the past which are such that it *is* within our power so to act. As we just explained, necessary states of affairs indexed to past times are soft facts about those times which are such that it is not within our power so to act. An example of a *contingent* state of affairs which is both intuitively and by our analysis a soft fact about the past and which has the same property is this: *in 1492 God knows that the Milky Way will exist in 1983*. Hence, some soft facts share this crucial characteristic with hard facts, while others do not. Of course, Ockhamists are most interested in those soft facts which do *not* have this property in common with hard facts.

Another state of affairs which, according to our analysis, is both a soft fact and fixed, is any past-tense state of affairs indexed to a past time. For example, *Columbus walked in 1492*. This past-tense state of affairs contains a kernel which is not *URP*, and hence the whole state of affairs fails to satisfy condition (2) of (IV). Yet we have asserted that the state of affairs *Columbus walks in 1492 is* a hard fact about 1492. Why the distinction: are these not the same facts? Our approach here is nominally to deny hard fact status to the past-tense fact so that a cogent analysis of the hard fact/soft fact distinction can be formulated. Since we do not claim that all soft facts are such that we can act so that they would never have occurred at all, no vital intuitions are offended by our drawing the distinction where we do draw it. Furthermore, there is a sense in which the past-tense state of affairs *Columbus walked in 1492* is not an ontologically fundamental or basic fact. Rather, it is logically dependent on a more fundamental state of affairs, namely, the corresponding present-tense or tenseless kernel state of affairs indexed to *t*, which *is* a hard fact about *t*. In other words, it is only true that Columbus walked in 1492 because it is true that in 1492 Columbus walks. Thus on our view, the present tense or the tenseless is the ontologically primal state of affairs, and past-tense and future-tense states of affairs are to be "cashed out" or understood in terms of the former. All that ever really contingently happens are *URP* states of affairs. To illustrate this further, consider a second, more complicated, example which goes as follows. Take the state of affairs, *Socrates walked for the first time in 400 B.C.* Because the kernel of this state of affairs is not *URP*, the whole state of affairs is a soft fact about 400 B.C. This complex state of affairs is equivalent to the following one: *(Socrates walks and Socrates never walked before) in 400 B.C.* This in turn is equivalent to: *(Socrates walks in 400 B.C.) and (t) [(t < 400 B.C.) → ~(Socrates walks at t)]*. And the latter is equivalent to an infinite conjunction of simple states of affairs whose kernels are *URP*: *(Socrates walks in 400 B.C.) and ~(Socrates walks in 401 B.C.) and ~(Socrates walks in 402 B.C.) and. . . .* It is these kernel states of affairs which ultimately really happen or fail to happen in the world at those various times to make the original state of affairs and its equivalents obtain. One different sort of example of a state of affairs which on our analysis is a soft fact but which gets "cashed out" in terms of a hard fact is: *[(2 + 2 = 5) or (Socrates walks)] at t.* This state of affairs is "cashed out" in terms of the hard fact about *t* that at *t* Socrates walks. Since, as we pointed out earlier, a hard fact about a past time *t* is a state of affairs which occurs or obtains at (in) *t* in the fundamental sense of 'occurring or obtaining at (in) *t*', our classifying such examples as the ones above as soft facts seems justified.

CHAPTER EIGHT

Accidental Necessity and Logical Determinism

Alfred J. Freddoso

Take some truth about the past, such as that Socrates drank hemlock. It is natural to believe that this proposition is necessary, i.e., no longer possibly such that it will be false. But just what kind of necessity are we dealing with here? It is clearly not logically—metaphysically—necessary that Socrates drank hemlock. Nor is this physically necessary, where a proposition is physically necessary just in case it is a law of nature. Of course, a causal determinist might contend that it is now causally necessary that Socrates drank hemlock, where p is causally necessary at t just in case, for some q (relevant causal conditions), q is true at t and it is physically, but not logically, necessary that if q is true, then p is true. But it should be clear that the sort of necessity in question here is independent of any special assumptions about causality. It attaches to the past simply in virtue of its being past.

Medieval logicians commonly called this modality necessity *per accidens*, i.e., accidental necessity. My goal in this paper is to construct a systematic and plausible account of accidental necessity. In so doing I will follow the lead of William of Ockham, who fashioned in rough outline a theory of *per accidens* modality which was explicitly intended to yield a non-Aristotelian re-

Reprinted by permission from the *Journal of Philosophy*, 80 (1983): 257–78. I wish to thank Thomas Flint, Richard Foley, Jorge Garcia, James Garson, Penelope Maddy, Philip Quinn, and an anonymous referee for their helpful remarks on earlier versions of this paper.

sponse to the challenge of logical determinism.[1] However, despite the fact that the recent literature on logical determinism contains a few detailed, as well a many superficial, discussions of the Ockhamistic position, no one has formulated a convincing version of that position.[2] Specifically, the philosophers in question have failed on two counts. First, they have not articulated precisely the central Ockhamistic thesis of the primacy of the pure present. And, second, they have not drawn clearly the important distinction between the necessity of the past and causal necessity. These failures are all the more lamentable in view of the fact that the Ockhamistic response to logical determinism is actually much more attractive than its more popular competitors—or so, at least, I shall argue.

In Section I of this paper I will first describe some general features of *per accidens* modality and then show how the most common construal of the claim that the past is necessary leads directly to a very strong argument for logical determinism. Then, in Section II, I will show that the Ockhamistic solution to this argument, with its insistence on the primacy of the pure present, has a firmer intuitive foundation than any other proposed solution. Next, in Section III, I will take up the neglected task of giving a precise analysis of the notion of the pure present, and then I will use this analysis to formulate an account of accidental necessity which thwarts the argument for logical determinism, but which, as I will show in Section IV, is clearly neutral with respect to the debate over causal determinism.

I

The first thing to notice is that accidental necessity is as respectable and well-behaved a modality as logical, physical, or causal necessity. To make this clear I will begin with the simplifying assumption that all propositions are tensed.[3] Though this assumption seems to me both natural and true, it is not crucial to my argument. But I will leave it to the friends of "tenseless" propositions to translate what I will say into their own idiom. The assumption in question has two consequences that will be relevant below. The first is that some logically contingent propositions may be true at some times and false at others. Examples are the present-tense proposition that David is sitting, the past-tense proposition that Plato taught Aristotle, and the future-tense proposition that someone will cook an omelet. The second consequence is that some present-tense propositions can be true at just one moment. Examples are the proposition that Mary is reading at t, and the proposition that t is present [or: that it is (now) t], where t is a single determinate moment of time. These propositions can be true only at t.

Let me now list some of the basic properties of *per accidens* modality. First, a proposition that is necessary *per accidens* is, as the name suggests, such that its being necessary is an accidental feature of it. So only logically contingent propositions can be necessary *per accidens* or, consequently, impossible *per accidens*. This is a property that accidental modality shares with physical and causal modality as characterized above.

Second, as we should expect, a proposition's being necessary (impossible) *per accidens* is relative to a time, since a proposition typically becomes necessary (impossible) *per accidens* after not having been necessary (impossible). For instance, it is, let us assume, now necessary *per accidens* that Socrates drank hemlock, but this proposition was false when Socrates was a child. Similarly, it is now impossible *per accidens* that Socrates never drank hemlock, but this proposition was true when Socrates was a child. So accidental modality resembles causal modality and, arguably, physical modality in being time-relative.

From these first two points it follows that, for any moment t, logically contingent propositions may be divided into three jointly exhaustive and mutually exclusive groups, viz., those which are necessary *per accidens* at t, those which are impossible *per accidens* at t, and those which are neither necessary *per accidens* at t nor impossible *per accidens* at t. We can say that each of the members of the last group is *temporally contingent* at t.

Third, a proposition's being necessary (impossible) *per accidens* at a moment t entails that it remains necessary (impossible) *per accidens* at every moment after t. This, again, is what we should expect to be true of the necessity of the past. And since it seems logically possible for a proposition to be a law of nature at one time and not at some later time, this feature of accidental necessity distinguishes it from both physical and causal necessity. (This is an important point to which I will return below.) So some logically contingent propositions, e.g., that Socrates drank hemlock, are not now and never will be possibly false, and their negations are not now and never will be possibly true, where the impossibility in question is accidental impossibility. One corollary is that if *p* is necessary *per accidens* at *t*, then no one can have the power at or after *t* to bring it about that *p* is or will be false; and if *p* is impossible *per accidens* at *t*, then no one can have the power at or after *t* to bring it about that *p* is or will be true. In short, the unalterability of the past follows from its necessity.

Fourth, when we limit the consequents to logically contingent propositions, then accidental necessity, like other kinds of necessity, is closed under entailment.[4] That is,

(A) If *p* entails *q*, and *q* is logically contingent, and *p* is necessary *per accidens* at *t*, then *q* is necessary *per accidens* at *t*.

Moreover, given what was said in the preceding paragraph, it is evident that the conjunction of (A) with the obvious truth that no one can have the power to make a logically necessary proposition false, entails:

(B) If *p* entails *q*, and *p* is necessary *per accidens* at *t*, then no one has the power at or after *t* to bring it about that *q* is or will be false.

(B) is unassailable. If *p* cannot be false at or after *t*, then no proposition entailed by *p* can be false at or after *t*—and so no one has the power at or after *t* to make such a proposition false. Likewise, it is easy to show that if *p* is impossible *per accidens* at *t*, then no proposition that entails *p* can be true at or after *t*—and so no one has the power at or after *t* to make such a proposition true.

What has been said so far provides us with a framework for talking about the necessity of the past, but it does not answer the question of just which propositions are in fact necessary *per accidens* at any given moment. And, of course, this is the heart of the matter. Some philosophers, appealing to the alleged possibility of time travel, have recently argued, in effect, that very few propositions are either necessary *per accidens* or impossible *per accidens*.[5] For many true past-tense propositions are, they claim, at least conceivably such that someone may now have the power to make them false. For instance, a time traveler might now transport himself to Socrates's death scene and find himself in a position to prevent Socrates from drinking the hemlock. We now know, of course, that he will (did?) not exercise this power, but he may have such power nonetheless. However one reacts to such flights of fancy, their coherence invariably depends on further metaphysical assumptions, e.g., about the structure of time or the nature of persons, which most sober-minded thinkers would find outlandish at best. Though oddity does not entail falsity, it is at least fair to say that the philosophers in question have not won many converts.

In fact, the most popular rendition of the thesis that the past is necessary goes in just the opposite direction. Philosophers from Aristotle to Arthur Prior have, at least implicitly, accepted the following:

(C) If p is true at t, then the proposition that p was the case is necessary *per accidens* at every moment after t, and the proposition that p was never the case is impossible *per accidens* at every moment after t.

That is, if p is true now, then it will always be necessary afterwards that p was once true, and always impossible afterwards that p has never been true. And, the proponent of (C) contends, this amounts to saying, in possible-worlds jargon, that, in every world just like ours up to and including the present moment t, the proposition that p was the case is true at every moment after t. Given (C), we can go on to state the thesis that the past is necessary succinctly as follows: for any p, if it is now the case that p was once true, then the proposition that p was true is necessary *per accidens* now; and if it is not now the case that p has never been true, then the proposition that p has never been true is impossible *per accidens* now.

The popularity of (C) forces us to acknowledge the initial plausibility of this conception of the necessity of the past. At the very least, there is no plausible alternative that stands out clearly. Yet, a moment's reflection reveals that the combination of (B) and (C) gives us all we need to construct the strongest possible (and, to my mind, the clearest possible) argument for logical determinism. In fact, I think it is fair to say that there is no strong argument for logical determinism which does not presuppose the truth of both (B) and (C). Take an arbitrary proposition describing what we would ordinarily consider to be a free action performed at a given moment, e.g., Katie's washing her car at some determinate moment t. Then we can formulate the deterministic argument as follows:

(P1) The proposition that Katie will wash her car at *t* is true now, long before *t*. (assumption)

(P2) So the proposition that it was the case that Katie will wash her car at *t* will be necessary *per accidens* at every future moment, including every moment that precedes or is identical with *t*. (from (P1) and (C))

(P3) But the proposition that it was the case that Katie will wash her car at *t* entails the proposition that if *t* is present, then Katie is washing her car. (assumption)

(P4) Therefore, no one (including Katie) will have the power at or before *t* to bring it about that it is or will be false that if *t* is present, then Katie is washing her car. That is, no one will have the power at or before *t* to bring it about that it is or will be true that Katie is not washing her car when *t* is present. (from (P2), (P3), and (B))

Given (C), the move from (P1) to (P2) is straightforward. (P3) simply reflects the usual assumption that if it has ever been the case that *p* will be true at a moment *t*, then either *p* has already been true at *t* or *p* is true now (at *t*) or *p* will be true at *t*— depending on whether *t* is now in our past, our present, or our future. In short, if it has ever been the case that *p* will be true at *t*, then *p* is true whenever *t* occurs. But if this is so, then, given (B), the necessity of the past-tense proposition that it was the case that Katie will wash her car at *t* entails our inability to affect the present truth-value of the proposition that when *t* is present, Katie is washing her car.

So (B) and (C) enable us to reason validly from the present truth of the proposition that Katie will wash her car at *t* to the conclusion that no one will ever have the power to bring it about that it is false at *t* that she is washing her car. (Notice that this is so regardless of whether the notion of power is given a libertarian or a compatibilist interpretation.) Further, this argument is perfectly general, since similar deterministic consequences follow whenever we substitute for the proposition that Katie will wash her car at *t* any other future-tense proposition whose present-tense counterpart can be true at just one moment.

II

There are only three philosophically interesting lines of response to this rather compelling argument. "Aristotelian" responses all deny assumption (P1), claiming either (a) that where *p* is a future contingent proposition, both *p* and its negation are neither true nor false, or (b) that where *p* is a contingent proposition, it is false both that *p* will be true and that the negation of *p* will be true. The first claim is commonly attributed to Aristotle, while Prior is responsible for the second claim.[6] The fact that such claims have issued readily from the mouths of contemporary as well as classical philosophers should not blind us to how counterintuitive they are. Both (a) and (b) commit their proponents to saying, for instance, that even if the present-tense proposition that Katie is washing her car turns out to be true at *t*, it is still not true now (before *t*) that Katie will wash her car at *t*. But what else, we want to know, could the future-tense verb signify? When we begin to notice that these philosophers mean by 'will be true' what most of us mean by 'is now inevitable', it is hard to suppress the suspicion that they have merely changed the subject without helping us understand why we were disturbed by the deterministic argument in the first place. Moreover, the mere fact that we can construct formal logical systems in which (a) or (b) can apparently be accommodated without inconsistency is not sufficient to allay our discomfort.

A second line of response, suggested by Peter Geach in some recent work on divine omniscience, is to deny assumption (P3) on the ground that all assertions ostensibly about the future are really only about present intentions, dispositions, tendencies, or trends.[7] So, for instance, it might have been true before *t* that Katie was going to wash her car at *t*, even if the present-tense proposition that Katie is washing her car is false when *t* occurs. For she may have intended to wash her car at *t*, but then changed her mind. This response has more initial appeal than the first, since we often do use future-tense sentences, e.g., 'I will wash my car tomorrow' or (perhaps) 'Jones is going to do well on the upcoming exams', to express propositions about our present intentions or about ways in which the world is presently tending. Still, it seems reasonably clear that we also use sentences of this sort in ways which are not so readily amenable to such an analysis. When Katie, full of self-knowledge, ruefully admits "Though I now intend to quit smoking tomorrow, I probably won't," she is, for all her weakness of will, hardly in as peculiar a logical position as she would be if she were to say "Though I will quit smoking tomorrow, I probably won't." And when a latter-day

Hobbes brashly predicts "Someday I will square the circle," we can be confident that he has uttered a falsehood even if we do not doubt for a moment his intention to make his prediction come true.

These brief and somewhat tendentious remarks are not meant to constitute a refutation of any of the positions discussed so far. I simply want to contrast their initial implausibility with what I take to be the initial attractiveness of the Ockhamistic alternative. It is, after all, hard to imagine that anyone would embrace either version of the Aristotelian response willingly, i.e., without being compelled to in the face of a very strong argument for determinism. And, perhaps to a slightly less degree, the same is true of the response adumbrated by Geach.

The Ockhamistic solution, put simply, is to deny the inference from (P1) to (P2) on the ground that (C), despite its popularity and *prima facie* plausibility, is a needlessly and unacceptably strong explication of our pre-analytic beliefs about the necessity of the past. For, the Ockhamist claims, from the fact that it is true now before t that Katie will wash her car at t, it simply does not follow that the proposition that it was the case that Katie will wash her car at t is necessary *per accidens* at every future moment. And, in general, from the fact that it is the case before a given moment t that p will be true, it does not follow that the proposition that it was the case that p will be true is necessary *per accidens* at t and every moment after t. That is, it does not follow that in every possible world just like ours prior to t, it is true at t and every moment after t that it was the case that p will be true. The most pressing task facing the Ockhamist, then, is to explicate the phrase 'just like ours prior to t' in a way which is (a) strong enough to preserve the claim that the worlds in question share the same history at t and (b) weak enough not to engender deterministic consequences when combined with assumptions like (P1) and (P3).

Although, as we shall see, the detailed articulation of this position is rather complicated, the intuition which grounds it is the familiar, but often misunderstood, claim that a future-tense proposition is true now *because* the appropriate present-tense proposition or propositions will be true in the future. For example, the future-tense proposition that Katie will wash her car at t is true now *because* the present-tense proposition that Katie is washing her car will be true at t. But, as many an undergraduate will hasten to assure you, the converse does not hold. That is, it is false that the present-tense proposition that Katie is washing her car will be true at t *because* the future-tense proposition that Katie will wash her car at t is true now. So there is an asymmetric dependence of the truth-values of future-tense and, as we shall see, past-tense propositions on the future and past truth-values of the appropriate present-tense propositions. And, as I have argued elsewhere, this insistence on the centrality of present-tense propositions is the salient feature of Ockham's own account of the truth conditions for past-tense and future-tense propositions.[8] However, this is not to say that the past and future are not "real," since the Ockhamist holds that every past-tense and every future-tense proposition is either true now (even if in principle unverifiable) or false now (even if in principle unfalsifiable).[9] Rather, we can characterize the Ockhamistic position most accurately by the assertion that the pure present is metaphysically primary, since what is true at any given moment t is true at t *because* of what, at t, has been or is or will be purely present. With this insight in hand, the Ockhamist then substitutes for (C) the claim that p is necessary *per accidens* at t just in case p is a logically contingent proposition that is true at every moment at or after t in every possible world which shares all of our world's "presents" prior to t. And this, as I will show in more detail below, invalidates the move from (P1) to (P2).

As I noted above, however, the basic insight in question is often misunderstood. The reason is that the occurrences of the term 'because' in the preceding paragraph are frequently taken to signal a *causal* dependence of the past and future on what has been or will be purely present. Ockhamists themselves sometimes make this mistake and then sit in embarrassed silence when badgered with questions like: How can the future truth of a present-tense proposition have causal effects now? And, even if it can, doesn't this in itself show that the future is already 'real' in a sense which has deterministic consequences? The inability of the Ockhamists in question to give convincing replies to these queries accounts in part for the specious plausibility which has been assumed by the other responses to the argument for logical determinism.

The correct reply, however, is simply to deny that the asymmetric dependence in question is causal. It may seem evasive to insist that this 'temporal' dependence is *sui generis*, but many philosophers today accept, willingly or not, the similar claim that causal dependence is itself *sui generis*. Moreover, as I hope to show, our intuitions about temporal dependence are fine-grained enough to enable us to analyze this dependence in terms of more familiar notions. Regrettably, Ockhamists have not, as far as I can tell, successfully carried out this analysis before now. Some have even been content to take the notion of the pure present as primitive. So it is not surprising that their opponents have suspected them of preferring, in Russell's words, the advantages of theft over honest toil. But once we have such an analysis, it is hard to imagine what more could be demanded. The Ockhamist, as we have seen, is operating from a position of strength, since his conception of the necessity of the past has a firmer intuitive foundation than any of its competitors. Once these intuitions are articulated coherently in a way which thwarts the determinist's argument, the most reasonable course will be to accept the Ockhamistic response to that argument.

III

The Ockhamist, then, holds that every future-tense proposition is either true now or false now (*pace* Aristotle), that some contingent propositions are now such that they will be true (*pace* Prior), and that at least many future-tense sentences are commonly used to express propositions "about" the future rather than simply "about" the present (*pace* Geach). Moreover, as just noted, the Ockhamist's central thesis is that the pure present is metaphysically primary. This thesis, I hope to show, can serve as the basis for a plausible analysis of what it is for two possible worlds to share the same history at a given moment, and hence as the basis for an intuitively satisfying explication of accidental necessity.

It will be helpful here to outline my general strategy informally before introducing the modicum of formal machinery that I will use in what follows. I take the claim that the pure present is metaphysically primary to be tantamount to the assertion that for any moment t and any logically possible world w there is a set k of purely present-tense propositions such that (a) each member of k is true at t in w and (b) k determines what is true at t in w in a temporally independent way, i.e., in a way which does not temporally depend on what has been or will be true at moments of w other than t. I will call this set the *submoment* of t in w, and I will say that a given submoment obtains when and only when each of its members is true. Then, to put it roughly, I will claim that two worlds share the same history at a moment t just in case they share all and only the same submoments, obtaining in exactly the same order, prior to t. Finally, building on this claim, I will say that a proposition p is necessary *per accidens* at t in w just in case p is true at t and at every moment after t in every possible world which shares the same history (in the above sense) with w at t.

Given this general strategy, my first task is to specify which propositions are themselves purely present tense, i.e., temporally independent, and thus eligible for membership in some submoment. To avoid confusion, I will hereafter call such propositions 'immediate' rather than 'present-tense'. For, as Ockham himself realized, some grammatically present-tense sentences are used to express propositions about the past or about the future.

The division of propositions into immediate ones and non-immediate ones will be guided and constrained by what I take to be our shared intuitions about the notions of temporal dependence and independence. Roughly speaking, the truth or falsity of an immediate proposition is temporally (as opposed to, say, logically or causally) independent of what has been or will be true, while the truth conditions of a non-immediate proposition involve an essential reference to what has been true at past moments or will be true at future moments. Alternatively, the immediate propositions true at a given moment, unlike their non-immediate counterparts, determine what is "really occurring" at that moment and what will become part of our history after that moment.

To begin, it seems clear that every proposition which is either logically necessary or logically impossible is immediate, since the present truth or falsity of any such proposition is wholly independent of considerations about the past or about the future. But how are we to divide logically contingent propositions? Before we address this question directly, it will be helpful to list some intuitively obvious examples of immediate propositions which are logically contingent:

(1) David is sitting.
(2) David is sitting or Katie is not standing.
(3) David is standing and it will never be the case that David has never stood.

and

(4) David believes that Katie will travel to Rome next week.

(1) requires little comment, and there are innumerable simple propositions just like it. Again, although (2) is a complex proposition, each of its components is immediate, and its truth conditions are independent of what is true at times other than the present. (3) is somewhat more problematic, since one of its components is a proposition that is about the future and hence non-immediate. But on closer inspection we see that (3) is logically equivalent to its first conjunct, which is clearly immediate. (Note that the second conjunct of (3) is true if there are no future moments.) Hence, the truth or falsity of (3) depends only on what is immediately true in the present. Propositions like (4), which involve present-tense propositional attitudes directed toward non-immediate propositions, play an especially interesting role in the history of the Ockhamistic treatment of future contingents. Ockham himself seems to have counted such propositions as (to use my terminology) non-immediate and hence as ineligible for membership in submoments. But this is clearly a mistake—and one which would render implausible the Ockhamistic response to the argument for logical determinism. Immediate propositions, as noted above, are the key to determining what our history is at a given moment and which possible worlds share the same history with our world at that moment. But the past hopes, fears, beliefs, desires, predictions, etc., of historical agents are clearly unalterable elements of our past and must be counted as part of our history by any explication of what it is for two worlds to share the same history at a given time. No world w can claim to share the same history with our world now if in w Chamberlain did not fear that Hitler would not keep his word, or if in w Ernie Banks did not hope (and predict) every spring that the Cubs would win the pennant. So (4) must be counted as immediate if

the Ockhamistic position is to retain its intuitive advantage over its competitors.

On the other hand, the following logically contingent propositions are clearly non-immediate:

(5) David will sit;
(6) David is standing if and only if Katie has never been to Rome;
(7) Katie is 30 years old;

and

(8) David mistakenly believes that Katie will be in Rome next week.

(5), like all simple past- and future-tense propositions, is obviously non-immediate. Its present truth or falsity depends on whether the immediate proposition that David is sitting will be true at any future moment. (6) is a bit more subtle, but its present truth-value does depend, at least in part, on whether the immediate proposition that Katie is in Rome has ever been true in the past. (7), though expressed by a present-tense sentence, clearly depends for its present truth-value on whether the immediate proposition that Katie exists began to be true 30 years ago. And (8), unlike (4) above, depends in part for its present truth or falsity on whether the immediate proposition that Katie is in Rome will be true at any time next week. (As a general rule, a proposition involving a present-tense propositional attitude directed at a past- or future-tense proposition p is immediate unless it entails p or the negation of p. Hence, whereas:

(9) David believes that Katie will go to Rome

and

(10) David fears that Katie has gone to Rome

are immediate, the propositions

(11) David correctly believes that Katie will go to Rome

and

(12) David mistakenly fears that Katie has gone to Rome

are non-immediate.)

I will now introduce the formal mechanism which will allow us to systematize these intuitions. It consists of a propositional language *L* and a model theory for *L*. I will first describe it and then make some remarks about its intended interpretation. Suppose that *L* has a stock of letters representing propositions, together with the truth-functions, an alethic modality *M* (logical possibility), and tenses *P* and *F* (past tense and future tense, respectively). Now let *C* be a linearly ordered set, the set of times, and let *W* be the set of logically possible worlds. A model structure *R* for *L* is a subset of the logical product $W \cdot C$ such that for every $w \in W$, the class of pairs (w, t), where $t \in C$, forms a sequence of *C*. (I am assuming, consistent with this model structure, that some possible worlds have a first moment of time and some have a last moment of time.) A model with model structure *R* is given by an assignment of classical truth-values, for each (w, t) in *R*, to the proposition-letters. The truth-functional connectives behave in the usual way, while the tenses are given the following Ockhamistic definitions, where '*A*' is replaceable by any well-formed formula of *L*:

P (*A*) is true at (w, t) iff for some $t^* < t$, *A* is true at (w, t^*);
F (*A*) is true at (w, t) iff for some $t^* > t$, *A* is true at (w, t^*).

In addition, the modality *M* is defined as follows:

M (*A*) is true at (w, t) iff for some $(w^*, t^*) \in R$, *A* is true at (w^*, t^*).

In order to give an intuitively adequate account of immediacy, it is necessary for us to make the following three stipulations about the interpretation of *L* under which that account is to be formulated:

First, the proposition-letters of *L*, which I will call its atomic constituents, represent only propositions that may be expressed in English by grammatically present-tense sentences. This stipulation is entirely natural, since the past-tense and future-tense counterparts of such propositions can then be adequately represented in *L* by formulas which involve operations on the atomic constituents of *L*.

Second, no proposition is represented by an atomic constituent of *L* if it is, intuitively, most properly represented in *L* by a formula which involves operations on *L*'s atomic constituents. This stipulation is somewhat stronger and also somewhat more vague than the first. Nevertheless, it can be defended on intuitively attractive grounds. For instance, since *L* contains no operators that represent propositional attitudes, a simple present-tense proposition like

(13) David believes that Katie will at some time be in Rome

is represented by an atomic constituent of L, say 'p'. But now consider the proposition:

(14) David correctly believes that Katie will at some time be in Rome.

How is (14) to be represented? Let 'q' stand for the proposition that Katie is in Rome. The second stipulation dictates that (14) be represented not by an atomic constituent of L but rather by the non-atomic formula 'p and Fq'. Again, even though

(15) David is standing and Katie is sitting

is, arguably, expressed in English by a present-tense sentence, it is intuitively natural to represent it in L by a non-atomic formula like 'r and s'. While I realize that in some cases there will be disagreement about what the proper structural representation of a given proposition might be, I do not believe that any such disagreement will be sufficient to undermine my account of immediacy.[10]

The third, and initially the least intuitive, stipulation is that no atomic constituent of L represents a proposition whose proper philosophical analysis contains quantifiers, unless those quantifiers fall within the scope of a propositional attitude. Thus, no proposition like the following is represented by an atomic constituent of L:

(16) David has no true beliefs;
(17) Katie is omniscient;[11]
(18) Every manatee is ugly;
(19) David is such that he is acquainted with many people in North Liberty, Indiana;

and

(20) David has more than three children.

On the other hand, propositions like

(21) David believes that every manatee is ugly

and

(22) David fears that Katie is omniscient

may be represented by atomic constituents of L. As I will explain below, this stipulation, despite first appearances to the contrary, has firm intuitive footing. Moreover, even though it limits the expressive power of L (since it has as a consequence that many propositions cannot be represented in L), this limitation is both necessary and harmless.[12] I will return to this point shortly.

The account of immediacy that I will now formulate presupposes the interpretation of L determined by these three stipulations. Once we have an explication of immediacy, we can then resort to a less stringent interpretation under which L has the resources to represent any proposition.

It seems unproblematic to claim that any logically contingent immediate proposition is such that it, as well as its negation, is (a) possibly such that it is true at a first moment of time and (b) possibly such that it is true at a last moment of time and (c) possibly such that it is true at an intermediate (i.e., neither first nor last) moment of time. That is, a proposition is temporally independent only if its present truth or falsity is indifferent both to the question of whether there are any past moments and to the question of whether there are any future moments. Given our intended interpretation of L, we can define this notion of temporal indifference for the formulas of L as follows:

A is *temporally indifferent* iff either (a) A or its negation is not logically possible or (b) A, as well as its negation, is such that it (i) is true at some (w,t) where t is the first moment in w, and (ii) is true at some (w,t) where t is the last moment in w, and (iii) is true at some (w,t) where t is an intermediate moment in w.

Then we can say that a proposition is temporally indifferent if it is represented in L (under the intended interpretation) by a temporally indifferent formula.

Even though every formula for the form $F(A)$ or $P(A)$ is such that neither it nor its negation is temporally indifferent, not every temporally indifferent formula is also immediate (consider the formula representing the disjunctive proposition that David is standing or Katie has been to Rome). Nor is it the case that every atomic constituent of L is immediate (consider the atomic constituent representing the proposition that Katie is Tony's granddaughter). However, given the three stipulations made above, it does seem clearly to be the case that every temporally indifferent atomic constituent of L is indeed immediate. For each such formula represents a singular affirmative present-tense proposition which is also temporally indifferent.[13] Conversely, it seems clear that, given our intended interpretation, the only non-immediate temporally indifferent formulas in L will be non-atomic. Such formulas will represent propositions like

(23) David correctly believes that Katie will never be in Rome;
(24) David was standing if and only if Katie will sit;

and

(25) David is standing or Katie will at some time be in Rome.

So we have a core of atomic formulas which are also immediate. Let S be the set of such formulas, and let $V(S)$ be any valuation which assigns a classical truth-value to each of the members of S at a given (w, t). Then we can explicate immediacy as follows:

A is *immediate* iff both (a) for any (w, t), if A is true at (w, t), then A is true at every (w^*, t^*) such that $V(S)$ at $(w^*, t^*) = V(S)$ at (w, t); and (b) if A is false at (w, t), then A is false at every (w^*, t^*) such that $V(S)$ at $(w^*, t^*) = V(S)$ at (w, t).

Intuitively, the truth-value of an immediate formula at any (w, t) is wholly a function of the assignment of truth-values for (w, t) to the temporally indifferent atomic constituents of that formula. Its truth-value, in short, does not temporally depend on what is true or false at other moments.

Finally, to revert to talk of propositions, we can say that a proposition p is immediate if and only if either (a) p is represented by an immediate formula of L, where L is taken under the interpretation determined by the three stipulations made above, or (b) p is logically equivalent to a proposition which meets condition (a).

The following consequences follow straightforwardly from this account of immediacy: (a) p is immediate if and only if the negation of p is immediate; (b) p and q are each immediate only if their conjunction and disjunction are also immediate; (c) p is immediate if and only if every proposition logically equivalent to p is also immediate; and (d) every logically necessary proposition is immediate, as is every logically impossible proposition. Each of these consequences is patently desirable. In addition, each of our original examples, (1)–(12), is classified correctly on this account of immediacy.

We can now see why the third stipulation made above is both necessary and harmless. Consider the proposition:

(26) David has no false beliefs and David believes that Katie will never be in Rome.

Intuitively, (26) is non-immediate, since its present truth-value depends in part on whether the immediate proposition that Katie is in Rome will ever be true. However, in the absence of the third stipulation, the first conjunct of (26) would be represented in L by a temporally indifferent atomic constituent of L, and so (26) itself would be represented by a conjunction of two immediate formulas. So without the third stipulation, (26) would turn out to be immediate, even though it is obviously non-immediate. But given the third stipulation, the first conjunct of (26) cannot be represented in L and so we are not forced to count (26) as immediate.

On the other hand, the limitation on L's expressive power imposed by the third stipulation is harmless. For even though the proposition that David has no false beliefs cannot be represented in L under the interpretation presupposed above, still its truth-value at any given $(w,t) \in R$ is wholly determined by the valuations $V(S)$ for every t^* such that $(w,t^*) \in R$. Each proposition expressed by an English sentence of the form 'David believes that _____', where the blank is filled by a declarative sentence, is immediate. So even under the intended interpretation, L can express all truths about what David believes at (w,t). And the valuations $V(S)$ for (w,t) and all the other moments of w are sufficient to determine whether or not all of the beliefs that David has at (w,t) are true. Similar considerations hold for (16)–(20) and other propositions involving quantifiers that cannot be represented in L under the intended interpretation. Furthermore, even though a proposition like

(27) Every armadillo is vicious,

which is intuitively immediate and not troublesome in the way that the first conjunct of (26) is, turns out not to be immediate, still its truth or falsity at any given moment is completely dependent on the truth-values for that moment of the officially immediate propositions. Hence, nothing is lost by counting this proposition and others like it as non-immediate. Moreover, now that we have used our intended interpretation of L to isolate the set of immediate propositions, we can abandon this interpretation in favor of one under which L has the resources to represent any proposition.

We can now return to our main objective. Given the above account of immediacy, we can simply define the *submoment* for any (w,t) as the set of immediate formulas (or propositions) true at (w,t). (Below I will, for the sake of simplicity, speak of propositions rather than the formulas of L that represent them.)

In Section II of this paper I noted that the Ockhamist rejects (C) as a needlessly and unacceptably strong construal of the necessity of the past. The underlying reason for (C)'s inadequacy is that it presupposes the following "natural," though ultimately implausible, explication of what it is for two possible worlds to share the same history at a given time:

(D) w shares the same history with w^* at t iff for any $t^* < t$, both (a) $(w,t^*) \in R$ iff $(w^*,t^*) \in R$, and (b) for any proposition p, p is true at (w,t^*) iff p is true at (w^*,t^*).

(D) has as a consequence that if it is now a truth about the future that Katie will wash her car at t, then even before t it is part of our *history* that it has been the case that Katie will wash her car at t. The Ockhamist's opponents accept this consequence, but go on to deny that there are now any such (contingent) truths about the future.[14] The Ockhamist, by contrast, insists that the consequence itself should be rejected because it reflects outrageously inflated ideas of actuality and history. Instead, he offers the following alternative to (D):

(E) w shares the same 1˙story with w^* at t iff for any $t^* < t$, both (a) $(w,t^*) \in R$ iff $(w^*,t^*) \in R$, and (b) for any submoment k, k obtains at (w,t^*) iff k obtains at (w^*,t^*).

Though weaker than (D), (E) is clearly sufficient to capture the intuitive sense of the claim that w and w^* share the same *history* at t. For suppose that they do share at t the same history in the sense explicated by (E). It then follows, for instance, that all and only the individuals that exist in w before t also exist in w^* before t—and each has exactly the same life-story before t. Again, it follows that all and only the events which occur before t in w also occur before t in w^*—and each occurs at exactly the same time in each world. Moreover, it follows that w and w^* share all and only the same scientific laws at every time before t. Persons do exactly the same things at the same time, and have exactly the same things happen to them. The same political and social upheavals occur at exactly the same time in both worlds. In short, (E)—supported by the above explication of immediacy—seems to capture perfectly what philosophers or historians have in mind when they ask us to imagine a world "just like ours prior to t," or when they ask us to consider two worlds with "identical initial segments prior to t."

But, of course, from the fact that w and w^* share the same history at t in this sense it does not follow that they also share the same present and future at t—even if we accept the law of bivalence and reject the views of Prior and Geach. That is, it does not follow from (E), as it does from (D), that all and only the same future tense propositions true at a given moment t^*, before t, in w are also true at t^* in w^*. And so (E) provides us with the basis for an intuitively satisfying account of accidental necessity:

(F) p is necessary *per accidens* at (w,t) iff (a) p is logically contingent and (b) p is true at t and at every moment after t in every world w^* such that w^* shares the same history with w at t (in the sense explicated by (E)).

So, for instance, the past-tense proposition that Socrates drank hemlock is now necessary *per accidens*, since the immediate proposition that Socrates is drinking hemlock is a member of some submoment which has already obtained. It follows that this submoment also obtains at some moment before t in every possible world which shares the same history with our world at t, where t is the present moment. So in every such world the proposition that Socrates drank hemlock is true at t and at every moment after t.

On the other hand, suppose that it is now the case, long before t, that the future-tense proposition that Katie will wash her car at t has always been true. Since t has not yet occurred, the immediate proposition that Katie is washing her car at t has not yet been true and hence is not a member of any submoment that has already obtained. So there is a possible world w that shares the same history with our world at the present moment and yet is such that it is *never* true in w that Katie will wash her car at t. From this it follows that the past-tense proposition that it was the case that Katie will wash her car at t, though now true, is not necessary *per accidens* now or at any other moment before t. But this, as claimed above, is sufficient to defuse the argument for logical determinism.

IV

We can now see that the deterministic argument initially confounded us only because we could not immediately envision any plausible alternative to the construal of the necessity of the past embodied in (C) above. But at this point it should be clear that (C) was indeed the culprit, and so we are not forced to ingest the dubious remedies prescribed by Aristotle, Prior, and Geach in order to ward off the determinist. Rather, a careful articulation of our natural response to the argument, viz., that it is now true (before t) that it was the case that Katie will wash her car at t only because it will be true at t that Katie is washing her car, has yielded a more palatable solution.

We are also in a position now to appreciate the often ignored distinction between *per accidens* modality and causal modality. Suppose that w and w^* share the same history at a determinate moment t^*. And suppose that prior to t^* in w it is not only true but also causally necessary that Hurricane Xenophon will strike Key West at t^*. Does it follow that:

(28) It was the case that Xenephon will strike Key West at t^*

is necessary *per accidens* before t^* in w? Our previous discussion shows clearly that this does not follow. For even though w^* shares the same history with w at t^*, it is at least conceivable that the laws of nature change at t^* in w^*, or that God or some other supernatural agent intervene to save Key West at t^* in w^* by violating or suspending the relevant laws of nature. This suggests that the classical notion of a "future contingent" is insidiously ambiguous. In a weak sense p is a future contingent at t just in case *p* is future-tense and temporally contingent at *t*. In this sense (28) is a future contingent at *t**. But to be a future contingent in the stronger sense *p* must also be causally contingent at *t*. Yet while this stronger sense is dominant in the philosophical literature, only the weaker sense is, strictly speaking, relevant to the issues surrounding the debate over logical determinism. In fact, it is precisely my use of the weaker sense that distinguishes my notion of accidental necessity from Prior's notion of what is "now-unpreventable."[15] My contention, in its barest terms, is that Prior and others have conflated questions pertinent to the debate over logical determinism with questions pertinent to the debate over causal determinism. But this conflation prevents us from coming to a deeper understanding of the relation between the two debates. This is clearly illustrated by the fact that we can use the proposed account of *per accidens* modality to formulate a necessary condition on an agent's power which is both (a) the strongest condition on power that can emanate from the mere claim that the past is necessary and (b) perfectly neutral with respect to the debate over causal determinism:

(G) *S* has the power at (w,t) to bring it about that *p* is true only if for some world *w** such that *w** shares the same history with *w* at *t*, at (w^*,t) *S* brings it about that *p* is true.

We can then use (G) to formulate a corresponding condition for freedom. It should be clear that (G) expresses an extremely weak condition which is acceptable to both libertarians and compatibilists. The differences that separate these two groups surface only when we ask the further question of whether we can correctly add to (G) the condition that the causal laws shared by *w* and *w** just before *t* are also shared by them (with no violations) at *t*. Libertarians will insist that we can add this condition, while compatibilists will deny this. But regardless of how we resolve this issue, the neutrality of (G) at least enables us to see clearly what is often obfuscated, viz., exactly how it is possible to be a causal determinist without at the same time being a logical determinist. Interestingly, a moment's reflection also reveals that a causal determinist can avoid being a logical determinist only by espousing an Ockhamistic response to the argument for logical determinism. For the responses suggested by Aristotle, Prior, and Geach cannot even count as responses unless the truth-values of some future-tense propositions are not now fixed in the way demanded by a thoroughgoing causal determinism.

Finally, there are two further issues that would naturally be addressed here if it were not for lack of space. The first is whether my view commits me to the claim that we can have power over the past, specifically over those "future-infected" past-tense propositions that are neither necessary *per accidens* nor impossible *per accidens* at the present moment. In another paper I have argued that anyone who accepts an Ockhamistic account of accidental necessity should also accept the general thesis that an agent S has the power to bring it about that p is or will be true at t only if S has at the same time the power to bring it about that it has always been the case that p would be true at t.[16] However, this argument involves assumptions that are not integral to an Ockhamistic account of the necessity of the past, and so dissenters on this issue need not reject what I have said above.

Second, my account of the necessity of the past has obvious relevance to the still lively debate over the alleged incompatibility between divine foreknowledge and human freedom. Briefly, if God is, as is frequently held, essentially omniscient, then it can be argued persuasively, I believe, that every proposition attributing to God a belief about the future is nonimmediate and hence not a member of any submoment. Thus divine foreknowledge would pose no new problems for one who accepts my explication of accidental necessity. But, of course, this contention requires more elaborate support, which I hope to provide in another place.

CHAPTER NINE

Hard Facts and Theological Fatalism

William Hasker

It is sometimes thought that the distinction between hard and soft facts is needed only because of the problem of theological fatalism, but this is a mistake. Consider the following three propositions:

(1) If event E occurs at t_2, then "E will occur at t_2" is true at any previous time t_1.

(2) Some propositions about the future are such that it is now in someone's power to determine whether or not they are true.

(3) No propositions about the past are such that it is now in someone's power to determine whether or not they are true. (When I say that it is in someone's power to determine whether or not a proposition is true, I mean that, if it is true, it is in someone's power to bring it about that it is false, and if it is false, it is in someone's power to bring it about that it is true.)

Propositions (1) through (3) can easily seem to generate a contradiction. Suppose, for example, that John had a cup of tea for lunch. It follows, according to (1), that "John will have a cup of tea for lunch" was true at any arbitrarily chosen past time—for instance, it was true at 6:00 this morning. So now we have:

(4) It was true at 6:00 this morning that John would have a cup of tea for lunch.

Reprinted by permission from *Noûs*, 22 (1988): 419–36. My thanks to Gary Rosenkrantz and Joshua Hoffman for their extremely valuable comments on an earlier draft of this paper.

But from this it follows, according to (3), that

(5) It was not in anyone's power at 6:01 this morning to determine whether or not John would have a cup of tea for lunch.

And since the same reasoning can be followed for any time prior to lunch, and indeed for any arbitrarily chosen action or event, it follows that (2) is false; what is true instead is rather

(6) No proposition is ever such that it is in anyone's power to determine whether or not it is true.

This, of course, is the problem of logical determinism or fatalism, and it is clear what must be done to solve it: if one accepts both (1) and (3), then one must explicate the phrase "propositions about the past" in such a way that (4) does not qualify as being "about the past," so that the inference from (4) to (5) is blocked. That is to say, we need to be able to classify (4) as a "soft fact" about the past rather than as a "hard fact."

So the distinction between hard and soft facts is needed for the solution of the problem of logical fatalism. To be sure, this distinction may also be thought relevant to the problem of theological fatalism. But it needs to be appreciated that this is a further difficulty, not the same difficulty over again. To solve the problem of logical fatalism, it suffices that (4) be classified as a soft fact rather than a hard fact, but this is not enough to avoid theological fatalism, because philosophers concerned with theological fatalism typically accept not only (1)–(3) but also

(7) If event E occurs at t_2, then "God believes that E will occur at t_2" is true at any previous time t_1.

And from this, together with the fact that John has tea for lunch, it follows that

(8) God believed at 6:00 this morning that John would have a cup of tea for lunch.

And from this together with (3), it would seem to follow that

(9) It was not in anyone's power at 6:01 this morning to determine whether or not God believed at 6:00 this morning that John would have a cup of tea for lunch.

But, given that God is essentially infallible, God's having believed this at 6:00 entails John's drinking the cup of tea, so that

(9) entails (5). And by the process of generalization, we arrive once again at the fatalistic conclusion (6). So in order to avoid theological fatalism it is essential that not only (4) but also (8) be classified as soft facts.

Now this creates an interesting situation. The hard/soft fact distinction is being used to solve two separate problems: logical fatalism and theological fatalism. But there is no guarantee that it will be equally successful in resolving both of them. It is possible that the distinction may be adequate for avoiding logical fatalism, in that it classifies (4) as a soft fact and also classifies other relevant propositions in an intuitively plausible way, and yet it may fail for theological fatalism: it may turn out that (8) is after all a hard fact about the past. In fact, I shall argue that this is indeed the case, that *any adequate way of drawing the distinction between hard and soft facts will fail to solve the problem of theological fatalism*.

In trying to establish this rather sweeping conclusion, one is confronted with an obvious difficulty. The distinction between hard and soft facts has some intuitive plausibility, but the task of formulating the distinction in detail turns out to be surprisingly complex. No one way of doing this even comes close to being obviously right; in fact, several analyses have been proposed that differ in significant ways, and it is likely that still others may appear in the future. So how is it possible to justify a *general* claim (such as the one made above) stating what the consequences of *any* such distinction must be?

The difficulty is a genuine one, but I believe it can be circumvented. I shall begin by expounding two recent attempts to formulate the hard/soft fact distinction, and showing how these analyses attempt to resolve the problems of logical and theological fatalism. I then go on to give a counterargument showing that, contrary to their authors' intentions, these analyses fail to solve the problem of theological fatalism. Finally, I argue that this failure can be generalized—that the argument by which these particular analyses are shown to be unsuccessful against theological fatalism will apply to any others that may be presented.

Before launching into all this, however, it will be helpful to reflect a bit more about the underlying significance of the distinction between hard and soft facts. Just what difference is this distinction intended to capture? Examples such as (4) above suggest that it is the *pastness* of facts that makes them "hard"; we want to say that (4) is not "really about the past," and therefore that it is to be classified as a "soft fact" rather than as a "hard fact." Viewing the distinction in this light, we are inclined to see hard facts as those that are "about the past" in some particular way, and the purpose of our analysis will be to spell out this "pastness" in detail.

But the ultimate rationale for our interest in the hard/soft fact distinction may lead us in another direction. The reason for concerning ourselves with the distinction is at bottom the desire to avoid fatalism, as expressed in (6), whether that fatalism is engendered by purely logical considerations, such as (1), or by theological beliefs, such as (7). What we want is to establish the coherence with our other beliefs of the claim, expressed in (2), that there are some propositions which are such that it is or may be in someone's power to determine whether or not they are true. From this perspective, we might want to say that these propositions, the ones such that it may be in someone's power to determine whether or not they are true, are, if they are true, the soft facts. The hard facts, on the other hand, will be those true propositions such that it is not possible that it should be in anyone's power to bring it about that they are false.

Which of these two ways of understanding the hard/soft fact dichotomy is preferable? For our present purposes it is better not to decide between them; we may instead recognize two different dichotomies, marking the distinction by a difference in notation. So let us term "SOFT" and "HARD," respectively, those facts which are, and which are not, such that someone may now have the power to bring it about that they are false. The "hard" facts, on the other hand, will be those that are about the past in the requisite way, and the "soft" facts those that are not. And a "hard fact with respect to t" is one that is true at t and that after t is "about the past" in the way in question.

Now that we have the two dichotomies before us, some observations can be made about the relations between them. First of all, note that although all hard facts are HARD and all SOFT facts are soft, there will be HARD facts that are not hard and soft facts that are not SOFT. (For instance, the truths of logic are HARD but not hard.) In other words, a fact's being hard is a sufficient but not a necessary condition of its being HARD. And this is of importance as we consider the results of various analyses of the hard/soft fact distinction. If a fact is classified as soft according to a given analysis, it does not immediately follow that someone might have the power to bring it about that it is false. For there may be other considerations which determine that the fact is HARD, even though it is not about the past in the relevant way. Only when we have determined that a fact is soft *and also* that there are no other relevant considerations available in view of which it might be classified as HARD, can we with some confidence conclude that the fact is indeed SOFT.

The other point to be noted is this: the set of HARD facts, but not that of hard facts, is closed under entailment. The set of hard facts is not thus closed, because any hard fact will entail the tautologies of logic, none of which is a hard fact. But if we have two or more true propositions, each of which is such that it cannot possibly be in anyone's power to bring it about that it is false, then the conjunction of those propositions as well as their logical consequences are also such that it cannot be in anyone's power to bring it about that they are false. This is so in virtue of the following principle, which is itself a necessary truth:

(10) If "p" is true and entails "q," then if it is not in N's power to bring it about that "p" is false it is also not in N's power to bring it about that "q" is false.

This point will turn out to be of considerable importance in the ensuing discussion.

I

At this point we are ready to examine two proposals for the analysis of the hard/soft fact dichotomy. These proposals, advanced by Alfred J. Freddoso (Chapter 8 in this volume) and by Joshua Hoffman and Gary Rosenkrantz (Chapter 7 in this volume), are as careful and thorough as any that have appeared, and they have the additional advantage, for our purposes, that they differ considerably from each other.[1] In expounding these proposals I shall make rather free use of paraphrase, and I will omit some technicalities that are not essential to our present concerns, but I think the result will faithfully represent the authors' intentions. We begin with Freddoso.

Freddoso does not use the terminology of hard and soft facts, preferring to borrow from Ockham the term "necessity *per accidens*" or "accidental necessity." Accidentally necessary propositions are, roughly, those logically contingent propositions that are true in any possible world that *shares the same history* with the actual world up to the present moment. But what is it that qualifies a proposition as "part of our history"? In answering this, Freddoso singles out a class of "immediate" propositions that, for any given moment of time, "determine what is 'really occurring' at that moment and what will become part of our history after that moment" (p. 146). We arrive at these immediate propositions in the following way:[2]

(AF1) We single out the class of present-tense propositions that are "atomic" in the sense that they are not quantifications, truth-functions, or in some other way logically complex. (The atomic propositions do, however, include those that state propositional attitudes, such as "David believes that Katie will at some time be in Rome" [pp. 149–50].)

(AF2) Among the atomic propositions we further single out those that are "temporally indifferent," meaning that the present truth or falsity of such a proposition "is indifferent both to the question of whether there are any past moments and to the question of whether there are any future moments" [p. 151].

(AF3) All atomic propositions that are temporally indifferent are *immediate*, as are all truth-functional compounds formed from these propositions [pp. 148–53].

Freddoso points out that by these criteria no quantified propositions will count as immediate, even though it would seem intuitively that some such propositions ought to be immediate. ("Every armadillo is vicious" is his example.) But he thinks this is harmless, since such a proposition's "truth or falsity at any given moment is completely dependent on the truth-values for that moment of the officially immediate propositions" (pp. 153–54).

Freddoso goes on to explain how it is that immediate propositions are "part of our history":

(AF4) For any possible world w and time t, we define the *submoment* as the set of immediate propositions true at (w,t) [p. 154].

(AF5) The *history* of a possible world w at time t then consists of the complete set of submoments of that world prior to t, and any two worlds *share the same history* at t if and only if they have the same submoments for all times prior to t [p. 154].

Freddoso claims that this explication "seems to capture perfectly what philosophers or historians have in mind when they ask us to imagine a world 'just like ours prior to *t'*, or when they ask us to consider two worlds with 'identical initial segments prior to *t'''* (p. 155). And now we are ready for the notion of necessity *per accidens*:

(AF6) A proposition is necessary *per accidens* at (*w*,*t*) just in case the proposition is contingent and is true at *t* and forever after in all worlds that share the same history with *w* at *t* [p. 155].

The notion of a proposition that is necessary *per accidens* is, then, Freddoso's reconstruction of our notion of a hard fact; he notes that "when we limit the consequents to logically contingent propositions, then accidental necessity . . . is closed under entailment" (p. 139). When we add to the set of such propositions all those that are logically necessary, we have the set of HARD facts.

It remains to show how Freddoso's analysis deals with logical and theological fatalism. It follows from this analysis that

(11) John is drinking a cup of tea

is an immediate proposition, and if it is true then its past-tense counterpart will be part of the history of our world from now on. But

(12) It is now true that John will drink a cup of tea

cannot be immediate, because it is not temporally indifferent; it could not be true if this were the last moment of time. So the past-tense counterpart of (12) does not become part of our history, the inference from (4) to (5) is blocked, and logical fatalism is averted. But now consider

(13) God now believes that John will drink a cup of tea.

Freddoso states, "if God is, as is frequently held, essentially omniscient, then it can be argued persuasively, I believe, that every proposition attributing to God a belief about the future is non-immediate and hence not a member of any submoment" (p. 158). And this seems true enough: If God is essentially omniscient, (13) cannot be true unless John actually drinks the tea, so (13) no more than (12) could be true at the last moment of time. Freddoso concludes, "Thus divine foreknowledge would pose no new problems for one who accepts my explication of accidental necessity."[3]

The other proposed analysis of the hard/soft fact distinction to be considered comes from Joshua Hoffman and Gary Rosenkrantz. Like Freddoso, they proceed by identifying, for any given moment in time, a special set of propositions (or, as they prefer to say, of states of affairs) that determine what is "really happening" at that moment; but their way of going about this differs considerably from Freddoso's. Once again, we proceed in a series of steps:

(HR1) We begin by identifying a set of states of affairs that are *present tense*;[4] examples are *Jones walks*, *Jones is seated*, and *Smith believes that Jones will walk*. The sentences expressing these states of affairs contain no expression for tense except for the present tense (unless, as in the third example, within the scope of a verb of psychological attitude) [pp. 128–29].

(HR2) We next identify, within the set of present-tense states of affairs, the class of states of affairs that are *unrestrictedly repeatable*. An unrestrictedly repeatable state of affairs is one that "may obtain, then fail to obtain, then obtain again, indefinitely many times *throughout all of time*." So we now have the set of *unrestrictedly repeatable present-tense* (*URP*) states of affairs [pp. 127–28].

(HR3) When one state of affairs is indexed to a time to form another state of affairs (e.g., *Socrates walks at t_1*) then the former state of affairs (*Socrates walks*) is a *kernel* state of affairs. A *URP kernel* state of affairs is one that is either a simple (atomic) *URP* state of affairs or a complex state of affairs that is itself *URP* and all of whose parts are *URP* [p. 129].[5]

A certain difficulty of understanding presents itself here. Hoffman and Rosenkrantz state that a complex state of affairs may be constructed "by use of the logical apparatus of first-order quantification theory enriched with whatever modalities one chooses to employ" (pp. 129–30). But all of the examples they give are truth-functional compounds of atomic *URP* states of affairs—e.g., *Socrates is wise and Socrates is ugly*. This leaves us somewhat in the dark with regard to what the more complicated sorts of complex kernel states of affairs might look like. This difficulty is, however, not crucial; for our purposes it is sufficient to consider those complex states of affairs that are truth-functional compounds.

And now we are ready for hard facts:

(HR4) A state of affairs *r* is *hard fact about a time t* if and only if (a) *r* is the state of affairs *s at* (*in*) *t*; (b) *s* obtains throughout (all or some part of)

t; (c) s is a *URP* kernel state of affairs; (d) neither r nor s nor any of s's parts entails a *URP* kernel state of affairs indexed to any time that does not overlap with t; and (e) t is a past time [see p. 129].

Several comments are in order here. First, note that t may be either a moment of time or an interval; this allows the hard facts to include states of affairs that require a period of time in order to occur. Freddoso's immediate propositions, on the other hand, must be those that can be true at a moment of time. (Note that the expression "in t," under (a), is meant to apply in cases in which s obtains only through part of t.)

Note also that condition (d) provides some insight into the reason for the focus on *URP* states of affairs. Consider, for example, the state of affairs *Socrates walks at t_1*. Intuitively, once t_1 has passed this should be a hard fact about t_1, but it does entail a fact about a later time t_2, namely the state of affairs, $\sim$(*Socrates walks for the first time*) *at t_2*. But the kernel of the entailed state of affairs, $\sim$(*Socrates walks for the first time*), is not *UR*. "It may obtain (because Socrates has never walked), then fail to obtain (because Socrates takes his first walk), and then obtain again (he stops walking), but then it must obtain forever after" (p. 131). So our intuition that *Socrates walks at t_1* ought to be a hard fact is vindicated. Hoffman and Rosenkrantz remark, "Thus on our view it is not enough merely for a state of affairs about a time t to entail a state of affairs about a later time to prevent it from being a hard fact; it must entail the right sort of state of affairs" (p. 131).

Finally, it should be noted that this analysis, unlike Freddoso's, does not contain any provision whereby a *past-tense* state of affairs can qualify as a hard fact. And this has some peculiar consequences; it means, for instance, that *Columbus walked in 1492* is *not* a hard fact about 1492 even though *Columbus walks in 1492* *is* a hard fact about 1492. About this Hoffman and Rosenkrantz say several things:

Our approach here is nominally to deny hard fact status to the past-tense fact so that a cogent analysis of the hard fact/soft fact distinction can be formulated. Since we do not claim that all soft facts are such that we can act so that they would never have occurred at all, no vital intuitions are offended by our drawing the distinction where we do draw it. Furthermore, there is a sense in which the past-tense state of affairs, *Columbus walked in 1492*, is not an ontologically fundamental or basic fact. Rather, it is logically dependent on a more fundamental state of affairs, namely, the corresponding present-tense or tenseless kernel state of affairs indexed to t, which *is* a hard fact about t. In other words, it is only true that Columbus walked in 1492 because it is true that in 1492 Columbus walks. . . . All that ever really contingently happens are *URP* states of affairs [pp. 134–35].

Assuming that this analysis has been sufficiently clarified, we again turn to the issue of fatalism. First, consider the state of affairs

(14) *John drinks a cup of tea at t_1.*

The kernel state of affairs here is *URP*, and neither (14) nor its kernel entails a *URP* state of affairs indexed to a time other than t_1, so (14) will be a hard fact about t_1. But now consider

(15) *(John drinks a cup of tea at t_2) obtains at t_1. ($t_1 < t_2$)*

This cannot be a hard fact, for two reasons. The kernel of (15) is *John drinks a cup of tea at t_2*. But this state of affairs is not *UR*; it is rather an *eternal* state of affairs, one such that, if it obtains at all, it obtains for all of time. Furthermore, (15) entails a *URP* state of affairs indexed to a time other than t_1, namely *John drinks a cup of tea at t_2*. So (15) is not a hard fact, and logical fatalism is defeated. But now we must consider

(16) *(God believes that John drinks a cup of tea at t_2) at t_1.*

This also cannot be a hard fact, for reasons that parallel those given above. The kernel state of affairs is not *UR* but rather timeless, the reason in this case being that God, who is essentially omniscient, cannot change his mind about the truth of "John drinks a cup of tea at t_2." Furthermore (16), like (15), entails a *URP* state of affairs indexed to a time other than t_1, namely *John drinks a cup of tea at t_2*. So (16) is not a hard fact, and theological fatalism is undermined.

II

The two analyses we have examined seem to me to be admirable both in their conception and in their execution, carried out in each case with a degree of formal rigor that is only partially suggested by my summaries. The two analyses are, so far as I can see, equally successful in resolving the problem of logical fatalism. And I am able to agree with Freddoso that (13) is not an immediate proposition, and with Hoffman and Rosenkrantz that (16) is not a hard fact. Nevertheless, the problem of theological fatalism is not resolved. But before I explain the reason for this, it is necessary to discuss the notion of entailment.

Both the Freddoso and Hoffman-Rosenkrantz analyses use the notion of entailment (or the interdefinable notion of logical consistency) in explicating the idea of a hard fact (see (AF2) and (HR4)). But there are at least two different concepts of entailment that could apply here, and the difference between them is important. In either case, "*p*" entails "*q*" if and only if it is necessarily true that, if *p*, then *q*. The two concepts of entailment differ, however, with respect to the concept of necessity that is involved. The narrower view of entailment interprets "necessarily" in the formula given to mean *conceptual necessity*, where a proposition is conceptually necessary if and only if it is true in virtue of the meanings of the terms in which it is expressed. The truth of a conceptually necessary proposition, then, is determined by the laws of logic together with the meanings of the non-logical terms employed in stating the proposition. Let us call entailment in this narrower sense *conceptual entailment*.

In the second, broader view of entailment, "*p*" entails "*q*" just in case the conditional "if *p*, then *q*" is *metaphysically necessary*, true in all possible worlds. Let us term this *metaphysical entailment*. The two concepts of entailment diverge when we are dealing with certain propositions concerning essential properties both of natural kinds and of individual entities. Take Kripke's example: "This table is not made of ice." [6] Clearly, this statement is not analytic or conceptually necessary; no amount of skill at logic and conceptual analysis will enable us to recognize its truth. But if it *is* true, Kripke says (and I agree) that it is necessarily true; in no possible world does *this table* exist made of ice. [7] The statement is metaphysically necessary but not conceptually necessary.

Now that we have these two concepts of entailment before us, which should be applied to the matter in hand? Neither of the articles we are considering is explicit on this point. [8] I believe, however, that we shall do best to interpret entailment (and consistency) in this context in terms of conceptual necessity, rather than the broader metaphysical necessity. The reason for this can be briefly stated here, though the justification of the reason depends on the rest of this essay. I claim that, by using the notion of conceptual entailment, we can arrive at a distinction between hard and soft facts that solves the problem of logical fatalism, though (as I shall argue) it fails to resolve the issue of theological fatalism. If, on the other hand, we employ the notion of metaphysical entailment, the distinction between hard and soft facts does not even solve the problem of logical fatalism; indeed, it collapses altogether. Accordingly, I shall use the notion of conceptual entailment throughout the remainder of the present section; the implications of adopting metaphysical entailment will be considered in the following section.

And now for the argument. The proposition

(17) Mary believed at 6:00 this morning that John would have a cup of tea for lunch

is a hard fact about 6:00 on both the Freddoso and Hoffman-Rosenkrantz analyses, whereas

(8) God believed at 6:00 this morning that John would have a cup of tea for lunch

is not. (I shall from now on write in the language of propositions, usually leaving it to the reader to translate into the idiom of states of affairs.) But the only difference between them is that in (8) "Mary" is replaced by "God." And the reason why this makes a difference is that the word "God" *expresses our concept of God*, a concept that includes the attribute of *essential infallibility*, so that in no possible world does God hold a false belief. It is this that prevents a statement about God's beliefs from being immediate (Freddoso) or from expressing a hard fact (Hoffman and Rosenkrantz).

But consider the name "Yahweh," which was used by the ancient Hebrews to refer to their God. They used this name (as a reading of Genesis will confirm) with no thought or connotation of such metaphysical attributes as essential omniscience, essential everlastingness, and the like. For a variety of reasons, this name for the deity is not in common use among present-day Christians or Jews, but nothing prevents us from reviving its use for a special purpose. And as we do so we will take care to avoid importing into the name's significance such metaphysical notions as essential everlastingness and essential infallibility. We will use the name, as the ancient Hebrews did, simply as a non-connotative proper name referring to that individual who in fact was, and is, the God of Abraham, Isaac, and Jacob.

Understood in this way,

(18) Yahweh believes that John will have a cup of tea for lunch

is, in Freddoso's sense, an immediate proposition, and if it is true at 6:00 then at any subsequent time

(19) Yahweh believed at 6:00 on (today's date) that John would have a cup of tea for lunch

is accidentally necessary; it is part of the history of our world. For neither (18) nor (19) entails anything about what happens at times other than 6:00. Similarly,

(20) *(Yahweh believes that John will have a cup of tea for lunch) at 6:00*

will be a hard fact about 6:00 on the Hoffman-Rosenkrantz analysis; it has a *URP* kernel, and entails no *URP* kernel indexed to any time other than 6:00.

To be sure, this does not yet give us theological fatalism. But now consider

(21) If Yahweh exists, Yahweh is God.

Given our stipulation about the name "Yahweh," (21) is not a conceptually necessary truth; its truth does not follow from the meaning of the terms in which it is expressed. But it is a metaphysically necessary truth: it expresses an *essential property* of Yahweh, so that in no possible world does Yahweh exist without being God. It is not possible that anyone, not even God himself and certainly no human being, should bring it about that Yahweh exists and is not God. (21) is a HARD fact *par excellence*.

But since (19) and (21) are both HARD facts, so is the proposition they jointly entail, namely

(8) God believed at 6:00 this morning that John would have a cup of tea for lunch.

And although "God now believes that John will have a cup of tea for lunch" is not an immediate proposition, (8) is all the same accidentally necessary, since it is jointly entailed by an accidentally necessary proposition and a necessary truth. Similarly, (20) together with (21) jointly entail

(22) (*God believes that John will have a cup of tea for lunch*) *at 6:00*.

(22) still does not qualify as a hard fact on the Hoffman-Rosenkrantz analysis, but that is of no help: they admit that some soft facts are not "such that we can act so that they would never have occurred," and (contrary to their expectation) (22) turns out to be such a fact—entailed by the conjunction of two HARD facts, it is itself as HARD as can be. So theological fatalism is triumphant.[9]

But now we can easily see that the argument presented in this section is general, and can be applied to any analysis of the hard/soft fact distinction that is otherwise acceptable. We have seen that, on both the Freddoso and Hoffman-Rosenkrantz analyses,

(17) Mary believed at 6:00 this morning that John would have a cup of tea for lunch

is a hard fact about 6:00. But this must be so also on any other analysis of the distinction that makes any pretension to being adequate. As Freddoso says,

[T]he past hopes, fears, beliefs, desires, predictions, etc., of historical agents are clearly unalterable elements of our past and must be counted as part of our history. . . . No world *w* can claim to share the same history with our world now if in *w* Chamberlain did not fear that Hitler would not keep his word, or if in *w* Ernie Banks did not hope (and predict) every spring that the Cubs would win the pennant [p. 147].

So any adequate analysis must classify (17) as a hard fact. But the only difference between (17) and (8) lies in the replacement of "Mary" with "God." If however we employ the name "Yahweh" instead of "God," as was done in the preceding argument, we produce the proposition

(19) Yahweh believed at 6:00 on (today's date) that John would have a cup of tea for lunch

which is similar to (17) in all logically relevant respects, and must like (17) be classified as a hard fact. And given this, theological fatalism cannot be avoided. The truth of the matter is that the triad consisting of (2), (3), and (7) simply *is* inconsistent, and if (2) is to be retained one must give up either (3) or (7).

III

I know of only one serious objection to the argument presented in Section II, and the remainder of this paper will be devoted to it. The objection comes in two distinct forms, of which the first might be expressed as follows: "You claim that by replacing 'God' in (8) with 'Yahweh' you have removed the implication of essential infallibility, so that (19) qualifies as a hard fact. But this simply will not work. Proper names, including 'Yahweh', express *essences* of their bearers and entail all of the bearers' essential properties. So you cannot get rid of essential infallibility, and (19) is not a hard fact."

It is not necessary to spend too much time on this version of the objection. The doctrine that proper names express essences seems to be one that involves considerable difficulties and has few good arguments in its favor.[10] But even if it were correct, the argument of the previous section could still go through in a slightly altered form. Instead of replacing "God" with "Yahweh," we could replace it with a pronoun or a demonstrative; perhaps something like

(23) *That one* believed at 6:00 this morning that John would have a cup of tea for lunch

where *"that one"* is accompanied by a gesture toward the heavens to indicate who it is that is being talked about. I do not know that anyone has claimed that pronouns and demonstratives entail the essential properties of their referents, and the claim would have bizarre consequences: it would entail, for instance, that the question "What's *that*?" (asked about a noise in the dark) already expresses its own answer! To be sure, along with (23) we will also need

(24) The being mentioned in (23), if it exists, is God.

And in spite of its unpromising appearance, this proposition also, like (21) is a metaphysically necessary truth; it expresses an *essential property* of the being in question, who is now being viewed more as the Unknown God than as the God of Abraham, Isaac, and Jacob. So (8) is after all a HARD fact, and theological fatalism is still viable.

The second version of the objection is more formidable, and

may be stated as follows: "All right, have it your own way about the name 'Yahweh'; that does not really matter. For whatever is or is not expressed by the *name* 'Yahweh', you are forced to admit that infallibility is an essential property *of Yahweh himself*. As you yourself admit, there is no possible world in which Yahweh holds a false belief, no possible world in which he believes John will drink that tea but the tea is not drunk. So (19) *does* entail a fact about a time other than 6:00, and it cannot be a hard fact. It does no good at all first to pretend to forget this, as you do in order to classify (19) as hard, and then suddenly to remember it in order to derive (8) from (19)."

The objector here is criticizing my way of applying the hard/soft fact distinction. She embraces the metaphysical conception of entailment (discussed in Section II above) and maintains that

(A) If in stating a proposition an individual is referred to by a rigid designator, all essential properties of that individual must be considered in classifying the proposition as a hard or soft fact.

I agree that if (A) is followed then neither (19) nor (23) will qualify as a hard fact. But I reject (A), insisting instead that

(B) In classifying a proposition as a hard or a soft fact, only such essential properties of individuals are to be considered as are expressed in stating the proposition.

How is this disagreement to be adjudicated? I shall show that (B) must be followed rather than (A) by showing that if (A) is accepted the whole distinction between hard and soft facts will collapse, leaving few if any hard facts behind. In particular, if (A) is accepted then

(25) John drank a cup of tea for lunch today,

which ought to be a hard fact if there are any hard facts, will turn out to be soft.

Admittedly it is not easy to establish this point in its full generality, because of the wide variety of theoretical approaches that would need to be considered. There are not only the various ways of analyzing the hard/soft fact distinction, but also a variety of views about what kinds of essential properties are had by various types of entities. In the face of this variety, the best I am able to do is to give some examples of the way in which the acceptance of (A) would undermine the hard/soft fact distinction. But I think the examples will prove striking enough to render my general claim extremely plausible.

What essential properties does John possess? We are to assume that John is a mature human being, who was born in the normal way to human parents. If so, then I would maintain that his having come into existence in this way, his having the very parents that he in fact has, and indeed his originating from a particular pair of male and female reproductive cells, are all among John's essential properties. The view that this is so is not of course uncontroversial, but it is both inherently plausible and fairly widely accepted. If this is so, then

(11) John is drinking a cup of tea

will, according to (A), entail a whole host of propositions about times other than the present; it will not be temporally independent or immediate, nor will its corresponding state of affairs qualify as the kernel of a hard fact.

Other examples follow more directly from theological considerations. If theism is true, it is extremely plausible to suppose that each non-divine contingent entity has essentially the property, *being created by God*. If John has this property essentially then John's existence entails God's existence and, since God is essentially everlasting, this alone disqualifies (11) from being temporally independent or immediate: it is not logically possible that (11) be true at the first or last moment of time, because it is not logically possible that both God exists and there *is* a first or last moment of time.

The particular example, however, is effective only against the Freddoso analysis and not against Hoffman and Rosenkrantz. For as they say, "on our view it is not enough merely for a state of affairs about a time *t* to entail a state of affairs about a later time to prevent it from being a hard fact; it must entail the right sort of state of affairs" (p. 131). And although

(14) *John drinks a cup of tea at t_1*

metaphysically entails

(26) *God exists at t_2,*

this does not disqualify (14) from being a hard fact, for the kernel of (26) is not *URP* but rather eternal. To be sure, (26) is not the only fact about God at t_2 that is entailed by (14); it also entails

(27) (*God believes that John drinks a cup of tea at* t_1) *at* t_2

as well as

(28) (*God remembers that John drank a cup of tea at* t_1) *at* t_2.

But neither of these will do the job; the kernel of (27) is eternal, and though the kernel of (28) is not eternal neither is it *UR*, since it begins to obtain at t_1 and continues forever after. But now consider

(29) (*God believes that John drank a cup of tea exactly n time-units ago*) *at* t_2
      (where n time-units = the exact time between t_1 and t_2).

The kernel of (29) is not eternal, like that of (27), nor is it like the kernel of (28) in obtaining forever once it has begun to obtain. The kernel of (29) obtains at those times, and only at those times, that are exactly n time-units subsequent to a time at which John was drinking tea—and since John's drinking is *UR*, so is God's believing this. So the kernel of (29) is a *URP* kernel, and (14), since it entails (29), cannot be a hard fact.

I trust that the lesson in all this is clear. In determining whether a proposition is a hard fact, is temporally independent, or is *URP*, we must consider what is derivable, by appropriate logical techniques, *from that proposition* and exclude from consideration essential properties that are not represented or implied in the proposition. Violating this restriction leads, as we have seen, to the general collapse of the distinction between hard and soft facts. But even apart from this, the restriction is intuitively plausible. If some agent has performed an action or if some event has occurred at some past time, then that action or event is finished and must be counted, as Freddoso says, as part of our history. Whatever essential properties may belong to an agent or other entity was also determined in the past, either eternally or when that agent or entity came into existence. There is, I suggest, very little intuitive plausibility in the idea that, because of its essential properties, the past actions or events involving an entity are somehow not really past, not really part of our history. This, however, was the basis for the defense against theological fatalism based on the distinction between hard and soft facts. But if essential properties are to be used in this way in reasoning about God's (or Yahweh's) past beliefs, the same approach must be applied to all other agents and entities—and this, as we have seen, leads to the collapse of the entire enterprise. The distinction between hard and soft facts cannot solve the problem of theological fatalism.

CHAPTER TEN

On Ockham's Way Out

Alvin Plantinga

Two essential teachings of Western theistic religions—Christianity, Judaism, and Islam—are that God is omniscient and that human beings are morally responsible for at least some of their actions. The first apparently implies that God has knowledge of the future and thus has foreknowledge of human actions; the second, that some human actions are *free*. But divine foreknowledge and human freedom, as every twelve-year-old Sunday school student knows, can seem to be incompatible; and at least since the fifth century A.D. philosophers and theologians have pondered the question whether these two doctrines really do conflict. There are, I think, substantially two lines of argument for the *incompatibility thesis*—the claim that these doctrines are indeed in conflict; one of these arguments is pretty clearly fallacious, but the other is much more impressive. In Part I, I state these two arguments; in Part II, I explain (and endorse) Ockham's reply to them; in Part III, I point out some startling implications of Ockham's way out; and finally in Part IV, I offer an account of accidental necessity. There is also an appendix on possible worlds explanations of ability.

Reprinted from *Faith and Philosophy*, 3 (1986): 235–69, by permission of the editors. I am especially grateful to Edward Wierenga for penetrating comments on an ancestor of this paper. I am grateful for similar favors to many others, including Lawrence Powers, Alfred Freddoso, Mark Heller, Peter van Inwagen, William Alston, David Vriend, the members of the Calvin College Tuesday Colloquium, and especially Nelson Pike.

I. Foreknowledge and the Necessity of the Past

In *De Libero Arbitrio* Augustine puts the first line of argument in the mouth of Evodius:

That being so, I have a deep desire to know how it can be that God knows all things beforehand and that, nevertheless, we do not sin by necessity. Whoever says that anything can happen otherwise than as God has foreknown it, is attempting to destroy the divine foreknowledge with the most insensate impiety. If God foreknew that the first man would sin—and that anyone must concede who acknowledges with me that God has foreknowledge of all future events—I do not say that God did not make him, for he made good, nor that the sin of the creature whom he made good could be prejudicial to God. On the contrary, God showed his goodness in making man, his justice in punishing his sin, and his mercy in delivering him. I do not say, therefore, that God did not make man. But this I say. Since God foreknew that man would sin, that which God foreknew must necessarily come to pass. How then is the will free when there is apparently this unavoidable necessity?[1]

(Replies Augustine: "You have knocked vigorously.") Evodius's statement of the argument illustrates one parameter of the problem: the conception of freedom in question is such that a person S is free with respect to an action A only if (1) it is within S's power to perform A and within his power to refrain from performing A, and (2) no collection of necessary truths and causal laws—causal laws outside S's control—together with antecedent conditions outside S's control entails that S performs A, and none entails that he refrains from doing so. (I believe that the first of these conditions entails the second, but shall not argue that point here.) Of course if these conditions are rejected, then the alleged problem dissolves.

The essential portion of Evodius's argument may perhaps be put as follows:

(1) If God knows in advance that S will do A, then it must be the case that S will do A.
(2) If it *must* be the case that S will do A, then it is not within the power of S to refrain from doing A.
(3) If it is not within the power of S to refrain from doing A, then S is not free with respect to A.

Hence

(4) If God knows in advance that *S* will do *A*, then *S* is not free with respect to *A*.

Augustine apparently found this argument perplexing. In some passages he seems to see its proper resolution; but elsewhere he reluctantly accepts it and half-heartedly endorses a compatibilist account of freedom according to which it is possible both that all of a person's actions be determined and that some of them be free.

Thomas Aquinas, however, saw the argument for the snare and delusion that it is:

If each thing is known by God as seen by Him in the present, what is known by God will then have to be. Thus, it is necessary that Socrates be seated from the fact that he is seen seated. But this is not absolutely necessary or, as some say, with the *necessity of the consequent*; it is necessary conditionally, or with the *necessity of the consequence*. For this is a necessary conditional proposition: *if he is seen sitting, he is sitting*.[2]

Aquinas's point may perhaps be put more perspicuously as follows. (1) is ambiguous as between

(1a) Necessarily, if God knows in advance that *S* will do *A*, then *S* will do *A*

and

(1b) If God knows in advance that *S* will do *A*, then it is necessary that *S* will do *A*.

Now consider

(1c) If God knows in advance that *S* will do *A*, then *S* will do *A*.

(1a), says Aquinas, is a true proposition expressing "the necessity of the consequence"; what it says, sensibly enough, is just that the consequent of (1c) follows with necessity from its antecedent. (1b), on the other hand, is an expression of the necessity of the *consequent*; what *it* says, implausibly, is that the necessity of the consequent of (1c) follows from its antecedent. Aquinas means to point out that (1a) is clearly true but of no use to the argument. (1b), on the other hand, is what the argument requires; but it seems flatly false—or, more modestly, there seems not the slightest reason to endorse it.

If the above argument is unconvincing, there is another, much more powerful, that is also considered by Aquinas.[3] The argument in question has been discussed by a host of philosophers both before and after Aquinas; it received a particularly perspicuous formulation at the hands of Jonathan Edwards:

1. I observed before, in explaining the nature of necessity, that in things which are past, their past existence is now necessary: having already made sure of existence, 'tis now impossible, that it should be otherwise than true, that that thing has existed.

2. If there be any such thing as a divine foreknowledge of the volitions of free agents, that foreknowledge, by the supposition, is a thing which already has, and long ago had existence; and so, now its existence is necessary; it is now utterly impossible to be otherwise, than that this foreknowledge should be, or should have been.

3. 'Tis also very manifest, that those things which are indissolubly connected with other things that are necessary, are themselves necessary. As that proposition whose truth is necessarily connected with another proposition, which is necessarily true, is itself necessarily true. To say otherwise, would be a contradiction; it would be in effect to say, that the connection was indissoluble, and yet was *not so*, but might be broken. If that, whose existence is indissolubly connected with something whose existence is now necessary, is itself not necessary, then it may possibly not exist, notwithstanding that indissoluble connection of its existence.—Whether the absurdity ben't glaring, let the reader judge.

4. 'Tis no less evident, that if there be a full, certain and infallible foreknowledge of the future existence of the volitions of moral agents, then there is a certain infallible and indissoluble connection between those events and that foreknowledge; and that therefore, by the preceding observations, those events are necessary events; being infallibly and indissolubly connected with that whose existence already is, and so is now necessary, and can't but have been.[4]

Edwards concludes that since "God has a certain and infallible prescience of the acts and wills of moral agents," it follows that "these events are necessary" with the same sort of necessity enjoyed by what is now past.

The argument essentially appeals to two intuitions. First, although the past is not necessary in the broadly logical sense (it is possible, in that sense, that Abraham should never have existed), it *is* necessary in *some* sense; it is fixed, unalterable, outside anyone's control. And second, whatever is "necessarily connected" with what is necessary in some sense, is itself necessary in that sense; if a proposition *A*, necessary in the way in which the past is necessary, entails a proposition *B*, then *B* is necessary in that same way. If Edwards's argument is a good one, what it shows is that if at some time in the past God knew that I will do *A*, then it is necessary that I will do *A*—necessary in just the way in which the past is necessary. But then it is not within my power to refrain from doing *A*, so that I will not do *A* freely. So, says Edwards, suppose God knew, eighty years ago, that I will mow my lawn this afternoon. This foreknowledge is, as he says, a "thing that is past." Such things, however, are now necessary; "'tis now impossible, that it should be otherwise than true, that that thing has existed." So it is now necessary that God had that knowledge eighty years ago; but it is also *logically* necessary that if God knew that I will mow my lawn today, then I will mow my lawn today. It is therefore now necessary that I will mow; it is thus not within my power to refrain from mowing; hence though I will indeed mow, I will not mow freely.

Edwards's argument is for what we might call "theological determinism"; the premise is that God has foreknowledge of the "acts and wills of moral agents" and the conclusion is that these acts are necessary in just the way the past is. Clearly enough the argument can be transformed into an argument for *logical* determinism, which would run as follows. It was true, eighty years ago, that I will mow my lawn this afternoon. Since what is past is now necessary, it is now necessary that it was true eighty years ago that I will mow my lawn today. But it is logically necessary that if it was true eighty years ago that I will mow my lawn today, then I will mow my lawn today. It is therefore necessary that I will mow my lawn—necessary in just the sense in which the past is necessary. But then it is not within my power not to mow; hence I will not mow freely.

Here a Boethian bystander might object as follows. Edwards's argument involves a divine *fore*knowledge—God's having known at some time in the past, for example, that Paul will mow his lawn in 1995. Many theists, however, hold that God is *eternal*,[5] and that his eternity involves at least the following two properties. First, his being eternal means, as Boethius suggested, that everything is *present* for him; for him there is no past or future. But then God does not know any such propositions as *Paul will mow in 1995*; what he knows, since everything is present for him, is just that Paul mows in 1995. And secondly, God's being eternal means that God is atemporal, "outside of time"—outside of time in such a way that it is an error to say of him that he knows some proposition or other *at a time*. We thus cannot properly say that God *now* knows that Paul mows in 1995, or that at some time in the past God knew this; the truth, instead, is that he knows this proposition *eternally*. But then Edwards's argument presupposes the falsehood of a widely accepted thesis about the nature of God and time.

I am inclined to believe that this thesis—the thesis that God is both atemporal and such that everything is present for him—is incoherent. If it *is* coherent, however, Edwards's argument can be restated in such a way as not to presuppose its falsehood. For suppose in fact Paul will mow his lawn in 1995. Then the proposition *God (eternally) knows that Paul mows in 1995* is now true. That proposition, furthermore, was true eighty years ago; the proposition *God knows (eternally) that Paul mows in 1995* not only *is* true *now*, but *was* true *then*. Since what is past is necessary, it is now necessary that this proposition was true eighty years ago. But it is logically necessary that if this proposition was true eighty years ago, then Paul mows in 1995. Hence his mowing then is necessary in just the way the past is. But, then it neither now is nor in future will be within Paul's power to refrain from mowing.

Of course this argument depends on the claim that a proposition can be true *at a time*—eighty years ago, for example. Some philosophers argue that it does not so much as make sense to suggest that a proposition *A* is or was or will be true at a time; a proposition is true or false *simpliciter* and no more true at a time than, for example, true in a mail box or a refrigerator.[6] (Even if there is no beer in the refrigerator, the proposition *there is no beer* is not true in the refrigerator.) We need not share their scruples in order to accommodate them; the argument can be suitably modified. Concede for the moment that it makes no sense to say of a *proposition* that it was true at a time; it nonetheless makes good sense, obviously, to say of a sentence that it expressed a certain proposition at a time. But it also makes good sense to say of a sentence that it expressed a truth at a time. Now eighty years ago the sentence

(5) God knows (eternally) that Paul mows in 1995

expressed the proposition that God knows eternally that Paul mows in 1995 (and for simplicity let us suppose that proposition was the only proposition it expressed then). But if in fact Paul will mow in 1995, then (5) also expressed a truth eighty years ago. So eighty years ago (5) expressed the proposition that Paul will mow in 1995 and expressed a truth; since what is past is now necessary, it is now necessary that eighty years ago (5) expressed that proposition and expressed a truth. But it is necessary in the broadly logical sense that if (5) then expressed that proposition (and only that proposition) and expressed a truth, then Paul will mow in 1995. It is therefore necessary that Paul will mow then; hence his mowing then is necessary in just the way the past is.

Accordingly, the claim that God is outside of time is essentially irrelevant to Edwardsian arguments. In what follows I shall therefore assume, for the sake of expository simplicity, that God does indeed have foreknowledge and that it is quite proper to speak of him both as holding a belief at a time and as having held beliefs in the past. What I shall say, however, can be restated so as to accommodate those who reject this assumption.

In 1965 Nelson Pike proposed an interesting variant of Edwards's argument for theological determinism from the stability of the past. (Those not interested in a detailed anatomy of Pike's argument are invited to skip to the beginning of Part II.) More exactly, what he proposed was an interesting variant of the argument for the conclusion that divine foreknowledge is incompatible with human freedom. What he argued is not that human freedom is incompatible with divine foreknowledge *simpliciter*, but that it is incompatible with the claim that God is *essentially* omniscient and has foreknowledge of human actions. To say that God has the property of being omniscient *essentially* is to say that he is indeed omniscient and furthermore could not have failed to be so. It is to say that God is omniscient and that it is not possible that he should have existed and failed to be omniscient: there is no possible world in which he exists but is not omniscient. It follows that it is impossible that God holds or has held a false belief.

To argue his case, Pike considers the case of Jones, who mowed his lawn at t_2—last Saturday, say. Now suppose God is essentially omniscient. Then at any earlier time t_1—eighty years ago, for example—God believed that Jones would mow his lawn at t_2. Furthermore, since he is essentially omniscient, it is not possible that God falsely believe something; hence his having believed at t_1 that Jones would mow at t_2 entails that Jones does indeed mow at t_2. The essential premise of the argument, as Pike puts it, goes as follows:

(vi) If God existed at t_1 and if God believed at t_1 that Jones would do X at t_2, then if it was within Jones's power at t_2 to refrain from doing X, then (1) it was within Jones's power at t_2 to do something that would have brought it about that God held a false belief at t_1, or (2) it was within Jones's power at t_2 to do something which would have brought it about that God did not hold the belief He held at t_1, or (3) it was within Jones's power at t_2 to do something that would have brought it about that any person who believed at t_1 that Jones would do X at t_2 (one of whom was, by hypothesis, God) held a false belief and thus was not God—that is, that God (who by hypothesis existed at t_1) did not exist at t_1.[7]

Another way to put the claim Pike makes in (vi), I think, is to claim that

(6) God existed at t_1 and believed at t_1 that Jones would do X at t_2 and it was within Jones's power at t_2 to refrain from doing X

entails

(7) Either (7.1) it was within Jones's power at t_2 to do something that would have brought it about that God held a false belief at t_1, or (7.2) it was within Jones's power at t_2 to do something which would have brought it about that God did not hold the belief he held at t_1, or (7.3) it was within Jones's power at t_2 to do something that would have brought it about that God did not exist at t_1.

The rest of the argument then consists in suggesting that each of (7.1), (7.2), and (7.3) is necessarily false. If so, however, then (6) is necessarily false and divine foreknowledge is incompatible with human freedom.

Now everyone will concede, I think, that it was not possibly within Jones's power at t_2 to do something that would have brought it about that God did not exist at t_1; nor, if God is essentially omniscient, was it possibly within Jones's power at t_2 to do something that would have brought it about that God held a false belief at t_1.[8] But what about (7.2), the second disjunct of (7)? Was it—could it have been—within Jones's power to do something that would have brought it about that God did not hold the belief he held at t_1? We must ask a prior question. How shall we *understand*

(7.2) It was within Jones's power at t_2 to do something that would have brought it about that God did not hold the belief he held at t_1?

If God is essentially omniscient, it is clearly necessary that if Jones had refrained from doing X at t_2, then God would not have believed at t_1 that Jones would do X at t_2. Hence (6) entails that it was within Jones's power at t_2 to do something—namely refrain from doing X—which is such that if he had done it, then God would not have held a belief that in fact he *did* hold. This suggests that Pike intends (7.2) as ascribing to Jones the power to do something that would have brought it about that God would not have held a belief that in fact he did hold. So construed, what (7.2) asserts is that God held a certain belief at t_1, and it was within Jones's power at t_2 so to act that God would not have held that belief then. Presumably, therefore, (7.2) must be understood as

(7.2*) God held a certain belief B at t_1, and at t_2 it was within Jones's power to perform an action which is such that if he had performed it, then at t_1 God would not have held B.[9]

Accordingly, (7.2) is to be read at (7.2*). Now Pike's strategy here is to claim first that (6) entails (7) and then that each of the disjuncts in (7) is necessarily false. The premise proclaiming the falsehood of (7.2) is

(iv) It is not within one's power at a given time to do something that would bring it about that someone who held a certain belief at a time prior to the time in question did not hold that belief at the time prior to the time in question.[10]

If the argument is to succeed, then of course (iv) must be construed in such a way as to contradict (7.2*)—perhaps as (iv*) For any persons *S* and *S**, if at some time in the past *S** held a certain belief, then it is not within the power of *S* to perform any action which is such that if he were to perform it, then *S** would not have held that belief then.

The relevant specification of (iv*) withholds from Jones, not the absurd power of bringing it about that God did and did not hold a given belief, but the power, at t_2, to do a thing X which is such that if he *had* done it, then God would not have held a belief that as a matter of fact he did hold. But of course the question is, what do (iv*) and its specification have to recommend them? Why should we be inclined to accept them? Perhaps, Pike thinks, because the proposition *God believed at t_1 that Jones would mow at t_2* is a fact about the past relative to t_2; and it is not within anyone's power so to act that what is *in fact* a fact about the past would not have been a fact about the past. That is, for any fact *f* about the past, it is not within anyone's power to perform an action which is such that if he were to perform it, then *f* would not have been a fact about the past. More likely, the claim is that there is a certain *kind* of proposition about the past such that it is never within anyone's power so to act that a true proposition of *that* kind would have been false; a proposition specifying what someone believed at an earlier time, furthermore, is a proposition of just that sort. In either case Pike's argument for the incompatibility of divine foreknowledge and human freedom is rightly seen as in the company of the argument Aquinas, Ockham, Edwards, and others consider for that conclusion—the argument from the fixedness of the past.

II. Ockham's Way Out

As Edwards (and perhaps Pike) sees things, then, "in things which are past, their existence is now necessary. . . . 'Tis too late for any possibility of alteration in that respect: 'tis now impossible that it should be otherwise than true that that thing has existed." Nor is Edwards idiosyncratic in this intuition; we are all inclined to believe that the past, as opposed to the future, is fixed, stable, unalterable, closed. It is outside our control and outside the control even of an omnipotent being. Consider, for example, Peter Damian, often (but mistakenly) cited as holding that the power of God is limited by nothing at all, not even the laws of logic. In *De Divina Omnipotentia*, a letter to Desiderio of Cassino, Damian recalls and discusses a dinner conversation with the latter, a conversation that touched off a centuries-long discussion of the question whether it was within the power of God to restore to virginity someone who was no longer a virgin. The topic is God's power over the past:

> . . . I feel obliged to respond to an objection that many put forward. They say: "If God," as you affirm, "is omnipotent in all things, can he so act that things that are made, are not made? He can certainly destroy all things that have been made, so that they exist no more: but it is impossible to see how he can bring it about that those things which were made should never have been made at all. He can bring it about that from now and henceforth Rome should no longer exist, but how can the opinion be maintained that he can bring it about that it should never have been built of old?" [11]

Damian's response is not entirely clear. In his chapter 15, which is substantially his concluding chapter, he suggests that "it is much the same thing to ask 'How can God bring it about that what once happened did not happen?' or 'Can God act in such a way that what he made, he did not make?' as to assert that what God has made, God did not make." [12] (Damian takes a relatively strong line with respect to this last; anyone who asserts it, he says, is contemptible, not worthy of a reply, and should instead be branded.) Here it is not clear whether he is holding that the proposition *what has happened is such that God can bring it about that it has not happened* is equivalent to the proposition *God can bring it about that what has happened has not happened* and is thus false, or whether he simply fails to distinguish these propositions. He goes on to make heavy weather over the relation of God's eternity to the question under discussion, apparently holding that "relative to God and his unchangeable eternity," it is correct to say that God *can* bring it about that Rome was never founded; "relative to *us*," on the other hand, the right thing to say is that God *could have* brought it about that Rome was never founded. [13]

Damian's views on the matter are not altogether clear; what *is* clear is that he, like the rest of us, saw an important asymmetry between past and future. This asymmetry consists in part in the fact that the past is outside our control in a way in which the future is not. Although I now have the power to raise my arm, I do not have the power to bring it about that I raised my arm five minutes ago. Although it is now within my power to think about Vienna, it is not now within my power to bring it about that five minutes ago I was thinking about Vienna. The past is fixed in a way in which the future is open. It is within my power to help determine how the future shall be; it is too late to do the same with respect to the past.

Edwards, indeed, speaks in this connection of the *unalterability* of the past; and it is surely natural to do so. Strictly speaking, however, it is not alterability that is here relevant; for the future is no more alterable than the past. What after all, would it be to alter the past? To bring it about, obviously, that a temporally indexed proposition which is true and about the past before I act, is false thereafter. On January 1, 1982, I was not visiting New Guinea. For me to change the past with respect to that fact would be for me to perform an action *A* such that prior to my performing the action, it is true that on January 1, 1982, I was not in New Guinea, but after I perform the action, false that I was not in New Guinea then. But of course I cannot do anything like that, and neither can God, despite his omnipotence.

But neither can we alter the future. We can imagine someone saying, "Paul will in fact walk out the door at 9:21 A.M.; hence *Paul will walk out at 9:21 A.M.* is true; but Paul has the power to refrain from walking out then; so Paul has the power to alter the future." But the conclusion displays confusion; Paul's not walking out then, were it to occur, would effect no alteration at all in the future. To alter the future, Paul must do something like this: he must perform some action *A* at a time *t* before 9:21 such that prior to *t* it is true that Paul will walk out at 9:21, but after *t* (after he performs *A*) false that he will. Neither Paul nor anyone—not even God—can do something like that. So the future is no more alterable than the past.

The interesting asymmetry between past and future, therefore, does not consist in the fact that the past is unalterable in a way in which the future is not; nonetheless this asymmetry remains. Now, before 9:21, it is within Paul's power to make it false that he walks out at 9:21; after he walks out at 9:21 he will no longer have that power. In the same way in 1995 B.C. God could have brought it about that Abraham did not exist in 1995 B.C.;

now that is no longer within his power. As Edwards says, it's too late for that.

Recognizing this asymmetry, Ockham, like several other medieval philosophers, held that the past is indeed in some sense necessary; it is *necessary per accidens*:

I claim that every necessary proposition is *per se* in either the first mode or the second mode. This is obvious, since I am talking about all propositions that are necessary *simpliciter*. I add this because of propositions that are necessary *per accidens*, as is the case with many past tense propositions. They are necessary *per accidens*, because it was contingent that they be necessary, and because they were not always necessary.[14]

Here Ockham directs our attention to propositions about the past: past tense propositions together with temporally indexed propositions, such as

(8) *Columbus sails the ocean blue* is true in 1492,[15]

whose index is prior to the present time. Such propositions, he says, are accidentally necessary if true; they are *accidentally* necessary because they *become* necessary. Past tense propositions become necessary when they become true; temporally indexed propositions such as (8), on the other hand, do not become true—(8) was always true—but they become necessary, being necessary after but not before the date of their index. And once a proposition acquires this status, says Ockham, not even God has the power to make it false.

In *Predestination, God's Foreknowledge and Future Contingents*, Ockham goes on to make an interesting distinction:

Some propositions are about the present as regards both their wording and their subject matter (*secundum vocem et secundum rem*). Where such propositions are concerned, it is universally true that every true proposition about the present has (corresponding to it) a necessary one about the past:—e.g., 'Socrates is seated', 'Socrates is walking', 'Socrates is just', and the like.

Other propositions are about the present as regards their wording only and are equivalently about the future, since their truth depends on the truth of propositions about the future. Where such (propositions) are concerned, the rule that every true proposition about the present has corresponding to it a necessary proposition about the past is not true.[16]

Ockham means to draw the following contrast. Some propositions about the present "are about the present as regards both their wording and their subject matter"; for example,

(9) Paul is seated.

Such propositions, we may say, are *strictly* about the present; and if such a proposition is now true, then a corresponding proposition about the past—

(10) Paul was seated—

will be accidentally necessary from now on. Other propositions about the present, however, "are about the present as regards their wording only and are equivalently about the future"; for example,

(11) Paul correctly believes that the sun will rise on January 1, 2000.

Such a proposition is "equivalently about the future," and it is not the case that if it is true, then the corresponding proposition about the past—

(12) Paul correctly believed that the sun will rise on January 1, 2000,

in this case—will be accidentally necessary from now on. (Of course we hope that (12) will be accidentally necessary after January 1, 2000.)

What Ockham says about the present, he would say about the past. Just as some propositions about the present are "about the present as regards their wording only and are equivalently about the future," so some propositions about the past are about the past as regards their wording only and are equivalently about the future; (12) for example, or

(13) Eighty years ago, the proposition *Paul will mow his lawn in 1999* was true,

or (to appease those who object to the idea that a proposition can be true at a time)

(14) Eighty years ago, the sentence "Paul will mow his lawn in 1999" expressed the proposition *Paul will mow his lawn in 1999* and expressed a truth.

These propositions are about the past, but they are also equivalently about the future. Furthermore, they are not necessary *per accidens*—not yet, at any rate. We might say that a true proposition like (12)–(14) is a *soft* fact about the past, whereas one like

(15) Paul mowed in 1981

—one *strictly* about the past—is a *hard* fact about the past.[17]

Now of course the notion of aboutness, as Nelson Goodman has reminded us,[18] is at best a frail reed; *a fortiori*, then, the same goes for the notion of being *strictly* about. But we do have *something* of a grasp of this notion, hesitant and infirm though perhaps it is. It may be difficult or even impossible to give a useful criterion for the distinction between hard and soft facts about the past, but we do have *some* grasp of it, and can apply it in many cases. The idea of a hard fact about the past contains two important elements: *genuineness* and *strictness*. In the first place, a hard fact about the past is a genuine fact about the past. This cannot be said, perhaps, for (13). It is at least arguable that if (13) is a fact about the past at all, it is an *ersatz* fact about the past; it tells us nothing about the past except in a Pickwickian, Cantabridgian sort of way. What it really tells us is something about the future: that Paul will mow in 1999. (12) and (14), on the other hand, do genuinely tell us something about the past: (12) tells us that Paul believed something and (14) that a certain sentence expressed a certain proposition. But (12) and (14) are not *strictly* about the past; they also tell us something about what will happen in 1999. It may be difficult to give criteria, or (informative) necessary and sufficient conditions, for either genuineness or strictness; nevertheless we do have at least a partial grasp of these notions.

Accordingly, let us provisionally join Ockham in holding that there is a viable distinction between hard and soft facts about the past. The importance of this distinction, for Ockham, is that it provides him with a way of disarming the arguments for logical and theological determinism from the necessity of the past. Each of those arguments, when made explicit, has as a premise

(16) If *p* is about the past, then *p* is necessary

or something similar. Ockham's response is to deny (16); *hard* facts about the past are indeed accidentally necessary, but the same cannot be said for soft facts. Such propositions as (13) and (14) are not hard facts about the past; each entails that Paul will mow his lawn in 1999, and is therefore, as Ockham says, "equivalently about the future." Not all facts about the past, then, are hard facts about the past; and only the hard facts are plausibly thought to be accidentally necessary. (16), therefore, the general claim that all facts about the past are accidentally necessary, is seen to be false—or at any rate there seems to be no reason at all to believe it. And thus dissolves any argument for theological determinism which, like Edwards's, accepts (16) in its full generality.

I believe Ockham is correct here; furthermore, there is no easy way to refurbish Edwards's argument. Given Ockham's distinction between hard and soft facts, what Edwards's argument needs is the premise that such propositions as

(17) God knew eighty years ago that Paul will mow in 1999

are hard facts about the past. Clearly, however, (17) is not a hard fact about the past; for, like (13) and (14), it entails

(18) Paul will mow his lawn in 1999;

and no proposition that entails (18) is a hard fact about the past.

Let me be entirely clear here; I say that none of (13), (14), and (17) is a hard fact about the past, because each entails (18). In so saying, however, I am not endorsing a *criterion* for hard fact-hood; in particular I am not adopting an "entailment" criterion, according to which a fact about the past is a hard fact about the past if and only if it entails no proposition about the future. No doubt *every* proposition about the past, hard fact or not, entails *some* proposition about the future; *Socrates was wise*, for example, entails *It will be true from now on that Socrates was wise*; and *Paul played tennis yesterday* entails *Paul will not play tennis for the first time tomorrow*. What I *am* saying is this: No proposition that entails (18) is a hard fact about the past, because no such proposition is *strictly* about the past. We may not be able to give a criterion for being strictly about the past; but we do have at least a rough and intuitive grasp of this notion. Given our intuitive grasp of this notion, I think we can see two things. First, no conjunctive proposition that contains (18) as a conjunct is (now, in 1986) strictly about the past. Thus *Paul will mow his lawn in 1999 and Socrates was wise*, while indeed a proposition about the past, is not *strictly* about the past. And second, hard facthood is closed under logical equivalence: any proposition equivalent (in the broadly logical sense) to a proposition strictly about the past is itself strictly about the past.[19] But any proposition that entails (18) is equivalent, in the broadly logical sense, to a conjunctive proposition one conjunct of which is (18); hence each such proposition is equivalent to a proposition that is not a hard fact about the past, and is therefore itself not a hard fact about the past. Thus the Edwardsian argument fails.

Similar comments apply to Pike's argument (above, pp. 61–64) for the incompatibility of essential divine omniscience with human freedom. Pike puts his argument in terms, not of God's fore*knowledge*, but, so to speak, of God's fore*belief*; and the essential premise of the argument, as you recall, is

(iv*) For any persons S and S^*, if at some time in the past S^* held a certain belief, then it is not within the power of S to perform an action such that if he were to perform it, then S^* would not have held that belief then.

His essential insights, I think, are two: first, it seems natural to think of propositions of the sort *eighty years ago, S believed p* as hard facts about the past (and thus as plausible candidates for accidental necessity); and secondly, if God is essentially omniscient, then such a proposition as *God believed eighty years ago that p* entails *p*. (To these insights he adds the idea, not in my view an insight, that it is not within anyone's power to perform an action which is such that if he were to perform it, then what is *in fact* a hard fact about the past would not have been a fact at all.)

Unfortunately, the second of these insights is incompatible with the first. If God is essentially omniscient, then

(19) Eighty years ago, God believed the proposition that Paul will mow his lawn in 1999

entails that Paul will mow in 1999. By the above argument, then, (19) is not strictly about the past and is therefore not a hard fact about the past. But then we no longer have any reason to accept (iv*). Perhaps it is plausible to accept (iv*) for S^* stipulated not to be essentially omniscient, or stipulated to be such that propositions of the sort *S* believed that p* are hard facts about the past.[20]

But given the possibility of essential divine omniscience, (iv*) in its full generality has nothing whatever to recommend it; for if God is essentially omniscient, then such propositions as (19) are not hard facts about the past.

We can see the same point from a slightly different perspective. Pike is assuming, for purposes of argument, that God is essentially omniscient. Suppose we add, as classical theism also affirms, that God is a necessary being. What follows is that God both exists and is omniscient in every possible world; hence in every possible world God believes every true proposition and believes no false propositions. But then *truth* and *being believed by God* are equivalent in the broadly logical sense; it is then necessary that for any proposition p, p is true if and only if God believes p. It follows that

(20) Eighty years ago, God believed that Paul will mow in 1999

is equivalent in the broadly logical sense to

(21) Eighty years ago, it was true that Paul will mow in 1999.

Here again we can accommodate our colleagues ("atemporalists," as we may call them) who do not believe that propositions can be true at times; for (20), given the plausible (but widely disputed) assumption that necessarily, for any time t there is a time t^* eighty years prior to t, is also equivalent to

(22) Paul will mow in 1999.

Even without the "plausible assumption," (20) is equivalent to

(23) There is (i.e., is, was, or will be) such a time as eighty years ago, and Paul will mow in 1999.

Clearly enough none of (21), (22), and (23) is a hard fact about the past; but (20) is equivalent in the broadly logical sense to at least one of them; hence (20) is not a hard fact about the past. Furthermore, (20) is inconsistent with Paul's being free to mow in 1999 only if (23) is; and no one, presumably, except for the most obdurate logical fatalist, will hold that (23) is incompatible with Paul's being free to mow in 1999.[21] So if, as traditional theism affirms, God is both a necessary being and essentially omniscient, then theological determinism is logically equivalent to logical determinism; divine foreknowledge is incompatible with human freedom only if the latter is inconsistent with the existence of true propositions detailing future free actions.

Ironically enough, from Ockham's perspective it is the suggestion that God is omniscient but *not* essentially omniscient that is plausibly thought to create a problem. Return, once more, to

(20) Eighty years ago, God believed that Paul will mow in 1999.

If God is not essentially omniscient, then (20) does not entail that Paul will mow in 1999; at any rate we no longer have any reason to suppose that it does. But then we are deprived of our only reason for denying that (20) is strictly about the past; we shall then presumably have to hold that (20) is a hard fact about the past. From an Ockhamist perspective, it follows that (20) is accidentally necessary. But an Ockhamist would also certainly hold that even if God is not *essentially* omniscient, nevertheless his omniscience is counterfactually independent of Paul's actions; that is to say, there is not anything Paul can do such that if he were to do it, then God would not have been or would no longer be omniscient. If Paul were to refrain from mowing his lawn in 1999, therefore, God would not have believed, eighty years ago, that Paul will mow then. But Ockham also thinks it is or will be within Paul's power to refrain from mowing then. From Ockham's point of view, then, the facts are these: if God is not essentially omniscient, then there is an accidentally necessary proposition p—(20), as it happens—and an action Paul can perform, such that if he were to perform it, then p would have been false. Ockham is not very explicit about accidental necessity; nevertheless he would have held, I think, that it is not within anyone's power to perform an action which is such that if he were to perform it, then a proposition which is in fact accidentally necessary would have been false. From Ockham's point of view, therefore, divine foreknowledge threatens human freedom only if God is not essentially omniscient.

What I have argued, then, is that Ockham's way out gives us the means of seeing that neither Edwards's nor Pike's argument is successful. Edwards's argument fails because, essentially, God's having *known* a certain proposition is not, in general, a hard fact about the past; but only hard facts about the past are plausibly thought to be accidentally necessary. Pike's argument fails for similar reasons: if God is essentially omniscient, then the facts about what God *believed* are not, in general, hard facts about the past; but then there is no reason to suppose that none of us can act in such a way that God would not have believed what in fact he does believe. In Parts III and IV, therefore, I shall assume, with Ockham, that divine foreknowledge and human freedom are not incompatible.

III. On Ockham's Way Out

As we have seen, Ockham responds to the arguments for theological determinism by distinguishing hard facts about the past—facts that are genuinely and strictly about the past—from soft facts about the past; only the former, he says, are necessary *per accidens*. This response is intuitively plausible. It is extremely difficult, however, to say precisely what it is for a proposition to be strictly about the past, and equally difficult to say what it is for a proposition to be accidentally necessary. According to Ockham, a proposition is not strictly about the past if its "truth depends on the truth of propositions about the future" (above, p. 190). This suggests that if a proposition about the past *entails* one about the future, then it is not strictly about the past; we might therefore think that a proposition is strictly about the past if and only if it does not entail a proposition about the future. We might then concur with Ockham in holding that a proposition about the past is accidentally necessary if it is true and *strictly* about the past. But as John Fischer points out [in Chapter 4 of this volume], difficulties immediately rear their ugly heads. I shall mention only two. In the first place, suppose we take 'about the future' in a way that mirrors the way we took 'about the past'; a proposition is then about the future if and only if it is either a future-tense proposition or a temporally indexed proposition whose index is a date later than the present. Then obviously any proposition about the past will entail one about the future;

(24) Abraham existed a long time ago

and

(25) Abraham exists in 1995 B.C.

entail, respectively,

(26) It will be the case from now on that Abraham existed a long time ago

and

(27) It will always be true that Abraham exists in 1995 B.C.

But then the distinction between propositions strictly about the past and propositions about the past *simpliciter* becomes nugatory.

Perhaps you will reply that propositions like (26) and (27) are at best *ersatz* propositions about the future, despite their future tense or future index; on a less wooden characterization of 'about the future' they would not turn out to be about the future. Perhaps so; I will not dispute the point here. But other and less tractable difficulties remain. First, (24) and (25) both entail that Abraham will not begin to exist (i.e., exist for the first time) in 1999 (Fischer, p. 92 in this volume); and that is not, or is not obviously, an *ersatz* fact about the future. Second, on that more adequate characterization, what ever exactly it might be, it will no doubt be true that

(28) It was true eighty years ago either that God knew that Friesland will rule the world in A.D. 2000 or that Paul believed that Friesland will rule the world in A.D. 2000.[22]

entails no non-*ersatz* future propositions and is thus strictly about the past. Now suppose, *per impossibile*, that Friesland will indeed rule the world in A.D. 2000. Then (28) (given divine omniscience) will be true by virtue of the truth of the first disjunct; the second disjunct, however, is false (by virtue of Paul's youth). And then on the above account (28) is accidentally necessary; but is it really? Is it not still within someone's power—God's, say—to act in such a way that (28) would have been false (Fischer, p. 91 in this volume)?

Necessary *per accidens* and *being strictly about the past* thus present difficulties when taken in tandem in the way Ockham takes them. The former, furthermore, is baffling and perplexing in its own right; and this is really the fundamental problem here. If, as its proponents claim, accidental necessity is not any sort of logical or metaphysical or causal necessity, what sort of necessity is it? How shall we understand it? Ockham, Edwards, and their colleagues do not tell us. Furthermore, even if they (or we) had a plausible account of *being strictly about the past*, we could not sensibly *define* accidental necessity in terms of being strictly about the past; for the whole point of the argument for theological determinism is just that propositions about the future that are entailed by accidentally necessary propositions about the past will themselves be accidentally necessary. So how shall we understand accidental necessity?

Perhaps we can make some progress as follows. In explaining accidental necessity, one adverts to facts about the power of agents—such facts, for example, as that not even God can now bring it about that Abraham did not exist; it is too late for that. Furthermore, in the arguments for logical and theological determinism, accidental necessity functions as a sort of middle term. It is alleged that a proposition of some sort or other is about or strictly about the past; but then, so the claim goes, that proposition is accidentally necessary—in which case, according to the argument, it is not now within the power of any agent, not even God, to bring it about that it is false. Why not eliminate the middle man and *define* accidental necessity in terms of the powers of agents? If a proposition p is accidentally necessary, then it is not possible—possible in the broadly logical sense—that there be an agent who has it within his power to bring it about that p is false; why not then define accidental necessity as follows:

(29) p is accidentally necessary at t if and only if p is true at t and it is not possible both that p is true at t and that there is a being that at t or later has the power to bring it about that p is false?[23]

But how shall we understand this "has the power to bring it about that p is false"? Pike speaks in this connection of "its being within Jones's power to do something that would have brought it about that" p, and Fischer of "being able so to act that p would have been false." This suggests

(30) S has the power to bring it about that p is false if and only if there is an action it is within S's power to perform such that if he were to perform it, p would have been false.

(30) is perhaps inadequate as a *general* account of what it is to have the power to bring it about that a proposition is false. For one thing, it seems to imply that I have the power with respect to necessarily false propositions (as well as other false proposi-

tions whose falsehood is counterfactually independent of my actions) to bring it about that they are false; and this is at best dubious. But here we are not interested, first of all, in giving an independent account of having the power to bring it about that p is false; even if (30) is not a satisfactory general account of that notion, it may serve acceptably in (29). Incorporating (30), therefore, (29) becomes

(31) p is accidentally necessary at t if and only if p is true at t and it is not possible both that p is true at t and that there exists an agent S and an action A such that (1) S has the power at t or later to perform A, and (2) if S were to perform A at t or later, then p would have been false.[24]

Now so far as I know, Ockham gave no explicit account or explanation of accidental necessity; nevertheless it is not implausible to see him as embracing something like (31). On this definition, furthermore (given common-sense assumptions), many soft facts about the past will not be accidentally necessary: for example.

(32) Eighty years ago it was true that Paul would not mow his lawn in 1999.

Even if true, (32) is not accidentally necessary: it is clearly possible that Paul will have the power, in 1999, to mow his lawn; but if he were to do so, then (32) would have been false. The same goes for

(33) God believed eighty years ago that Paul would mow his lawn in 1999

if God is essentially omniscient; for then it is a necessary truth that if Paul were to refrain from mowing his lawn during 1999, God would not have believed, eighty years ago, that he would mow then. (32) and (33), therefore, are not accidentally necessary.

Since (32) and (33) are not hard facts about the past, Ockham would have welcomed this consequence. But our account of accidental necessity has other consequences—consequences Ockham might have found less to his liking. Let us suppose that a colony of carpenter ants moved into Paul's yard last Saturday. Since this colony has not yet had a chance to get properly established, its new home is still a bit fragile. In particular, if the ants were to remain and Paul were to mow his lawn this afternoon, the colony would be destroyed. Although nothing remarkable about these ants is visible to the naked eye, God, for reasons of his own, intends that it be preserved. Now as a matter of fact, Paul will not mow his lawn this afternoon. God, who is essentially omniscient, knew in advance, of course, that Paul will not mow his lawn this afternoon; but if he had foreknown instead that Paul *would* mow this afternoon, then he would have prevented the ants from moving in. The facts of the matter, therefore, are these: if Paul were to mow his lawn this afternoon, then God would have foreknown that Paul would mow his lawn this afternoon; and if God had foreknown that Paul would mow this afternoon, then God would have prevented the ants from moving in. So if Paul were to mow his lawn this afternoon, then the ants would not have moved in last Saturday. But it is within Paul's power to mow this afternoon. There is therefore an action he can perform such that if he were to perform it, then the proposition

(34) That colony of carpenter ants moved into Paul's yard last Saturday

would have been false. But what I have called "the facts of the matter" certainly seem to be possible; it is therefore possible that there be an agent who has the power to perform an action which is such that if he were to perform it, then (34) would have been false—in which case it is not accidentally necessary. But (34), obviously enough, is strictly about the past; insofar as we have any grasp at all of this notion, (34) is about as good a candidate for being an exemplification of it as any we can easily think of. So, contrary to what Ockham supposed, not all true propositions strictly about the past—not all hard facts—are accidentally necessary—not, at any rate, in the sense of (31).

Another example: a few years ago Robert Nozick called our attention to *Newcomb's Paradox*. You are confronted with two opaque boxes, box A and box B. You know that box B contains $1,000 and that box A contains either $1,000,000 or nothing at all. You can choose to take both boxes or to take just box A; no other action is possible. You know, furthermore, that the money was put there eighty years ago by an extremely knowledgeable agent according to the following plan: if she believed that you would take both boxes, she put $1,000 in box B and nothing in box A; if on the other hand, she believed that you would exercise a decent restraint and take only box A, she put $1,000 in box B and $1,000,000 in box A. You know, finally, that this being has an amazing track record. Many other people have been in just your situation and in at least a vast majority of such cases, if the person in question took both boxes, he found box A empty; but if he took just box A, he found it to contain $1,000,000. Your problem is: given your depleted coffers and acquisitive nature, what should you do? Should you take both boxes, or just box A? And the puzzle is that there seem to be strong arguments on both sides. First, there seems good reason to take just box A. For if you were to take just box A, then the being in question would have known that you would take just box A, in which case she would have put $1,000,000 in it. So if you were to take just box A, you would get $1,000,000. If you were to take both boxes, on the other hand, then the being in question would have known that you would take both, in which case she would have put nothing in box A and $1,000 in box B. If you were to take both boxes, therefore, you would get $1,000. So if you were to take just box A you would get $1,000,000 and if you were to take both boxes you would get $1,000. Obviously, then, you ought to take just box A.

But there seems an equally plausible argument on the other side. For the money in the boxes has been there for a long time—eighty years, say. So if in fact there is $1,001,000 in those boxes, then there is nothing you can do now to alter that fact. So if there is $1,001,000 there, then if you were to take both boxes, you would get $1,001,000. On the other hand, if there is $1,001,000 there, then if you were to take just box A, you would get only $1,000,000, thus missing out on the extra $1,000. So if there is $1,001,000 there, you would get more if you took both boxes than if you took only one. But a similar argument shows that the same holds if there is just $1,000 there; in that case you would get $1,000 if you took both boxes but nothing at all if you took just box A. The only prudent course, then, is to take both boxes.

Now the fact is, as I think, that neither of these arguments is conclusive; each takes as a premise a proposition not obviously true and not entailed by the puzzle conditions. Thus the two-boxer appears to argue that if there is $1,001,000 there, then it follows that if you were to take both boxes, there (still) would have been $1,001,000 there. But of course that does not follow; the argument form *A: therefore, if p were true A would be true* is invalid. Or perhaps he argues that since it is true that if there were $1,001,000 there and you were to take both boxes, you would get $1,001,000, it follows that if there were $1,001,000 there, then if you were to take both boxes, you would get $1,001,000. But that does not follow either; exportation does not hold for counterfactuals. The one-boxer, I think, has a better time of it. He does claim, however, that if you were to take both boxes, then the being in question would have known that you would take both boxes; but of course this is not entailed by the puzzle conditions. The best we can say is that it is *probable*, relative to the puzzle conditions, that if you were to take both, then she would have known that you would take both. This is the best we can say; but can we say even as much as that? How does one determine the probability of such a counterfactual on the basis of such evidence as the puzzle conditions provide?

But suppose we strengthen the puzzle conditions. Suppose it is not just some knowledgeable being with a splendid track record that puts the money in the boxes, but God. Suppose furthermore, that God is omniscient; and add one of the following further conditions (in order of decreasing strength): God is essentially omniscient; God is omniscient in every world in which you exist; God is omniscient both in the worlds in which you take just box A and the worlds in which you take both; God's being omniscient is counterfactually independent of your decision, so that God would have been omniscient if you were to take box A and would have been omniscient if you were to take both boxes. Add also that the other puzzle conditions are counterfactually independent of your actions. Then there is a knock-down drag-out argument for taking just box A (and no decent argument at all for taking both). For then both

(35) If you were to take both boxes, then God would have believed that you would take both boxes

and

(36) If you were to take both boxes and God had believed that you would take both boxes, then God would have put nothing in box A

follow from the puzzle conditions; from (35) and (36) it follows by counterfactual logic that

(37) If you were to take both boxes, then God would have put nothing in box A;

and from (37) (together with the puzzle conditions) it follows that if you were to take both boxes, then you would get only $1,000. But a precisely similar argument shows that if you were to take just box A, you would get $1,000,000. So if you were to take just box A, you would get a lot more money than you would if you were to take both. This argument will be resisted only by those whose intellects are clouded by unseemly greed.

But something further follows. The puzzle conditions, thus strengthened, seem possible. But they entail that there is a true proposition p strictly about the past and an action you can perform such that if you were to perform it, then p would have been false. For suppose in fact that you will take both boxes, so that in fact

(38) There was only $1,000 there eighty years ago

is true. According to the puzzle conditions, it is within your power to take just box A; but they also entail that if you were to take just box A, then (38) would have been false. (38), however, is strictly about the past; hence there is a proposition strictly about the past that is not necessary *per accidens*.

So here are a couple of propositions—(34) and (38)—that are hard facts about the past, but are not accidentally necessary. Of course there will be many more. It is possible (though no doubt unlikely) that there is something you can do such that if you were to do it, then Abraham would never have existed. For perhaps you will be confronted with a decision of great importance—so important that one of the alternatives is such that if you were to choose *it*, then the course of human history would have been quite different from what in fact it is. Furthermore, it is possible that if God had foreseen that you would choose *that* alternative, he would have acted very differently. Perhaps he would have created different persons; perhaps, indeed, he would not have created Abraham. So it is possible that there is an action such that it is within your power to perform it and such that if you were to perform it, then God would not have created

Abraham. But if indeed that *is* possible, then not even the proposition *Abraham once existed* is accidentally necessary in the sense of (31). By the same sort of reasoning we can see that it is possible (though no doubt monumentally unlikely) that there is something you can do such that if you were to do it, then the Peloponnesian War would never have occurred.

It follows, then, that even such hard facts about the past as that Abraham once existed and that there was once a war between the Spartans and Athenians are not accidentally necessary in the sense of (31). Indeed, it is not easy to think of *any* contingent facts about the past that are accidentally necessary in that sense. Of course there are limits to the sorts of propositions such that it is possibly within my power so to act that they would have been false. It is not possible, for example, that there be an action I can perform such that if I were to do so, then I would never have existed.[25] But even if it is necessarily not within *my* power so to act that I would not have existed, the same does not go for *you*; perhaps there is an action you can take which is such that if you were to take it, then I would not have existed. (I should therefore like to ask you to tread softly.) Neither of us (nor anyone else) could have the power so to act that there should never have been any (contingently existing) agents; clearly it is not possible that there be an action *A* some (contingently existing) person could perform such that if he were to do so, then there would never have been any contingent agents. So the proposition *there have been* (contingent) *agents* is accidentally necessary; but it is hard indeed to find any stronger propositions that are both logically contingent and accidentally necessary.

IV. Power over the Past

The notion of accidental necessity explained as in (31) is, I think, a relevant notion for the discussion of the arguments for theological determinism from the necessity of the past; for the question at issue is often, indeed ordinarily, put as the question, Which propositions about the past are such that their truth entails that it is not within anyone's power so to act that they would have been false. Accidental necessity as thus explained, however, does little to illumine our deep intuitive beliefs about the asymmetry of past and future—the fact that the future is within our control in a way in which the past is not; for far too few propositions turn out to be accidentally necessary.[26] What is the root of these beliefs and what is the relevant asymmetry between past and future? Is it just that the scope of our power with respect to the past is vastly more limited than that of our power with respect to the future? That is, is it just that there are far fewer propositions about the past than about the future which are such that I can so act that they would have been false? I doubt that this is an important part of the story, simply because we really know very little about how far our power with respect to either past or future extends. With few exceptions, I do not know which true propositions about the past are such that I can so act that they would have been false; and the same goes for true propositions about the future.

So suppose we look in a different direction. Possibly there is something I can do such that if I were to do it, then Abraham would not have existed; but it is not possible—is it?—that I now *cause* Abraham not to have existed. While it may be within Paul's power so to act that the colony of ants would not have moved in last Saturday, surely it is not within his power now—or for that matter within God's power now—to *cause* it to be true that the colony did not move in. Perhaps we should revise our definition of accidental necessity to say that a proposition is (now) accidentally necessary if it is true and also such that it entails that it is not (now) within anyone's power (not even God's) to cause it to be false. And perhaps we could then see the relevant asymmetry between past and future as the fact that true propositions strictly about the past—unlike their counterparts about the future—are accidentally necessary in this new sense.

The right answer, I suspect, lies in this direction; but the suggestion involves a number of profound perplexities—about agent causation, the analysis of causation, whether backwards causation is possible, the relation between causation and counterfactuals—that I cannot explore here. Let us instead briefly explore a related suggestion. In our first sense of accidental necessity, a proposition p is accidentally necessary if and only if p is true and such that it is not possible that p be true and there be an agent and an action such that (1) the agent is now or will in the future be able to perform the action and (2) if he were to do so, then *p* would have been false. Then such propositions as *Abraham existed in 1995 B.C.* turn out not to be accidentally necessary because of the possibility of divine foreknowledge and, so to speak, divine fore-cooperation. Perhaps if I were to do *A*, then God would have foreseen that I would do *A* and would not have created Abraham. My doing *A*, however, is not by *itself* sufficient for Abraham's not existing; it requires God's previous cooperation. So suppose we strengthen the counterfactual involved in the above definition; suppose we say

(39) *p* is accidentally necessary at *t* if and only if *p* is true at *t* and it is not possible both that *p* is true at *t* and that there exists an action *A* and an agent *S* such that (1) *S* has the power at *t* or later to perform *A*, and (2) *necessarily* if *S* were to perform *A* at *t* or later, then *p* would have been false.

While it may be within Paul's power to do something—namely, mow his lawn—such that if he were to do so, then that colony of ants would not have moved in, his performing that action does not *entail* the falsehood of the proposition that the ants did move in; and it looks as if there is nothing he or anyone can do that does entail its falsehood.

Permit me a couple of comments on this definition. First, although it involves the idea of a proposition's being true at a time, it is easily revised (as are (42) and (44) below) so as to accommodate our atemporalist friends. Second, I am thinking of the notion of an *agent*, as it enters into the definition, broadly, in such a way as to include agents of all sorts; in particular it is to include God. Third, propositions that are necessary in the broadly logical sense turn out accidentally necessary (see note 24). Fourth, accidental necessity thus characterized is closed under entailment but not under conjunction; see under Appendix, below, p. 213. Fifth, many contingent propositions about the past turn out to be accidentally necessary, but so do some contingent propositions about the future. And finally, Ockham's claim that necessity *per accidens* is connected with what is strictly about the past seems to be vindicated on (39); barring a couple of complications (see below, pp. 208–10), it looks as if a logically contingent proposition about the past is accidentally necessary in the sense of (39) if and only if it is true and strictly about the past. So, for example,

(40) Eighty years ago, the sentence "Paul will mow his lawn in 1995" expressed the proposition *Paul will mow his lawn in 1995* and expressed a truth

is true (let us suppose), but not strictly about the past. Here there is indeed something someone can do that entails its falsehood: Paul can not mow his lawn in 1995. But it is not possible that there be an action Paul (or anyone) can or will be able to perform such that his performing it entails that

(41) Paul did not mow his lawn in 1984

is false. We may thus say, with Ockham, that propositions strictly about the past are accidentally necessary; and the relevant asymmetry between past and future is just that contingent propositions strictly about the past are accidentally necessary, while their colleagues about the future typically are not.

Unfortunately, there is a residual perplexity. For what shall we count, here, as *actions*? Suppose it is in fact within Paul's power so to act that the ants would not have moved in; is there not such an action as *bringing it about that the ants would not have moved in* or *so acting that the ants would not have moved in*? If there is (and why not?) then it is both an action he can perform and one such that his performing it entails that the ants did not move in; but then *the ants moved in* is not accidentally necessary after all. Here what we need, clearly enough, is the idea of a *basic* action, what an agent can in some sense do *directly*. *Moving my arm*, perhaps, would be such an action; starting a world war or so acting that the ants would not have moved in would not. Let us say that an action is one I can *directly* perform if it is one I can perform without having to perform some other action in order to perform it. Starting a war would not be an action I can directly perform; I cannot start a war without doing something like pushing a button, pulling a trigger, or making a declaration. According to Roderick Chisholm, the only actions I can directly perform are *undertakings*.[27] I cannot, for example, raise my arm without trying or endeavoring or undertaking to do so; more exactly (as Chisholm points out, p. 57), I cannot raise it without undertaking to do *something*—scratch my ear, for example. I am inclined to think he is right: more generally, I cannot perform an action which is not itself an undertaking, without undertaking some action or other. (What I say below, however, does not depend on this claim.) But he is also right in thinking that undertakings are not undertaken. If so, however, it will follow that the only actions I can directly perform are undertakings.

Now some actions I can perform are such that my undertaking to perform them and my body's being in normal conditions are together causally sufficient for my performing them; raising my hand and moving my feet would be an example. "Normal conditions" here includes, among other things, the absence of pathological conditions as well as the absence of such external hindrances as being locked in a steamer trunk or having my hands tied behind my back. Of course more should be said here, but this will have to suffice for now. Let us say, then, that an action A is a basic action for a person S if and only if there is an action A^* that meets two conditions: first, S can directly perform A^*, and secondly, S's being in normal conditions and his directly performing A^* is causally sufficient for his performing A. Then we may revise (39) by appropriately inserting "A is basic for S":

(42) p is accidentally necessary at t if and only if p is true at t and it is not possible both that p is true at t and that there exists an agent S and an action A such that (1) A is basic for S, (2) S has the power at t or later to perform A, and (3) necessarily if S were to perform A at t or later, then p would have been false.

There is one more complication.[28]

(43) God foreknew that Smith and Jones will not freely cooperate in mowing the lawn

should not turn out to be accidentally necessary; but on (42) it does. The problem is that (42) does not properly accommodate cooperative ventures freely undertaken; it must be generalized to take account of multiple agency. This is easily enough accomplished:

(44) p is accidentally necessary at t if and only if p is true at t and it is not possible both that p is true at t and that there exist agents $S_1 \ldots$, S_n and actions $A_1 \ldots$, A_n such that (1) A_i is basic for S_i, (2) S_i has the power at t or later to perform A_i, and (3) necessarily, if every S_i were to perform A_i at t or later, then p would have been false.[29]

And now we may say, perhaps, that the way in which the future but not the past is within our control is that contingent propositions strictly about the past are accidentally necessary, while those about the future typically are not.

By way of summary and conclusion, then: the two main arguments for the incompatibility of divine foreknowledge with human freedom are both failures. The Ockhamite claim that not all propositions about the past are hard facts about the past seems correct; among those that are not hard facts would be propositions specifying God's (past) foreknowledge of future human actions, as well as propositions specifying God's past beliefs about future human actions, if God is essentially omniscient. Only hard facts about the past, however, are plausibly thought to be accidentally necessary; hence neither God's foreknowledge nor God's forebelief poses a threat to human freedom. Accidental necessity is a difficult notion, but can be explained in terms of the power of agents. The initially plausible account of accidental necessity—(31)—is defective as an account of the intuitively obvious asymmetry between past and future; for far too few propositions turn out to be accidentally necessary on that account. (44), however, is more satisfying.

Appendix: Ability and Possible Worlds

What is it to have the *ability* to do something—to mow the lawn, for example? What is it for an action to be within my power? Can we get any insight into this question by thinking about it in terms of possible worlds? It is initially obvious that I have the ability to perform an action at a time only if there is a possible world in which I perform that action then. Of course this condition is not *sufficient*; what it is within my power to do and what it is logically possible that I do, sadly enough, do not coincide. But what would be the right condition? Can we give an illuminating account of ability in terms of possible worlds?

In replying to a criticism I made[30] of his argument for the incompatibility of human freedom with essential divine foreknowledge, Pike ventures such an account. He points out first that "when assessing what is within my power at a given moment, I must take into account the way things are and the way things have been in the past" and goes on:

If we assume that what is within my power at a given moment determines a set of possible worlds, all of the members of that set will have to be worlds in which what has happened in the past relative to the given moment is precisely what has happened in the past relative to that moment in the actual world.[31]

He then applies this account to Jones and the question whether it was within his power to refrain from mowing at t_2 if at t_1 God believed that he would mow at t_2:

Going back now to the original problem, we have assumed that Jones does X at t_2 and that God exists and is everlasting and essentially omniscient. It follows that God believes at t_1 that Jones does X at t_2. The question before us is whether it is within Jones's power at t_2 to refrain from doing X. Plantinga assumes that this is to ask whether there is a possible world in which Jones refrains from doing X at t_2. His answer is that there is—it is a world in which God does not believe at t_1 that Jones does X at t_2. But Plantinga has not formulated the question correctly. He has not taken account of the restrictions that must be respected if one is to employ a possible worlds analysis of what it is for something to be within one's power. The question is not whether there is just some possible world or other in which Jones refrains from doing X at t_2. What must be asked is whether there is a possible world, having a *history prior to t_2 that is indistinguishable from that of the actual world*, in which Jones refrains from doing X at t_2. The answer is that there is not. All such worlds contain an essentially omniscient being who believes at t_1 that Jones does X at t_2. There is no possible world of this description in which Jones refrains from doing X at t_2.[32]

Now on one point Pike is wholly correct: (broadly) logical possibility, as he says, is quite insufficient for ability. There are plenty of actions I cannot perform, despite the fact that there are possible worlds in which I do perform them: composing poetry in Japanese is an example, as is, say, memorizing Kant's *Critique of Pure Reason* in half an hour. Ability and logical possibility do not coincide; and (contrary to what Pike says) I have never assumed or suggested otherwise. Indeed, as I have argued elsewhere, ability and possibility do not coincide even for God. There are many possible worlds God could not have weakly actualized, despite the fact that it is logically possible that he weakly actualize them—despite the fact, that is, that there are possible worlds in which he does weakly actualize them.[33]

Pike's positive proposal as to what it is to have the ability to do or refrain from doing X, however, is vastly more problematic. The suggestion is that

(1) S has the power to refrain from doing X at t if and only if there is a possible world W that has a history up to t indistinguishable from the actual world and in which S refrains from doing X at t.

And given (1), it follows that at t_2 Jones does not have the power not to mow. For a world in which there is no essentially omniscient being who believes at t_1 that Jones will do X at t_2 does not (given our supposition that God is essentially omniscient and. believes at t_1 that Jones will do X at t_2) have a history prior to t_2 that is indistinguishable from that of the actual world; every world in which there is such a being, furthermore, is one in which, clearly enough, Jones does X at t_2. Accordingly, there is no possible world that meets the above two conditions with respect to Jones's doing X; it therefore follows, Pike thinks, that Jones's having the power to refrain from doing X at t_2 is inconsistent with God's being essentially omniscient and believing at t_1 that Jones would do X at t_2.

Now it is not wholly clear what it is for a pair of worlds to have indistinguishable histories prior to t;[34] but (1) seems initially much too strong. First, what is so special about *essential* omniscience? According to Pike, a pair of worlds have distinguishable histories prior to t if one but not the other contains an essentially omniscient being who prior to t believes that Jones will mow; but would not the same go for a pair of worlds one but not the other of which contains a being who is omniscient *simpliciter* and believes that proposition prior to t? If so, on Pike's showing human freedom is incompatible with God's being omniscient *simpliciter*. Further, would not a pair of worlds have distinguishable histories prior to t if one but not the other contained a being, omniscient or not, who prior to t *knew* the proposition in question?[35] Or a being who *correctly believed* the proposition, whether or not he knew it? Indeed, would not W and W* have distinguishable histories prior to t if in one but not the other the proposition in question was *true* prior to t, whether or not anyone knew or believed it? Or if one but not the other contained a being who prior to t had the property *mows his lawn at t*? But then on Pike's account it will follow that a person is free with respect to an action A at a time t only if it is not true prior to t

that he will perform A then, and only if he does not have, prior to t, the property of being such that he performs A at t. And then Pike's account of ability, together with the assumption that propositions about the future have truth value, will imply logical determinism.

An Ockhamite bystander might suggest that what Pike needs here is the distinction between those propositions about the past that are accidentally necessary and those that are not. It is only the former, he says, that are relevant to a pair of worlds having indistinguishable histories prior to t; a pair of worlds have indistinguishable histories prior to t if and only if no proposition is accidentally necessary, in the sense of (44), at t in one but not the other. Then the fact that, say, in W but not W^* Smith knows at $t - n$ that Jones will mow at $t + n$ does not suffice to show that W and W^* have distinguishable histories prior to t; for

(2) Smith knows at $t - n$ that Jones will mow at $t + n$

while true in W is not accidentally necessary in W at t.

Sadly enough, however, this suggestion is unsatisfactory; for

(3) Every proposition Paul believed at noon yesterday was true

and

(4) At noon yesterday Paul believed that Jones will not mow his lawn for the next three days

are both true (let us suppose). If so, they are also accidentally necessary; each is such that there is nothing anyone can now do that entails its falsehood. (Their conjunction, however, is another matter; accidental necessity is not closed under conjunction, as this example shows.) Clearly enough, however, there is no possible world in which (3) and (4) are both true and in which Jones mows his lawn tomorrow; but surely this does not imply that it is not or will not be within his power to mow then.

Here the Ockhamite bystander might make another suggestion: what Pike needs here, he might say, is not the idea of accidental necessity, but the distinction between hard and soft facts about the past. What we should say, he suggests, is that I have the ability to do X if and only if there is a possible world that shares its hard facts about the past with the actual world and in which I do X. This suggestion, however, is doubly deficient.

First it is of no use to Pike. For on this suggestion a pair of worlds can have histories that are indistinguishable prior to t even if the one but not the other contains an essentially omniscient God who prior to t believes that Jones will mow at t; as we have already noted, if God is essentially omniscient, then *God believed at t_1 that Jones will mow at t_2* is not strictly about the past. Secondly, the suggestion is dubious in its own right. The fact that there is a possible world that shares its hard facts with the actual world and in which I do X, does not, I think, suffice to show that it is within my power to do X. Return to the Newcomb situation, and suppose that the knowledgeable agent involved is extremely knowledgeable but not essentially omniscient. Suppose this person (call her Michelle) knows whether you will take one box or two, and suppose her knowledge is counterfactually independent of your action: it is true (but not necessarily true) that if you were to take both boxes, then Michelle would have known that, but if you were to take just one, then she would have known *that*. More generally, it is true (but not necessarily true) that there is nothing you can do which is such that if you were to do it, then Michelle would have held a false belief as to what you would do. I take it the case as so far set out entails that it is not within your power to bring it about that Michelle holds a false belief on the topic in question. It is consistent with these conditions, I think, to add that the conjunction of all the hard facts about the past with the proposition that Michelle believes that you will take both boxes, does not entail that you will in fact take both. It is therefore possible that this conjunction be true but you take just one box. If this conjunction were true and you took only one box, however, then in so doing you would bring it about that Michelle had a false belief. Now I am inclined to think that all this is possible; but if it is, then there is a possible world that shares its hard facts about the past with the actual world and in which you bring it about that Michelle held a false belief—and this despite the truth that it is not in fact within your power to bring it about that Michelle held a false belief. I am therefore inclined to think that this suggestion—the suggestion that S has the power to do X if and only if there is a possible world that shares its hard facts about the past with the actual world and in which she does X—is at best dubious.

What I can do depends upon what I can *directly* do, together with the facts, with respect to each of the actions A^* I can directly perform, as to what would happen if I were to perform A^*. What I can do depends (among other things) on two things: (a) my repertoire of direct actions, and (b) the question which counterfactuals are true—which counterfactuals whose antecedents specify that I perform some action or series of actions that are direct for me. Now of course possible world thought has been abundantly illuminating and clarifying with respect to the second. It is hard to see, however, how it can help us with the first; it is hard to see, that is, how to give an illuminating account in terms of possible worlds of what it is within a person's power to do directly.

CHAPTER ELEVEN

Foreknowledge and Necessity

William Hasker

The modern controversy over divine foreknowledge and human freedom, begun two decades ago by Nelson Pike and A. N. Prior,[1] has yet to reach a satisfactory conclusion. Probably most philosophers who have considered the issue have reached their own conclusions, but no sort of general consensus has emerged. Furthermore, the principal arguments of the opposing sides in the controversy seem to pass by each other almost without contact, so that there is much discussion, but little apparent progress.

It is not immediately obvious why this should be so. There do not appear to be any systematic differences in philosophical style or methodology between the opposing sides which might explain their differing conclusions. Nor does the issue seem to be one which marks the difference between major competing world-views—like, for example, the controversies over scientific determinism or mind-body dualism. To be sure, the role of religious belief in the controversy cannot be denied, but it would be premature to explain the philosophical disagreements solely in terms of prior religious commitments.

While the issues surrounding the disagreement are complex, it will be argued here that what lies at the root of them is disagree-

Reprinted from *Faith and Philosophy*, 2 (1985): 121–57, by permission of the editors. I wish to thank George Mavrodes for comments on an earlier version of this paper, as well as for his collaboration in a lengthy correspondence that has been the source of many of the ideas contained in it.

ment over a fundamental intuition or metaphysical datum—the intuition often expressed by saying, "You cannot change the past." Perhaps no one involved in the controversy denies this outright, but there are wide differences about what its significance is perceived to be. And clustered around this fundamental disagreement are a host of other disagreements, problems, and perplexities, all combining to guarantee that a discussion of the topic rarely follows a straight path from premises to conclusion.

If this description of the state of the controversy is even approximately correct, it would seem that no simple, straightforward argument is likely to contribute much towards its resolution. Such an argument might, to be sure, capture effectively what one side in the discussion perceives as the grounds for its position. But the complexity of the surrounding issues, and especially the disagreement over a central intuition, make it unlikely that such a straightline approach will convince those who need to be convinced.

I believe, therefore, that an illuminating treatment of this topic must take a more subtle and dialectical approach. The aim must be to strip away, one by one, the surrounding complexities in order to reveal the core disagreement. Formal arguments will have their role to play in this, but only as part of a larger process which seeks to elucidate the total philosophical context within which the arguments must function.

Specifically, the procedure in the present paper will be as follows: We shall begin with a brief, straightforward argument for the incompatibility of free will and divine foreknowledge. (Henceforth I shall refer to proponents of this view as *incompatibilists*, and to its opponents as *compatibilists*. This is the only way these terms will be used in this essay.) After a brief criticism, this simple argument will be replaced by a somewhat more complex argument for the same conclusion. This is followed by a discussion of this argument and of some clearly inadequate compatibilist replies to it. Here, also, we will consider briefly alternative ways proposed by incompatibilists for dealing with God's knowledge of the future—e.g., the doctrine of divine timelessness. Finally, we shall consider the strongest, most serious arguments advanced by the compatibilists in their attempt to overcome the argument for incompatibilism.

I. Two Arguments

As has become customary in this discussion, the arguments for incompatibilism will be presented in terms of specific examples; since the examples will not be unique in any way that is relevant to the soundness of the arguments, the results can easily be generalized. But philosophers who have become weary of following Jones through his interminable project of mowing the lawn will be happy to learn that a new example is in the offing: our concern in the following pages will be with Clarence, an aficionado of cheese omelets, and with the question, will Clarence have such an omelet for breakfast tomorrow morning, or won't he?

The first argument for incompatibilism begins by assuming that Clarence will, in fact, have a cheese omelet tomorrow morning, and it argues that Clarence's eating that omelet is necessary, hence not a matter of free choice. The argument goes like this:

(A1) Necessarily, God has always believed that Clarence would have a cheese omelet tomorrow morning. (premise)
(A2) Necessarily, if God has always believed that a certain thing will happen, then that thing will happen. (premise: divine infallibility)
(A3) Therefore: Necessarily, Clarence will have a cheese omelet tomorrow. (from 1, 2)

This argument has some impressive merits. It is complete, with no suppressed premises, and as concise as one could ask. Its validity is beyond reasonable doubt, and it will be sound if any incompatibilist argument for this conclusion is sound. Yet its very conciseness works against its usefulness as a tool for analyzing the controversy. The purpose of the argument, after all, is to say something about free will and therefore about what Clarence has it in his power to do—but these topics are present in argument (A) only by implication. Also, the first premise makes assumptions about the relation of God's knowledge to events in time, and these assumptions need to be made explicit so they can be examined. But the most serious deficiency of argument (A) concerns the modal operator in the first premise. 'Necessarily' here does not refer to logical necessity, as it does in the second premise; it is not claimed that God has the belief in question in all possible worlds. Rather, 'necessarily' in the first premise refers to the "necessity of the past"; God's having held this belief is *now* necessary because it has *already happened*. And it is this necessity which is, as it were, transmitted across the entailment stated in the second premise to appear again in the conclusion. But it is crystal clear that this notion, the idea of the necessity of the past, is the most crucial, difficult, and contentious element in the entire controversy. Clearly, an argument which is to throw light on the controversy must do more with this notion than baldly assert it.

With these considerations in mind, let us try another argument:

(B1) It is now true that Clarence will have a cheese omelet for breakfast tomorrow. (premise)

(B2) It is impossible that God should at any time believe what is false, or fail to believe anything which is true. (premise: divine omniscience)

(B3) Therefore, God has always believed that Clarence will have a cheese omelet for breakfast tomorrow. (from 1, 2)

(B4) If God has always believed a certain thing, it is not in anyone's power to bring it about that God has not always believed that thing. (premise: the unalterability of the past)

(B5) Therefore, it is not in Clarence's power to bring it about that God has not always believed that he would have a cheese omelet for breakfast. (from 3, 4)

(B6) It is not possible for it to be true both that God has always believed that Clarence would have a cheese omelet for breakfast, and that he does not in fact have one. (from 2)

(B7) Therefore, it is not in Clarence's power to refrain from having a cheese omelet for breakfast tomorrow. (from 5, 6) So Clarence's eating the omelet tomorrow is not an act of free choice.

II. Comments and Objections

Clearly this argument could be further expanded; still, it can serve as a basis for analysis. It does meet the objections raised against argument (A): it speaks explicitly about what it is in Clarence's power to do, it makes explicit the conception of divine omniscience which the argument assumes, and it deals with the necessity (or unalterability) of the past in a way which is at least somewhat less opaque than (A). We now proceed to some further comments on argument (B), together with some compatibilist answers to the argument.

First, note that the conception of free will implicit in (B7) is a libertarian conception; it can be formulated as follows:

(FW) N is free at t with regard to performing A = df.
    It is in N's power at t to perform A, and it is in N's power at t to refrain from performing A.

(Note that 'power' is used here in such a way that if it is in a person's power to perform a certain action in given circumstances, there is nothing in those circumstances which prevents or precludes that action's being performed. This conception of free will is basic to the whole discussion: if it were held that free will is compatible with causal determination, there would be no significant additional problem in reconciling free will with divine foreknowledge.)

It will be noted that arguments (A) and (B), while ostensibly about divine foreknowledge, refer explicitly to God's *belief*. The reason for this should be obvious: in general,

(1) N knows at t that p

entails

(2) (N believes at t that p) & p.

Now, the necessity asserted in (A1), and the unalterability asserted in (B4), are held to attach to God's past beliefs *because they are past*. But to assert that either (1) or (2) is thus necessary would be to assume that the state of affairs described by 'p' is itself necessary, *even if it lies in the future*. This of course is what the argument is trying to establish; it will not do to simply assume it as a premise. The arguments do however assume that God holds these beliefs *with absolute certainty* rather than probabilistically.

This is, perhaps, an appropriate place to mention an objection to incompatibilism which is fairly frequent: sometimes we ourselves know what another person is going to do (say, in anticipating a friend's reaction to some situation which has arisen), and we do not suppose that our knowing this is incompatible with their acting freely—so why suppose such an incompatibility when it is God who knows? The short answer to this is that arguments (A) and (B) do not proceed from God's knowledge as a premise but from God's belief, and no one supposes that a human being's believing something entails the truth of what is believed. But there may be more to the objection than this. If Susan, his wife, knows that Clarence will have an omelet for breakfast tomorrow, it must be true not only that she believes this but also that she has *adequate evidence* for her belief (she knows about his addiction to cheese omelets, he came home yesterday with a new hunk of sharp cheddar, and so on). And (it may be supposed) this justifying evidence must be sufficient to exclude the possibility that Clarence will *not* have an omelet; otherwise she could not be said to know that he will. In general, however, this need not be true. We often ascribe knowledge in situations where the justifying evidence is insufficient to warrant absolute certainty. And surely this is one of those situations: whatever evidence Susan may have is surely compatible with its being possible that Clarence will decide not to have an omelet tomorrow, and therefore with its being a matter of free choice whether he has one or not. If on the other hand the requirement for knowledge is strengthened to absolute certainty, then it is perfectly plausible to suppose that we never do have knowledge of future free actions.

Another frequent objection against incompatibilism is that this view wrongly assumes that God's prior knowledge of what a person will do *causes* the subsequent action. But if I know (for instance) that you are walking across the street, this does not *cause* you to walk across the street, so why assume that it is different with God? This is true enough, but a careful examination of arguments (A) and (B) will reveal that neither argument makes the claim that God's knowledge (or belief) causes the event which He knows. They merely assert that it is impossible that God should believe that an event will happen and yet the event not occur. And this is certainly true. But what, if anything, *causes* Clarence to eat the omelet is left as a problem for further study. (It may further be observed that (A) and (B) are both compatible with the assumption that God's belief is caused retroactively by the future action.)

Another important point about arguments (A) and (B) is that neither one raises the question of *how* God is able to know future actions. One might argue that God can do this only if sufficient causal conditions of the actions already exist; thus a world in which such knowledge is possible for God is of necessity a deterministic one. Such an argument might possibly be sound, but its major premise is exceedingly difficult to establish. Alternative accounts of God's knowledge of future actions are available, accounts which do not involve the presence of sufficient causal conditions. (To mention two examples, God's knowledge might result through retroactive causation from the actual future events—or, he might know future actions in virtue of his knowledge of the "counterfactuals of freedom" (Plantinga).) The task of disposing of such alternative accounts is formidable enough to make the suggested argument unattractive. But, to repeat the point, neither (A) nor (B) relies on assumptions about how God is able to know what he knows.

There is one further objection to incompatibilism which should be mentioned here. The incompatibilist claims that if God foreknows a person's action, then the action is not free. But, it is pointed out, if God foreknows that some person will *freely* choose a certain action, what follows is that the action will be done *freely*, which is the reverse of the conclusion desired by the incompatibilist. I mention this argument because I have heard it from reputable philosophers, but a moment's thought will reveal its vacuity. Certainly, "God believes that N will freely do A" entails "N will do A freely." But arguments (A) and (B) claim to establish that this same premise also entails "N will do A of necessity." And the new entailment does not cancel the old, nor does this argument do anything to undermine either (A) or (B). (In general, whenever it is claimed that "p" entails "q," one can truly assert that "p & $\sim q$" entails "$\sim q$," but this has no tendency whatever to show that "p" does *not* entail "q.")[2]

III. Some Incompatibilist Solutions

Before we consider still more objections to incompatibilism, it will be well to examine some of the solutions given by incompatibilists to the problem which is posed by the (alleged) success of their argument. That there is such a problem cannot be denied. There are a number of Scriptural passages for which the most obvious interpretation would seem to be that God knows in advance the free actions of human beings. And this also seems to be a fairly straightforward inference from the basic theological doctrine of divine omniscience. The incompatibilist who does not wish to reject these important elements of Scripture and theology must provide his own interpretations at these points. It lies beyond the scope of this essay to engage in a detailed examination of Biblical passages, but we will survey the various theological answers to the problem of divine omniscience and free action.

No doubt the most direct solution is simply to deny that free will, in the libertarian sense, exists at all. This is Jonathan Edwards's reaction to the argument—or rather, this was the prior conviction that made him receptive to the argument in the first place. It seems to me that much of the charm of Edwards's presentation of incompatibilism comes from the undisguised gusto with which he rams home the conclusions of his arguments. He does not (like Boethius and Aquinas) view incompatibilism as a problem for which a solution must be found. Rather, he finds in it a ready-made club with which to beat his Arminian opponents over the head. Do they find the consequences of his doctrine of predestination repellent and obnoxious? Very well, he will prove to them that the very same consequences follow from a doctrine which they themselves cannot deny, namely foreknowledge.

Most incompatibilists, however, have wished to affirm free will in precisely the libertarian sense which Edwards denied. The incompatibilist arguments claim to show that free will, in this sense, is incompatible with foreknowledge, so that to affirm free will one must deny foreknowledge. The problem is to show how this is compatible with divine omniscience.

It will be helpful to approach this problem by way of argument (B). The incompatibilist holds this argument to be valid, so if the conclusion is to be avoided at least one of the premises must be false. Since the incompatibilist is in no way willing to give up (B4), which affirms the unalterability of the past, the remaining possibilities are (B1) and (B2).

Suppose, then, that we deny (B1), the premise which says that it is now true that Clarence will eat an omelet tomorrow. To deny this is not to say that Clarence *will not* eat an omelet, but rather that it is not now true *either* that he will eat one or that he will not. If Susan were to conjecture, on the basis of his known addiction to cheese omelets, that "Clarence will have an omelet tomorrow," then what she says may *come true* tomorrow morning but it is not true now; as of now, there just is not any truth about what Clarence will eat for breakfast tomorrow.

The view that there are no truths about future contingent events is traced back to Aristotle; it was adopted (with certain complications) by Thomas Aquinas, and has been revived in our day by A. N. Prior and Peter Geach.[3] It has been my observation that philosophers often react against it with a vehemence that bears little relation to any demonstrated logical inadequacies.[4] It is somehow bizarre, or outrageous, or just downright offensive to suggest that this view might be correct. It seems to me that this is an over-reaction. In all likelihood what is at stake here is not a matter of logical correctness or incorrectness, but rather a matter of terminology: just how shall we use the words 'true', 'truth', and so on?[5] And it does not seem to me that our ordinary, pre-philosophical usage of these words clearly settles the matter one way or the other. (For example, we sometimes say of a pre-diction that it has "come true," which is not quite the same as saying that it was true all along. I note, also, that philosophi-cally unsophisticated students do not, on the whole, find the Aristotle-Prior view especially odd or bizarre when it is pre-sented to them in class.) So perhaps this is an appropriate point at which to invoke Rudolph Carnap's "Principle of Tolerance": "Let us be cautious in making assertions and critical in examin-ing them, but tolerant in permitting linguistic forms."[6]

However this may be, it is clear that many theists will find this view unacceptable for theological reasons: it implies that there are significant aspects of the future, especially those concerning the future free actions of persons, about which God as yet has neither definite beliefs nor knowledge. Still, the view we are considering affirms God's omniscience; premise (B2) is accepted without reservation. The matters God does not yet know about are matters about which there is not, as yet, any truth to be known. As soon as there are such truths, God will be the first to know!

It has been pointed out by Richard Swinburne that results which are essentially similar can be reached in another way, namely by modifying the definition of omniscience.[7] There is an interesting parallel here with omnipotence: many philosophers would now agree that God's omnipotence means that he has the power to do, not indeed everything, but everything which it is logically possible for him to do. Should we not, then, define omniscience by saying that God knows everything which it is logically possible for him to know? If we modify (B2) in accordance with this suggestion, the result is:

(B2′) It is impossible that God should at any time believe what is false, or fail to believe any true proposition such that his knowing that proposition at that time is logically possible.

It seems to me that (B2′) has considerable appeal even apart from incompatibilism's problem with foreknowledge. It will be noted that (B2′) does not affirm or presuppose that there *are* truths which it is logically impossible for God to know, but by leaving this possibility open it achieves a generality which is lacking in (B2) itself. And on the other hand, most compatibilists presumably do not want to claim that there are truths which God knows in spite of its being logically impossible for him to know them!

When argument (B) is modified along the lines of this suggestion—call the new argument (B′)—the results are interesting. The revised argument starts out with (B1) and (B2′). The text of the next step is the same as that of (B3), but it is not derivable from (B1) and (B2′), because it is not known whether (B1) satisfies the restriction in (B2′). So we have

(B3′) God has always believed that Clarence will have a cheese omelet tomorrow. (assumption for indirect proof)

(B4) through (B7) are taken over intact from the original proof. We then add:

(B8′) Clarence will act freely when he eats the omelet for breakfast tomorrow. (premise)

This of course contradicts (B7), so we can proceed to the conclusion:

(B9′) It is not the case that God has always believed that Clarence will have a cheese omelet for breakfast tomorrow. (from 3–8, indirect proof)

This argument suggests what may be a promising strategy for resolving the entire controversy. Perhaps the compatibilist and the incompatibilist should begin by agreeing to accept (B2′) as their definition of omniscience: this ought to be possible, since (as noted above) the formula entails nothing to which either party has reason to object. They will then proceed to resolve their differences about the validity of the incompatibilist arguments (B) and (B')—admittedly, not an easy task! But once this has been done, essentially complete agreement will have been reached; there will be no occasion (in view of the prior agreement to (B2')) for any further disputes about the meaning of 'omniscient'.

There is another way of avoiding the conclusion of (B) which historically has won much more acceptance than the views we have been considering. The reference, of course, is to the doctrine of divine timelessness. It lies beyond the scope of this paper either to expound this doctrine or to defend it against objections.[8] The doctrine of timelessness is frequently rejected as unintelligible, but attempts to demonstrate the unintelligibility do not seem to have been successful. Our present concern, however, is limited to seeing how the doctrine of timelessness resolves the problem of free will and foreknowledge.

Unlike the views just considered, the doctrine of timelessness affirms God's comprehensive knowledge of our future instead of removing from that knowledge events which are as yet contingent and indeterminate. But this knowledge is not, literally, *fore*knowledge at all; rather it is eternal knowledge, knowledge which exists at no time whatever, but only in the eternity of God's own timeless being. (Note that it is a cardinal error to consider God's eternal present as simultaneous with our present moment, or indeed with any moment at all of our time. Once this error is committed, the doctrine of timelessness collapses into chaos and contradiction.) By denying that God's eternal knowledge has a place in our time-sequence, the doctrine of timelessness removes an essential premise in the argument from foreknowledge to theological fatalism.

It is instructive to view this solution, also, in relation to argument (B). Once again, the definition of omniscience (B2) will have to be modified, this time to:

(B2*) It is impossible that God should believe anything false, or fail to believe timelessly anything that is true.

From this, together with (B1), we get:

(B3*) Therefore, God timelessly believes that Clarence will have a cheese omelet for breakfast tomorrow.

But in order to avoid the deterministic conclusion, we must affirm instead of (B4) that:

(B4*) It may sometimes be true that God timelessly believes a certain thing, and yet it is in someone's power to bring it about that God does not timelessly believe that thing.

Here we see the importance of the point that God's timeless present is not identical with any moment of our time. If God believes *now*, at the present time, that Clarence will have an omelet, then it is already *too late* for Clarence to do anything that would prevent God from having had that belief. But, to repeat this once more, God does *not* (according to the doctrine of timelessness) believe this, or anything else, *at the present time*. Rather, he believes things timelessly, entirely outside of our time-sequence. And what it is that God timelessly believes depends, in part, on what Clarence will freely choose to do tomorrow morning.

The doctrine of divine timelessness is surely a strange and difficult one, and nothing like a comprehensive assessment of it can be attempted in the present paper. But it does present a way, and perhaps (if the incompatibilist arguments are valid) the only way, to affirm consistently both that God has comprehensive knowledge of our future, and that we ourselves shall freely determine what, in certain respects, that future will be.

IV. God's Beliefs as "Soft Facts"

In a sense, everything to this point is preliminary to the main task of this paper. We have stated, in two different versions, the main argument for incompatibilism, rejected some clearly inadequate compatibilist replies to it, and reviewed various methods which are available to the incompatibilist for handling the theological problem created by his position. But the most serious and formidable replies to the incompatibilist arguments remain to be dealt with. All of these replies challenge, in different ways, the use made by the incompatibilist of the fundamental intuition which lies at the heart of his position—the intuition, namely, that the past is necessary, fixed, and unalterable in some way in which the future is not. In the present section we shall examine the contention that God's beliefs about the future are "soft facts," while the next two sections deal with various claims about our power over the past.

The view that God's beliefs are "soft facts"[9] accepts without question the intuition that the past is fixed, unpreventable, and beyond our control in a way in which the future is not. As Alvin Plantinga puts it:

Although I now have the power to raise my arm, I do not have the power to bring it about that I raised my arm five minutes ago. Although it is now within my power to think about Vienna, it is not now within my power to bring it about that five minutes ago I was thinking about Vienna. The past is fixed in a way in which the future is open. It is within my power to help determine how the future shall be; it is too late to do the same with respect to the past.[10]

So far, the incompatibilist is in hearty agreement, and it may seem just a small step from these remarks of Plantinga's to (A1), which affirms that God's believing that Clarence will eat a cheese omelet for breakfast tomorrow is necessary. But the compatibilist refuses to take this step. He points out, quite correctly as we shall see, that the necessity of the past must be restricted in its scope if it is not to generate some implausible and wildly counterintuitive consequences. For instance, consider

(3) A new U.S. president will be elected in 1984.

This may or may not be true, but if it is true so is

(4) It was true in 1976 that a new U.S. president would be elected in 1984.

This is in some sense a proposition about the past (I am writing this in 1983), but is it therefore necessary? Was it already "too late" in 1976 (and indeed long before that) for any of us to help determine who will be elected president in 1984? This of course is the problem of logical determinism or fatalism, and if fatalism is to be avoided (as intuitively it must be) there must be some way to exclude propositions such as (4) from those propositions about the past which are necessary, not within our power, and so on. We must, in other words, distinguish "hard facts" about the past from "soft facts."

One's first reaction is likely to be that there is something shady and disreputable about "facts about the past" such as (4). This proposition, we want to say, is not "really about" the past; it does not describe anything that "really happened" in the past. And this may well be true; intuitively there does seem to be a relevant difference between (4) and

(5) Jimmy Carter was elected president in 1976

with respect to pastness. The problem is that while phrases like "really about the past" and "really happened" evoke an intuitive response, they are not sufficient to delineate the (supposed) logical distinction between (4) and (5) which qualifies (5) as a hard fact and (4) as a soft fact. And not all of the problem cases are as transparent as (4). For instance,

(6) David said yesterday that Sandra will arrive tomorrow.

This seems to be really about the past, but consider:

(7) David yesterday said truly that Sandra will arrive tomorrow.

If (7) is true, should we conclude that Sandra's arrival is already necessary, unpreventable, beyond anyone's control, and so on? And consider

(8) Everything David said yesterday was true.

This, again, speaks about what happened yesterday, and unlike (7) it does not even entail any propositions about the future. Yet when conjoined with (6), which intuitively should be a hard fact about the past, it entails

(9) Sandra will arrive tomorrow.

Just one other example will be considered:

(10) Either David has already arrived or he will arrive tomorrow.

Assuming this to be true, is it a hard fact or a soft fact? The first disjunct by itself, if true, is a hard fact; the second disjunct, if true, is a soft fact. What then shall we say of the entire disjunction?

These examples show, I think, that the project of distinguishing between hard facts and soft facts is both necessary and nontrivial. And the compatibilist believes that this distinction can be used to thwart the arguments for incompatibilism. For, he argues, whatever other problems may be involved in the distinction, it should at least be clear that propositions "about" the past which entail propositions concerning the future—such as (4) and (7)—cannot be counted as hard facts.

But now consider once again

(B3′) God has always believed that Clarence will have a cheese omelet for breakfast tomorrow.

If God is essentially omniscient—that is, if (A2) and (B2) are true—then (B3′) entails

(11) Clarence will have a cheese omelet for breakfast tomorrow,

and this is clearly about the future, so (B3′) cannot be a hard fact; it cannot be necessary in the sense in which many other propositions about the past are necessary.

Is this conclusion correct? Perhaps the answer to this must wait until we have devised an adequate criterion for distinguishing hard from soft facts. But it is not at all evident that the compatibilist is drawing the right conclusion from the situation. There seems to be no doubt that (B3′), unlike (4), is "really about the past"; it asserts that God has performed a certain mental act (or perhaps, been in a certain mental state) throughout all ages past. It is, in this sense, just as much a part of the past that God believed this about Clarence as that David said that Sandra would arrive tomorrow. It is true that God, unlike David, is essentially omniscient. But how is this relevant to the question of whether God's past beliefs, like David's past statements, are now fixed and unalterable? How does God's omniscience give us a power over God's past beliefs that we do not have over David's past statements? To be sure, it follows from God's omniscience that (B3′) and (11) are either both soft facts or both hard facts, in spite of our natural tendency to think that (B3′) is hard and (11) soft. But which way does the inference go—from the softness of (11) to the softness of (B3′), or from the hardness of (B3′) to the hardness of (11)? This is what the whole controversy is about, and it is at least not obvious that the compatibilist's way of drawing the inference is the correct one.

But how shall we distinguish the hard facts?[11] A hard fact may be defined as a proposition which is true (that is its factuality) and which is such that it is impossible that anyone should have the power to bring it about that it is false (that is its hardness, which in the most typical case is a result of its being about the past). Our strategy here is to begin by delimiting a class of *future-indifferent propositions* whose truth or falsity cannot be affected by anything which happens after the present moment. The future-indifferent propositions which are true, along with some others, will then be our hard facts.

We begin by identifying a set of propositions which are "elementary" or "atomic" roughly in the sense of the *Tractatus* or the early Russell—propositions which say of some individual that it has a certain property, or of two or more individuals that they stand in a certain relation. (Many of these propositions will state that an individual has a property at a specified *time*; they will be of the form, '*S* has *p* at *t'*.) These elementary propositions will not include any whose most natural representation is as quantifications or truth-functions. (I am well aware that it is possible to contrive examples in which extremely complex propositions are represented in what appears to be simple subject-predicate form. For the time being all I am able to do is to rule out these examples on an *ad hoc* basis.) Having identified the elementary propositions, we proceed as follows:

(C1) An elementary proposition is future-indifferent iff it is consistent with there being no times after the present, and also consistent with there being times after the present.

The intuitive idea here is that a future-indifferent proposition must permit, but not require, that the entire universe should disappear and there be nothing at all after the present moment. One further point must be noted: the consistency mentioned in (C1) is to be determined through the ordinary methods of logical inference, without recourse to *de re* modalities, i.e. to truths about the essential properties of individual entities. The reason for this should be clear after a little reflection. Our aim is to delineate the future-indifferent propositions, those which are really about the past, and (C1) does this in the way noted. But it seems very likely that many if not all individuals have essential properties which imply things about them at times other than the present. Just what these essential properties are depends in part on which overall view of the world is true, but consider the following examples: If some form of scientific naturalism is true, then it is plausible that each spatio-temporal entity has essentially the property of *being such that it will continue in existence until it ceases to exist through natural transformations*. And these natural transformations both take time to happen, and leave something else in existence in place of the entity that has perished—so a presently existing stone (for example) has essential properties which are inconsistent with the world's ceasing to exist at this moment. Yet intuitively this should have no bearing on whether "this stone has existed for three billion years" is a fact about the past rather than the future. For another example: if theism is true, then each contingent individual has essentially the property, *being a creature of God*. But this entails God's existence, which in turn (since God is essentially everlasting) entails that there will be times after the present. If considerations of this sort are relevant to the notion of a future-indifferent proposition, then there will be few such propositions—but clearly, they are not relevant.

We now proceed as follows:

(C2) A truth-functional proposition is future-indifferent if each of its component propositions is future-indifferent.
(C3) An existentially quantified proposition is future-indifferent if each of its possible instances is future-indifferent.
(C4) Any proposition equivalent to a future-indifferent proposition is itself future-indifferent.

Now we are ready for hard facts:

(C5) Any future-indifferent proposition which is true is a hard fact.
(C6) Any necessary truth is a hard fact.

Here we include truths which are logically necessary both *de dicto* and *de re*. In (C1) our concern was with those truths which are "really about the past," and (for the reasons given) *de re* modal principles are not relevant to this. A hard fact, on the other hand, is a proposition such that it is not possible that anyone whatever should have the power to bring it about that it is false, and to this *de re* modalities *are* relevant: no one (not even

God) can bring it about that a given individual exists but lacks one of its essential properties.

Finally,

(C7) Any proposition which is entailed by one or more hard facts is a hard fact.

It is interesting to see how these criteria handle the examples given earlier. Clearly (5) will be a hard fact whereas (3) and (4) will not. (That is to say: (3) and (4) appear not to be hard facts on the basis of the information which is presently available. But, in virtue of (C7), they might turn out to be hard facts after all, if it turns out that they are entailed by some conjunction of hard facts. And so for the other examples.) (6) will also be a hard fact, since it entails nothing about the truth or falsity of the embedded proposition. (7) is equivalent to

(12) David said yesterday that Sandra will arrive tomorrow, and Sandra will arrive tomorrow.

The first conjunct, if true, is a hard fact, but the second is not, so neither is (12) or (7) a hard fact. (8) is equivalent to

(13) $\sim(Ep)((\text{David said yesterday that } p) \& \sim p)$.

When (13) is instantiated, the first conjunct will be future-indifferent, but for many values of 'p' the second will not. So (8) and (13) are not future-indifferent and, even if true, are not hard facts. In (10) the first conjunct is future-indifferent but the second is not, so (10) is not future-indifferent. It will however be a hard fact in virtue of (C7), if the first conjunct is true.

Now, what about (B3')? Is this proposition future-indifferent? In order to answer this, we need to know what is expressed by 'God'. Does it function simply as a non-connotative proper name, which serves to refer to the bearer but conveys no information about him? Or is 'God' like a title or a common noun in that it expresses something about the nature and status of the divine being?

My inclination is to say that the term 'God' as we ordinarily use it does indeed express, if not God's essence, at least our conception of God. In view of this I would say that a principle such as (A2) is not only necessary *de re*, in that it formulates one of God's essential properties, but is also necessary *de dicto* in virtue of the meaning of the term 'God'. If this is so, (B3') will *not* be future-indifferent, since it will entail (11), a fact about the future. But (B3') is by no means unique in this. Propositions such as "God spoke to Abraham" and even "God exists" will not be future-indifferent, for reasons analogous to those given in the discussion under (C1). If we use the word 'God' in such a way that God must be an essentially everlasting being, then any proposition which entails God's existence entails that there is no last moment of time.

Does this mean that "God exists" and "God created the universe out of nothing" are *soft* facts? The intention of the distinction between soft and hard facts was to distinguish between those propositions which are such that it might be in someone's power to make them false, from those for which this is impossible. But it is absurd—isn't it?—to suggest that anyone, even God, should now have the power to bring it about that God does not exist or that he did not create the universe out of nothing. Do we then need a third category of facts? A colleague suggested to me that besides hard facts and soft facts, there may also be facts sunny-side-up. But why stop there? Why not scrambled facts, poached facts, and even facts Benedict?

There is a better way. Consider the name 'Yahweh', which was used by the ancient Hebrews to refer to their God. They used this name (as a reading of Genesis will confirm) with no thought or connotation of such metaphysical attributes as essential omniscience, essential everlastingness, and the like. For a variety of reasons, this name for the deity is not in common use among present-day Christians or Jews, but nothing prevents us from reviving its use for a special purpose. And as we do so we will take care to avoid importing into the name's significance such metaphysical notions as essential everlastingness. We will use the name, as the ancient Hebrews did, simply as a non-connotative proper name referring to that individual who in fact was, and is, the God of Abraham, Isaac, and Jacob.

Given this use of the name 'Yahweh', the proposition "Yahweh spoke to Abraham" is a future-indifferent proposition; unlike "God spoke to Abraham," it entails nothing about the existence of times later than the present. But by the same token,

(14) Yahweh has always believed that Clarence will have a cheese omelet for breakfast tomorrow

is a future-indifferent proposition; unlike (B3′), it entails nothing about Clarence's breakfast tomorrow, or Clarence's existence tomorrow, or even about whether there will *be* a tomorrow. And since we are assuming that (14) is true, it will also be a hard fact.

Now the truth of (14), by itself, will not make (11) a hard fact. But now consider:

(15) If Yahweh exists, Yahweh is God.

This proposition is not logically necessary *de dicto*: its truth is not implied by the meanings of the terms in which it is expressed. And the proposition will not be future-indifferent, because its consequent entails God's existence. But it is, in a sense, a necessary truth: it expresses an *essential property* of Yahweh. There is no possible world in which Yahweh exists but is not God; no one, not even God himself and certainly no human being, could bring it about that Yahweh exists but is not God. So although (15) is not a future-indifferent proposition it is, in virtue of (C6), a hard fact.

And now the denouement becomes clear. As hard facts, we have the following:

(14) Yahweh has always believed that Clarence will have a cheese omelet for breakfast tomorrow.
(15) If Yahweh exists, Yahweh is God.
(A2) Necessarily, if God has always believed that a certain thing will happen, then that thing will happen.

But of course, these jointly entail

(11) Clarence will have a cheese omelet for breakfast tomorrow.

So (11), which is jointly entailed by a set of hard facts, is itself a hard fact: it is now unpreventable, so that it is utterly impossible that anyone at all, even God himself, should now have the power to bring it about that Clarence does not eat that omelet for breakfast tomorrow.

If the analysis of "hard facts" which we have given is sound, the incompatibilist is triumphant. No doubt, however, it would be overly optimistic to expect the compatibilist at this point to fold his tents and steal silently away. For one thing our principles (C1)–(C7), while they are logically coherent and well-motivated, are certainly too complex to qualify as either obvious or self-evident. So the possibility remains that the incompatibilist may develop his own analysis of hard facts, according to which it will turn out that (11) cannot after all be derived as a hard fact.

But even if the claim that God's beliefs are soft facts must be given up, the compatibilist's resources are not exhausted. For compatibilists have also made claims about powers we have over the past—claims which do not depend on the distinction between hard and soft facts. To these claims we now turn.

V. Counterfactual Power over the Past

The next compatibilist view to be examined holds that we have powers over the past of a rather special sort, powers which are most adequately expressed by counterfactual propositions. This view was first advanced by Alvin Plantinga, in his criticism of Nelson Pike's argument for incompatibilism,[12] and has since been endorsed by a number of other philosophers.

In Pike's article, "Divine Omniscience and Voluntary Action," a pivotal role is played by the following premise:

(P6) If God existed at t_1 and if God believed at t_1 that Jones would do X at t_2, then if it was within Jones's power at t_2 to refrain from doing X, then (1) it was within Jones's power at t_2 to do something that would have brought it about that God held a false belief at t_1, or (2) it was within Jones's power at t_2 to do something which would have brought it about that God did not hold the belief He held at t_1, or (3) it was within Jones's power at t_2 to do something that would have brought it about that any person who believed at t_1 that Jones would do X at t_2 (one of whom was, by hypothesis, God) held a false belief and thus was not God—that is, that God (who by hypothesis existed at t_1) did not exist at t_1.[13]

Pike's argument contains three additional premises, each of which states that the kinds of powers attributed to Jones in subpoints (1)–(3) of (P6) are such that no one can have them; thus, he is able to conclude that under the stated conditions it cannot be in Jones's power at t_2 to refrain from doing X. The additional premises are as follows:

(P3) It is not within one's power at a given time to do something having a description that is logically contradictory.

(P4) It is not within one's power at a given time to do something that would bring it about that someone who held a certain belief at a time prior to the time in question did not hold that belief at the time prior to the time in question.

(P5) It is not within one's power at a given time to do something that would bring it about that a person who existed at an earlier time did not exist at that earlier time.[14]

In his response to Pike's argument, Plantinga does not challenge the premises (P3)–(P5); he agrees that Jones cannot have any of the powers ruled out by those premises. Plantinga's challenge is directed at (P6), which he regards as false on the grounds that subpoints (1)–(3) of (P6) do not exhaust the possible ways in which Jones might have the power at t_2 to refrain from doing X. Pike himself had admitted, "I do not know how to argue that these are the only alternatives, but I have been unable to find another."[15] Plantinga comes to his assistance at this point, pointing out not one but three additional alternatives (each corresponding to one of the subpoints (1)–(3)), each of which would enable Jones to have the power in question without violating the restraints imposed by premises (P3)–(P5). These additional alternatives are not, however, independent of each other, and for our purposes it will be sufficient to examine one of them—the one which corresponds to subpoint (2) of (P6).

In discussing this premise, Plantinga suggests that it is Pike's view that

(PL51) God existed at t_1, and God believed at t_1 that Jones would do X at t_2, and it was within Jones's power to refrain from doing X at t_2

entails

(PL53) It was within Jones's power at t_2 to do something that would have brought it about that God did not hold the belief He did hold at t_1.

Plantinga, however, finds (PL53) to be ambiguous. It might, conceivably, mean the same as

(PL53a) It was within Jones's power at t_2, to do something such that if he had done it, then at t_1 God would have held a certain belief and also *not* held that belief.

Plantinga goes on to say that "(53a) is obviously and resoundingly false, but there is no reason whatever to think that (51) entails it. What (51) entails is rather

(PL53b) It was within Jones's power at t_2 to do something such that if he had done it, then God would not have held a belief that in fact he did hold.

This follows from (51) but is perfectly innocent."[16] Plantinga then goes on to discuss the situation in terms of possible worlds:

Suppose again that (51) is true, and consider a world W in which Jones refrains from doing X. If God is essentially omniscient, then in this world W He is omniscient and hence does not believe at t_1 that Jones will do X at t_2.[17]

I think it is fairly clear what kind of power over the past Plantinga is attributing to Jones (and, by implication, to all of us). And we also can see where the plausibility of Pike's argument (a specious plausibility, according to Plantinga) comes from. We notice that God's having believed at t_1 that Jones will do X at t_2 is inconsistent with Jones's refraining from doing X at t_2, and we conclude from this that it was not within Jones's power to refrain. What we fail to notice is that if Jones were to refrain from doing X at t_2 then God *would not have believed* at t_1 that Jones would do X at t_2. Our mistake is that we have changed our supposition about what Jones does (from acting to refraining) without changing our supposition about what God believed.

Note, however, that Jones's power over the past has to be formulated very carefully. Plantinga does not attribute to Jones the power to do something which would *bring about* that God, who at t_1 believed that Jones would do X, did not believe this at t_1. Jones's having this power would be inconsistent with Pike's premise (P4). (It would also be inconsistent with Plantinga's own statements about the fixity and stability of the past, quoted in the previous section.)[18] No, the power attributed to Jones is the power to do something such that *if he had done it, God would not have held* a belief that in fact he did hold. The counterfactual form is essential for stating this power that Jones has: it is *counterfactual power over the past*.

Nor is Jones's power to affect the past limited to God's past beliefs. A world in which Jones refrained from doing X would necessarily be different from the actual world with respect to God's beliefs about what Jones would do, but it might well be different in other respects as well. For if God had foreknown that Jones would refrain from doing X, he might well have arranged other things differently than they are in the actual world. To take a historical example, if God had not known in advance that the Allied armies would be encircled at Dunkirk in June 1940, he might not have prearranged the unusually calm weather which permitted the evacuation to be carried out with minimal loss of life. Thus, it may well be true not only that

(16) If the Allied armies had not been encircled at Dunkirk in June 1940, then God would not have believed, prior to 1940, that this would happen

but also that

(17) If the Allied armies had not been encircled at Dunkirk in June 1940, then God would not have arranged the weather prior to that time in the way in which he actually did arrange it.

In supposing that this sort of thing is possible (the particular example is my own) Plantinga is assuming a certain principle which I will call the *Principle of Foreknowledge and Providence*:

(PFP) If God has always known that a certain person will perform a particular free action at a given time, then God may have acted at any previous time in the light of that knowledge in a way that is different from the way he would have acted if he had known that the person would perform a different action at that time.

It should be noted that (PFP) is not a direct consequence of the doctrine of foreknowledge or of God's essential omnipotence. It is, I think, conceivable that God might possess comprehensive foreknowledge but never allow himself to be influenced by it in choosing his course of action. It may even be conceivable that God *could not* determine his course of action in view of future events which may themselves, in part, be consequences of that very action. But these possibilities have little appeal for the believer in foreknowledge, because they do not give him the theological benefits which he wishes to derive from foreknowledge. Surely one of the main advantages of foreknowledge lies in the thought that God, having known in advance everything that will happen, has also prearranged circumstances in view of this knowledge, so as to secure the fulfillment of his ultimate purposes. If God's knowledge does not have this result, then (to put the matter crudely) what good is it—either to him or to us? So while (PFP) is not entailed by either foreknowledge or essential omniscience, it seems to be something that most if not all believers in foreknowledge would want to affirm.

But if (PFP) is accepted, the potential scope of our power over the past becomes very large indeed. To be sure, it may be that we are very seldom in a position to know, or even plausibly conjecture, that God has arranged things in a certain way because of his foreknowledge of some particular human action. (My example concerning Dunkirk is perhaps as plausible as most that could be thought of. But it involves assumptions about the justification of war in general, and about the righteousness of the Allied cause in World War II, which are highly contestable.) But it is also true that there are very, very few facts about the past which are such that we can confidently say that they could not have been different, had God foreknown that people would choose freely in ways differently than they actually did choose. To take Plantinga's own example:

It is possible (though no doubt unlikely) that there is something you can do such that if you were to do it, then Abraham would never have existed. For perhaps you will be confronted with a decision of great importance—so important that one of the alternatives is such that if you were to choose *it*, then the course of human history would have been quite different from what in fact it is. Furthermore, it is possible that if God had foreseen that you would choose *that* alternative, he would have acted very differently. Perhaps he would have created different persons; perhaps, indeed, he would not have created Abraham. So it is possible that there is an action such that it is within your power to perform it and such that if you were to perform it, then God would not have created Abraham.[19]

So the scope of our power over the past is, potentially at least, very extensive. Yet this is still *counterfactual* power over the past, rather than power to *bring about* the past. As Plantinga says:

Possibly there is something I can do such that if I were to do it, then Abraham would not have existed; but it is not possible—is it?—that I now *cause* Abraham not to have existed.[20]

And his subsequent remarks indicate that, in his view, not even God now has it in his power to cause Abraham not to have existed. So much of the past may lie within our power, but it is counterfactual power and not power to bring about the past.

No one who is familiar with the literature can doubt that

Plantinga has given us a fascinating and provocative account of divine foreknowledge and providence. Of necessity much has been omitted here, and even the points that have been considered invite far more discussion than space will allow for. So we will confine our critical discussion of Plantinga to one point: his distinction between counterfactual power over the past and power to bring about the past. As we saw, the thing Plantinga objects to in Pike's original argument is Pike's contention that

(PL51) God existed at t_1, and God believed at t_1 that Jones would do X at t_2, and it was within Jones's power to refrain from doing X at t_2

entails

(PL53) It was within Jones's power at t_2 to do something that would have brought it about that God did not hold the belief he did hold at t_1.

Plantinga is able to avoid Pike's conclusion only after he has replaced (PL53) with the "perfectly innocent"

(PL53b) It was within Jones's power at t_2 to do something such that if he had done it, then God would not have held a belief that in fact he did hold.

Now, is this replacement justified? Why did Pike suppose in the first place that (PL51) entails (PL53)? Was it a mere oversight, resulting from his failure to notice that (PL53b) is the correct conclusion to draw from (PL51)? One thing is certain: if (PL51) does after all entail (PL53), Plantinga's main argument against Pike is invalidated and he will have to begin all over again.

Another way to see the importance of this distinction is to compare Plantinga's view with our argument (B). If I understand Plantinga's position correctly, he does not deny any of the premises of argument (B). What he does deny is the validity of the inference from (B5) and (B6) to (B7). (This is, of course essentially the same inference as that from (PL51) to (PL53).) If the inference from (B5) and (B6) to (B7) is in fact valid, Plantinga will have to reconsider his whole position.

Philip Quinn, in a forthcoming paper discussing the Pike-Plantinga controversy, has suggested a way in which this question might be settled. If the incompatibilist could vindicate a logical principle of a certain type (I will call such principles *Power Entailment Principles*), he could then use it to justify such inferences as the one from (PL51) to (PL53). Quinn himself proposes two candidates for such a principle, of which the first is

(PEP1) If it is within S's power to bring it about that p and if that p entails that q, then it is within S's power to bring it about that q.[21]

(PEP1) is obviously false: Neil Armstrong's being the first human to walk on the moon entails that $2 + 2 = 4$, but neither Armstrong nor anyone else has ever had the power to bring it about that this arithmetical proposition is true. Nor are matters any better for

(PEP2) If it is within S's power to bring it about that p and if that p entails that q and if it is contingent that q, then it is within S's power to bring it about that q.[22]

For Neil Armstrong's being the first human to walk on the moon entails that there is a moon, but certainly Armstrong never had the power to bring *that* about. At this point Quinn gives up the search for a true Power Entailment Principle: he says, "I have been unable to discover such a principle, and I very much doubt that there is one."[23]

The quest for such a principle has been taken up by Thomas Talbott in a recent paper. After reviewing the principle we have labeled (PEP1) and rehearsing its deficiencies, he proposes one of his own:

(PEP3) If (a) it is within S's power to bring it about that p is true and (b) it is within S's power to bring it about that p is false and (c) p entails q *and not-p entails not-q*, then it is within S's power to bring it about that q is true.[24]

About this principle, Talbott says that it "seems not only true but obviously true. Where p and q are logically equivalent, it could hardly be up to me whether or not p is true unless it were also up to me whether or not q is true."[25] It seems to me that this is absolutely correct. And since, given Plantinga's assumption that God is a logically necessary being, "p" is logically equivalent to "God has always believed that p," it follows that (*PEP3*) *shows that Plantinga's position is wrong*.

Talbott recognizes this, but he still goes on to look for a stronger principle, because there are valid cases of "power entailment" which are not instances of (PEP3). For instance, my having the power to draw a triangle certainly entails my having the power to draw a plane figure, in spite of the fact that "I draw a triangle" and "I draw a plane figure" are not equivalent. And such a principle is indeed available: it is

(PEP4) If (a) it is within S's power to bring it about that p is true, (b) p entails q, and (c) q is not a necessary condition of S's having the power to bring it about that p is true, then it is within S's power to bring it about that q is true.[26]

Talbott's proof of this principle is both elegant and conclusive:

If p entails q, then it is within the power of a person S to bring it about that p is true *only if* at least one of these conditions is met: either q is true *or*, if not true, then it is within S's power to bring it about that q is true. Suppose, then, that p entails q and it is *not* within S's power to bring it about that q is true. It immediately follows that, unless q is true, it is not within S's power to bring it about that p is true either; it follows, in other words, that q is a necessary condition of S's having the power to bring it about that p is true.[27]

Now, apply this to (PL51). Is God's having believed at t_1 that Jones would refrain from doing X at t_2 a necessary condition of Jones's having the power to refrain from doing X at t_2? If it is, then it follows immediately that Jones did not have this power. But (PL51) says that he *did* have such a power, so we are forced to the other alternative: that Jones at t_2 had it in his power to bring it about that God did not hold the belief he did hold at t_1. And this, of course, is just what (PL53) says. So (PL51) *does* entail (PL53); of that there can be no reasonable doubt. And by similar reasoning, (B5) and (B6) entail (B7).[28]

These Power Entailment Principles show that, with respect to our power over God's past beliefs, the distinction between counterfactual power over the past and power to bring about the past collapses: it is a distinction which fails to distinguish. These principles do not, however, apply to such cases as our alleged power to act in such a way, that if we were to act in that way Abraham would never have existed. But there is another principle which, if true, would collapse the distinction in that case also. It is:

(PEP5) If (a) it is within S's power to bring it about that p and (b) if it were the case that p it would be the case that q and (c) its being the case that q is not a necessary condition of S's having the power to bring it about that p, then it is within S's power to bring it about that q.

Is (PEP5) true? I believe it is, and I believe that an argument for (PEP5) which parallels Talbott's proof of (PEP4) would be a sound argument. Such an argument would, however, encounter certain complexities (such as the so-called "counterfactuals of freedom") which are not present in the case of (PEP4). And our central concern in the present section is with our power to bring about God's past beliefs, not with our power to bring about good weather on the English Channel or the non-existence of Abraham. So while I believe that (PEP5) is true, I shall forbear at this point any further attempt to prove it.

But concerning (PEP3) and (PEP4) there can be no reasonable doubt. And given those principles, there can be no reasonable doubt, either, that if we are to have the power to act in ways other than those in which God has always believed we would act, we must also have the power to bring it about that God has not believed the things which in fact he always has believed.

VI. Preventing the Past

Do we have power over the past? Among the very few philosophers who have considered this question and given an unequivocal affirmative answer must be numbered George Mavrodes.[29] We do indeed have power over the past. This power is not limited to the counterfactual power over the past discussed in the previous section; it is the power to directly, and indeed causally, bring about past events and also to prevent past events. And the past events to which this power extends are not limited to those involving God's knowledge or belief about future events; rather, the power in question is quite general, so that in principle we may be able to bring about or prevent all of the same kinds of events in the past that we are able to bring about or prevent in the future. (A qualification is needed here. Mavrodes does not necessarily want to claim that we *actually have* power over all of these past events. He is, in fact, quite cautious in his claims about the powers which we actually have over past events; his point is that we *could* have such powers, that there is nothing *logically incoherent* in the idea that we might have them. There may very well be specific reasons why I cannot (for example) prevent Abraham's birth, just as there are specific reasons why I cannot swim from San Francisco to Honolulu. Mavrodes's claim, however, is that there is nothing logically incoherent in supposing that I might have either of these powers.)

One more point needs to be added. It might be supposed that Mavrodes is claiming merely that we may, now, have the power to bring about those past events which *have already occurred*, and to prevent those events which have already failed to occur. Such powers as these would be remarkable enough, involving as they do retroactive causality. But Mavrodes is claiming more than this: in addition to the powers just mentioned, he claims that we also have the power to bring about past events which have *not* occurred, and to prevent events which have *already* occurred.

In making these claims, Mavrodes is attacking the arguments for incompatibilism in a profound and fundamental way, by rejecting the fundamental intuition on which all such arguments are built—the intuition of the necessity of the past. If he is right in rejecting this intuition, then incompatibilism cannot be defended. And on the other hand, it seems likely (and this is supported by the arguments in the previous sections) that no compatibilist position which does not reject this intuition can succeed.

It will not be necessary to compare Mavrodes's position in a detailed way with the incompatibilist arguments which have been featured in this paper. For Mavrodes does not just nibble around the edges of premises such as (A1) and (B4); he rejects them outright. And without these premises, or others like them, the argument for incompatibilism cannot get off the ground. What remains to be done, then, is first to *understand* Mavrodes's claims about our powers over the past, and secondly to *assess* those claims, to determine as best we can whether they are true or false.

What would it mean to bring about the past? What sort of power is this? I think it makes a difference here whether we are thinking of the power to bring about past events which have in fact taken place, or of the power to bring about events which might have taken place in the past but which in fact did not. Understanding the first kind of power is not difficult, if we are prepared to contemplate the possibility of retroactive causation: it is the power to perform an action some of whose consequences are events in the past. Do we ever exercise this power? Mavrodes's claim is that we do this every day of our lives. For by performing any free action, I bring it about that God has always believed that I would perform that action, and by freely refraining from an action I prevent God from having believed I would perform it.[30] (These are the only specific examples of power over the past to which Mavrodes commits himself. It may be reasonable to assume that he would accept the Principle of Foreknowledge and Providence and thus would agree that we sometimes have the power to influence the past indirectly in the way suggested by Plantinga. I think that Mavrodes would also want to say that there may be any number of other ways in which we have power over the past, only we do not at present know what those ways are.)

But how shall we understand that other kind of power, the power to bring about events which might have taken place in the past but which in fact have not? In answering this question I shall proceed somewhat indirectly. We shall first consider several interpretations of Mavrodes's claim which might appear somewhat plausible, but which must be rejected. Only then will we turn to what I think is the correct interpretation of that claim. My reason for this roundabout procedure is that I find that claim to be extremely difficult to interpret, and I hope that consideration of several inadequate interpretations will help to motivate the acceptance of the correct one. (Readers who find claims about bringing about the past to be unproblematic are therefore invited to skip over the next few pages until they reach what they view as the "correct" interpretation!)

One way of understanding this power is suggested by the counterfactual power over the past discussed in the last section: the power to bring about past events which have not in fact occurred may simply be the power to do something such that, if I were to do it, an event which in fact has not taken place in the past would have taken place.

This is absolutely correct, but also totally unilluminating. We saw in the last section that Plantinga conceived of counterfactual power over the past as an *alternative* to power to bring about the past: he thought it possible to affirm our counterfactual power over God's past beliefs, while accepting Pike's premise

(P4) It is not within one's power at a given time to do something that would bring it about that someone who held a certain belief at a time prior to the time in question did not hold that belief at the time prior to the time in question.

But we have seen that the notion of counterfactual power over the past as an alternative to power to bring about the past is a snare and a delusion: the compatibilist, if he is to be consistent, must affirm our power to *bring about* the past, and if counterfactual power over the past is something less than this it is not the power we need if compatibilism is to be true. If on the other hand counterfactual power over the past is simply *the same as* power to bring about the past, what is gained by the change in wording? And why make a point of describing just our powers over the *past* in counterfactual terms, rather than all of our other powers? Why not describe my power to greet the postman as the power to do something, such that if I were to do it then the postman would be greeted by me? Such a description would not be inaccurate, but what would be gained by it? I conclude, then, that while it is not inaccurate to describe our powers over the past in counterfactual terms, there is no reason to suppose that such a description conveys any additional illumination or brings us any closer to understanding what such powers really amount to.

Plantinga, to be sure, also suggests a second possible interpretation of our power to bring about God's past beliefs. It is, he suggests, conceivable that Jones's "power at t_2 to do something that would have brought it about that God did not hold the belief he held at t_1," might be interpreted as Jones's "power, at t_2, to do something such that if he had done it, then at t_1 God would have held a certain belief and also *not* held that belief." [31] But this has nothing to recommend it as an interpretation of Jones's power. The reason for this is not simply that such a power would be logically absurd, for it may well turn out that the power to bring about God's past beliefs *is* logically absurd; indeed the incompatibilist believes that it is. But *this* interpretation of Jones's power would not perform, and would not even seem to perform, the function which it has in Pike's premise (P6). That premise enumerates three different kinds of powers, such that if it were possible for Jones to have powers of one or more of these kinds, it would be possible for Jones to be acting freely even though God knows beforehand what Jones is going to do. But the power to bring it about that God both has and does not have a certain belief would not fulfill this role: even if Jones (absurdly) had this power and exercised it, it would still be true that God believed at t_1 that Jones would do X at t_2 (although it would also be true that God did *not* have that belief), and so it would still be impossible for Jones to refrain from doing X at t_2.

So this suggestion is unacceptable, yet reflecting on it may suggest to us yet another possible interpretation of our power over the past. For why is it that Jones (apparently) lacks freedom with respect to doing X at t_2? The answer is, because there is a circumstance which obtains (namely, God's having always believed that Jones would do X at t_2) which logically *precludes* Jones's refraining from doing X at t_2, and since it is not possible for Jones to refrain from doing X at t_2, it is also not possible for him to do X freely. (Let us call circumstances of this sort *precluding circumstances*.)

Now, the precluding circumstances which affect our lives are not by any means limited to God's past beliefs. And perhaps considering how we deal with some other kinds of precluding circumstances will help us to see how Jones might be free to refrain from doing X even though God has always believed that he would do X. Suppose, for example, that I am going on a trip to Romania, and in order to get the most out of my visit I promise myself that I will take the opportunity to converse with as many Romanians as possible. But there is a snag: I have never learned Romanian. However, a remedy is available; some intensive work at my friendly neighborhood Berlitz school will soon equip me to carry on a passable conversation. It may be helpful to state this situation formally:

(18) If at t_1 N had never learned Romanian, and it was in N's power to t_2 to converse freely in Romanian, then it was in N's power to bring it about that whereas it *v*as true at t_1 that N had never learned Romanian it was no longer true at t_2 that N had never learned Romanian.

It should be noted that in order to have the power in question, N must be able to bring it about that a certain past-tense proposition—in this case, "N has never learned Romanian"—is true at one point in time but false at a later point in time. But now consider:

(19) If at t_1 God had always believed that Jones would do X at t_2, and it was in Jones's power to refrain from doing X at t_2, then it was in Jones's power to bring it about that whereas it was true at t_1 that God had always believed that Jones would do X at t_2 it was no longer true at t_2 that God had always believed that Jones would do X at t_2.

The parallelism between (18) and (19) is close and (I believe) also instructive. In one case, it is N's never having learned Romanian which precludes his conversing in that language; in the other case, it is God's always having believed that Jones would do X at t_2 which precludes his refraining from doing X. In each case, if the precluding circumstance can be removed (i.e., if the past-tense proposition which was formerly true can become false), the precluded action may become possible. In the case of N this can probably be done, but what about Jones? Here there is a complication. If the "believer" in (19) were anyone other than God, we might be able to persuade him to change his mind, and after the change of mind it would no longer be true that he had always believed that Jones would do X at t_2. But with God, things are somewhat different: by hypothesis, whatever God believes at one time he believes at all times, so the only way for Jones to bring it about that God has not *always* believed that Jones would do X at t_2 is for him to bring it about that God has *never* believed this. This is true enough. Nevertheless, I maintain that the power attributed to Jones in the consequent of (19) is indeed the power that Jones must have if he is to be free in the face of God's prior belief: it is the power to bring it about that God has not believed the things which in fact he always has believed.

At this point certain objections can be anticipated. Someone will say, "But that power would be the power to *change the past!*" I agree; I can think of no better expression for describing the kind of power mentioned in the consequent of (19). "But," the objector continues, "that is absurd; *no one* could possibly have the power to change the past!" Again, I agree; I am in no way an advocate for powers of this kind. But, I add, a reader of the writings of George Mavrodes might easily receive the impression from certain passages that this philosopher *does* advocate the power to change the past. One of his examples is the coronation of Elizabeth II as Queen of England, and he asserts repeatedly that this event may even now be preventable. He explicitly rules out "sensible" interpretations of this, such as our now discovering that her coronation in 1953 was invalid due to some technicality. "No," he says, "I mean that, assuming that she has been Queen for many years, we might now be able to do something which would bring it about that she has never, up to the present time, been Queen."[32] But if she has in fact been Queen for many years, and we can now bring it about that she has never been Queen, would that not be to change the past?

I said that a reader of Mavrodes might receive this impression, but I must add at once that it would be a mistaken impression. Mavrodes explicitly rules out powers of the kind implied by (19)—the power to bring it about that there was "a time at which it was true that *E has occurred*, and a later time at which it was not true that *E has occurred*."[33] And he lays great emphasis on the difference between the power to *change* the past and the power to *determine* the past—to *bring about* or to *prevent* past events. It is the latter power, and not the former, that he wishes to affirm.

Now it is my contention that by admitting that we cannot have powers of the kind specified in the consequent of (19)— powers describable as powers to alter the past—Mavrodes in effect concedes the central premise of the incompatibilist argument, as expressed, for example, in

(B4) If God has always believed a certain thing, it is not in anyone's power to bring it about that God has not always believed that thing.

Mavrodes, however, would disagree; he holds that our inability to *change* the past, in the sense indicated by (19), is completely irrelevant to the necessity of the past as this is affirmed by the incompatibilist. For, he goes on to say, no one can change the future, either.[34] We can, to be sure, change our plans for the future, but the future itself—roughly, the set of states of affairs subsequent to the present that actually obtain—is what results after all such changes have been made. So to say that we cannot change the past marks no genuine contrast and is not to the point.

I think this is a red herring, but we must follow it up briefly lest someone be led astray by it. First, with regard to the argument of this paper, it may be said that the expression "changing the past" is of no importance whatever. I have argued that if compatibilism is to be true we humans must have powers of a certain kind, the kind specified in the consequent of (19). These powers, I agree, are aptly characterized as powers to change the past. But this characterization is of no importance for my argument: what matters is not what these powers are called but whether or not we have them. So far as the argument is concerned, they could be called powers to bring about the past, or powers to prevent the past, or powers to facilitate the past, or anything else you like. Now, if someone defines a set of powers which could be aptly characterized as powers to change the future, and shows that some important philosophical point hinges on whether we have these powers or do not have them, then the question of whether or not we can change the future will be of philosophical interest. But so far as the present argument is concerned, the question simply does not arise.

That really should be sufficient, but I am going to abandon for a moment the formal context of my argument and comment on the notion of "changing the past" in its broader cultural context. For us in this culture (I cannot speak about others) it seems natural to think of the past as a determinate totality of some kind, consisting of all the facts and happenings up until now—it includes everything that would be written about in a complete history of the entire universe. Having before our minds the idea of such a totality, a natural question is whether anything can now be done to change it—and the answer we all give (including George Mavrodes!) is that it cannot be changed. Now the question about whether the future can be changed does not seem to be a natural question in the same way—I do not think I have ever so much as encountered it, except in the writing of philosophers. To be sure, if we think of the future as a determinate totality—say, as written in the book of Fate, or as a plan in the mind of God—then it makes sense to ask whether it can be changed—can we erase some of the writing in the book, or induce God to change his plan? But outside the context of such religious or philosophical doctrines, I submit that we simply do not operate with the idea of the future as a determinate totality. The future is seen rather as a realm of possibility, where all sorts of things *can* or *might* happen, but in which only the hazy outlines are discernible of a few things that *will definitely* happen. But in general, the future is not made yet, so what sense would it make to talk about *changing* it? So in this context also, I want to say that the question of changing the future is one that does not arise.

Let us briefly review our progress to date. We are trying to understand Mavrodes's claim that we can have power over the past—in particular, power to prevent events which have in fact already occurred. We considered the possibility of expressing this power in counterfactual terms, and we saw that this move gives no help whatever in our attempt to understand what such powers might be. We also considered, and rejected, the notion that the power in question might be the power to bring it about that a certain event *both* has and has not occurred (e.g., to bring it about that God both held and did not hold a certain belief). Finally, we considered the possibility that the power might be the power to bring it about that whereas it was true at one time that a certain event had occurred, it was at a later time no longer true that this event had occurred—for example, to bring it about

that whereas it was true at t_1 that God had always believed that Jones would do X at t_2 it was no longer true at t_2 that God had always believed that Jones would do X at t_2.

I believe, and have argued above, that this is indeed the kind of power we must have if we are to be free in the face of God's past beliefs, i.e., if compatibilism is to be true. Nevertheless, this cannot possibly be the correct interpretation of Mavrodes's claim about our power over the past. For Mavrodes repudiates powers of the kind specified above—powers describable as powers to change the past—and nevertheless he continues to claim that we may have the power to prevent events which have already occurred—for example, he claims that someone may, even now, have the power to prevent Elizabeth's coronation as the Queen of England. So the question becomes acute: *How is this claim to be understood*?

I believe the right way to understand it is this. When he says that someone might even now have the power to prevent Elizabeth's coronation, he means that there may be a kind of action such that (1) someone has, or could have, all of the abilities, personal qualities, etc., which are requisite for performing such an action, and (2) such an action, if performed in 1983 or later, would have the effect that Elizabeth would never have become

Queen. Mavrodes does not, however, think that it is possible that the actual world, the state of affairs which actually obtains and contains everything which has happened up to the present moment (including Elizabeth's coronation), should also contain this preventing action.[35] It is not now possible that someone *actually will* prevent Elizabeth's coronation, given that she has in fact been crowned, any more than it is now possible that I should converse in Romanian, given that I have never learned Romanian. Just as my failure to learn Romanian precludes that act of conversing, so Elizabeth's coronation precludes that act of preventing. There is, however, an important difference between the cases: the condition of my never having learned Romanian is one that can be removed, so that even though it is not *now* possible for me to converse in that language, this may well *become* possible in the future. But Elizabeth's coronation *cannot* be removed from our past history, for that would be to change the past. So in this case, the circumstance which precludes the preventing action is permanent: it will not and cannot be removed.

But how can Mavrodes say that someone *might* perform the preventing act, or that someone may have the *power* to do so? We have to keep in mind that there is a sense of 'power' according to which a person's powers (normally) remain more or less constant, while the possibilities of their being exercised come and go.[36] If I complete my project of learning Romanian, I will have the power to converse in that language, but I will be able to exercise that power only when I am in the company of another Romanian-speaker. Now, suppose I am being questioned about my abilities. (The questioner is a Japanese exchange student who is working hard on learning his English modal auxiliaries.)

"Can you carry on a conversation in Romanian?"

"Yes, I can; actually I'm fairly fluent."

"Excellent! Please demonstrate your ability!"

"Well, I can't do it *now*. I mean, you don't speak Romanian, and neither does anyone else who is present."

"But you just said that you *can* converse in Romanian."

"No, but you didn't understand me. When I said that I *can* converse in Romanian, I didn't mean that I can do it *now*. What I meant was that I *could* converse in that language, *if* there were someone else present with whom to do so. Now do you see?"

"Ah, so! Thank you very much!"

It should be clear by now that when Mavrodes says that we *can* prevent Elizabeth's coronation, he is using this word as I used it when in my first reply I said that I can converse in Romanian—not as I used it in my second reply, when I said that I cannot do this in the absence of other speakers of the language. His 'can', like mine, is really a 'could . . . if'. And what goes for 'can' goes also for power'. And understanding this, we can also understand how Mavrodes can say that we have the power to prevent Elizabeth's coronation even though (as we have seen) it is not possible, given that she was in fact crowned, for us to exercise that power.

At this point a pattern has begun to emerge—a pattern which the reader may already have identified. It is, in fact, the beginning of a familiar dialectic which results when a soft determinist is invited to discuss free will. Perhaps someone has committed a misdeed, and the soft determinist is asked whether the person could have done otherwise. The answer is that nothing compelled the commission of the misdeed, and that the culprit could have acted otherwise if he had willed to. Ah, but could he have willed to? He could have, if his character had been different than it is. But could *that* have been different? It could have, if some of his experiences earlier in life had been different. . . . At some point, a hard determinist (or a libertarian) breaks in to say that, at each stage, what would have to have been different in order for the person to respond differently *could not* have been different, and that therefore the supposed "freedom" to act otherwise is an illusion. It is not my present purpose to enter into this dialectic. My purpose, rather, is to point out that the uses of 'can', 'power', 'ability', and similar words which generate this dialectic are *exactly the same* as the uses of these words employed by Mavrodes when he is explaining our power to prevent the past.

Am I saying that Mavrodes is a soft determinist? Certainly he does not want to be and does not intend to be. But would it not be a striking confirmation of the incompatibilist's thesis if it turns out that a compatibilist who wishes to affirm our power *over* the past but to deny our power to *change* the past, finds himself compelled to use crucial terms like 'can' and 'power' in a way which generates "free will" only in the soft determinist sense and not in the libertarian sense of that term?

What I have been saying about Mavrodes in this connection

will apply to other compatibilists as well. Take Plantinga, for instance: when he affirms that

(PL53b) If was within Jones's power at t_2 to do something such that if he had done it, then God would not have held a belief that in fact he did hold,

does he really think it possible that the actual world, the world which in fact contains God's belief that Jones would do X at t_2, should also contain Jones's refraining from doing X? Assuredly not, for this would mean that a belief of God's would be false. Is it possible, then, that Jones can bring it about that the past does *not* contain that belief of God's? This also is impossible, for it would involve changing the past. But how then can Jones have the power to refrain? The answer is that Plantinga, like Mavrodes, is using 'power' in a general sense here, the sense in which I use it when I say that I have the power to converse in Romanian, though my exercise of that power may sometimes be precluded by the absence of other speakers of that language. Similarly, Jones has the power to refrain from doing X, and no doubt does so on many occasions (a life of continual X-ing would probably be pretty monotonous!), but his refraining therefrom on this occasion is precluded by God's belief that at t_2 he will in fact do X.

And what is true of Mavrodes and Plantinga will, I believe, turn out to be true of other compatibilists as well. When their positions are analyzed as far as they can be, it will turn out that either they affirm our ability to alter the past (and I know of none that does affirm this), or they speak of our "powers" in the soft determinist sense, the sense such that it may be in my power to do something even though precluding circumstances make it impossible that I should actually do it.

Let me reinforce this by pointing out that the compatibilist position very clearly *is* a variety of determinism according to some quite standard definitions of determinism. According to Richard Taylor, for instance,

Determinism is the general philosophical thesis which states that for everything that ever happens there are conditions such that, given them, nothing else could happen.[37]

And Brand Blanshard says

By indeterminism I mean the view that there is some event B that is not so connected with any previous event A that, given A, B must occur.[38]

It is quite clear that, in the light of these definitions, the views of compatibilists such as Mavrodes and Plantinga qualify as a version of determinism rather than indeterminism. Of course, they may want to say that these are not the right definitions of determinism and indeterminism. But if so it is up to them to tell us what the right definitions are, and why we should prefer them to those given by Taylor and Blanshard.

VII. Conclusion

We have examined some arguments for the incompatibility of free will and comprehensive divine foreknowledge, and rejected some ineffective replies to those arguments. We have seen how theists who affirm this incompatibility deal with the resulting theological problem. We then considered the distinction between "hard facts" and "soft facts," and developed an analysis of that distinction according to which "God believed that p" will be a hard fact even if "p" is a proposition concerning the future. We then examined the contention that our power over the past is counterfactual power rather than power to bring about the past, and we saw that this attempted distinction collapses—demonstrably so in the case of power over God's past beliefs, but probably in all other cases as well. Finally, we considered the most profound and fundamental challenge to the incompatibilist arguments—the challenge which rejects altogether the necessity of the past. We saw that this rejection, when pressed to its conclusion, requires that we have the ability actually to alter God's past beliefs—to bring it about that whereas it has always been true that God has always believed a certain thing, it will now no longer be the case that God has always believed that thing. We also saw that compatibilists do not in fact affirm this. Instead, they use crucial terms like 'can' and 'power' in a way which in effect commits them to a soft determinist conception of free will. And so the incompatibilist analysis of the situation is strikingly confirmed: those who seek to maintain the compatibility of free will and foreknowledge are in the end forced to abandon, implicitly if not explicitly, the libertarian conception of freedom with which the discussion began.

It was noted at the beginning of this essay that the controversy over free will and foreknowledge has failed to reach a satisfactory conclusion. It is my hope that compatibilists who read the essay will find that their positions have been fairly represented, that their arguments have been addressed, and that relevant questions have been raised. If so, then perhaps we can proceed together in the task of answering those questions.

CHAPTER TWELVE

Divine Foreknowledge and Alternative Conceptions of Human Freedom

William P. Alston

I

Nelson Pike's important 1965 paper, "Divine Omniscience and Voluntary Action"[1] presents an interestingly novel version of the old argument from divine foreknowledge to our inability to do (choose) other than what we in fact do.

1. "God existed at t_1" entails "If Jones did X at t_2, God believed at t_1 that Jones would do X at t_2."
2. "God believes X" entails "'X' is true."
3. It is not within one's power at a given time to do something having a description that is logically contradictory.
4. It is not within one's power at a given time to do something that would bring it about that someone who held a certain belief at a time prior to the time in question did not hold that belief at the time prior to the time in question.
5. It is not within one's power at a given time to do something that would bring it about that a person who existed at an earlier time did not exist at that earlier time.
6. If God existed at t_1 and if God believed at t_1 that Jones would do X at t_2, then if it was within Jones's power at t_2 to refrain from doing X, then (1) it was within Jones's power at t_2 to do something that would have brought it about that God held a false belief at t_1, or (2) it was within Jones's power at t_2 to do something which would have brought

Reprinted by permission from the *International Journal for Philosophy of Religion*, 18 (1985): 19–32. I have greatly profited from discussing the issues of this paper with Jonathan Bennett, Nelson Pike, Alvin Plantinga, and Peter van Inwagen.

it about that God did not hold the belief He held at t_1, or (3) it was within Jones's power at t_2 to do something that would have brought it about that any person who believed at t_1 that Jones would do X at t_2 (one of whom was, by hypothesis, God) held a false belief and thus was not God—that is, that God (who by hypothesis existed at t_1) did not exist at t_1.

7. Alternative 1 in the consequent of item 6 is false. (from 2 and 3)
8. Alternative 2 in the consequent of item 6 is false. (from 4)
9. Alternative 3 in the consequent of item 6 is false. (from 5)
10. Therefore, if God existed at t_1 and if God believed at t_1 that Jones would do X at t_2, then it was not within Jones's power at t_2 to refrain from doing X. (from 6 through 9)
11. Therefore, if God existed at t_1, and if Jones did X at t_2, it was not within Jones's power at t_2 to refrain from doing X. (from 1 and 10)[2]

This argument has stimulated a flurry of discussion that shows no signs of abating.[3] But in this literature there is little attempt to spell out the intended sense of such crucial terms as 'power', 'ability', 'could have done otherwise', 'free', and 'voluntary'. And even where some attention is given to these terms there is no recognition that they might be used differently by different parties to the discussion. This is all the more surprising since, in another part of the forest, one finds elaborate analyses of competing senses of these terms. I refer, of course, to the extensive literature on free will. It is high time the fruits of this latter activity were brought to bear on Pike's argument, which, after all, is concerned to show that human actions are not free in some sense, that human beings lack the power, in some sense, to do other than what they do. I will be asking (1) what concepts of power, etc., Pike and other participants in the controversy mean to be using, and (2) how such concepts will have to be construed if their arguments are to be successful, or as successful as possible.

Rather than attempt to follow all the twists and turns in the free will literature, I will focus on the crucial distinction between a "libertarian" and a "compatibilist" understanding of terms like 'within one's power'. I will not attempt a full characterization of either interpretation. Instead I will focus on one basic respect in which they differ, viz., on whether its being within one's power to do A at t requires that it be "really possible" that one do A at t. What is *really possible* at t is what is "left open" by what has happened up to t; it is that the non-occurrence of which is not necessitated by what has happened up to t. Now there are various ways in which previous states of the world can necessitate, prevent, or leave open a state of affairs. It is the causal way that has dominated the free will discussion. A previous state of affairs, F, *causally* necessitates E at t if the necessitation is by virtue of causal laws.

I. E is causally necessitated by a previous state of affairs, F = df. E is entailed by the conjunction of F and some causal laws, and E is not entailed by either conjunct alone.[4]

And to say that E is *causally possible* is to say that not-E is not causally necessitated by any previous states of affairs.

II. E is causally possible at t = df. There is no state of affairs prior to t, F, such that not-E is entailed by the conjunction of F and some causal laws without being entailed by either conjunct alone.

Being causally ruled out by the past is not the only threat to real possibility. Contemporary thinkers who suppose that God's foreknowledge rules out human free choice do not typically suppose that divine knowledge causes us to act as we do.[5] They think, rather, that since God is necessarily infallible the fact that God believes at t_1 that Jones will do X at t_2 *by itself* logically entails that Jones will do X at t_2, and hence is, by itself, logically incompatible with Jones's refraining from doing X at t_2. Let us say that a state of affairs is "situationally logically necessitated" when it is entailed by a previous state of affairs alone.

III. E is situationally logically necessitated by a previous state of affairs, F = df. E is entailed by F alone.

And let us say that a state of affairs is "situationally logically possible" ('S-logically possible') when its non-occurrence is not entailed by past facts alone.

IV. E is S-logically possible at t = df. There is no state of affairs prior to t, F, such that not-E is entailed by F.

We may think of an event as "really possible" when it is both causally and S-logically possible.

V. E is really possible at t = df. There is no state of affairs prior to t, F, such that either (a) not-E is entailed by the conjunction of F and

some causal laws without being entailed by either conjunct alone, or
(b) E is entailed by F alone.

This formulation can be simplified. Clearly if E is entailed by the
conjunction of F and some causal laws, this covers both the case
in which both conjuncts are needed for the entailment and the
case in which E is entailed by F alone. Hence the following is
logically equivalent to V.

VI. E is really possible at t = df. There is no state of affairs prior to t, F,
such that E is entailed by the conjunction of F and some causal laws.

However, IV is more perspicuous in that it brings out the way
in which a really possible event escapes being ruled out by the
past in both of two ways.

Since the basic claim of the libertarian is that I am not really
free to do X at t if doing X is ruled out by what has already happened, she will want to use the broader notion of real possibility
for a necessary condition of freedom. She will want to make it a
necessary condition of being free to do E (having it within one's
power to do E) that E is neither causally nor S-logically necessitated by past events.

Recently, under the influence of William of Ockham, a distinction between "hard" and "soft" facts has been injected into
the discussion of these and related issues.[6] Roughly, a dated fact
is a "hard" fact about the time in question if it is wholly about
that time, if it is completely over and done with when that time
is over. Otherwise it is a "soft" fact about that time. Thus the
fact that I was offered the job at t is a hard fact about t; it embodies only what was going on then and is fully constituted by the
state of the world at t. On the other hand, the fact that I was
offered the job two weeks before declining it is not a hard fact
about t, even if t is when I was offered the job. That fact is not
fully constituted until two weeks past t. This distinction is relevant to our account of real possibility in the following way. A
soft past fact can entail the occurrence of non-E without thereby
preventing E from being really possible. The fact that I was offered the job two weeks before declining it at t entails that I did
not accept it at t; but this obviously fails to show that it was not
really possible for me to accept the job at t. Of course my not
accepting the job at t is entailed by any fact that includes my de-

clining it as a conjunct; but that has no bearing on whether accepting it was a real possibility for me at the moment of choice. Thus III–VI must be understood as restricted to states of affairs that have completely obtained before t, i.e., to *hard* facts about times prior to t.

Some recent thinkers, again following Ockham, have sought to draw the teeth of arguments like Pike's by claiming that a divine belief at t is not a hard fact about t; and hence that the fact that 'God believes at t_1 that Jones will do X at t_2' entails 'Jones will do X at t_2' does not show that Jones's refraining from doing X is not a real possibility for Jones at t_2.[7] If that contention is accepted, Pike's argument never gets out of the starting gate, and the question of the kind of freedom it shows to be impossible does not arise. Since the issue is controversial, I feel free to preserve my problem by simply assuming, for purposes of this discussion, that a divine belief at t_1 is a hard fact about t_1. Setting aside this additional complication will enable us to focus on the differential bearing of the argument on different conceptions of freedom.

The "compatibilist" interpretation of 'within one's power', by contrast, was specifically devised to ensure a compatibility of free will and determinism. It does this by adopting the following account of what it is for something to be within an agent's power.

VII. It is within S's power at t to do A = df. If S were to will (choose, decide, . . .) at t to do A, S would do A.

In other words, its being within S's power to do A at t is simply a matter of S's being so constituted, and his situation's being such, that choosing to do A at t would have led to A's actually being done at t. As far as A is concerned, S's will would have been effective. To have been able to do other than what one actually did, in this sense, is obviously compatible with causal determinism. Even if my choice and action were causally necessitated by antecedent factors, it could still be the case that *if* I had chosen to do otherwise that choice would have been implemented. That counterfactual could be true even if it were causally impossible for me to choose or to do anything else. This is all quite analogous to the following physical analogue. Where only ball A hit ball C at t, it could still be true that *if* ball B had hit ball C at t instead, C would have moved differently from the way it in fact moved; and this can be true even if all these motions are causally determined.

Thus in the compatibilist's sense of '*A* is within one's power' the causal possibility of *A* is not a necessary condition. And, by the same token, the S-logical possibility of *A* is not, either. Even if Jones's mowing his lawn logically follows from God's antecedent beliefs, that would seem to be compatible with the claim that *if* Jones *had* decided not to mow his lawn nothing would have prevented that decision from being implemented.[8] Hence we may say that neither form of real possibility is a necessary condition of *A*'s being within one's power in a compatibilist sense of the term.

II

Turning now to the application of this distinction to the debate over foreknowledge and free will, I first want to ask what concept of 'within one's power' Pike was employing. He is not very forthcoming about this. In the original article his focal term was 'voluntary', and about this he says:

Although I do not have an analysis of what it is for an action to be *voluntary*, it seems to me that a situation in which it would be wrong to assign Jones the *ability* or *power* to do *other* than he did would be a situation in which it would also be wrong to speak of his action as voluntary.[9]

This makes 'voluntary' depend on 'within one's power', but it gives no hint as to the understanding of the latter. Nor does Pike offer any further clues in his responses to critics.

Faced with this situation we should perhaps follow Wittgenstein's dictum: "If you want to know *what* is proved, look at the proof."[10] In that spirit, let us ask: in what sense of 'within one's power' does Pike's argument show that divine foreknowledge is incompatible with its being in anyone's power to do anything other than what one does? Or, not to take sides between Pike and his critics, in what sense of 'in one's power' is Pike's argument the strongest?

There would seem to be a clear answer to this question. We have distinguished the two concepts in terms of whether its being within one's power to do *A* requires that one's doing *A* is really possible. But Pike's argument is naturally read as being designed to show that, given God's forebelief that Jones mows his lawn at t_2, it is *not* really possible that Jones refrain from mowing his lawn at t_2. Underneath all its complexities Pike's argument essentially depends on the thesis that *God's believing at t_1 that Jones will do X at t_2 entails that Jones will do X at t_2*, and hence that Jones's not doing X at t_2 is not really possible. It is because of this entailment that in order for Jones to have the power at t_2 to refrain from doing X he would have to have the power to bring it about that the entailing fact did not occur, either because God did not exist at t_1 ((3) of Pike's step 6), or did not believe at t_1 that Jones would do X at t_2 ((2) of step 6), or would have to have the power to bring it about that the entailment does not hold ((1) of step 6). But if this entailment is the heart of the matter, the argument can be construed as an attempt to show that Jones's refraining at t_2 is not really possible, from which we conclude that it is not within his power to refrain. But we get this last conclusion only on a conception of *within one's power* that, like the libertarian conception, takes real possibility as a necessary condition. On the compatibilist conception the real impossibility of Jones's refraining cuts no ice. Thus it seems that Pike's argument shows, at most, that it is not within Jones's power to refrain from mowing his lawn in a libertarian sense of that term.

This may be contested. It may be claimed that the argument shows that Jones cannot refrain even in a compatibilist sense. For if a necessarily infallible deity believes in advance that Jones mows his lawn at t_2, then Jones would do that even if he did decide to refrain. A mere momentary human decision surely would not over-ride eternal divine foreknowledge in the determination of what will happen. Hence if God believes in advance that Jones will do X at t_2, then even if Jones were to decide not to do X he would still do it. And so Pike's argument shows that it is not within Jones's power to refrain, even in a compatibilist sense.[11]

Thus we have plausible-looking arguments on both sides. This is not an unusual situation with counterfactuals, which are notoriously slippery customers. If Jones had made a decision different from the one he in fact made, what would have ensued depends on what else would have been different from the actual world. It is clear that there cannot be a world different from the actual world only in that Jones decided at t_2 to refrain from doing X. For the actual decision will have resulted from certain causes and will in turn contribute to the causation of subsequent events.[12] Hence if Jones had decided at t_2 to refrain from X, the causal influences on his decision-making would have been different; otherwise that decision to refrain would not have been forthcoming. And, in turn, the consequences of the decision to refrain from X will be different from the consequences of a decision to do X. The only alternative to this would be a change in causal laws that would permit this decision to refrain to be inserted into precisely the actual causal context. Hence a world in which Jones decides at t_2 to refrain from doing X will be different in *some* other respects from the actual world. And whether the counterfactual 'If Jones had decided to refrain from X, he would have refrained from X' is true depends on just what additional differences from the actual world are being presupposed, implied, or allowed for. If we hang onto the actual causal laws and keep the causal context as similar as possible, then the decision to refrain would lead to refraining, and God's forebelief that Jones does X at t_2 would have to be different.[13] On the other hand, if we keep God's actual beliefs unaltered so far as possible then Jones will still do X at t_2, which implies either that some further causal influences on his behavior are different or that causal laws are not as they are in the actual world. So which is it to be?

I believe that it can be shown fairly easily that as the compatibilist understands his counterfactual, and as causal counterfactuals like this are commonly understood, the question of whether the proposition is true *is* the question of what would be the case if causal laws and causal factors were as much like the actual world as possible. When we wonder what Jones would have done had he decided differently, or whether that match would have lit if it had been struck, or whether Smith would have fallen from the ledge had the fireman not rescued him, we want to know what further difference this difference would have made, given our actual causal laws, and given the actual situation so far as it is logically compatible with this difference. If we are told that Jones still would have done X, despite the decision to refrain, if his behavior had been under radio control from Mars and the Martians in question had decided that Jones should do X, or if Jones's brain were organized in a quite different way, or if causal laws were quite different, that is all irrelevant to what we are asking. And it is equally clear that this is the way in which the compatibilist understands the counterfactual. For when the compatibilist maintains that, even given causal determinism, Jones *could* have refrained, in the sense that if he *had* decided to refrain he would have done so, what she is concerned to insist on is the point that the actual situation in which Jones found himself is such that a contrary decision, inserted into *that situation*, would give rise to a contrary action. Hence, as the compatibilist understands 'in one's power', divine forebelief that Jones does X at t_2 has no tendency to imply that it is not within Jones's power to refrain from doing X at t_2. The crucial counterfactual will still be true, even though in the counterfactual situation God's belief as to what Jones does at t_2, as well as God's belief as to what Jones decides at t_2, will be different.

It may be useful to look at the matter from another angle. It is often held that when we wonder whether Y would have happened if X had happened, what we want to know is whether Y happens in a situation in which X happens and which is otherwise as similar as possible to the actual situation. In a recently popular possible-worlds formulation, the question is as to whether Y is the case in all the X-worlds (worlds containing X) that are "closest" to the actual world. (For purposes of this highly compressed discussion let us understand 'closeness' as 'similarity'.) Now it may look as if there is a real contest on this point between those who think Pike's argument does apply to freedom in the compatibilist sense (extremists) and those who think that it does not (moderates). For the moderate will say that a Jones-decides-to-refrain world in which causal laws are the same and the causally relevant surroundings of Jones's decision are as much like the actual world as possible (but where God's belief about what Jones does at t_2 is different) is closer to the actual world than a Jones-decides-to-refrain world in which God's belief that Jones does X at t_2 is the same, but there are differences in causal laws or causally relevant factors. And the extremist will make the opposite judgment. This looks like a thorny issue as to which makes the *larger* difference from the actual world: (a) differences in causal laws or causal factors, or

(b) differences in God's beliefs. And how do we decide a question like that?

But this appearance of a deep impasse is deceptive. There is really no contest. This can be seen once we set out the differences from the actual world that obtain in the worlds claimed by each side to be closest. The worlds favored by the extremist as closest we will call 'Set I' and the worlds favored by the moderate as closest we will call 'Set II'. Let us begin by enumerating the differences apart from God's beliefs.[14]

Differences from the Actual World

Set I	Both	Set II
Some additional causally relevant features of Jones's situation, or some causal laws, to block the implementation of the decision	Jones's decision to refrain at t_2, together with whatever changes in the past are required to produce this decision, and some differences that result from the decision	Jones refrains from doing X at t_2

Intuitively it looks as if Set I worlds are farther from the actual world than Set II worlds. But, says the extremist, it only looks that way until we realize that Set II, but not Set I, worlds will also differ from the actual world by the fact that God believes that Jones refrains from doing X at t_2. Hence, at the very least, it is not clear that Set II worlds are closer to the actual world. However, a moment's reflection should assure us that this observation cuts no ice. Just as we have to add to the differences specified above for Set II the additional difference that God believes that Jones refrains from doing X at t_2, so we have to add to the differences specified above for Set I the additional difference that God believes that all these differences obtain. Thus bringing in differences in God's beliefs *could not* affect a previously existing difference in closeness. If world A is closer to the actual world than world B on all counts other than God's beliefs, then it cannot be further away with God's beliefs taken into account.

For since the beliefs of an omniscient and infallible deity will exactly mirror what is the case, the differences introduced by God's beliefs will exactly mirror differences in other respects. And so if Set II worlds have the edge in closeness with God's beliefs left out, they will necessarily retain that edge with God's beliefs taken into account.

III

On this basis I will take it that Pike's argument is designed to show that it is not within anyone's power to do otherwise in a libertarian sense of that term. In what sense of the term are his critics contesting this?

The earliest published criticism of Pike's 1965 article was John Turk Saunders's "Of God and Freedom."[15] In considering the three alternatives embedded in step 6 of Pike's argument, Saunders concedes that Jones cannot have the first power, but he finds no bar to attributing the second or third. However, he first reformulates these powers, since he takes Pike to have been construing them as powers to causally influence the past.

[I]t is contradictory to speak of a later situation causing an earlier situation, and consequently, it is contradictory to speak of its being in Jones's power to do something at t_2 which causes God not to exist, or not to have a certain belief, at t_1. But, while such powers are contradictory, there is no good reason to think that Jones must possess such powers if he has the power to refrain from X at t_2. The power to refrain from X at t_2 is, indeed, the power so to act at t_2 that either God does not exist at t_1 or else God does not at t_1 believe that Jones will do X at t_2. But Jones's so acting at t_2 would not bring it about that God does not exist at t_1, or that God does not hold a certain belief at t_1, any more than Jones's doing X at t_2 brings it about that God believes, at t_1, that Jones will do X at t_2. Jones's power so to act at t_2 is simply his power to perform an act such that if that act were performed, then certain earlier situations would be different from what in fact they are.[16]

Backwards causation turns out to be a non-issue, however, since in his reply to Saunders, Pike disavows any causal interpretation of 'bring it about' and acknowledges that Saunders's formulations might well do a better job of expressing his intent.[17]

Thus it looks as if there is a head-on confrontation between Pike and Saunders with respect to the possibility that Jones has the second and third powers mentioned in step 6. But this is so only if they are using 'within one's power' in the same sense. And this is definitely not the case, for it is clear from Saunders's article that he understands such terms in a compatibilist way.

[S]uppose that at t_1 I decide to skip at t_2 rather than run at t_2, that conditions are "normal" at t_1 and t_2 (I have not been hypnotized, drugged, threatened, manhandled, and so forth), and that I have the ability (know-how) both to skip and to run. Suppose, too, that the world happens to be governed by empirical laws such that if ever a man in my particular circumstances were to make a decision of this kind, then he would not change his mind and do something else but would follow through upon his decision: suppose, that is, that, under the circumstances which prevail at t_1, my decision is empirically sufficient for my skipping at t_2. Clearly, it is in my power to run at t_2, since I know how to do so and the conditions for the exercise of this ability are normal. If I were to exercise this power then I would not, at t_1, have decided to skip at t_2, or else the circumstances at t_1 would have been different.[18]

[A]lthough it (logically) cannot be both that my decision, under the circumstances, is empirically sufficient for my doing what I decide to do and also that I change my mind and do not do it, it does not follow that it is not in my power to change my mind and run instead. It follows only that I do not change my mind and run instead: for the fact that I know how to run, together with the fact that it is my own decision, under normal conditions, which leads me to persevere in my decision and to skip rather than to run, logically guarantees that I skip of my own free will and, accordingly, that it is in my power to change my mind and run. To maintain the contrary would be to suppose that some sort of indeterminism is essential to human freedom, on grounds that if ever, under normal conditions, my own decision is empirically sufficient for my doing what I do, then my own decision compels me to do what I do.[19]

Saunders plainly does not take the real possibility of S's doing A at t to be a necessary condition of its being within S's power to do A at t. He insists that even if antecedent events are causally sufficient for my doing B at t it could still be within my power to do A at t instead, and, indeed, that this will be within my power, provided I know how to do A, conditions are normal, and nothing is preventing whatever choice I make between A and B from issuing in action. This is obviously compatibilism; we even have the standard compatibilist line that to require indeterminism for freedom is to confuse causation with compulsion.

Thus Saunders and Pike are arguing past each other. The conclusion of Pike's argument is to be construed, as we have seen, as the claim that it is not within Jones's power at t_2 to refrain from doing X in a libertarian sense of 'within one's power', whereas Saunders holds that it is often within our power to do other than what we actually do in a compatibilist sense of 'within one's power'. They are simply not making incompatible claims.

IV

The other exchange I wish to examine is that between Pike and Alvin Plantinga. In *God, Freedom and Evil*,[20] Plantinga contends, like Saunders, that the powers Jones must have in order to be able to refrain are not, when properly understood, impossible at all. From now on let us concentrate on Pike's (2), the power, as Pike originally put it, to bring it about that God did not hold the belief He held at t_1.[21] In working toward his own version of this power, Plantinga does not, like Saunders, first set aside a backwards causation interpretation. Instead he first considers the following version.

It was within Jones's power, at t_2, to do something such that if he had done it, then at t_1 God would have held a certain belief and also *not* held that belief.[22]

Quite sensibly rejecting the supposition that Jones has any such power as this, Plantinga proposes instead the following as quite sufficient for Jones's having the power at t_2 to refrain from doing X.

It was within Jones's power at t_2 to do something such that if he had done it, then God would not have held a belief that in fact he did hold.[23]

Let us call the power so specified, 'P'. The attribution of P, Plantinga says, would be "perfectly innocent." Note that this is substantially equivalent to Saunders's formulation.

We have seen that Saunders is a card-carrying compatibilist. This enables us to understand how he can regard P as "innocent." For, as we have seen, even if a necessarily infallible God believed at t_1 that Jones would do X at t_2, it could still be true that Jones could have refrained from doing X at t_2, in the sense that *if* he had decided to refrain nothing would have prevented the implementation of that decision. Hence in *that* sense he could, given God's antecedent infallible belief that he would do X, have the power so to act that one of God's antecedent beliefs would have been other than it was in fact. But how can Plantinga regard the attribution as innocent? It cannot be for the same reason. Plantinga has made it abundantly clear that he takes what I have been calling the "real possibility" of S's doing A to be a necessary condition of its being within S's power to do A, and the real possibility of both doing A and refraining from doing A to be a necessary condition of S's freely doing A, or freely refraining from doing A.

If a person is free with respect to a given action, then he is free to perform that action and free to refrain from performing it; no antecedent conditions and/or causal laws determine that he will perform the action, or that he won't. It is within his power, at the time in question, to take or perform the action and within his power to refrain from it.[24]

But if Jones's having a power to do A at t_2 requires that "no antecedent conditions and/or causal laws" determine that Jones does not do A at t_2, how can Jones have power P? For clearly *God believes that p at t_1 entails Jones does not do something at t_2 such that if he had done it God would not have believed that p at t_1.* And so if divine beliefs are "antecedent conditions" in the relevant sense, i.e., hard facts about the time at which a given such belief is held,[25] then Plantinga's condition for something's being within a person's power is not met by Jones and power P. Hence Plantinga, and anyone else who takes real possibility as a necessary condition for something's being within one's power, cannot regard the attribution of P to Jones as "innocent," at least not without denying that divine beliefs are "hard facts."

In support of this verdict, look at the way Plantinga defends his "innocence" claim. As a preliminary, let us specify the proposition Plantinga numbers (51).

(51) God existed at t_1, and God believed at t_1 that Jones would do X at t_2, and it was within Jones's power to refrain from doing X at t_2.[26]

Now the defense:

For suppose again that (51) is true, and consider a world W in which Jones refrains from doing X. If God is essentially omniscient, then in this world W He is omniscient and hence does not believe at t_1 that Jones will do X at t_2. So what follows from (51) is the harmless assertion that it was within Jones's power to do something such that if he had done it, then God would not have held a belief that in fact (in the actual world) He did hold.[27]

We can see that there is something wrong with a libertarian's taking this line when we reflect that just the same case could be made for holding that its being within Jones's power to refrain from doing X at t_2 is compatible with *Jones's doing X at t_2* being causally determined. Here is that parallel case. Instead of (51) we will have its analogue for causal determinism.

(51A) Causal factors obtained prior to t_2 that determined Jones to do X at t_2, and it was within Jones's power to refrain from doing X at t_2.

Suppose that (51A) is true, and consider a world W in which Jones refrains from doing X. If causal determinism holds in this world W then either causal laws in W are different from what they are in the actual world or some of the causal factors that affect what Jones does at t_2 are different from what we have in the actual world. So what follows from (51A) is the harmless assertion that it was within Jones's power to do something such that if he had done it, then (assuming causal determinism still holds) either causal laws or causal factors would have been different from what they are in the actual world.

This is at least as strong as the case for the compatibility of divine foreknowledge of Jones's doing X, and Jones's power to refrain. If Jones can have it within his power to do something such that if he had done it then what God believed prior to that time would have been somewhat different, then surely Jones can have it within his power to do something such that if he had done it causal factors or causal laws would have been somewhat different.[28] Thus if Plantinga were in a position to argue as he does for the compatibility of *Jones's being able to do otherwise* with divine foreknowledge, he would equally be in a position to argue for the compatibility of *Jones's being able to do otherwise* with causal determinism. And that is just to say, once more, that Plantinga's argument goes through only on a compatibilist conception of 'within one's power'. It is not surprising, then, that in his paper, "On Ockham's Way Out," Plantinga finds a different way to oppose Pike's argument—by arguing that the beliefs of a necessarily infallible being at t are not hard facts about t.

V

The moral of all this is a simple but important one. If we are to consider attempts to show that it is within no one's power to do other than what one does, we had better attend to the variant possibilities for understanding 'within one's power', and we had better make explicit how it is being understood in a particular context. Else we run the risk of arguing to no purpose.

CHAPTER THIRTEEN

Boethius and Others on Divine Foreknowledge

Martin Davies

Some say 'If God sees everything before
It happens—and deceived he cannot be—
Then everything must happen, though
    you swore
The contrary, for He has seen it, He'.
And so I say, if from eternity
God has foreknowledge of our thought
    and deed,
We've no free choice, whatever books we
    read.[1]

What warring cause does thus disjoin
The bonds of things? What God has set
Such enmity between two truths,
That things established separately
Refuse a common yoke to bear?
Or is there no discord of truths
Which ever sure in union join?[2]

1. Is there an argument which establishes a *prima facie* incompatibility between the existence of a foreknowing God and free action? Let us have an example before us. Suppose that I raise my hand at time t_2 (say, noon on 19-8-1982). Then a foreknowing God would already believe at an earlier time t_1 (say, noon on 1-1-4004 B.C.) that I shall raise my hand at t_2.

As Susan Haack has pointed out,[3] no interest attaches to an argument in which the assumption of divine foreknowledge or omniscience merely idles. Thus no interest attaches to an argument which proceeds from

P: I raise my hand at t_2

to

Reprinted by permission from the *Pacific Philosophical Quarterly*, 64 (1983): 313–29. I am grateful to John Martin Fischer, Lloyd Humberstone, Mark Sainsbury, and Ralph Walker for comments and conversations.

It is true at t_1 that P,

then, by the assumption of omniscience, to

God knows at t_1 that P,

and thence, by the principle that knowledge entails truth, back to

It is true at t_1 that P.

Such an argument is not relevantly different from more austerely logical arguments for fatalism.

Nor does any interest attach to arguments in which the assumption of divine foreknowledge or omniscience is not idle, but which turn on the notorious modal fallacy. Suppose that we abbreviate

Bel(P): God believes at t_1 that P.

Then, given omniscience and the assumption that P, one can justify the premises of the following argument; but the inference is clearly fallacious.

$$\Box(\text{Bel}(P)\rightarrow P)$$
$$\underline{\text{Bel}(P)}$$
$$\Box P$$

Perhaps the best way to guard against the modal fallacy is to make explicit in the argument the relevant instance of the acceptable modal principle

(M1)$\Box(A\rightarrow B)\rightarrow(\Box A\rightarrow\Box B)$.

For nobody would be taken in by the following argument.

$$\Box(\text{Bel}(P)\rightarrow P)\rightarrow(\Box\text{Bel}(P)\rightarrow\Box P)$$
$$\Box(\text{Bel}(P)\rightarrow P)$$
$$\underline{\text{Bel}(P)}$$
$$\Box P$$

The argument could, of course, be rehabilitated if one had available, instead of 'Bel(P)', the stronger premise '$\Box$Bel(P)'. But, if '$\Box$' expresses metaphysical, or broadly logical, necessity then that stronger premise is intuitively false.

We move towards an argument which is not so obviously flawed if we employ, instead of '$\Box$', a temporally modified necessity operator. The idea is that '$\square_{now}$', should be roughly equivalent to Prior's 'now-unpreventably'. . . .[4] We should accept, for example, the principle

$$\square A \rightarrow \square_t A$$

for any time t: what is necessary *tout court* is necessary, inevitable, or unpreventable from the point of view of time t. And we should not accept, for example, the principle

$$\square \sim A \rightarrow \square_t A$$

even though what is necessarily false is, in a sense, un*prevent*able from the point of view of time t: there is nothing anyone can *do* at t to *make* false what is *necessarily* false.

Let us assume, then, that the sense of this operator is clear enough for present purposes, and let us fix upon a time t between t_1 and t_2. The operator '$\square_t$' expresses necessity or inevitability from the point of view of that intermediate time. Then, I claim, the following argument has something to be said for it.

Argument A

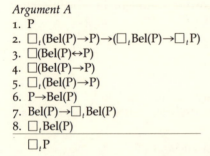

1. P
2. $\square_t(\mathrm{Bel}(P) \rightarrow P) \rightarrow (\square_t \mathrm{Bel}(P) \rightarrow \square_t P)$
3. $\square(\mathrm{Bel}(P) \leftrightarrow P)$
4. $\square(\mathrm{Bel}(P) \rightarrow P)$
5. $\square_t(\mathrm{Bel}(P) \rightarrow P)$
6. $P \rightarrow \mathrm{Bel}(P)$
7. $\mathrm{Bel}(P) \rightarrow \square_t \mathrm{Bel}(P)$
8. $\square_t \mathrm{Bel}(P)$

$\quad \square_t P$

The conclusion rests on lines 1, 2, 3, and 7. As for the other lines: 4 and 6 follow uncontroversially from 3, and 8 from 1, 6, and 7; 5 follows from 4 by the principle mentioned in the last paragraph. Line 2 is an instance of the apparently acceptable temporally modified version of (M1)

$$(\mathrm{M1t}) \square_t(A \rightarrow B) \rightarrow (\square_t A \rightarrow \square_t B).$$

Line 3 is justified by the doctrine that God is essentially omniscient. Line 7 depends on the idea that facts about t_1 are inevitable from the point of view of the later time t. Line 1 is just the assumption that I do in fact raise my hand at t_2. According to

Argument A, in that case it is inevitable from the point of view of the earlier time t that I raise my hand at t_2.

This does seem to establish a *prima facie* incompatibility between the existence of a foreknowing God and free action. For the conclusion of Argument A seems intuitively inconsistent with my raising my hand freely at t_2. It is natural to say that if I raise my hand freely at t_2—if I could, say, have put my hand on the desk instead—then surely it was not necessary or inevitable or unpreventable from the point of view of the earlier time t that I raise my hand at t_2. Whether there is a real inconsistency here is, of course, one of the main concerns of the present paper.

Argument A is not very different from an argument presented by Nelson Pike;[5] and responses to Pike's argument might be directed against Argument A, too. In particular, cannot line 7 be attacked on the grounds that the fact expressed by 'Bel(P)' is not a *hard fact* about the past from the point of view of time t? Let us consider that worry.

Suppose that, instead of using 'Bel(P)' as in Argument A, we had abbreviated

Bel*(P): God believes *correctly* at t_1 that P.

Then it would be natural to say that the fact expressed by 'Bel*(P)' is in part a fact about t_1 but also in part a fact about t_2.[6] If we had used 'Bel*(P)' to construct an argument like Argument A, then someone could have reasonably objected to the premise

7'. $Bel*(P) \rightarrow \Box_t Bel*(P)$.

For any instance of

$$A \rightarrow \Box_t A$$

is justified by claiming that A expresses a fact that is genuinely about some time earlier than t, so that, given the 'fixity' of the past, A expresses an unpreventable fact about the past from the point of view of t: a hard fact about the past. But 'Bel*(P)' clearly does not express a fact that is genuinely about a time earlier than t.

Argument A is designed to avoid any corresponding objection. But, in the discussion of Pike's argument, Marilyn McCord Adams[7] pointed out, in effect, that the idea that 'Bel(P)' avoids the problem posed for 'Bel*(P)' is in apparent conflict with line 3 of the argument:

$$\Box(Bel(P)\leftrightarrow P).$$

Roughly, the idea is this. We say that 'Bel*(P)' expresses a fact in part about t_1 and in part about t_2 because it is equivalent to

$$Bel(P) \& P.$$

But by line 3 this is just equivalent to 'Bel(P)'. So is it not an illusion that 'Bel(P)' itself expresses a hard fact about the past?

Adams laid the matter out rather more precisely. Her definition of a hard fact can be paraphrased as follows.[8]

Statement p expresses a 'hard' fact about a time t = df. It is not the case that for any time t' future relative to t the happening or not happening . . . of something at t' is a necessary condition of the truth of p.

Clearly, given this definition, and given line 3 of Argument A, 'Bel(P)' does not express a hard fact about time t_1 (a fact genuinely about t_1), and so does not express a hard fact about the past from the point of view of time t.

There are at least two possible lines of response to this objection against line 7 of the argument. The first is that Adams's point demonstrates that one should not give a definition of hard facts or of 'aboutness' in terms of necessary conditions. Suppose that A putatively expresses a hard fact about t_1 and that the truth of B is a necessary condition of the truth of A, where B is superficially about t_2. Clearly, whether A really expresses a hard fact about t_1 (a fact genuinely about t_1) depends on whether B is genuinely, and not just superficially, about t_2. On Adams's account this question about B is to be answered by invoking the phrase 'the happening of something at t_2'. But if that is right then the original question about A could have been answered without using Adams's definition.

The problem for this first line of response is that it involves an obligation to give a better account of the intuitive notion of a hard fact. One naturally reaches for the idea of a sentence being *true in virtue of* a certain occurrence at a time, or a certain state of affairs obtaining at a time. But then that latter idea would have to be explicated without the reintroduction of necessary conditions.

Let us then turn to a second line of response. Suppose it is agreed that 'Bel(P)' is in part about t_2. Surely it is also in part about t_1. So what we expect is that the fact expressed by 'Bel(P)' can be divided into a hard part and a soft part, from the point of view of t. Such a division is just what Adams proposes. The idea is that it is a fact genuinely about t_1, and so a hard fact about the past relative to t, that the being in question (namely God) believed at t_1 that P. But it is a soft fact about the past relative to t that the being in question is God at t_1. For whether that being is God is, on Adams's account, in part a matter of how things turn out at t_2.

As John Martin Fischer has pointed out, it is quite unclear that Adams's definition allows there to be any hard facts at all. But suppose, for a moment, that we accept that the fact expressed by 'Bel(P)' can be divided into a hard part and a soft part, from the point of view of t, and ask what is the point of this division in the context of Argument A. What, in particular, is the point of uncovering a soft component in the fact expressed by 'Bel(P)'? The answer is that it is supposed to enable us to reject line 7 of the argument: once we see that it is a soft fact about the past relative to t that the believer is God, we see that we cannot maintain that it is inevitable from the point of view of t that God believed at t_1 that P. The second line of response consists in maintaining that it is a metaphysically necessary property of the being who is in fact God at t_1 that that being exists and is God at t_1 and at all other times. So, whether it is a hard fact or a soft fact about the past relative to t that the believer is God, it is necessary or inevitable from the point of view of t that that being is God.

Thus, I want to set aside the hard fact/soft fact distinction and defend line 7 of Argument A on the grounds that (i) the fact that the being which is in fact God at t_1 believed at t_1 that P is a fact genuinely about t_1 and so is inevitable from the point of view of t; and (ii) the fact that the being which is in fact God at t_1 is God at t_1 is a metaphysically necessary fact and so is inevitable from the point of view of t.

Let us turn to consider line 3 of the argument. There are various reasons why this line might be rejected, but I think none of them is very appealing. Here briefly are three.

(i) One might hold that although God is in fact omniscient

this is not an essential property of God, so that instead of line 3 we should have only the weaker principle

$$Bel(P) \leftrightarrow P.^9$$

(ii) One might hold that, although an omniscient being believes everything that is true, propositions about the future are neither true nor false. So an omniscient being need not believe at t_1 that P.[10]

(iii) One might hold that God, being eternal, is 'outside' time. So it is not literally true that God believed *at* t_1 that P.[11]

Of these reasons why line 3 might be rejected, (i) is incompatible with one reasonable conception of God's nature, and (ii) is independently implausible and in any case invites reformulation of the argument in terms of propositions which will become true. What shall we say of (iii)? According to Anthony Kenny, it is incoherent to maintain that God inhabits 'a timeless eternity, the whole of which is simultaneous with every part of time'. That seems to be correct, given the usual understanding of simultaneity. But it is not so clear that it would be incoherent to maintain, simply, that predications of God cannot be temporally modified; to maintain, in particular, that the application of the temporal modifier 'at t_1', to 'God believed that P' is a kind of category mistake. However, as Kenny points out, to maintain that is not to take a step towards establishing the compatibility of divine foreknowledge and human freedom. It is, rather, to deny that there is such a thing as divine *fore*knowledge. So, if we are interested in the compatibility question, then we should not adopt reason (iii) for rejecting line 3.

There is a fourth reason, of a more complex kind, why line 3 might be rejected. Someone might hold that a proper definition of omniscience does not require that God should believe all truths, any more than a proper definition of omnipotence requires that God should be able to actualize each possible state of affairs. As Argument ʌ in effect shows, such a person might go on, it could be that an agent will act freely in a certain way but that it is not possible both that the agent act freely in that way and that God believe in advance that the agent will act in that way. A proper definition of omniscience will allow that God's (infallible) beliefs may be restricted in the interests of human freedom.[12]

This reason depends on accepting that Argument A does establish the incompatibility of divine foreknowledge and free action. Since that is precisely what I am concerned to question, I can scarcely adopt this reason for rejecting line 3. Also, more generally, this way of rejecting line 3 leaves God with rather more ignorance than might be expected of an omniscient being. So it does not seem unreasonable to reject all four reasons, and to defend line 3 of the argument.

But if we do defend line 3, then we seem to be left with this choice: either reject the temporally modified version (M1t) of the acceptable modal principle, or else accept the incompatibility of divine foreknowledge and free action. How we should respond to this apparent choice is the question for the next section.

2. The modal principle (M1) is a theorem schema of the very weak modal logic *K*. In the heuristically appealing terminology of possible worlds it says this: if in every possible world if A is the case then B is also the case, then if A is the case in every world then also B is the case in every world. That sounds utterly uncontroversial.

There are ways of interpreting the temporally modified operator '$\Box_t$' in possible worlds terminology, so that the principle (M1t) is also clearly acceptable. Suppose that we interpret '$\Box_t A$' as saying that A is the case in every possible world that is just like the actual world up to some time just before t. (Let us abbreviate: A is the case in every $<t$-actual world.) Then the principle says this: if in every $<t$-actual world if A is the case then B is also the case, then if A is the case in every $<t$-actual world then also B is the case in every $<t$-actual world. That sounds utterly uncontroversial. And the principle is also acceptable if we interpret '$\Box_t A$' as saying that A is the case in every possible world that is just like the actual world up to and including time t. (Let us abbreviate: A is the case in every $\leq t$-actual world.)

Provided that the temporally modified operator is interpreted in one or other of these ways, we cannot reject the principle (M1t). But I wish to deny that we are therefore obliged to accept the incompatibility of divine foreknowledge and free action. What we are obliged by Argument A to accept is that if there is a foreknowing God and if I in fact raise my hand at t_2 then there is no $<t$-actual world and no $\leq t$-actual world in which I do not

raise my hand at t_2. In that sense it is necessary or inevitable from the point of view of time t that I raise my hand at t_2. But it does not follow immediately that there is no good sense of 'free' in which I raise my hand freely at t_2, or in which I am free at t not to raise my hand at t_2 but, say, to put my hand on the desk instead.

The position I wish to defend is thus analogous to soft determinism. It is a consequence of determinism that if I in fact raise my hand at t_2 then there is no possible world with the same laws as the actual world and just like the actual world up to some time t earlier than t_2, but in which I do not raise my hand at t_2. A compatibilist maintains that nevertheless there is a good sense of 'free' in which I raise my hand freely at t_2, and in which I am free at t not to raise my hand at t_2. An incompatibilist may then respond in one of two ways. On the one hand, he may simply *insist* that there can be no such good sense of 'free'; that if I raise my hand freely at t_2 then there is some possible world with the same laws as the actual world and just like the actual world up to time t, but in which I do not raise my hand at t_2. If the compatibilist responds in that way then we rapidly reach a standoff. On the other hand, he may argue that it is an absurd consequence of soft determinism that I am either free to influence the past or else free to break the laws of nature. If the incompatibilist responds in this second way then we must uncover some flaw in his argument. David Lewis has recently pointed out just what the flaw is,[13] and I want to maintain that there is a somewhat similar flaw in the corresponding argument against the position that, despite Argument A, divine foreknowledge and free action are compatible.

The argument I have in mind is an attempted *reductio ad absurdum* of the claim that, despite divine foreknowledge, I raise my hand freely at t_2. The rough idea behind the argument is that if we hold that I raise my hand freely at t_2, then we hold also that I was free not to raise my hand at t_2 but, say, to put my hand on the desk instead. But then we are bound to hold that I was free to bring it about that God did not, after all, believe at t_1 that I would raise my hand at t_2. And this is absurd, since I am not free to change the past.

Suppose then, that in some good sense of 'free', I raise my hand freely at t_2. Then, surely, there are times earlier than t_2

such that it is possible or open (to me) from the point of view of those times that I did not raise my hand at t_2 but, say, put my hand on the desk at t_2. We can assume that our intermediate time t is such a time. Suppose, too, that some such claim as that it is possible or open (to me) from the point of view of t that I put my hand on the desk at t_2, or that I am free at t to put my hand on the desk at t_2, can be represented using a temporally modified possibility operator '$\Diamond_t$'. Then, if we abbreviate

Q: I put my hand on the desk at t_2

we have the first line of the following argument.

Argument B
1. $\Diamond_t Q$
2. $\Box_t(Q \rightarrow \sim\mathrm{Bel}(P)) \rightarrow (\Diamond_t Q \rightarrow \Diamond_t \sim\mathrm{Bel}(P))$
3. $\Box(Q \rightarrow \sim P)$
4. $\Box(\mathrm{Bel}(P) \leftrightarrow P)$
5. $\Box(Q \rightarrow \sim\mathrm{Bel}(P))$
6. $\Box_t(Q \rightarrow \sim\mathrm{Bel}(P))$

$\qquad \Diamond_t \sim\mathrm{Bel}(P)$

Given the way we introduced the operator '$\Diamond_t$' the conclusion of this argument represents an apparently absurd claim. But line 3 is uncontroversial, and lines 4, 5, and 6 are as acceptable as lines 3, 4, and 5 of Argument A. So if we are to avoid the *reductio*, it seems that we must reject line 2. But that is an instance of the temporally modified version (M2t) of the acceptable modal principle

$$(\text{M2}) \quad \Box(A \rightarrow B) \rightarrow (\Diamond A \rightarrow \Diamond B).$$

I am not attributing Argument B to anyone, and it is obviously suspect at least to the extent that the interpretation of '$\Diamond_t$' has been left indeterminate. But before I respond to Argument B, I want to consider a different attempted *reductio*. This time the rough idea is that if we hold that I was free not to raise my hand at t_2 then we are bound to hold, absurdly, that I was free to bring it about that God is mistaken. I shall lead up to that attempted *reductio* by looking at an argument involving free action and the principle (M2t), but not concerned with divine foreknowledge.

In a discussion of an argument which David Wiggins gave, for the incompatibility of causal determinism and the ability to do otherwise than one actually does, Kenny gives the following example, paraphrasing Duns Scotus.[14]

Suppose I am carrying my own suitcase, A. In these circumstances, to carry my wife's suitcase B, would be to carry both A and B. But though I can carry B, I can't carry both A and B.

The relevance of this for present purposes is that it can be organized as a counterexample to the principle (M2t). Let us abbreviate.

R: I carry suitcase A at t.
S: I carry suitcase B at t.

Then consider the following argument.

Argument C
1. R
2. R→$\Box_t$R
3. $\Box_t$R
4. $\Box_t$(R→(S→(S & R)))→($\Box_t$R→$\Box_t$(S→(S & R)))
5. $\Box_t$(R→(S→(S & R)))
6. $\Box_t$R→$\Box_t$(S→(S & R))
7. $\Box_t$(S→(S & R))
8. $\Box_t$(S→(S & R))→($\Diamond_t$S→ $\Diamond_t$(S & R))
9. $\Diamond_t$S→ $\Diamond_t$(S & R)
10. $\Diamond_t$S
    —————————————————
    $\Diamond_t$(S & R)

According to the Kenny/Duns Scotus example, lines 1 and 10 of this argument are true, given an appropriate interpretation of '$\Diamond_t$': 'I am carrying my own suitcase A', 'I can carry B'. But the conclusion is false: 'I cannot carry both A and B'. Lines 2–7 are clearly acceptable if '$\Box_t$A' is interpreted as saying that A is the case in every ≤t-actual world. And line 9 follows from 7 and 8. So line 8, an instance of principle (M2t), must be at fault.

This may seem puzzling for, as we have already noted, principle (M2t) is the temporally modified version of the acceptable modal principle (M2). Indeed, (M2) like (M1) is a theorem schema of the modal logic K. But in that logic, the operator '$\Diamond$' is interpreted as being the *dual* of '$\Box$'; that is, it is interpreted so as to preserve the equivalence schema

$$\Diamond A \leftrightarrow \sim\Box\sim A.$$

And it is clear that it is just because '◇' is so interpreted that principle (M2) shares the intuitive acceptability of (M1). Similarly, if '◇$_t$' is interpreted as being the dual of '□$_t$' then principle (M2t) will inherit the intuitive acceptability of (M1t). Suppose that '□$_t$A' is interpreted as saying that A is the case in every ≤t-actual world, as it must be if line 3 of Argument C is to be true. If '◇$_t$A' is interpreted dually as saying that A is the case in *some* ≤t-actual world, then principle (M2t) will be acceptable. But, if line 10 of Argument C, '◇$_t$S', is to be true in the Kenny/Duns Scotus example, then '◇$_t$' clearly *cannot* be interpreted as the dual of '□$_t$'. For it is built into the example that '□$_t$~S' is also true. And given the failure of duality consequent upon the required interpretation of the two temporally modified operators, it should not be surprising that principle (M2t) has to be rejected.

As Kenny points out, Duns Scotus was in fact concerned with principle (M2t) in the context of the problem of divine foreknowledge. He rejected (M2t) in order to reject the absurd conclusion that I can bring it about that God is mistaken. Thus consider the following argument.

Argument D
1. □$_t$Bel(P)
2. □$_t$(Bel(P)→(Q→(Bel(P) & Q))) →
   (□$_t$Bel(P)→□$_t$(Q→(Bel(P) & Q)))
3. □$_t$(Q→(Bel(P) & Q))
4. □$_t$(Q→(Bel(P) & Q))→(◇$_t$Q→◇$_t$(Bel(P) & Q))
5. ◇$_t$Q→◇$_t$(Bel(P) & Q)
6. ◇$_t$Q

   ◇$_t$(Bel(P) & Q)

If '□$_t$A' is interpreted as saying that A is the case in every <t-actual world, then line 1 is justified just as line 8 of Argument A, line 2 is an instance of the acceptable principle (M1t), and line 3 is analogous to line 7 of Argument C. According to the position I wish to defend, there is a good sense of 'free' in which I am free at t to put my hand on the desk at t_2. Consequently, I allow that there is *some* interpretation of '◇$_t$' according to which line 6 is true. But there is *no* reasonable interpretation of '◇$_t$' according to which the conclusion is true, for there is *no* possible world at all in which God has a false belief. So, if we are to avoid a *reductio ad absurdum* of the position I wish to defend, then we must reject line 4, an instance of principle (M2t).

It should be clear that in Argument D, as in Argument C, however '$\Diamond_t$' is interpreted it cannot be interpreted as the dual of '$\Box_t$'. For '$\Diamond_t Q$' is supposed to be true even though, as Argument A shows, '$\Box_t {\sim} Q$' is also true. So we can indeed reject principle (M2t).

It is important to understand the dialectical situation here. The imagined opponent does not baldly insist that, given Argument A, there can be no good sense of 'free' in which I raise my hand freely at t_2. That way leads to a standoff. Rather, he claims that from premises to which I am committed a conclusion which I acknowledge to be absurd follows. I reply that I am committed to lines 1–3 of Argument D if '$\Box_t A$' is interpreted in a certain way, and that I am committed to there being some interpretation of '$\Diamond_t$' for which line 6 is true. But on those interpretations the two operators are not mutually dual, so that line 4 is not available as a non-question-begging premise for a *reductio*. And if the opponent chooses to reinterpret '$\Box_t$' as dual to '$\Diamond_t$' then lines 1–3 will no longer be available as non-question-begging premises.

The fact that we can avoid the *reductio* threatened by Argument D by rejecting principle (M2t) may encourage the thought that the *reductio* threatened by Argument B can be as easily avoided. For there too, the two operators are not interpreted as mutually dual. But in another way our response to Argument D makes Argument B appear more disconcerting. For in explaining the non-duality of the temporally modified operators it is natural to say this: 'As things are, up to time t, God believes at t_1 that I shall raise my hand at t_2. I could put my hand on the desk at t_2. But if I were to put my hand on the desk at t_2 then some of the actual circumstances up to t would be different, for God would not in that case believe at t_1 that I shall raise my hand at t_2'. And is not that just the absurd consequence threatened by Argument B?

The reason why the point about non-duality does not, by itself, constitute an adequate response to Argument B is that the use of the temporally modified necessity operator in that argument is really inessential. The same apparently absurd conclusion '$\Diamond_t {\sim} \mathrm{Bel}(P)$' could be obtained from the assumption '$\Diamond_t Q$' *via* a simpler argument—Argument B'—in which line 6 is omitted and line 2 is replaced by the plausible looking premise

2'. $\Box(Q\rightarrow\sim Bel(P))\rightarrow(\Diamond_t Q\rightarrow \Diamond_t\sim Bel(P))$.

But does that conclusion really represent an absurd claim?

When Argument B was introduced, I left the interpretation of '$\Diamond_t$' somewhat indeterminate. The idea was that line 1 '$\Diamond_t Q$' should represent some such claim as that it is possible or open (to me) from the point of view of t that I put my hand on the desk at t_2, or that I am free at t to put my hand on the desk at t_2. But that idea hardly forces a unique interpretation of '$\Diamond_t\sim Bel(P)$'.

I said that the position I wish to defend is analogous to soft determinism. In response to the incompatibilist's claim that it is an absurd consequence of soft determinism that I am either free to change the past or else free to break the laws of nature, Lewis[15] has urged that we distinguish a weak thesis

I am able to do something such that, if I did it, a law would be broken

from a strong thesis

I am able to do something such that, if I did it, my act either would cause or would be a law-breaking event.

Although (according to Lewis) the weak thesis is indeed a consequence of soft determinism, it is only the strong thesis that is absurd.

I suggest that we can shed some light on Argument B', and its apparently absurd conclusion, if we similarly distinguish a weak thesis

It is open to me from the point of view of t to do something such that, if I did it, God would have had a belief in 4004 B.C. different from his actual belief then

from a strong thesis

It is open to me from the point of view of t to do something such that, if I did it, my act either would cause or would be an event of God's believing in 4004 B.C. something other than what he actually believed then.

The weak thesis is indeed a consequence of the position I wish to defend; it was implicit in our response to Argument D. But it is at most the strong thesis that can non-question-beggingly be held to be absurd. If '$\Diamond_t$' is interpreted in such a way that the conclusion of Argument B' represents only the weak thesis, then the plausible-looking line 2' is indeed acceptable. But if '$\Diamond_t$' is interpreted in such a way that the conclusion represents the strong, arguably absurd, thesis, then line 2' is not, after all, available as a non-question-begging premise for a *reductio*.

By making this distinction, we can fend off the *reductio* threatened by Argument B'. But it should be noted that our situation is not exactly similar to Lewis's. One difference is that it is not quite clear that even our strong thesis is absurd. What would be absurd, someone might say, is that an act of mine should cause an event of God's *coming to believe* in 4004 B.C. something other than what he actually believed then; but God does not come to believe things—what he believes he always believes. If even our strong thesis is not absurd then, of course, *a fortiori* the position I wish to defend is not threatened. But someone who thought that our strong thesis is indeed absurd might seek to reinstate the threat by pointing to another difference between our situation and Lewis's. In the case of Lewis's weak thesis, if I did what I am able to do then a law would be broken, and the law-breaking event would arguably be a causal antecedent of my act. But, in the case of our weak thesis we shall not wish to allow that if I did what I am able to do then God would have had a belief in 4004 B.C. which would be a causal antecedent of my act. If that is so, our imagined opponent might say, how is one to prevent the weak thesis from collapsing into the absurd strong thesis? This difference between our situation and Lewis's is quite genuine, and I think that we should accept that if I did what I am able to do then God would have had a particular belief in 4004 B.C. because of my so acting. That is, the direction of explanation is from my acting to God's believing and not *vice versa*. But, as a priori knowledge of truths about the future perhaps illustrates, not every case of backward 'because'-ation is a case of backward causation. So the weak thesis need not collapse into the strong thesis.

Lewis's distinction can be cast as a distinction between two senses of 'could have rendered false'. It is a consequence of soft determinism that, in the weak sense, I could have rendered false a law. But all that is absurd is that, in the strong sense, I could have rendered false a law. Similarly, it is a consequence of the position I wish to defend that, in the weak sense, I could have rendered false a proposition about the past. But the most that is absurd (I maintain) is that, in the strong sense, I could have rendered false a proposition about the past.

Lewis's imagined incompatibilist opponent is partly modeled on Peter van Inwagen.[16] André Gallois[17] replied to van Inwagen's argument, urging a distinction between two senses of 'could have rendered false'. Could we have adapted Gallois's distinction to our present purposes?

Gallois's weak sense of the phrase is essentially the same as Lewis's. His strong sense can be illustrated by the following example.[18]

It may be that a couple can render it false that they do not have a boy and do not have a girl. That is, the couple can bring it about that they have a child. However, even if it lies within the couple's power to have either a boy or a girl, it does not follow that they can render it false that they do not have a boy or that they can render it false that they do not have a girl.

This sense of the phrase is stronger than Lewis's strong sense. For the couple presumably can perform an action which in the circumstances is either causally sufficient for them to have a boy or else causally sufficient for them to have a girl. They cannot, however, perform an action which is both causally sufficient for them to have a boy and intentional under the description 'producing a boy'; nor similarly, for having a girl. Distinguishing this strong sense does not serve our present purposes. It is indeed correct that from the premises that I could have put my hand on the disk intentionally and that there is an essentially omniscient God, it does not follow that I could have influenced the past intentionally. But, if our strong thesis is indeed absurd, then it would be bad enough if it were a consequence of the position I wish to defend that I could have causally influenced the past intentionally or unintentionally. Thus, for a defense of that position we need Lewis's distinction rather than Gallois's.

In a response to Pike's argument, John Turk Saunders wrote[19]

Jones's power so to act at t_2 is simply his power to perform an act such that if that act were performed, then certain earlier situations would be different from what in fact they are.

And three pages later we find[20]

Pike's case rests . . . on the contention (which I repudiate) that it is contradictory to suppose that one has the power so to act that the past would be other than it is.

That looks like an anticipation of the point I have borrowed from Lewis. But in fact the situation is not so clear. For Saunders continued that the way to see that the power involves no contradiction is to consider this fact.[21]

Whenever one has the power to do Y but does X instead, one has the power so to act that the past would be other than it is: for if one were to do Y, then every past situation would be other than it is in that it would be followed by one's Y-ing at this time rather than by one's X-ing at this time.

Perhaps there is no problem about a power to render false a proposition that expresses only a soft fact about the past. But the point I have borrowed from Lewis is intended to show that there is no problem about a power to render false (in the weak sense) a proposition that expresses a hard fact about (a fact genuinely about) the past. And, if that is right, then we can maintain that, despite Argument A, divine foreknowledge and free action are compatible.

3. The problem of divine foreknowledge has a long philosophical history. But it seems that at least two different styles of argument have been considered under that general heading. Some philosophers have been primarily concerned with an argument that goes roughly as follows. If God is to know at t_1 that I shall raise my hand at t_2, then the way the world is at t_1 cannot leave it open whether or not I raise my hand at t_2. Rather, the way the world is at t_1 must be causally sufficient for my raising my hand at t_2: my raising my hand must be causally determined. But then—by the presumed incompatibility of causal determinism and free will—I shall not raise my hand freely at t_2.

This argument is quite different from any that we have been considering, for it is causal-epistemological rather than austerely modal. Clearly the argument turns upon two points: one is incompatibilism, the other is a particular model of God's knowledge of the future. So long as that model of God's knowledge was not questioned, the argument reduced to one about incompatibilism. Thus, Augustine complained against Cicero (an incompatibilist) that 'wishing to make men free, he makes them sacrilegious', and urged that the solution is to recognize that 'our wills themselves are included in that order of causes which is certain to God, and is embraced by His foreknowledge, for human wills are also causes of human actions'.[22]

Boethius, in his extended treatment of the topic,[23] offered a different solution to the problem in its causal-epistemological version, for he rejected the model of divine foreknowledge. If a man is to know at t_1 that an event will occur at t_2 then what is directly accessible to (present to) the man at t_1, namely the state of the world at t_1, must guarantee the occurrence of the later event. But God's knowledge of the future is not like that. According to Boethius it is more like knowledge gained by direct perception.[24]

We see many things before our eyes as they happen, like the actions we see charioteers performing in order to control and drive their chariots. . . . But no necessity forces any of them to happen in this way, does it? . . . so foreknowledge imposes no necessity on what is going to happen.

We might respond that, if it is taken seriously, the perceptual model raises the problem of backward causation. But it seems clear that Boethius did not intend the model to be taken so seriously. Rather, his talk of the differences amongst 'sense-perception, imagination, reason and intelligence'[25] suggests that a better analogue of God's foreknowledge would be our 'just seeing' that something is the case, by the most immediate kind of a priori knowledge.

Thus, it was in the context of a response to the causal-epistemological argument that Boethius made use of the idea that all times are present to God.[26]

His knowledge . . . embraces all the infinite recesses of past and future and views them in the immediacy of its knowing as though they are happening in the present. . . . it is far removed from matters below and looks forth at all things as though from a lofty peak above them.

According to Kenny,[27] Aquinas made use of this same idea (right down to the example of someone looking down from a hill), but used it against the austerely modal version of the problem: if

God is outside time then he does not literally know (or believe) at t_1 that certain things are going to happen. Kenny rejects that use of the idea, and I have followed him. And I think that Boethius would have rejected it, too.

Certainly Boethius had the causal-epistemological argument as his main concern. Also, he did not distinguish sharply between the causal-epistemological argument and the austerely modal argument. But after his lengthy reflections on God's knowledge, he proceeds to some briefer remarks which seem to be directed towards a version of the problem which is left standing, even after the unsatisfactory model of God's knowledge has been rejected. In these remarks he does not deny that God literally foreknows, and he considers in turn the modal fallacy, and versions of the two attempts at *reductio* which I regimented as Argument D and Argument B.

He begins like this.[28]

If you say at this point that what God sees as a future event cannot but happen, and what cannot but happen, happens of necessity . . . I shall answer that the same future event is necessary when considered with reference to divine foreknowledge, and yet seems to be completely free and unrestricted when considered in itself. For there are two kinds of necessity; one simple . . . and one conditional.

Then, after a paragraph beginning[29]

What does it matter, then, if they are not necessary, when because of the condition of divine foreknowledge it will turn out exactly as if they were necessary?

he turns to the two attempts at *reductio*. But here his account contains what we now perceive as a very unfortunate flaw. For Boethius did not employ the distinction between alethic and temporal modalities; between what is necessarily the case and what is merely always the case, for example. Consequently, where he should (from our point of view) have made use of the idea of actual and counterfactual circumstances, he instead makes use of the idea of different situations obtaining at different times.[30] As we shall see, this has serious consequences for his consideration of the second attempt at *reductio* (the one I regimented as Argument B).

The first attempt is this: if I am free to put my hand on the desk (instead of raising my hand) then I am free to bring it about that God is mistaken. Boethius's version concerns, not what I would have done under counterfactual circumstances, but a change over time in my proposed course of action. His comment is this.[31]

You can alter your plan, but . . . since this is possible, and since whether you do so or in what way you change it is visible to Providence . . . you cannot escape divine foreknowledge.

That reply could clearly be transposed to our modal version of the attempt. It would then remain to do what Duns Scotus did, namely identify the principle that is at fault in Argument D.

The second attempt is this: if I am free to put my hand on the desk then (since God cannot be mistaken) I am free to influence the past. Boethius's temporal version is this.[32]

Isn't divine knowledge changed as a result of my rearrangement [of my proposed course of action], so that as I change my wishes it, too, seems to change its knowledge?

Of course, the answer to that is rather obvious.

It does not change . . . with alternate knowledge of now this and now that, but with one glance anticipates and embraces your changes in its constancy.

Very clearly, that reply could not be transposed to our modal version of the attempt: constancy across times is one thing, but constancy across actual and counterfactual circumstances is another.

At this crucial point, Boethius's account is flawed. Because he lacked the needed conceptual distinction, we cannot—however sympathetic we may be—derive from his work any adequate response to our Argument B. Nevertheless, it is difficult not to be impressed by the extent to which he came close to a fully comprehensive treatment of the problem of divine foreknowledge, in both its causal-epistemological and its more austerely modal versions.

Reference Matter

Notes

Fischer: Introduction

1. Actually, the property of eternality is not necessary in order to generate the Basic Argument; the weaker assumption that God has existed at *some* point in the past is all that is necessary for the argument. But out of deference to tradition, I shall employ the assumption of eternality.

2. In my presentation of two versions of the argument, I shall assume that God is "counterfactually independent of possible human action." It is not absolutely evident, however, that this putative property of God is necessary in order to generate the Basic Argument; one might be able to dispense with it, given the Principle of the Fixity of the Past, which is developed below.

3. This view of God's eternality is found in, for example, William Paley, *Natural Theology* (London, 1802), ch. xxiv; John Calvin, *Institutes of the Christian Religion*, Bk. III, ch. xxi; and John Locke, *An Essay Concerning Human Understanding*, Bk. IV, ch. x.

4. This approach to God's eternality is articulated in, for example, St. Anselm, *Proslogium*, chs. xix, xxi–xxii; Boethius, *The Consolation of Philosophy*, Bk. V, secs. 4–6; St. Thomas Aquinas, *Summa Theologicae*, Pt. I, q. 10; Frederich Schleiermacher, *The Christian Faith*, Pt. I, sec. 2, par. 51; and Eleonore Stump and Norman Kretzmann, "Eternity," *Journal of Philosophy*, 78 (1981): 429–58.

5. This way of responding to the Basic Argument is developed in William Alston, "Does God Have Beliefs?" *Religious Studies*, 22 (1986): 287–306.

6. A modal version of the argument is presented in John Martin Fischer, "Introduction: Responsibility and Freedom," in Fischer, ed., *Moral Responsibility* (Ithaca, 1986). The power necessity operator is in-

troduced in Carl Ginet, "The Conditional Analysis of Freedom," in Peter van Inwagen, ed., *Time and Cause: Essays Presented to Richard Taylor* (Dordrecht, 1980); and Peter van Inwagen, *An Essay on Free Will* (Oxford, 1983).

7. There are discussions of this principle and related principles in Ginet, "The Conditional Analysis of Freedom," and "In Defense of Incompatibilism," *Philosophical Studies*, 44 (1983): 391–400; Michael Slote, "Selective Necessity and the Free-Will Problem," *Journal of Philosophy*, 79 (1982): 5–24; Fischer, "Responsibility and Freedom," and "Incompatibilism," *Philosophical Studies*, 43 (1983): 127–37; van Inwagen, *An Essay on Free Will*; and David Widerker, "On an Argument for Incompatibilism," *Analysis*, 47 (1987): 37–41.

8. Slote has rejected such a modal principle in his "Selective Necessity and the Free-Will Problem." See also Widerker, "On an Argument for Incompatibilism."

9. Robert Stalnaker, "A Theory of Conditionals," in Nicholas Rescher, ed., *Studies in Logical Theory* (Oxford, 1968); and David Lewis, *Counterfactuals* (Cambridge, 1973).

10. See, especially, Harry G. Frankfurt, "Alternate Possibilities and Moral Responsibility," *Journal of Philosophy*, 66 (1969): 829–39, and "Freedom of the Will and the Concept of a Person," *Journal of Philosophy*, 68 (1971): 5–20. For a selection of papers on this topic, see Fischer, *Moral Responsibility*.

11. St. Thomas Aquinas, *Summa Contra Gentiles*, Bk. 1, ch. 67, 10. St. Augustine (*On the Free Choice of the Will*) discussed a version of the Basic Argument, but he did not clearly see the distinction made by Aquinas. There is a discussion of Augustine's treatment of the issues in William L. Rowe, "Augustine on Foreknowledge and Free Will," *Review of Metaphysics*, 18 (1964): 356–63. For an excellent presentation of the history of the discussion of the Basic Argument, see Alvin Plantinga, "On Ockham's Way Out" (Chapter 10 in this volume).

12. For developments of this sort of argument, see, for example, Ginet, "The Conditional Analysis of Freedom," and van Inwagen, *An Essay on Free Will*.

13. David Lewis denies the fixity of the natural laws and thus adopts "local-miracle compatibilism" in his "Are We Free to Break the Laws?" *Theoria*, 47 (1981): 112–21.

14. John Turk Saunders, "Of God and Freedom," *Philosophical Review*, 75 (1966): 219–25, and "The Temptations of 'Powerlessness,'" *American Philosophical Quarterly*, 5 (1968): 100–108; Alvin Plantinga, *God, Freedom and Evil* (New York, 1974).

15. There is a discussion of these issues in Joshua Hoffman and Gary Rosenkrantz, "On Divine Foreknowledge and Human Freedom,"

Philosophical Studies, 37 (1980): 289–96; and William L. Rowe, "On Divine Foreknowledge and Human Freedom: A Reply," *Philosophical Studies*, 37 (1980): 429–30.

16. Thomas Talbott formulates this principle in his "On Divine Foreknowledge and Bringing About the Past," *Philosophy and Phenomenological Research*, 46 (1986): 455–69. There are also discussions of "power entailment principles" in Alfred J. Freddoso, "Accidental Necessity and Power over the Past," *Pacific Philosophical Quarterly*, 63 (1982): 54–68; and Phillip L. Quinn, "Plantinga on Freedom and Foreknowledge," in James Tomberlin and Peter van Inwagen, eds., *Alvin Plantinga* (Dordrecht, 1985).

17. Peter T. Geach, *Providence and Evil* (Cambridge, Engl., 1977).

18. This argument is in Jonathan Kvanvig, *The Possibility of an All-Knowing God* (New York, 1986).

19. Arthur Prior, "The Formalities of Omniscience," *Philosophy*, 37 (1962): 114–29.

20. Jan Lukasiewicz, "On Determinism" and "Philosophical Remarks on Many-Valued Systems of Propositional Logic," both in Storrs McCall, ed., *Polish Logic 1920–1939* (Oxford, 1967).

21. Freddoso discusses these issues in his "Introduction" in Luis de Molina, *On Divine Foreknowledge (Part IV of the "Concordia")*, trans. Alfred J. Freddoso (Ithaca, 1988).

22. Robert Adams, "Middle Knowledge and the Problem of Evil," *American Philosophical Quarterly*, 14 (1977): 110.

23. For this argument, see Charles A. Baylis, "Are Some Propositions Neither True Nor False?" *Philosophy of Science*, 3 (1936): 156–66. Also, I am indebted here to Freddoso, "Introduction."

24. Lukasiewicz, "On Determinism."

25. There are discussions of this issue in Rogers Albritton, "Present Truth and Future Contingency," *Philosophical Review*, 66 (1957): 1–28; Gilbert Ryle, "It Was to Be," in *Dilemmas* (Cambridge, Engl., 1954); Richard Gale, "Endorsing Predictions," *Philosophical Review*, 70 (1961): 376–85; John Turk Saunders, "Sea Fight Tomorrow?," *Philosophical Review*, 67 (1958): 367–78; Nelson Pike, *God and Timelessness* (New York, 1970); and van Inwagen, *An Essay on Free Will*.

26. Nelson Pike, "Divine Omniscience and Voluntary Action" (Chapter 2 in this volume).

27. Richard Swinburne, *The Coherence of Theism* (Oxford, 1977).

28. See Norman Kretzmann, "Omniscience and Immutability," *Journal of Philosophy*, 63 (1966): 409–21; and Kvanvig, *The Possibility of an All-Knowing God*.

29. There are various passages in both the Old Testament and the New Testament in which God is portrayed as having knowledge not

just of the past and present, but also of the future. There is a discussion of such passages and a defense of the claim that the dominant Biblical view of God implies that God possesses foreknowledge in William Lane Craig, *The Only Wise God* (Grand Rapids, 1987). There are, however, some passages in the Old Testament in which it is at least suggested that God does not have foreknowledge: Genesis 22:12, Genesis 18:21, Deuteronomy 8:2, and Deuteronomy 13:4. Note that Genesis 18:21 suggests that God does not know the past, and some of the other passages might be interpreted as implying that God does not know certain present facts. (I am grateful to David Widerker for bringing these passages to my attention.)

30. There is a good discussion of this passage in Plantinga, "On Ockham's Way Out" (Chapter 10 in this volume).

31. I develop this point in "Ockhamism," *Philosophical Review*, 94 (1985): 81–100.

32. See also P. Helm, "Divine Foreknowledge and Facts," *Canadian Journal of Philosophy*, 4 (1974): 305–15.

33. David Widerker develops this position in his "Two Fallacious Objections to Adams' Soft/Hard Fact Distinction," *Philosophical Studies* (forthcoming). For discussions of the issue of whether time can stop, see Arthur Prior, "On the Logic of Ending Time," in *Papers on Time and Tense* (Oxford, 1968); W. H. Newton-Smith, *The Structure of Time* (London, 1980); and Quentin Smith, "On the Beginning of Time," *Noûs*, 19 (1985): 579–84.

34. I discuss such facts in "Ockhamism." In this paper I argue that a position suggested by Pike is unacceptable because of the problem of hard-core soft facts; see Nelson Pike, "Fischer on Freedom and Foreknowledge," *Philosophical Review*, 93 (1984): 599–614.

35. For another account of the distinction between hard and soft facts, see Kvanvig, *The Possibility of an All-Knowing God*.

36. Peter T. Geach, *God and the Soul* (New York, 1969).

37. Nelson Goodman's famous examples, "grue" and "bleen," are such properties, as opposed to green and blue; see his *Fact, Fiction, and Forecast* (Cambridge, 1955).

38. Widerker has developed this example in an unpublished manuscript and also in conversation. Widerker believes that the Entailment Criterion of Soft Facthood should be rejected.

39. For discussion, see Zemach and Widerker (Chapter 6 in this volume); and Kvanvig, *The Possibility of an All-Knowing God*.

40. John Martin Fischer, "Hard-Type Soft Facts," *Philosophical Review*, 95 (1986): 591–601.

41. Ibid.

42. St. Thomas Aquinas, *Summa Theologicae*, Pt. I, q. 10.

43. Boethius, *The Consolation of Philosophy*, secs. 3–6. For an alternative interpretation of Boethius, see Davies, "Boethius and Others on Divine Foreknowledge" (Chapter 13 in this volume).

44. Kvanvig, *The Possibility of an All-Knowing God*.

45. This claim is defended as coherent in Stump and Kretzmann, "Eternity." For a discussion of the claim, see Paul Fitzgerald, "Stump and Kretzmann on Time and Eternity," *Journal of Philosophy*, 82 (1985): 260–69; and Eleonore Stump and Norman Kretzmann, "Atemporal Duration: A Reply to Fitzgerald," *Journal of Philosophy*, 84 (1987): 214–19.

46. There is a presentation of this sort of argument in Swinburne, *The Coherence of Theism*.

47. See also P. Helm, "Timelessness and Foreknowledge," *Mind*, 84 (1975): 516–27; and Linda Zagzebski, "Divine Foreknowledge and Human Free Will," *Religious Studies*, 21 (1985): 279–98.

48. For skepticism about the coherence of an atemporal God, see Anthony Kenny, "Divine Foreknowledge and Human Freedom," in Kenny, ed., *Aquinas: A Collection of Critical Essays* (London, 1969); and Pike, *God and Timelessness*.

49. For the claim that a compatibilist must confront the problem posed by God's providence, see Freddoso, "Introduction."

50. There is an argument that one cannot easily block incompatibilism even if one denies (FP) in John Martin Fischer, "Power over the Past," *Pacific Philosophical Quarterly*, 65 (1984): 335–50.

51. A defender of Alston's position might well insist that there is a strong analogy between "can" and "knows." Such a theorist might claim that "internalist" and "externalist" accounts of knowledge—or, perhaps, of justification—correspond to different senses of knowledge.

Pike: Divine Omniscience and Voluntary Action

1. Boethius, *Consolatio Philosophiae*, Bk. V, sec. 3, par. 6.

2. This position is particularly well formulated in St. Anselm's *Proslogium*, ch. xix, and *Monologium*, chs. xxi–xxii; and in Frederich Schleiermacher's *The Christian Faith*, Pt. I, sec. 2, par. 51. It is also explicit in Boethius, *Consolatio*, secs. 4–6, and in St. Thomas Aquinas's *Summa Theologicae*, Pt. I, q. 10.

3. This point is explicit in Boethius, *Consolatio*, secs. 4–6.

4. This position is particularly well expressed in William Paley's *Natural Theology*, ch. xxiv. It is also involved in John Calvin's discussion of predestination, *Institutes of the Christian Religion*, Bk. III, ch. xxi; and in some formulations of the first cause argument for the existence of God, e.g., John Locke's *An Essay Concerning Human Understanding*, Bk. IV, ch. x.

5. Calvin, *Institutes of the Christian Religion*, Bk. III, ch. xxi; this passage trans. by John Allen (Philadelphia, 1813), II, p. 145.

6. Ibid., p. 144.

7. Augustine, *City of God*, Bk. V, sec. 9.

8. The notion of someone being *able* to do something and the notion of something being *within one's power* are essentially the same. Traditional formulations of the problem of divine foreknowledge (e.g., those of Boethius and Augustine) made use of the notion of what is (and what is not) *within one's power*. But the problem is the same when framed in terms of what one is (and one is not) *able* to do. Thus, I shall treat the statements "Jones was able to do *X*," "Jones had the ability to do *X*," and "It was within Jones's power to do *X*" as equivalent. Richard Taylor, in "I Can," *Philosophical Review*, 69 (1960): 78–89, has argued that the notion of ability or power involved in these last three statements is incapable of philosophical analysis. Be this as it may, I shall not here attempt such an analysis. In what follows I shall, however, be careful to affirm only those statements about what is (or is not) within one's power that would have to be preserved on any analysis of this notion having even the most distant claim to adequacy.

9. In Bk. II, ch. xxi, secs. 8–11 of *An Essay*, Locke says that an agent is not *free* with respect to a given action (i.e., that an action is done "under necessity") when it is not within the agent's power to do otherwise. Locke allows a special kind of case, however, in which an action may be *voluntary* though done under necessity. If a man chooses to do something without knowing that it is not within his power to do otherwise (e.g., if a man chooses to stay in a room without knowing that the room is locked), his action may be voluntary though he is not free to forbear it. If Locke is right in this (and I shall not argue the point one way or the other), replace "voluntary" with (let us say) "free" in the above paragraph and throughout the remainder of this paper.

10. Aquinas, *Summa Theologicae*, Pt. I, q. 14, a. 8.

11. Richard Taylor, "Fatalism," *Philosophical Review*, 71 (1962): 56–66. Taylor argues that if an event E fails to occur at t_2, then at t_1 it was true that E would fail to occur at t_2. Thus, at t_1, a necessary condition of anyone's performing an action sufficient for the occurrence of E at t_2 is missing. Thus at t_1, no one could have the power to perform an action that would be sufficient for the occurrence of E at t_2. Hence, no one has the power at t_1 to do something sufficient for the occurrence of an event at t_2 that is not going to happen. The parallel between this argument and the one recited above can be seen very clearly if one reformulates Taylor's argument, pushing back the time at which it was true that E would not occur at t_2.

12. For a helpful discussion of difficulties involved here, see Rogers

Albritton's "Present Truth and Future Contingency," a reply to Richard Taylor's "The Problem of Future Contingency," both in *Philosophical Review*, 66 (1957): 1–28.

13. Gilbert Ryle interprets it this way. See "It Was to Be," in *Dilemmas* (Cambridge, Engl., 1954).

14. Richard Gale suggests this interpretation in "Endorsing Predictions," *Philosophical Review*, 70 (1961): 376–85.

15. This view is held by John Turk Saunders in "Sea Fight Tomorrow?," *Philosophical Review*, 67 (1958): 367–78.

16. G. W. Leibniz, *Théodicée*, Pt. I, sec. 37. This passage trans. by E. M. Huggard (New Haven, 1952), p. 144.

17. *De Libero Arbitrio*, Bk. III. This passage trans. by J. H. S. Burleigh, *Augustine's Earlier Writings* (Philadelphia, 1955).

18. Luis de Molina, *Concordia Liberi Arbitrii*. This passage trans. by John Mourant, *Readings in the Philosophy of Religion* (New York, 1954), p. 426.

19. Cf. Boethius's *Consolatio*, Bk. V, sec. 3, par. 2.

20. Emil Brunner, *The Christian Doctrine of God*, trans. by Olive Wyon (Philadelphia, 1964), p. 262.

21. Note: no comment here about *freely* doing X.

22. Schleiermacher, *The Christian Faith*, Pt. I, sec. 2, par. 55. This passage trans. by W. R. Matthew (Edinburgh, 1928), p. 228.

23. *De Libero Arbitrio*, Bk. III.

24. This last seems to be the position defended by Richard Taylor in "Deliberation and Foreknowledge," *American Philosophical Quarterly*, 1 (1964): 73–80.

25. The phrase "might have" as it occurs in this sentence does not express mere *logical* possibility. I am not sure how to analyze the notion of possibility involved here, but I think it is roughly the same notion as is involved when we say, "Jones might have been killed in the accident (had it not been for the fact that at the last minute he decided not to go)."

Adams: Is the Existence of God a "Hard" Fact?

1. John Turk Saunders, "Of God and Freedom," *Philosophical Review*, 75 (1966): 219–25.

2. Nelson Pike, "Of God and Freedom: A Rejoinder," *Philosophical Review*, 75 (1966): 369–79.

3. Ibid., pp. 377–78.

4. Ibid., pp. 369–70.

5. The following way of explaining the distinction was suggested to me by Robert Merrihew Adams.

6. This assumption is required to forestall the following objection. Suppose there are two individuals y and z who are alike in all respects except that y believed at t_1 that Jones would mow his lawn at t_2 and z believed at t_1 that Jones would refrain from mowing his lawn at t_2. Suppose further that the properties which y and z share include all the essential attributes of God except omniscience. Since Jones mowed his lawn at t_2, z was not God at t_1, though y may have been God at t_1 (if all the beliefs y and z share are true). Nevertheless, Jones's power at t_2 to refrain from mowing his lawn would not necessarily be the power at t_2 so to act that God would not have existed at t_1. For, if Jones had refrained from mowing his lawn at t_2, y would not have been God at t_1, but instead z might have been God at t_1 (if all the beliefs y and z share are true). (This objection was raised by Robert Merrihew Adams.) I think it is logically impossible that more than one individual have all the essential properties of God except omniscience, but I shall not defend this claim here.

7. Pike, "Of God and Freedom: A Rejoinder," p. 378.

Fischer: Freedom and Foreknowledge

1. Nelson Pike, "Divine Omniscience and Voluntary Action" (Chapter 2 in this volume); "Of God and Freedom: A Rejoinder," *Philosophical Review*, 75 (July 1966): 369–79; and "Divine Foreknowledge, Human Freedom and Possible Worlds," *Philosophical Review*, 86 (April 1977): 209–16. Pike also discusses the same basic argument in the fourth chapter of his book, *God and Timelessness* (New York, 1970).

2. Some examples are: Marilyn Adams, "Is the Existence of God a 'Hard' Fact?" (Chapter 3 in this volume), and William L. Rowe, *Philosophy of Religion* (Encino, Calif., 1978), pp. 154–69. The approach sketched below is called "Ockhamist" because William of Ockham distinguished between propositions about the past which are necessary and those which are not and argued that among those propositions about the past which are not now necessary are certain propositions about God. (Ockham, *Predestination, God's Foreknowledge and Future Contingents*, trans. Marilyn McCord Adams and Norman Kretzmann [New York, 1969], pp. 46–47, 92.) Roughly, Ockham claims that those propositions about the past which are true by virtue of contingent future events are not now necessary. Such propositions, it might be said, express "soft facts" about the past. A useful discussion of the Ockhamist approach can be found in Arthur Prior, *Past, Present and Future* (Oxford, 1967), pp. 121–27. John Turk Saunders agrees with the Ockhamist that certain propositions about God express soft facts (Saunders, "Of God and Freedom," *Philosophical Review*, 75 [April 1966]: 219–25). Saunders holds a position which is even stronger than Ockhamism, since he be-

lieves that neither soft facts nor hard facts need be fixed (Saunders, "The Temptations of 'Powerlessness,'" *American Philosophical Quarterly*, 5 [April 1968]: 104–7).

3. Adams, "Is the Existence of God a 'Hard' Fact?"

4. Pike, "Divine Omniscience," pp. 57–61 in this volume.

5. Thus Pike conceives of God's eternality as sempiternality—existence at all times. This conception is shared by the Ockhamist; it can be contrasted with the atemporal conception of eternality held by Boethius and Aquinas.

6. Pike makes this assumption explicit in "Omnipotence and God's Ability to Sin," *American Philosophical Quarterly*, 6 (1969): 208–16, esp. 208–9.

7. C. B. Martin argues for this approach in the fourth chapter of his *Religious Belief* (Ithaca, 1964).

8. Pike says in his original paper: "The important thing to be learned from the study of Smith's foreknowledge of Jones's action is that the problem of divine foreknowledge has as one of its pillars the claim that truth is *analytically* connected with God's *beliefs*. No problem of determinism arises when dealing with human foreknowledge of future actions. This is because truth is not analytically connected with human belief even when (as in the case of human knowledge) truth is contingently conjoined to belief" (Pike, "Divine Omniscience," pp. 70–71 in this volume). Thus it is clear that Pike as well as the Ockhamist *needs* the distinction between hard and soft facts.

9. Saunders, "Of God and Freedom," p. 224. Unfortunately, Saunders's arithmetic is wrong since there is no 0 B.C. or A.D. 0. Hence, Caesar's death preceded Saunders's writing his paper by 2,008 years! For simplicity's sake, however, I shall ignore this and proceed with Saunders, Pike, and Adams in adding a year to history.

10. Pike, "Of God and Freedom," pp. 369–70; Rowe makes a similar distinction between facts that are "simply about the past" and facts that are not (Rowe, *Philosophy of Religion*, pp. 162–65).

11. Pike, "Of God and Freedom," pp. 369–70.

12. Put in terms of possible worlds, the fixed past constraint is:

(FPC*) A possible world W^* (in which an agent does other than what he does in W at t) can establish that the agent had it in his power at t in W to do otherwise only if W and W^* have the same hard facts about the past relative to t.

In "Pike on Possible Worlds, Divine Foreknowledge, and Human Freedom," *Philosophical Review*, 88 (July 1979): 441–42, Joshua Hoffman criticizes Pike's interpretation of the fixity of the past. Hoffman construes Pike as claiming that the possession of every power *entails* the occurrence or nonoccurrence of past circumstances. That is, Hoffman attributes to Pike the claim that the truth of a statement ascribing a particular power to an agent at a time in a world *W entails* that the past be as it is in *W*. Pike himself puts the constraint in a misleading way, saying: "If we assume that what is within my power at a given moment determines a set of possible worlds, all of the members of that set will have to be worlds in which what has happened in the past relative to the given moment is precisely what has happened in the past relative to that moment in the actual world" (Pike, "Divine Foreknowledge," p. 215). But nothing in Pike's position requires acceptance of the radical doctrine attributed to him by Hoffman. Pike's fixed past constraint commits him to the claim that if an agent performs an act in world *W*, then any possible world *W** in which he refrains from performing the act must have the same past as *W*, if *W** is to establish that the agent can in *W* refrain from performing the act. But there may be possible worlds (including *W*) in which the agent can perform the act (and *does* perform the act) in which the past histories (relative to the time of the act) are all different from one another; hence, the truth of a power-ascription need not *entail* the past history. Hoffman's criticism of Pike misses the mark and leaves the fixed past constraint unscathed.

13. Adams, "Is the Existence of God a 'Hard' Fact?," pp. 75–76 in this volume.

14. Hilary Putnam, "The Meaning of 'Meaning,'" reprinted in Hilary Putnam, *Mind, Language, and Reality* (London, 1975), pp. 215–71, esp. pp. 223–27. Robert Stalnaker suggested to me the idea for the incompatibilist's constraint and pointed out the relevance of Putnam's point to it.

15. I borrow this sort of example from Rowe, *Philosophy of Religion*, p. 165.

Widerker: Two Forms of Fatalism

1. For an ancient version of this argument, see Peter de Rivo's version of it cited in Leon Baudry, ed., *La Querelle des Futurs Contingents* (Paris, 1950), pp. 80–81. For its recent versions, see Gilbert Ryle, ed., *Dilemmas* (Cambridge, 1954), p. 15; and Steven Cahn, *Fate, Logic, and Time* (New Haven, 1967), pp. 38–39, 82–83.

2. For a classic statement of this argument, see Jonathan Edwards, *Freedom of the Will*, eds. A. S. Kaufman and W. Frankena (Indianapolis, 1969), sec. 12. Its modern version has been stated by Nelson Pike, "Divine Omniscience and Voluntary Action" (Chapter 2 in this volume).

3. See, for example, F. Waismann, "How I See Philosophy," in H. D. Lewis, ed., *Contemporary British Philosophy* (London, 1956), p. 457; and A. J. Ayer, "Fatalism," in *The Concept of a Person and Other Essays* (London, 1963), p. 237.

4. Jan Lukasiewicz, "Philosophische Bemerkungen zu mehrwertigen Systemen des Aussagenkalkuls," *Comptes Rendus de Seances de la Société des Siences et des Lettres de Varsovie*, Classe III, vol. XXIII (1930), Fascicule 1–3, pp. 51–77. See also Ryle, *Dilemmas*, p. 20.

5. Arthur Prior, *Time and Modality* (Oxford, 1957), pp. 94–96. See also his *Past, Present and Future* (Oxford, 1967), pp. 128–34.

6. Joshua Hoffman and Gary Rosenkrantz, "On Divine Foreknowledge and Human Freedom," *Philosophical Studies*, 37 (1980): 292–93. For an approach to (NTF) that differs from those mentioned in the text, see Alfred Freddoso's "Accidental Necessity and Logical Determinism" (Chapter 8 in this volume). My approach to (NTF) is similar to Freddoso's, although my argument for it differs from his in important aspects.

7. Cf. Storrs McCall, "Temporal Flux," *American Philosophical Quarterly*, 3 (1966): 270–81. If one is ready to ignore the tensed aspect of (X1) and replace it with 'it is true at t_0 that Jack (tenselessly) pulls the trigger at t_{10}', then one can explicate (X1) more simply as follows: 'The time-moment t_0 has the property of being such that Jack pulls the trigger at t_{10}'.

8. This does not imply that one could not provide another motivation for adopting these views. A possible theological motivation might be this: in order for human freedom not to conflict with His knowledge, God creates a world whose future is essentially open.

9. This principle is an improved version of a principle used by Richard Taylor in his defense of fatalism; see his "Fatalism," *Philosophical Review*, 71 (1962): 58. Cf. William L. Rowe, "Fatalism and Truth," *Southern Journal of Philosophy*, 18 (1980): 217. A principle similar to (PRW) has been also suggested to me by Carl Ginet.

Another way of defending the inference from (1) to (2) is to appeal to the principle:

$$(\text{PRE}) \quad [\Box(p \equiv q) \cdot P^*_{a,t}(p)] \supset P^*_{a,t}(q)$$

10. Here, as well as in what follows, I shall take the term 'event' to refer to concrete, non-repeatable events. Also, I shall include under the rubric 'event' states of substances and processes.

11. The notion of truth as applied to sentences, though parasitic on the notion of truth as applied to propositions (or sentence-tokens) differs from the latter. Truth as applied to a sentence may vary with time and speaker.

12. Or expressing this condition even more cautiously in terms of:

$$\ulcorner \Box \{F^t(x^t, t^t) \supset (\exists y)(\exists G)(\exists t')[t' > t^t \cdot G(y, t')]\} \urcorner \text{ is true}$$

(where 'F^t', 'x^t', and 't^t' are rigid designators of F, x, and t).

13. Marilyn McCord Adams, "Is the Existence of God a 'Hard' Fact?" (Chapter 3 in this volume), pp. 75–76; and John Martin Fischer, "Freedom and Foreknowledge" (Chapter 4 in this volume), pp. 90–92.

14. By saying that (S1) does not entail the existence of times after t_1, I wish to indicate that it does not seem to me obvious that times are entities that exist necessarily. Such a strong claim about the nature of time would require an independent argument. For example, it does not seem to hold on the relational theory of time.

15. For another, more complicated way of handling Fischer's objection, see Hoffman and Rosenkrantz's improved account of the soft/hard fact distinction (Chapter 7 in this volume). Their theory, however, has some serious drawbacks. For example, it commits them to treating facts such as "Columbus walked in 1492" as soft facts about 1492. Their way out of this objection (see pp. 134–35), does not seem to me to be satisfactory.

16. For a similar conclusion, see Peter van Inwagen, *An Essay on Free Will* (Oxford, 1983), p. 42.

17. By divine knowledge, I mean here essential omniscience—that is, infallibility and essential all-knowingness. By 'freedom' I mean freedom in the incompatibilist's sense.

18. I prefer this version of the theological argument to that originally formulated by Pike ("Divine Omniscience," Chapter 2 in this volume). Unlike the latter, it precisely spells out the move from (i) Jack's having it within his power at t_9 to bring it about that it is not the case that Qt_{10}, to (ii) his having the power at t_9 to bring it about that God did not believe at t_0 that Qt_{10}.

19. The intuitive principle underlying this last inference is this: if p is the case, and q is a causally necessary condition for p, then if it is within an agent's power at t to bring it about that not-q, it is also within his power to bring it about that not-p.

20. For a related but still different argument, see Fischer, "Freedom and Foreknowledge," pp. 93–95 in this volume). For other aspects of the freedom-foreknowledge debate, see also Fischer's "Ockhamism," *Philosophical Review*, 94 (1985): 82–100.

21. For an attempt to work out such an account, see Eddy Zemach and David Widerker, "Facts, Freedom, and Foreknowledge" (Chapter 6 in this volume).

22. John Martin Fischer, "Hard-Type Soft Facts," *Philosophical Review*, 95 (1986): 591–601.

Zemach and Widerker: Facts, Freedom, and Foreknowledge

1. Among philosophers who espouse the Ockhamistic view are Marilyn McCord Adams, "Is the Existence of God a 'Hard' Fact?"

(Chapter 3 in this volume); Anthony Kenny, "Divine Foreknowledge and Human Freedom," in Kenny, ed., *Aquinas: A Collection of Critical Essays* (Garden City, 1969), pp. 255–70; and William L. Rowe, *Philosophy of Religion: An Introduction* (Encino, Calif., 1978), pp. 154–69. For an excellent presentation of the Ockhamistic view from a historical perspective, see Marilyn Adams and Norman Kretzmann's introduction to their translation of Ockham's *Predestination, God's Foreknowledge and Future Contingents* (New York, 1969).

2. John Martin Fischer, "Freedom and Foreknowledge" (Chapter 4 in this volume).

3. For other (non-identical) versions of this argument, see, for example, Nelson Pike, "Divine Omniscience and Voluntary Action" (Chapter 2 in this volume); Joshua Hoffman and Gary Rosenkrantz, "On Divine Foreknowledge and Human Freedom," *Philosophical Studies*, 37 (1980): 289–96. Hoffman and Rosenkrantz's objection to the principle of *power* entailment can be overcome by introducing the relevant scope distinctions. In (3) above we avoid this issue, for brevity's sake, by assuming that α and β contain no definite descriptions.

4. Fischer, "Freedom and Foreknowledge," pp. 90–92 in this volume. For Adams's account of the hard/soft fact distinction, see Adams, "Is the Existence of God a 'Hard' Fact?" pp. 75–76 in this volume.

5. The above definition of $C(w,t)$ can be strengthened, requiring members of $C(w,t)$ to share the same physical laws with w.

6. Another way of dealing with such compounds would be Van Fraassen's method of supervaluations, as expounded in his "Singular Terms, Truth-Value Gaps and Free Logic," *Journal of Philosophy*, 63 (1966): 481–85.

7. On Adams's account ("Is the Existence of God a 'Hard' Fact?," pp. 75–76 in this volume):

(C) "Statement p expresses a 'hard' fact about a time t" = df. "p is not at least in part about any time future relative to t,"

where "p is at least in part about time t" is defined as follows:

(B) "Statement p is at least in part about time t" = df. "The happening or not happening, actuality or non-actuality of something at t is a necessary condition of the truth of p."

Against this account of hard facts, Fischer argues that since (m2) is a necessary condition for the truth of (m1), (m1) is at least in part about t_2, in which case it does not express a hard fact about the past relative to t_2. This is counterintuitive. Similarly for (n1).

8. Cf. Rowe, *Philosophy of Religion*, p. 165.

9. Quoted by Aquinas, *Summa Theologicae*, IA, 14, 8.

Hoffman and Rosenkrantz: Hard and Soft Facts

1. Fischer, "Freedom and Foreknowledge," pp. 90–92 in this volume.

2. It should also be noted that in (C), Adams's definition of a hard fact, Adams should have stipulated that t is a past time.

3. For a discussion of sorts of repeatability which are intermediate between eternality and unrestricted repeatability, see Joshua Hoffman and Gary Rosenkrantz, "What an Omnipotent Agent Can Do," *International Journal for Philosophy of Religion*, 11 (1980): 1–19. In that paper it is argued that the concept of omnipotence can be analyzed in terms of the notion of an unrestrictedly repeatable state of affairs.

4. Where n ranges over all natural numbers, and where $t_1 \ldots t_n$ are non-overlapping.

5. Some philosophers have thought that John Locke claimed that a thing cannot have two beginnings of existence. This claim implies, contrary to what we have asserted, that the state of affairs *Mount St. Helens comes into existence* is not *UR*. However, Locke did not make such a claim, and an exegesis which demonstrates this can be found in Joshua Hoffman, "Locke on Whether a Thing Can Have Two Beginnings of Existence," *Ratio*, 22 (1980): 106–11. Furthermore, like Hume we simply fail to see any logical contradiction, incoherence, or absurdity in the supposition that Mount St. Helens goes in and out of existence indefinitely many times. In light of this, we shall assume that the state of affairs *Mount St. Helens comes into existence* is *UR*. Generally, contingent states of affairs of the forms '*a* comes into existence' and '*a* exists' are *UR*.

6. This dispute arises among philosophers who hold different theories about the ontological status of the present or the now. Such philosophers disagree about things like the nature of the "nexus of exemplification"—that is, whether it is tensed or tenseless, the correct analysis of the now, the reducibility of the now to other temporal properties or relations, and the nature of the relationship of the now to human thought. On one side are philosophers who hold that some present-tense states of affairs are repeatable, but all tenseless states of affairs are eternal. On the other side are those who maintain that some tenseless states of affairs are repeatable, but all present-tense states of affairs are eternal. In this latter camp is Ernest Sosa; see his "The Status of Becoming: What Is Happening Now?" *Journal of Philosophy*, 76 (1979): 26–42. Sosa argues that the most plausible account of the now implies that a repeatable state of affairs like *Socrates walks* is tenseless. Compare Alfred Freddoso, "Ockham's Theory of Truth Conditions," in Alfred Freddoso and Henry Schuurman, trans., *Ockham's Theory of Propositions:*

Part II of the Summa Logicae (Notre Dame, 1980), pp. 28–39. Freddoso attributes to Ockham the view that a repeatable state of affairs like *Socrates walks* is a present-tense state of affairs and that such present-tense states of affairs are what really happen in the world or are ontologically primal.

7. The following example helps to clarify our definition of a complex state of affairs. Call the state of affairs, *S walked*, *w*. Suppose *w* were analyzable as $(\exists t)$ ($t <$ now & *S* walks at *t*). Would this analysis show that *w* is complex? A state of affairs is complex if and only if it or its analysis can be exhibited as a conjunction, disjunction, etc., of other states of affairs. But open sentences like '$t <$ now' and '*x* is walking at *t*' (where '*x*' and '*t*' are free variables) do not express states of affairs because they are not literally true or false. Hence, the analysis above would not show that *w* is constructed out of other states of affairs by using conjunction and existential quantification. And since the quantifier in the analysans cannot be distributed to the conjuncts falling within the scope of that quantifier, the analysans is not a conjunction of two existentially quantified states of affairs. Thus, an analysis like the one above would not show that *w* is complex. However, if it were true that *w* is analyzable in terms of existential quantification, and if the highly questionable view that such quantification is analyzable in terms of infinite disjunction were also true, then *w* would be complex. This is because *w* would be analyzable into an infinite disjunction such as [(*S* walks one day earlier) or (*S* walks two days earlier) or (*S* walks three days earlier) or . . .]. The latter view is highly questionable because it is quite plausible to require of a successful philosophical analysis that it be of finite length or be humanly graspable. However, those who hold that quantifications are analyzable into infinitely long disjunctions or conjunctions may reply that we can grasp an infinitely long proposition of this kind just by grasping the corresponding quantified proposition, inasmuch as two such propositions are necessarily equivalent. The account we have given of the identity and analysis of propositions or states of affairs enables us to answer this in two ways. First, the necessary equivalence of two propositions is no guarantee that both of them are graspable if one of them is graspable. For example, the propositions *6 = the smallest perfect number* and *6 = 6* are necessarily equivalent, but the difference in cognitive content between them results in the latter being graspable by individuals who lack the conceptual resources to be able to grasp the former. Furthermore, because a (finite) quantified proposition is a proposition which we can fully survey, whereas an infinite disjunction or conjunction cannot be fully surveyed by us, there must be a difference in their cognitive content which results in only the former being graspable by us, even if they are necessarily equivalent.

This cognitive difference is one of the things which makes the former sort of proposition useful. Second, since grasping a proposition is a cognitive attitude, it seems that if one can grasp an infinitely long conjunction or disjunction *just by* grasping an equivalent (finite) quantified proposition, then such an infinite complex has the *same* cognitive content as the corresponding quantified proposition. This being so, in a so-called analysis of the latter in terms of the former, analysandum and analysans have the same cognitive content, implying that the so-called analysis is an uninformative tautology and not a genuine analysis at all.

Our definition of a complex state of affairs raises a second, epistemic problem. We know of a state of affairs that it is simple only if we know that it is not analyzable into a complex state of affairs. But can we ever know of a state of affairs that it is not analyzable into a complex state of affairs? Even if the answer is no, the view that a complex state of affairs is a compound of simple ones has considerable intuitive appeal—perhaps because there is serious doubt about the legitimacy of the infinite regress or circle which results if this view is false. And it is plausible that some of these simple states of affairs are *URP* and expressed by singular existential or predicative sentences of the form '*a* exists' or '*Fa*'. Furthermore, we can have increasingly good evidence that a particular *URP* state of affairs of this type is simple; for example, repeated failure by the best minds to analyze it into a complex. Whether such inductive evidence is ever sufficient for knowledge is debatable, but it is fair to say that we have this sort of evidence for attributing simplicity to many *URP* states of affairs of the type in question; for example, ones like *S exists*, *S walks*, and *S believes that Jones will sit*, etc. Since we have good inductive evidence for believing that *URP* states of affairs like these are simple, we shall attribute simplicity to such states of affairs. Nevertheless, our explications of the distinctions between complex and simple states of affairs and the notion of a hard fact in (IV) do not require that there be any simple states of affairs. To apply (IV) one need only to be able to say that there is a *URP* state of affairs like *S exists*, *S walks*, *S believes that Jones will walk*, etc., which is *either* simple *or* complex and composed only of *URP* parts. Given the presumption in favor of the simplicity of such states of affairs, the burden of proof is on those who would reject our account to produce plausible analyses of such states of affairs in terms of complexes containing a non-*URP* part.

8. Whether r_1 satisfies condition (4) of (IV) depends on the analyzability of knowledge. If r_1's kernel is analyzable into a conjunctive state of affairs consisting of eternal parts like God's believing that Jones walks at t_2, its being true that Jones walks at t_2, God's being justified in believing that Jones walks at t_2, and so forth, then r_1 seems not to satisfy (4) because r_1's kernel is a complex containing some parts which are not *URP*. But if r_1's kernel is simple, then r_1 satisfies (4).

9. For considerations bearing on the justification of the claim that these *URP* states of affairs are simple, see note 7 above. For an argument that a state of affairs like *Jones exists* is *UR*, see note 5 above.

10. Fischer, "Freedom and Foreknowledge," p. 91.

11. See note 8 above.

12. Likewise, it seems reasonable to suppose that any true conjunctive state of affairs, one of whose conjuncts is necessary, is not a hard fact about the past.

Freddoso: Accidental Necessity and Logical Determinism

1. Several of the relevant texts are found in English translation in William Ockham, *Predestination, God's Foreknowledge and Future Contingents*, trans. Marilyn McCord Adams and Norman Kretzmann (New York, 1969).

2. The most elaborate recent discussions of Ockham's position are found in the introduction to his *Predestination* and in Arthur Prior, *Past, Present and Future* (Oxford, 1967), esp. chap. 7.

3. For a recent defense of the view that all propositions are tensed, See Nicholas Wolterstorff, "Can Ontology Do Without Events?," in Ernest Sosa, ed., *Essays on the Philosophy of Roderick Chisholm* (Amsterdam, 1979), esp. pp. 183–88.

4. I will say that p entails q just in case it is logically impossible that there be a moment at which p is true and q is false. Similarly, p is *logically equivalent* to q just in case it is logically impossible that there be a moment at which p and q differ in truth value.

5. See, e.g., Jack W. Meiland, "A Two-Dimensional Passage Model for Time Travel," *Philosophical Studies*, 26 (1974): 153–73; and David Lewis, "The Paradoxes of Time Travel," *American Philosophical Quarterly*, 13 (1976): 145–52. To corroborate a point made below, Meiland's argument presupposes that there can be two independent time dimensions, and Lewis's argument presupposes that a person is (literally) a mereological sum of temporal parts, two of which could confront one another in a time-travel scenario.

6. See Aristotle, *On Interpretation*, chap. 9; and Prior, *Past, Present and Future*, pp. 128–36, and "The Formalities of Omniscience," *Philosophy*, 32 (1962): 119–29. I will assume for present purposes that this traditional interpretation of Aristotle is correct.

7. See Peter T. Geach, *Providence and Evil* (Cambridge, 1977), pp. 40–66. The most thorough explication of this position that I know of is contained in an unpublished paper by Jorge Garcia entitled "The Elimination of the Future."

8. See my "Ockham's Theory of Truth Conditions," in Alfred J. Freddoso and Henry Schuurman, trans., *Ockham's Theory of Propositions: Part II of the Summa Logicae* (Notre Dame, 1980), esp. pp. 28–39.

9. Geach contends that those who hold (A) that there are propositions "about" the future are committed to the dubious thesis (B) that there is a "futureland" populated by merely future beings. See *Providence and Evil*, pp. 51–57. But I have argued in "Ockham's Theory of Truth Conditions" that (A) is compatible with the negation of (B) and, further, that there are good reasons for thinking that Ockham himself rejected (B).

10. There are two points which merit special attention here. First, I am assuming that propositions like:

(a) David is now such that he will visit Rome

and

(b) Katie is now such that she has been to Rome

are not represented by atomic constitutents of L. This assumption is reasonable, since (a), for example, seems best analyzed as:

(c) David now exists and David will visit Rome,

which can be adequately represented in L by a formula like 'p and Fq'. Second, I accept the claim that if God exists, he is essentially omniscient—so that necessarily, God believes p just in case God correctly believes p. For present purposes I will simply assume that no proposition attributing a belief to God is represented by an atomic constituent of L. This will allow me to discuss logical determinism without having to tackle the problem of divine foreknowledge as well. However, it is important to note that the assumption in question would require a separate argument if we were dealing with divine foreknowledge. In short, the argument for determinism from divine foreknowledge is, contrary to what some have claimed, more difficult to contend with than is the argument for logical determinism.

11. I am assuming that the correct analysis of (17) is this: for any proposition p, if p is true, then Katie knows p. As is obvious, this analysis involves quantifiers.

12. At this point someone might suggest that it would be better for me to use a predicate language rather than a simple propositional language in explicating immediacy. However, as far as I can tell, this would simply complicate my presentation without making it any more accurate.

13. By a 'singular' proposition I simply mean one which involves no quantifiers or truth-functions which do not fall within the scope of a propositional attitude. Moreover, any proposition represented by an atomic constituent of L is affirmative, since any negative proposition representable in L is best represented (in accord with the second stipulation) by a formula involving the negation operator. I should also point

out in passing that among the propositions represented by atomic constituents of L there will be many which ascribe dispositional and other 'scientific' properties to individual objects.

14. The Aristotelian view is usually stated in such a way that bivalence is denied only for causally contingent future-tense propositions. So suppose that it is now causally necessary that Mt. Vesuvius will erupt at t, where t is in our future. Then, since they presuppose (D), most versions of Aristotelianism are committed to the claim that it is *now* part of our *history* that it has been true that Vesuvius will erupt at t. This result is by itself sufficient to cast doubt on both (D) and these versions of Aristotelianism. I will discuss the relationship between accidental and causal modality in more detail below.

15. Prior develops this notion in *Past, Present and Future* and in "The Formalities of Omniscience."

16. See my "Accidental Necessity and Power over the Past," *Pacific Philosophical Quarterly*, 63 (1982): 54–68.

Hasker: Hard Facts and Theological Fatalism

1. Most other writers who have employed the hard/soft fact distinction have been content to refer to it in general terms without attempting a precise explication. An early explication by Marilyn McCord Adams ("Is the Existence of God a 'Hard' Fact?" [Chapter 3 in this volume]) has been decisively criticized by John Fischer ("Freedom and Foreknowledge" [Chapter 4]). My own explication of the distinction will be found in "Foreknowledge and Necessity" (Chapter 11).

2. The following propositions summarizing Freddoso's position, as well as the series of propositions summarizing the Hoffman-Rosenkrantz analysis, represent at some points my paraphrase of the respective positions rather than direct citations from their authors. The authors of both papers have been kind enough to state that they find my formulations of their views to be accurate.

3. To be fair to Freddoso, I must cite his concluding words: "But, of course, this contention requires more elaborate support, which I hope to provide in another place" (p. 158). Nevertheless, I am confident that the explication I have given captures the essential thrust of what Freddoso would want to say about theological fatalism.

4. Here and elsewhere Hoffman and Rosenkrantz write "present tense or tenseless" in deference to the alternative position in logical theory according to which such states of affairs as *Jones walks* are tenseless rather than present tense. This alternative view is not without interest, but it plays no essential role in their subsequent discussion and for present purposes it will be ignored.

5. The term "*URP* kernel" is not found in the Hoffman and Rosenkrantz article. But the concept expressed by the term is present in the

article, and my introduction of the term serves to facilitate later references to this concept.

6. Saul Kripke, "Naming and Necessity," in Donald Davidson and Gilbert Harman, eds., *Semantics of Natural Language* (Dordrecht, 1972), pp. 332–33.

7. Perhaps I should write, "in no possible world does this table exist having been originally made of ice," in order to circumvent puzzles based on the gradual replacement of parts.

8. Hoffman and Rosenkrantz, however, inform me that their intention was to employ the notion of metaphysical entailment (private communication).

9. The Hoffman-Rosenkrantz analysis is subject to still more objections. Their explanations of the notions "analysis," "simple," and "complex" (see their note 7) have the result that many propositions involving descriptions or quantifications will be simple and atomic. I believe, in fact, that all of the states of affairs given below have by their account *URP* kernels and will, if true, qualify as hard facts:

(a) (*The being now worshipped by Cedric believes that John will have a cup of tea for lunch*) at 6:00.
(b) (*The being now worshipped by Cedric has no false beliefs*) at 6:00.
(c) (*Hector says that John will have a cup of tea for lunch*) at 6:00.
(d) (*Hector is saying nothing that is false*) at 6:00.

(Note that (a) and (b) are *UR*, not because it is possible for the being in question to change either his beliefs about John or his status as infallible, but because it is possible for Cedric to change his religious allegiance.) Now, if the being worshipped by Cedric is in fact God, and if God believes all true propositions, there will be analogues for (a) and (b) showing all facts to be HARD facts, and theological fatalism is again triumphant. And quite apart from theology, (c) and (d) show that any state of affairs that has at any time been affirmed by any person in the appropriate way is a HARD fact.

If correct, these arguments are decisive against the Hoffman-Rosenkrantz proposal as it stands. Yet they seem less important to me than those discussed in the main text. These arguments could be avoided by restricting states of affairs involving descriptions, quantifiers, etc., from being the kernels of hard facts (as is done, for example, by Freddoso). The arguments in the text, on the other hand, seem to have a more general application and to be harder to avoid.

10. The most convincing presentation of this view is Alvin Plantinga, "The Boethian Compromise," *American Philosophical Quarterly*, 15 (1978): 129–38. Plantinga's chief argument in support of his view is that it resolves problems in various other theories of proper names, but it is not at all clear that the problems cannot be solved in other ways.

Plantinga: On Ockham's Way Out

1. Augustine, *On Free Will*, in *Augustine: Earlier Writings*, vol. VI, trans. J. H. S. Burleigh (Philadelphia, 1953), bk. III, ii, 4.

2. Thomas Aquinas, *Summa Contra Gentiles*, bk. I, ch. 67, 10. The quoted passage involves Aquinas's view that the future is (in a sense hard to make clear) somehow *present* to God. This does not affect my point in quoting it, which is only to show that Aquinas notes the distinction between necessity of the consequent and necessity of the consequence—a distinction that enables us to see just how the argument in question goes wrong.

3. See *Summa Contra Gentiles*, I, 67, and *Summa Theologicae*, I, q. 14, a. 13.

4. Jonathan Edwards, *Freedom of the Will* (1745), sec. 12.

5. See Eleonore Stump and Norman Kretzmann, "Eternity," *Journal of Philosophy*, 78 (1981): 429–58.

6. See, for example, Peter van Inwagen, *An Essay on Free Will* (Oxford, 1983), pp. 35 ff.; and Nelson Pike, *God and Timelessness* (New York, 1970), pp. 67 ff. (Pike's objection is not to temporally indexed propositions as such, but to alleged propositions of the sort *It is true at t_1 that S does A at t_2*.

7. Nelson Pike, "Divine Omniscience and Voluntary Action" (Chapter 2 in this volume, p. 63).

8. Of course it does not follow that it was not within Jones's power, at t_1, so to act that a belief God *did* hold at t_1 *would have been false*. See my *God, Freedom and Evil* (New York, 1974; Grand Rapids, 1977), p. 70.

9. In principle, of course, (7.2) is subject to another reading, one in which "it is within Jones's power to do something that would have brought it about that" has wide scope, so that what is expressed could be put more explicitly as

(7.2**) It is within Jones's power at t_2 to do something that would have brought it about that the proposition *God did not hold the belief he held at t_1* would have been true.

The proposition *God did not hold the belief he held at t_1* would have been true if and only if there is a certain belief such that God held that belief at t_2 and furthermore did *not* hold that belief then. The power (7.2**) ascribes to Jones, therefore, is the absurd power of doing something such that if he had done that thing, then God would have held a certain belief at t_2 and furthermore would *not* have held that belief then. If we read (7.2) as (7.2**), however, then it is easy to show that (6) does not entail (7), so that Pike's claim that it *does* would be false.

10. Pike, "Divine Omniscience," p. 63 in this volume.

11. Peter Damian, *De Divina Omnipotentia*, ch. IV. In Migne's *Patrologia Latina*, vol. 145, 599. The translation of the last two sentences is from Anthony Kenny's *The God of the Philosophers* (Oxford, 1979), p. 101.

12. Damian, *De Divina Omnipotentia*, 618. The translation is by Owen J. Blum and is taken from John Wippel and Alan Wolter, *Medieval Philosophy* (New York, 1969), p. 147.

13. Damian, *De Divina Omnipotentia*, 619.

14. William of Ockham, *Ordinatio*, I, Prologue, q. 6.

15. I take it that (8) is equivalent to

(8*) *Columbus sails the ocean blue* is, was, or will be true in 1492;

I am here ignoring allegedly tenseless propositions, if indeed there are any such things.

16. William Ockham, *Predestination, God's Foreknowledge and Future Contingents*, trans. with Introduction, Notes, and Appendixes by Marilyn McCord Adams and Norman Kretzmann (New York, 1969), pp. 46–47.

17. See Nelson Pike, "Of God and Freedom: A Rejoinder," *Philosophical Review*, 75 (1966): 370, and Marilyn McCord Adams, "Is the Existence of God a 'Hard' Fact?" (Chapter 3 in this volume, pp. 74–76).

18. Nelson Goodman, "About," *Mind*, 70 (1962): 1–24.

19. I think it is clear that hard facthood *is* closed under broadly logical equivalence; this argument, however, does not require the full generality of that premise. All it requires is that no proposition strictly about the past is equivalent in the broadly logical sense to a conjunction one conjunct of which, like (18), is a contingent proposition paradigmatically about the future.

20. Even so restricted, (iv*) is by no means obviously true: What if I know my wife or child so well that I correctly believe that she will do *A*, though it is within her power to do *B* instead; and if she were to do *B*, then I would have believed that she will do *B*? It is not easy to see why this cannot be the case.

21. More exactly, anyone who thinks *both* that such propositions as (23) are either true or false *and* that (23) is incompatible with Paul's being free to mow in 1999, will be a logical fatalist.

22. I leave it to the reader to restate (28) in such a way as to accommodate those who hold that propositions are not true at times.

23. The appropriate atemporalist counterpart of (29) is

(29*) *p* is accidentally necessary if and only if *p* is true and it is not possible both that *p* is true and that there is or will be a being that has or will have the power to bring it about that *p* is false

of which (29) is a generalization. (31), (39), (42), and (44) below have similar counterparts.

24. (31) can be expressed a bit more precisely (if a bit less felicitously) as

(31) *p* is accidentally necessary at *t* if and only if *p* is true at *t* and it is not possible both that *p* is true at *t* and that there exists a time *t**, an agent *S* and an action *A* such that *t** is at least as late as *t*, at *t* S* has the power to perform *A*, and if *S* were to perform *A* at *t**, then *p* would have been false.

The atemporalist counterpart of (31) is

(31*) *p* is accidentally necessary if and only if *p* is true and it is not possible both that *p* is true and that there exists or will exist an action *A* such that (1) *S* has or will have the power to perform *A*, and (2) if *S* were to perform *A*, then *p* would have been false.

Note that on (31) propositions that are necessary in the broadly logical sense turn out to be accidentally necessary. If this is considered a defect, it can be remedied by adding an appropriate condition to the *definiens*. Similar comments apply to (39), (42), and (44) below.

25. Every action is necessarily such that if I were to perform it, I would have existed; so if there were such an action, it would be such that if I were to perform it, then I would have both existed and not existed.

26. We might be inclined to broaden (31) as follows:

(31*) *p* is accidentally necessary at *t* if and only if *p* is true at *t* and there is no action *A* and person *S* such that if *S* were to perform *A*, then *p* would have been false.

(31*) is indeed broader than (31). First, it is clearly necessary that any proposition satisfying the *definiens* of (31) also satisfies the *definiens* of (31*). Second, it seems possible that there be a true proposition *p* such that, while indeed it is *possible* that there be a person *S* and an action *A* such that *S* can perform *A* and such that if *S* were to perform *A*, then *p* would have been true, as a matter of act there is no such person and action. It is therefore possible that there be a proposition that is accidentally necessary in the sense of (31*) but not in the sense of (31). The problem with (31*), however, is a close relative of the problem with (31); under (31*) there will be far too few (contingent) propositions such that *we have any reason to think* them accidentally necessary.

27. Roderick Chisholm, *Person and Object* (LaSalle, Ill., 1976), p. 85. Chisholm's powerful discussion of agency (pp. 53–88 and 159–74) should be required reading for anyone interested in that topic. (Chisholm does not use the term "directly perform," and I am not here using the term "basic action" in just the way he does.)

28. Called to my attention by Edward Wierenga.

29. Again, (44) can obviously be recast so as to accommodate our atemporalist colleagues. What I claim for (44) is that propositions strictly about the past are accidentally necessary in the sense of (44), while their colleagues about the future typically are not; I do not claim that (44) is a satisfactory general analysis of our preanalytic notion of accidental necessity. So taken, it is subject to counterexamples of various kinds, including propositions of the form *PVQ* where *P* is a false contingent proposition strictly about the past and *Q* is a future proposition to the effect that some free agent *A* will perform some action (an action that is within *A*'s power). I think we do indeed *have* a general preanalytic notion of accidental necessity, although there are some hard puzzle cases, and the issues get complicated. Allow me to venture the following as a first approximation: say that *p* is *past* accidentally necessary if and only if *p* is a proposition about the past (not necessarily strictly about the past) and *p* is accidentally necessary in the sense of (44); and let *P* be a conjunction of the past necessary propositions.

Then

(44*) *p* is accidentally necessary *simpliciter* if and only if *p* is true and it is not possible that both (a) *P* but no proposition properly entailing *P* is past accidentally necessary, and (b) there is a past accidentally necessary proposition *q*, an agent *S* and an action *A* such that (1) *A* is basic for *S*, (2) *S* can perform *A* at *t* or later, and (3) necessarily, if *q* is true and *S* were to perform *A*, then *p* would have been false.

30. Plantinga, *God, Freedom and Evil*, pp. 66–73.

31. Nelson Pike, "Divine Foreknowledge, Human Freedom and Possible Worlds," *Philosophical Review*, 86 (1977): 216.

32. Ibid., p. 217.

33. See my *The Nature of Necessity* (Oxford, 1974), pp. 169–84, and my "Which Worlds Could God Have Created?" *Journal of Philosophy*, 70 (1973): 539–55.

34. See my *The Nature of Necessity*, pp. 175–76.

35. See Stephen T. Davis, "Divine Omniscience and Human Freedom," *Religious Studies*, 15 (1979): 303–16, and Joshua Hoffman, "Pike on Possible Worlds, Divine Foreknowledge, and Human Freedom," *Philosophical Review*, 88 (1979): 433–42.

Hasker: Foreknowledge and Necessity

1. Nelson Pike, "Divine Omniscience and Voluntary Action" (Chapter 2 in this volume); A. N. Prior, "The Formalities of Omniscience," *Philosophy*, 32 (1962): 119–29.

2. Here and throughout this essay I use the expression "*p*" to refer to the proposition that *p*.

3. See A. N. Prior, *Past, Present and Future* (Oxford, 1967), pp. 128–36; Peter T. Geach, *Providence and Evil* (Cambridge, Engl., 1977), pp. 40–66.

4. Perhaps an exception should be made to this for Alfred J. Freddoso ("Accidental Necessity and Logical Determinism," Chapter 8 in this volume), who does offer specific criticisms of Prior's scheme. I believe the criticisms can be answered, but there is no space to go into this here.

5. In "It Was to Be" (P. T. Geach and A. J. P. Kenny, eds., *Papers in Logic and Ethics* [Amherst, 1976], pp. 97–108), Prior discusses the two conceptions of truth and the resulting logical systems. The two systems are not quite intertranslatable, but the truth-conditions for assertions in each system can be explained in terms of the other.

6. See Rudolph Carnap, "Empiricism, Semantics, and Ontology," in *Meaning and Necessity*, enl. ed. (Chicago, 1956), p. 221.

7. See Richard Swinburne, *The Coherence of Theism* (Oxford, 1977), pp. 172–78.

8. See my "Concerning the Intelligibility of 'God is Timeless'," *New Scholasticism*, 57 (1983): 170–95; also Eleonore Stump and Norman Kretzmann, "Eternity," *Journal of Philosophy*, 78 (1981): 429–58.

9. This view was introduced into the modern debate by Marilyn Mc-Cord Adams ("Is the Existence of God a 'Hard' Fact?," Chapter 3 in this volume) and has been adopted by (among others) William Rowe (*Philosophy of Religion: An Introduction* [Encino, Calif., 1978], pp. 162–65); Alfred J. Freddoso ("Accidental Necessity and Logical Determinism"); and Alvin Plantinga ("On Ockham's Way Out," Chapter 10 in this volume). This solution stems historically from William of Ockham; it is no accident that both Adams and Freddoso are Ockham scholars. For an argument that this "Ockhamist" solution cannot succeed, see John Martin Fischer, "Freedom and Foreknowledge" (Chapter 4 in this volume).

10. "On Ockham's Way Out," p. 189 in this volume.

11. By far the most thorough treatment of this topic to date is Freddoso, "Accidental Necessity and Logical Determinism." While I adopt a somewhat different approach and terminology, my results at almost all points are consistent with Freddoso's.

12. Plantinga, *God, Freedom and Evil* (New York, 1974), pp. 66–73.

13. "Divine Omniscience," p. 63 in this volume. In this and subsequent quotations from Pike and Plantinga, the original numbering of propositions is retained, with initials added to indicate the source.

14. Ibid.

15. Ibid.

16. Plantinga, *God, Freedom and Evil*, pp. 70–71.

17. Ibid., p. 71.

18. There is an apparent inconsistency in what Plantinga says about this. He is clearly committed (in view of the considerations cited in the

text) to the view that (PL53) is false and cannot be entailed by (PL51). Yet he says that (PL53) is "ambiguous," seeming to leave open the possibility that, if properly interpreted, it might turn out to be true after all. Perhaps this can be reconciled by attributing to Plantinga the view that (PL53), while false if interpreted strictly, may nevertheless be taken to be an inaccurate and somewhat misleading way of ascribing to Jones the power which is more perspicuously expressed by (PL53b).

19. Plantinga, "On Ockham's Way Out," p. 204 in this volume.

20. Ibid., p. 206.

21. Philip L. Quinn, "Plantinga on Foreknowledge and Freedom," in James E. Tomberlin and Peter van Inwagen, eds., *Alvin Plantinga* (Dordrecht, 1985), p. 284.

22. Ibid., p. 285.

23. Ibid.

24. Thomas B. Talbott, "On Divine Foreknowledge and Bringing About the Past," *Philosophy and Phenomenological Research*, 46 (1986): 458. It will be noted that Talbott uses '*p*', '*q*', etc., in such a way that their substituends are not *sentences* but rather *noun phrases* which refer to propositions.

25. Ibid.

26. Ibid., p. 460. Talbott credits William Rowe with assistance in formulating this principle.

27. Ibid.

28. Yet another true Power Entailment Principle, discovered independently by the author, is the following: If (a) it is within S's power to bring it about that p and (b) "p" entails "q" and (c) it is false that q, then it is in S's power to bring it about that q.

29. See Mavrodes, "Is the Past Unpreventable?," *Faith and Philosophy*, 1 (1984): 131–46.

30. Ibid., pp. 144f.

31. Plantinga, *God, Freedom and Evil*, p. 71.

32. Mavrodes, "Is the Past Unpreventable?" p. 139.

33. Ibid., p. 137.

34. Ibid.; Plantinga, "On Ockham's Way Out"; Anthony Kenny, *The God of the Philosophers* (Oxford, 1979), pp. 55f.

35. Mavrodes makes it clear ("Is the Past Unpreventable?," pp. 143–44) that a world in which someone performed an action in 1984 or later that prevented Elizabeth's coronation would of necessity be a world in which Elizabeth was not in fact crowned in 1953. Such an act of prevention could occur only in a world which differs from the actual world with respect to events that already lie in the past.

36. See Kenny, *The God of the Philosophers*, p. 97.

37. Richard Taylor, "Determinism," in *The Encyclopedia of Philosophy*, vol. II, p. 359.

38. Brand Blanshard, "The Case for Determinism," in Sidney Hook, ed., *Determinism and Freedom in the Age of Modern Science* (New York, 1958), p. 20.

Alston: Divine Foreknowledge and Human Freedom

1. Chapter 2 in this volume.

2. Ibid., p. 63.

3. In addition to the contributions that will be discussed in this paper, see Marilyn McCord Adams, "Is the Existence of God a 'Hard' Fact?" (Chapter 3 in this volume); Joshua Hoffman, "Pike on Possible Worlds, Divine Foreknowledge, and Human Freedom," *Philosophical Review*, 88 (1979): 433–42; and John Martin Fischer, "Freedom and Foreknowledge" (Chapter 4 in this volume). At the March 1984 Pacific Regional meeting of the Society of Christian Philosophers, Pike presented a discussion of Fischer's paper, which was responded to by Marilyn Adams and Fischer, so that the conferees were treated to hearing Adams on Pike on Fischer on Adams on Pike, and Fischer on Pike on Fischer on Adams on Pike. "Enough!" you may well cry. And yet the beat goes on.

4. This last requirement is designed to prevent causal necessitation from ranging over logical necessitation, in which a previous state of affairs alone entails E.

5. Some classical theologians, e.g., St. Thomas Aquinas (*Summa Theologicae*, I, q. 14, a. 8), hold that divine knowledge causes what is known. But Aquinas never had the opportunity of discussing Pike's argument.

6. See, e.g., Adams, "Is the Existence of God a 'Hard' Fact?"; Fischer, "Freedom and Foreknowledge"; and Joshua Hoffman and Gary Rosenkrantz, "Hard and Soft Facts" (Chapter 7 in this volume).

7. Alfred J. Freddoso, "Accidental Necessity and Logical Determinism" (Chapter 8 in this volume); Alvin Plantinga, "On Ockham's Way Out" (Chapter 10 in this volume).

8. This may be contested. See the next section.

9. "Divine Omniscience," p. 62 in this volume.

10. Ludwig Wittgenstein, *Philosophical Grammar* (Berkeley, 1974), p. 369.

11. I am indebted to Pike for suggesting this line of argument, though he should not be taken as committed to it.

12. Since the compatibilist typically assumes causal determinism, we are conducting this discussion on that assumption. If decisions, actions, and so on are not strictly causally determined, similar points will hold, though the discussion would, perforce, be more complicated.

13. I am assuming that the actual situation is such that there is nothing to prevent either a decision to do X or a decision to refrain from doing X from being carried out. This is a situation in which human beings often find themselves. If divine foreknowledge were to rule out the power to do other than what one in fact does, it would have to rule it out in this kind of situation.

14. This is oversimplified a bit. For example, there may well be other differences in Set II that intervene between decision and execution. Moreover, each of the differences specified will ramify causally both backwards and forwards in time.

15. John Turk Saunders, "Of God and Freedom," *Philosophical Review*, 75 (1966): 219–25.

16. Ibid., p. 220.

17. Nelson Pike, "Of God and Freedom: A Rejoinder," *Philosophical Review*, 75 (1966): 371.

18. Saunders, "Of God and Freedom," p. 221.

19. Ibid., p. 222.

20. Alvin Plantinga, *God, Freedom and Evil* (New York, 1974).

21. I do so partly for the sake of greater focus in the discussion, and partly because more recent controversy over Pike's argument has centered around this part of the problem.

22. Plantinga, *God, Freedom and Evil*, p. 71.

23. Ibid.

24. Ibid., p. 29.

25. Plantinga does not question the "hardness" of divine beliefs in *God, Freedom and Evil*.

26. Ibid., p. 69.

27. Ibid., p. 71.

28. There are two significant differences between the two cases. First, Plantinga takes it that God necessarily exists; the non-existence of God in W does not constitute a possible difference between W and the actual world. Hence the non-existence of God is not one of the ways in which W could accommodate Jones's refraining from X at t_2. Whereas since causal determinism fails to hold in every possible world, its absence in W is one of the ways in which W could accommodate Jones's refraining from X at t_2. Second, even if determinism holds in W, the causal laws that hold there might be different in such a way as to permit Jones's refraining from X in the face of the same causal factors. But the theological analogue to the specific content of causal laws, viz., the infallibility of God, is taken to be necessary and so not to vary across possible worlds. Note that these two differences do nothing to shake the point that if Jones has the power to refrain from what is entailed by past facts he also has the power to refrain from what is causally necessitated

by past facts. On the contrary, the two differences mean that there is even more room for variations across possible worlds in what *causally* determines what actually happens than there is with respect to what *theologically* determines what actually happens.

Davies: Boethius on Divine Foreknowledge

1. Chaucer, *Troilus and Criseyde*, trans. Nevill Coghill (Baltimore, 1971), Bk. IV, p. 213. Chaucer puts into the mouth of Troilus a lightly edited version of Boethius, *The Consolation of Philosophy*, Bk. V, prose 3.

2. Boethius, *The Consolation of Philosophy*, trans. V. E. Watts (Baltimore, 1969), Bk. V, verse 3, p. 154.

3. S. Haack, "On a Theological Argument for Fatalism," *Philosophical Quarterly*, 24 (1974). See also P. Helm, "On Theological Fatalism Again," *Philosophical Quarterly*, 24 (1974); Haack, "On 'On Theological Fatalism Again' Again," *Philosophical Quarterly*, 25 (1975); and Helm, "Fatalism Once More," *Philosophical Quarterly*, 25 (1975).

4. See, e.g., A. Prior, "Time and Determinism," in *Past, Present and Future* (Oxford, 1967), p. 117.

5. N. Pike, "Divine Omniscience and Voluntary Action" (Chapter 2 in this volume). See also Pike, "Divine Foreknowledge, Human Freedom and Possible Worlds," *Philosophical Review*, 86 (1977).

6. Cf. A. Kenny, "Divine Foreknowledge and Human Freedom," in Kenny, ed., *Aquinas: A Collection of Critical Essays* (Garden City, 1970), esp. p. 268. See also P. Helm, "Divine Foreknowledge and Facts," *Canadian Journal of Philosophy*, 4 (1974), and D. C. Holt, "Foreknowledge and the Necessity of the Past" and P. Helm, "Foreknowledge and Possibility," *Canadian Journal of Philosophy*, 6 (1976).

7. M. Adams, "Is the Existence of God a 'Hard' Fact?" (Chapter 3 in this volume).

8. Ibid., pp. 75–76. For a discussion of the hard fact/soft fact distinction, similar in spirit to what follows, see J. M. Fischer, "Freedom and Foreknowledge" (Chapter 4 in this volume). In particular, see p. 92 of his paper for the point that on Adams's definition there do not seem to be any hard facts.

9. This was suggested to me by Lloyd Humberstone.

10. See G. Ryle, "It Was to Be," in *Dilemmas* (Cambridge, Engl., 1966), and M. Dummett, "Bringing About the Past," in *Truth and Other Enigmas* (London, 1978), pp. 339–40.

11. See Kenny, "Divine Foreknowledge," where this is attributed to Aquinas. For the points mentioned in the next paragraph, see p. 264 and p. 263.

12. Proponents of the free will defense against the problem of evil

maintain that there are possible states of affairs that God cannot actualize, such as states in which a person acts freely in a certain way. For a more sophisticated version of the fourth reason, see J. R. Lucas, *The Freedom of the Will* (Oxford, 1970), pp. 75–77.

13. D. Lewis, "Are We Free to Break the Laws?," *Theoria*, 47 (1981). I heard Lewis's paper when he read it at Monash University in 1981. Very similar points about the incompatibilist's position are made, independently, by Fischer in "Incompatibilism," *Philosophical Studies*, 43 (1983). See also note 15 below.

14. A. Kenny, *Will, Freedom and Power* (Oxford, 1975), p. 157. Cf. D. Wiggins, "Towards a Reasonable Libertarianism," in T. Honderich, ed., *Essays on Freedom of Action* (London, 1973), pp. 41–46. Note that in this example, only one time t is relevant. In this and some other respects the example is peculiar. But it is only intended to serve a limited purpose; it is not intended to demonstrate that *in the circumstances* I *can* carry suitcase B.

15. Lewis, "Are We Free to Break the Laws?" Following his "Counterfactual Dependence and Time's Arrow," *Noûs*, 13 (1979), Lewis maintains that if I had put my hand on the desk then the distant past would not have been different; rather, a law would have been broken. In "Incompatibilism," p. 130, Fischer distinguishes between (i) S has it in his power at t_1 to cause e's occurrence at t_0 and (ii) S has it in his power at t_1 to perform some act e^* such that if e^* were to occur, then e would have occurred at t_0. This is analogous to the distinction that I need.

16. See P. van Inwagen, "The Incompatibility of Free Will and Determinism," *Philosophical Studies*, 27 (1975).

17. A. Gallois, "Van Inwagen on Free Will and Determinism," *Philosophical Studies*, 32 (1977).

18. Ibid., p. 101.

19. J. T. Saunders, "Of God and Freedom," *Philosophical Review*, 75 (1966): 220.

20. Ibid., p. 223.

21. Ibid., p. 224.

22. St. Augustine, "The Freedom of the Will," extract in B. Berofsky, *Free Will and Determinism* (New York, 1966), pp. 271, 273.

23. Boethius, *The Consolation*, Bk. V, prose 3–6.

24. Ibid., prose 4, p. 156.

25. Ibid., p. 157. See also prose 3, p. 152: "But how absurd it is to say that the occurrence of temporal events is the cause of eternal prescience!"

26. Ibid., prose 6, p. 165.

27. Kenny, "Divine Foreknowledge and Human Freedom," p. 261.

28. Boethius, *The Consolation*, p. 166. The modal fallacy involves a confusion between simple and conditional necessity.

29. Ibid., p. 167.

30. I believe that the needed distinction was made, some 750 years later, by Duns Scotus.

31. Boethius, *The Consolation*, p. 168.

32. Ibid.

Bibliography

Compiled by Mark Ravizza in consultation with the volume editor. The works include most of those cited in the preceding chapters as well as a selection of books and articles with particular relevance to the issues raised in this volume. Classic works are cited without modern publication information because contributors may have referred to different editions.

Abbreviations

A	Analysis	P	Philosophy
APQ	American Philosophical Quarterly	PA	Philosophia
		PAS	Proceedings of the Aristotelian Society
CJP	Canadian Journal of Philosophy	PPQ	Pacific Philosophical Quarterly
DDSR	Duke Divinity School Review	PPR	Philosophy and Phenomenological Research
FP	Faith and Philosophy	PQ	Philosophical Quarterly
FS	Franciscan Studies	PR	Philosophical Review
IJPR	International Journal for Philosophy of Religion	PS	Philosophical Studies
JP	Journal of Philosophy	RM	Review of Metaphysics
M	Mind	RS	Religious Studies
N	Noûs	SJT	Scottish Journal of Theology
NDEJ	Notre Dame English Journal	T	Theoria
		TS	Theological Studies
NS	New Scholasticism		

Adams, Marilyn McCord. 1987. *William Ockham*. Notre Dame.
Adams, Robert. 1977. "Middle Knowledge and the Problem of Evil." *APQ*, 14 (April): 109–17.

————. 1985. "Alvin Plantinga on the Problem of Evil." In Tomberlin and van Inwagen (1985).

Ahern, Dennis M. 1979. "Foreknowledge: Nelson Pike and Newcomb's Problem." *RS*, 15 (December): 475–90.

Albritton, Rogers. 1957. "Present Truth and Future Contingency." *PR*, 66 (January): 1–28.

Alston, William P. 1985. "Divine-Human Dialogue and the Nature of God." *FP*, 2 (January): 5–20.

————. 1986. "Does God Have Beliefs?" *RS*, 22 (September/December): 287–306.

Anselm. *Monologium*.

————. *Proslogium*.

Aquinas, St. Thomas. *Summa Contra Gentiles*.

————. *Summa Theologicae*.

Augustine. *De Libero Arbitrio* [On the Free Choice of the Will].

Ayer, A. J. 1963. "Fatalism." In *The Concept of a Person and Other Essays*. London.

Bañez, Domingo. 1585. *Scholastica Commentaria in Primam Partum Summae Theologicae S. Thomae Aquinatis*. Ed. Luis Urbano. Madrid, 1934.

Basinger, David. 1984. "Divine Omniscience and Human Freedom: A 'Middle Knowledge' Perspective." *FP*, 1 (July): 291–302.

————. 1986. "Middle Knowledge and Classical Christian Thought." *RS*, 22 (September/December): 407–22.

————. 1987. "Middle Knowledge and Human Freedom: Some Clarifications." *FP*, 4 (July): 330–36.

Basinger, David, and Randall Basinger, eds. 1986. *Predestination and Free Will: Four Views of Divine Sovereignty and Human Freedom*. Downers Grove, Ill.

Baudry, Leon, ed. 1950. *La Querelle des Futurs Contingents*. Paris.

Baylis, Charles A. 1936. "Are Some Propositions Neither True Nor False?" *Philosophy of Science*, 3 (April): 156–66.

Bennett, Jonathan. 1984. "Counterfactuals and Temporal Dependence." *PR*, 93 (January): 57–91.

Boethius. *Consolatio Philosophiae* [The Consolation of Philosophy].

Burrell, David B. 1984. "God's Eternity," *FP*, 1 (October): 389–406.

Cahn, Steven M. 1967. *Fate, Logic, and Time*. New Haven.

Calvin, John. *Institutes of the Christian Religion*.

Campbell, C. A. 1951. "Is 'Free-Will' a Pseudo-Problem?" *M*, 60 (October): 441–65.

Chadwick, Henry. 1983. "Freedom and Necessity in Early Christian Thought." In David Tracy and Nicholas Lash, eds., *Cosmology and Theology*. New York.

Chapman, T. 1982. *Time: A Philosophical Analysis*. Dordrecht.

Cicero. *De Fato*.

Clark, David W. 1978. "Ockham on Human and Divine Freedom." *FS*, 38: 122–60.

Cook, Monte. 1982. "Tips for Time Travel." In Nicholas D. Smith, ed., *Philosophers Look at Science Fiction*. Chicago.

Cook, Robert R. 1987. "God, Time and Freedom." *RS*, 23 (March): 81–94.

Craig, William Lane. 1986. "Temporal Necessity; Hard Facts/Soft Facts." *IJPR*, 20: 65–91.

——. 1987a. "Divine Foreknowledge and Newcomb's Paradox." *PA*, 17 (October): 331–50.

——. 1987b. *The Only Wise God*. Grand Rapids.

——. 1988a. "Tachyons, Time Travel, and Divine Omniscience." *JP*, 85 (March): 135–50.

——. 1988b. *The Problem of Divine Foreknowledge and Future Contingents from Aristotle to Suarez*. Leiden.

Davis, Stephen T. 1979. "Divine Omniscience and Human Freedom." *RS*, 15 (September): 303–16.

——. 1983. *Logic and the Nature of God*. Grand Rapids.

Dummett, Michael. 1978. "Bringing About the Past." In *Truth and Other Enigmas*. London.

Edidin, Aron, and Calvin Normore. 1982. "Ockham on Prophecy." *IJPR*, 13: 179–89.

Edwards, Jonathan. *Freedom of the Will*.

Ehring, Douglas. 1982. "Causal Asymmetry." *JP*, 79 (December): 761–74.

Factor, R. Lance. 1978. "Newcomb's Paradox and Omniscience." *IJPR*, 9: 30–40.

Farrelly, Mark John. 1964. *Predestination, Grace and Free Will*. Westminster.

Feldman, Seymour. 1985. "The Binding of Isaac: A Test-Case of Divine Foreknowledge." In Rudavsky (1985a).

Fischer, John Martin. 1983. "Incompatibilism." *PS*, 43 (January): 127–37.

——. 1984. "Power over the Past." *PPQ*, 65 (October): 335–50.

——. 1985a. "Ockhamism." *PR*, 94 (January): 81–100.

——. 1985b. "Scotism." *M*, 94 (April): 231–43.

——. 1986a. "Hard-Type Soft Facts." *PR*, 95 (October): 591–601.

——. 1986b. "Introduction: Responsibility and Freedom." In Fischer (1986c).

——, ed. 1986c. *Moral Responsibility*. Ithaca.

——. 1986d. "Pike's Ockhamism." *A*, 46 (January): 57–63.

——. 1988. "Freedom and Actuality." In Morris (1988).

Fitzgerald, Paul. 1970. "Tachyons, Backwards Causation, and Freedom." In Roger C. Buck and Robert S. Cohen, eds., *Boston Studies in the Philosophy of Science*, vol. 8. Dordrecht.

———. 1974. "On Retrocausality." *PA*, 4 (October): 513–51.

———. 1985. "Stump and Kretzmann on Time and Eternity." *JP*, 82 (May): 260–69.

Flint, Thomas. 1983. "The Problem of Divine Freedom." *APQ*, 20 (July): 255–64.

Flint, Thomas P., and Alfred J. Freddoso. "Maximal Power." In Freddoso (1983).

Frankfurt, Harry G. 1969. "Alternate Possibilities and Moral Responsibility." *JP*, 66 (December): 829–39.

———. 1971. "Freedom of the Will and the Concept of a Person." *JP*, 68 (January): 5–20.

Freddoso, Alfred J. 1980. "Ockham's Theory of Truth Conditions." In Ockham (1980).

———. 1982. "Accidental Necessity and Power over the Past." *PPQ*, 63 (January): 54–68.

———, ed. 1983. *The Existence and Nature of God*. Notre Dame.

———. 1987. "The Necessity of Nature." In Peter French, Theodore E. Uehling, Jr., and Howard Wettstein, eds., *Midwest Studies in Philosophy*, vol. 11. Minneapolis.

———. 1988a. "Medieval Aristotelianism and the Case Against Secondary Causation in Nature." In Morris (1988).

———. 1988b. "Introduction." In Molina (1988).

Gale, Richard. 1961. "Endorsing Predictions." *PR*, 70 (July): 376–85.

Garrigou-Lagrange, Reginald. 1936. *God: His Existence and Nature*. St. Louis.

———. 1943. *The One God*. St. Louis.

Geach, Peter T. 1969. *God and the Soul*. New York.

———. 1972. *Logical Matters*. Berkeley.

———. 1977. *Providence and Evil*. Cambridge, Engl.

Geisler, Norman. 1986. "God Knows All Things." In Basinger and Basinger (1986).

Ginet, Carl. 1966. "Might We Have No Choice?" In Lehrer (1966).

———. 1980. "The Conditional Analysis of Freedom." In Peter van Inwagen, ed., *Time and Cause: Essays Presented to Richard Taylor*. Dordrecht.

———. 1983. "In Defense of Incompatibilism." *PS*, 44 (November): 391–400.

Goodman, Nelson. 1955. *Fact, Fiction, and Forecast*. Cambridge, Mass.

———. 1962. "About." *M*, 70 (January): 1–24.

Haack, S. 1974. "On a Theological Argument for Fatalism." *PQ*, 24 (April): 156–59.

————. 1975. "On 'On Theological Fatalism Again' Again." *PQ*, 25 (April): 159–61.

Hartshorne, Charles. 1941. *Man's Vision of God and the Logic of Theism*. Chicago.

Hasker, William. 1983. "Concerning the Intelligibility of 'God Is Timeless'." *NS*, 57 (Spring): 170–95.

————. 1986. "Simplicity and Freedom: A Response to Stump and Kretzmann." *FP*, 3 (April): 192–201.

————. 1987. "The Hardness of the Past: A Reply to Reichenbach." *FP*, 4 (July): 337–42.

Hebblethwaite, B. L. 1979. "Some Reflections on Predestination, Providence, and Divine Foreknowledge." *RS*, 15 (December): 433–48.

Helm, P. 1974a. "Divine Foreknowledge and Facts." *CJP*, 4 (December): 305–15.

————. 1974b. "On Theological Fatalism Again." *PQ*, 24 (October): 360–62.

————. 1975a. "Fatalism Once More." *PQ*, 25 (October): 289–96.

————. 1975b. "Timelessness and Foreknowledge." *M*, 84 (October): 516–27.

————. 1976. "Foreknowledge and Possibility." *CJP*, 6 (December): 731–34.

Hick, John. 1961. "Necessary Being." *SJT*, 14: 353–69.

Hill, William J. 1975. "Does God Know the Future: Aquinas and Some Moderns." *TS*, 36 (March): 3–18.

Hoffman, Joshua. 1979. "Pike on Possible Worlds, Divine Foreknowledge and Human Freedom." *PR*, 88 (July): 433–42.

Hoffman, Joshua, and Gary Rosenkrantz. 1980a. "On Divine Foreknowledge and Human Freedom." *PS*, 37 (April): 289–96.

————. 1980b. "What an Omnipotent Agent Can Do." *IJPR*, 11: 1–19.

Holt, Dennis C. 1976. "Foreknowledge and the Necessity of the Past." *CJP*, 6 (December): 721–30.

Hopkins, Jasper. 1977. "Augustine on Foreknowledge and Free Will." *IJPR*, 8: 111–26.

Horne, James R. 1983. "Newcomb's Problem as a Theistic Problem." *IJPR*, 14: 217–23.

Horwich, Paul. 1975. "On Some Alleged Paradoxes of Time Travel." *JP*, 72 (August): 432–44.

James, William. 1897. "The Dilemma of Determinism." In *The Will to Believe and Other Essays in Popular Philosophy*. New York.

Kapitan, Tomis. 1984. "Can God Make Up His Mind?" *IJPR*, 15: 37–47.

Kelly, Charles J. 1986. "God's Knowledge of the Necessary." *IJPR*, 20: 131–45.

Kenny, Anthony. 1969. "Divine Foreknowledge and Human Freedom." In Kenny, ed., *Aquinas: A Collection of Critical Essays*. Garden City.

————. 1975. *Will, Freedom and Power*. Oxford.

————. 1979. *The God of the Philosophers*. Oxford.

Khamara, Edward J. 1974. "Eternity and Omniscience." *PQ*, 24 (July): 204–19.

Kneale, Martha. 1968–69. "Eternity and Sempiternity." *PAS*, 69: 223–38.

Kneale, William. 1960–61. "Time and Eternity in Theology." *PAS*, 61: 87–108.

Kneale, William, and Mary Kneale. 1962. *The Development of Logic*. Oxford.

Kretzmann, Norman. 1966. "Omniscience and Immutability." *JP*, 63 (July): 409–21.

————. 1983. "Goodness, Knowledge, and Indeterminacy in the Philosophy of Thomas Aquinas." *JP*, 80 (Supplemental): 631–49.

Kvanvig, Jonathan. 1986. *The Possibility of an All-Knowing God*. New York.

La Croix, Richard R. 1976. "Omnipresence and Divine Determinism." *RS*, 12 (September): 365–81.

Lehrer, Keith, ed. 1966. *Freedom and Determinism*. New York.

Leibniz, G. W. 1952. *Théodicée*. Trans. E. M. Huggard. Ed. Austin Farrer. New Haven.

Lewis, David. 1973. *Counterfactuals*. Cambridge, Mass.

————. 1976. "The Paradoxes of Time Travel." *APQ*, 13 (April): 145–52.

————. 1979. "Counterfactual Dependence and Time's Arrow." *N*, 13 (November): 455–76.

————. 1981. "Are We Free to Break the Laws?" *T*, 47: 112–21.

Locke, Don. 1976. "The 'Can' of Being Able." *PA*, 6 (March): 1–20.

Locke, John. *An Essay Concerning Human Understanding*.

Lonergan, Bernard. 1971. *Grace and Freedom*. New York.

Lucas, J. R. 1970. *The Freedom of the Will*. Oxford.

Lukasiewicz, Jan. 1967a. "On Determinism." In McCall (1967).

————. 1967b. "Philosophical Remarks on Many-Valued Systems of Propositional Logic." In McCall (1967).

Mackie, J. L. 1955. "Evil and Omnipotence." *M*, 64 (April): 200–212.

————. 1966. "The Direction of Causation." *PR*, 75 (October): 441–66.

Mann, William. 1985. "Epistemology Supernaturalized." *FP*, 2 (October): 436–56.

Maritain, Jacques. 1966. *God and the Permission of Evil*. Trans. Joseph W. Evans. Milwaukee.

Marmura, Michael E. "Divine Omniscience and Future Contingents in Alfarabi and Avicenna." In Rudavsky (1985a).

Martin, Charles Burton. 1964. *Religious Belief*. Ithaca.

Mavrodes, George. 1977. "Aristotelian Necessity and Freedom." In Peter French, Theodore E. Uehling, Jr., and Howard Wettstein, eds., *Midwest Studies in Philosophy*, vol. 1. Minneapolis.

————. 1983. "Vestigial Modalities." *A*, 43 (March): 91–94.

————. 1984. "Is the Past Unpreventable?" *FP*, 1 (April): 131–46.

McCall, Storrs. 1966. "Temporal Flux." *APQ*, 3 (October): 270–81.

————, ed. 1967. *Polish Logic 1920–1939*. Oxford.

Meiland, Jack W. 1974. "A Two-Dimensional Passage Model for Time Travel." *PS*, 26 (November): 153–73.

Molina, Luis de. 1988. *On Divine Foreknowledge (Part IV of the "Concordia")*. Trans. Alfred J. Freddoso. Ithaca.

Morris, Thomas, ed. 1988. *Divine and Human Action: Essays in the Metaphysics of Theism*. Ithaca.

Morriston, Wesley. 1985. "Is God 'Significantly Free'?" *FP*, 2 (July): 257–64.

Nerlich, Graham. 1979. "How to Make Things Have Happened." *CJP*, 9 (March): 1–22.

Newton-Smith, W. H. 1980. *The Structure of Time*. London.

Normore, Calvin. 1982. "Future Contingents." In Norman Kretzmann, Anthony Kenny, and Jan Pinborg, eds., *Cambridge History of Later Medieval Philosophy*. Cambridge, Engl.

————. 1985. "Divine Omniscience, Omnipotence, and Future Contingents: An Overview." In Rudavsky (1985a).

Nozick, Robert. 1970. "Newcomb's Problem and Two Principles of Choice," In Nicholas Rescher, ed., *Essays in Honor of Carl G. Hempel*. Dordrecht.

Ockham, William. 1969. *Predestination, God's Foreknowledge and Future Contingents*. Trans. Marilyn McCord Adams and Norman Kretzmann. New York.

————. 1980. *Ockham's Theory of Propositions: Part II of the Summa Logicae*. Trans. Alfred J. Freddoso and Henry Schuurman. Notre Dame.

O'Connor, D. J. O. 1971. *Free Will*. Garden City.

Paley, William. 1802. *Natural Theology*. London.

Pegis, Anton. 1939. "Molina and Human Liberty." In Gerard Smith, ed., *Jesuit Thinkers of the Renaissance*. Milwaukee.

Penelhum, Terence. 1971. *Religion and Rationality*. New York.

Pike, Nelson. 1966. "Of God and Freedom: A Rejoinder." *PR*, 75 (July): 369–79.

————. 1969. "Omnipotence and God's Ability to Sin." *APQ*, 6 (July): 208–16.

————. 1970. *God and Timelessness*. New York.

————. 1977. "Divine Foreknowledge, Human Freedom and Possible Worlds." *PR*, 86 (April): 209–16.

————. 1984. "Fischer on Freedom and Foreknowledge." *PR*, 93 (October): 599–614.

Pinnock, Clark H. 1986. "God Limits His Knowledge." In Basinger and Basinger (1986).

Plantinga, Alvin. 1973. "Which Worlds Could God Have Created?" *JP*, 70 (October): 539–55.

———. 1974a. *God, Freedom and Evil*. New York.

———. 1974b. *The Nature of Necessity*. Oxford.

———. 1978. "The Boethian Compromise." *APQ*, 15 (April): 129–38.

———. 1980. "Does God Have a Nature?" *Aquinas Lecture*. Milwaukee.

———. 1985. "Replies to My Colleagues." In Tomberlin and van Inwagen (1985).

Pontifex, Mark. 1960. *Freedom and Providence*. New York.

Prior, Arthur. 1957. *Time and Modality*. Oxford.

———. 1959. "Thank Goodness That's Over." *P*, 34 (January): 12–17.

———. 1960. "Identifiable Individuals." *RM*, 13 (June): 684–96.

———. 1962. "The Formalities of Omniscience." *P*, 32 (April): 119–29.

———. 1967. *Past, Present and Future*. Oxford.

———. 1968. "On the Logic of Ending Time." In *Papers on Time and Tense*. Oxford.

Purtill, Richard. 1974. "Foreknowledge and Fatalism." *RS*, 10 (September): 319–24.

Quinn, Philip L. 1978. "Divine Foreknowledge and Divine Freedom." *IJPR*, 9: 219–40.

———. 1985. "Plantinga on Foreknowledge and Freedom." In Tomberlin and van Inwagen (1985a).

Raitt, Jill. 1978. "St. Thomas Aquinas on Free Will and Predestination." *DDSR*, 43 (Fall): 188–95.

Reichenbach, Bruce. 1984. "Omniscience and Deliberation." *IJPR*, 16: 225–36.

———. 1986. "God Limits His Power." In Basinger and Basinger (1986).

———. 1987. "Hasker on Omniscience." *FP*, 4 (January): 86–92.

Roberts, Lawrence D. 1978. "The Contemporary Relevance of Duns Scotus' Doctrine of Human Freedom." In *Regnum Homnis et Regnum Dei, Acta Quarti Congressus Scotistici*. Vol. 1. Rome.

Rosenthal, David M. 1977. "The Necessity of Foreknowledge." In Peter French, Theodore E. Uehling, Jr., and Howard Wettstein, eds., *Midwest Studies in Philosophy*, vol. 1. Minneapolis.

Ross, James. 1983. "Creation II." In Freddoso (1983).

Rowe, William L. 1964. "Augustine on Foreknowledge and Free Will." *RM*, 18 (December): 356–63.

———. 1978. *Philosophy of Religion: An Introduction*. Encino, Calif.

———. 1980a. "Fatalism and Truth." *Southern Journal of Philosophy*, 18 (Summer): 213–19.

———. 1980b. "On Divine Foreknowledge and Human Freedom: A Reply." *PS*, 37 (May): 429–30.

Rudavsky, Tamar, ed. 1985a. *Divine Omniscience and Omnipotence in Medieval Philosophy*. Dordrecht.

———. 1985b. "Divine Omniscience, Contingency and Prophecy in Gersonides." In Rudavsky (1985a).

Runzo, Joseph. 1981. "Omniscience and Freedom for Evil." *IJPR*, 12: 131–47.

Ryle, Gilbert. 1954. "It Was to Be." In Ryle, ed., *Dilemmas*. Cambridge, Engl.

Saunders, John Turk. 1958. "Sea Fight Tomorrow?" *PR*, 67 (July): 367–78.

———. 1965. "Fatalism and Ordinary Language." *JP*, 62 (April): 211–22.

———. 1966. "Of God and Freedom." *PR*, 75 (April): 219–25.

———. 1968. "The Temptations of 'Powerlessness.'" *APQ*, 5 (April): 100–108.

Schleiermacher, Frederich. 1928. *The Christian Faith*. Translation of the second German edition. Eds. H. R. Mackintosh and J. S. Stewart. Edinburgh.

Schwartz, Regina. 1983. "Free Will and Character Autonomy in the Bible." *NDEJ*, 15 (Winter): 51–74.

Slote, Michael. 1982. "Selective Necessity and the Free-Will Problem." *JP*, 79 (January): 5–24.

Smith, Gerard. 1966. *Freedom in Molina*. Chicago.

Smith, Quentin. 1985. "On the Beginning of Time." *N*, 19 (December): 579–84.

Sosa, Ernest. 1979. "The Status of Becoming: What Is Happening Now?" *JP*, 76 (January): 26–42.

Stalnaker, Robert. 1968. "A Theory of Conditionals." In Nicholas Rescher, ed., *Studies in Logical Theory*. Oxford.

Steuer, Axel D. 1983. "The Freedom of God and Human Freedom." *SJT*, 36: 163–80.

Streveler, Paul A. 1973. "The Problem of Future Contingents." *NS*, 47 (Spring): 233–47.

Stump, Eleonore, and Norman Kretzmann. 1981. "Eternity." *JP*, 78 (August): 429–58.

———. 1985. "Absolute Simplicity." *FP*, 2 (October): 353–82.

———. 1987. "Atemporal Duration: A Reply to Fitzgerald." *JP*, 84 (April): 214–19.

Suarez, Francisco. *De Divina Gratia*.

———. *De Scientia Quam Deus Habet de Futuria Contingentibus*.

———. *Opera Omnia*.

Swinburne, Richard. 1977. *The Coherence of Theism*. Oxford.

Talbott, Thomas B. 1986. "On Divine Foreknowledge and Bringing About the Past." *PPR*, 46 (March): 455–69.

Taliaferro, Charles. 1985. "Divine Cognitive Power." *IJPR*, 18: 133–40.

Taylor, Richard. 1957. "The Problem of Future Contingency." *PR*, 66 (January): 1–28.

———. 1960. "I Can." *PR*, 69 (January): 78–89.

———. 1962. "Fatalism." *PR*, 71 (January): 56–66.

———. 1964. "Deliberation and Foreknowledge." *APQ*, 1 (January): 73–80.

Thorp, John. 1980. *Free Will: A Defense Against Neuro-Physiological Determinism*. London.

Tomberlin, James E., and Peter van Inwagen, eds. 1985. *Alvin Plantinga*. Dordrecht.

Van Fraassen, Bas. 1966. "Singular Terms, Truth-Value Gaps and Free Logic." *JP*, 63 (September): 481–85.

Van Inwagen, Peter. 1983. *An Essay on Free Will*. Oxford.

Waismann, F. 1956. "How I See Philosophy." In H. D. Lewis, ed., *Contemporary British Philosophy*. London.

Walls, J. L. 1987. "A Fable of Foreknowledge and Freedom." *P*, 62 (January): 67–75.

Waterlow, Sarah. 1974. "Backward Causation and Continuing." *M*, 83 (July): 372–87.

Wertheimer, Roger. 1968. "Conditions." *JP*, 65 (June): 355–64.

Widerker, David. 1987. "On an Argument for Incompatibilism." *A*, 47 (January): 37–41.

———. Forthcoming. "Two Fallacious Objections to Adams' Soft/Hard Fact Distinction." *PS*.

Williams, C. J. F. 1978. "True Tomorrow, Never True Today." *PQ*, 28 (October): 285–99.

Wippel, John F. 1985. "Divine Knowledge, Divine Power and Human Freedom in Thomas Aquinas and Henry of Ghent." In Rudavsky (1985a).

Wolterstorff, Nicholas. 1982. "God Everlasting." In Steven M. Cahn and David Shatz, eds., *Contemporary Philosophy of Religion*. Oxford.

Wright, John H. 1977. "Divine Knowledge and Human Freedom: The God Who Dialogues." *TS*, 38 (September): 450–77.

Zagzebski, Linda. 1985. "Divine Foreknowledge and Human Free Will." *RS*, 21 (September): 279–98.

Index

Index

Ability and possible worlds, 210–15
Aboutness, 192, 197–98
Absolute necessity, 65
Absurdum, reductio ad, 282–89
Accidental impossibility, 138, 139–41
Accidental necessity: and accidental
impossibility, 139–41; and asymmetry of past and future, 205–10;
and the Basic Argument of the incompatibilists, 47–48; and beliefs
of God, 47–48; and causality, 138,
144–45, 156–58, 206; characteristics of, 137–41; and contingent
propositions, 138–48 *passim*,
155, 207, 210; and determinism,
136–58, 199–200; and entailment,
207; and Fischer, 40, 47–48, 197;
and fixity of the past, 47–48,
207–8; and Freddoso, 40, 136–58,
163–65, 171–72; and freedom/free
will, 157, 205–10; and the future,
141–42, 145–56, 157–58; and
hard/soft facts, 40, 163–65, 192–
93, 200–205, 210; and immediacy,
149–56; and logical determinism,
136–58; and necessity of the past,
138–41, 154, 158; and Ockhamists,
143, 144–45; and Ockham, 136–
37, 197, 207–8; and omniscience,
158, 165, 207; and Plantinga,
47–48, 190–92, 196–205, 213; and
power, 48, 141, 207–10; and the
pure present, 137, 141–45; and
tense/tenselessness, 137–38; and

truth, 141–44, 146–54, 157–58,
190–92, 206–7
Adams, Marilyn McCord: as an
Ockhamist, 33–36, 86–87, 96; and
Davies, 277–78; and Fischer,
33–36, 89–92, 96, 104–5, 113,
124–26, 131, 133; and Hoffman-
Rosenkrantz, 123–26, 131, 133;
and Widerker, 104–5. *See also
name of specific topic*
Adams, Robert, 16–17, 27–28
Alston, William P.: and Fischer,
54–55; and Pike, 258–59, 263–68,
270–72; and Plantinga, 270–72;
and Saunders, 268–70. *See also
name of specific topic*
Anselm [Saint], 9
Aquinas, Thomas, 13, 49–53, 64,
180–81, 224, 291–92
Aristotle, 64, 140, 141–42, 143, 156,
157–58, 224
Asymmetry of past and future,
189–91, 205–10
Attributes of God. *See name of specific
attribute*
Augustine [Saint], 61, 65–66, 68–69,
72, 179–80, 291

Basic Argument of the incompatibilists: and accidental necessity,
47–48; and bringing about the
past, 18–23; and causality, 16–18;
comments about the, 11–18; and
fixity of the past, 32–48, 54–56;